The Future of Economics

Classics in Economics Series
Warren J. Samuels, Series Editor

American Capitalism,
John Kenneth Galbraith. With an new introduction by the author

The Chicago School of Political Economy,
Edited by Warren J. Samuels. With a new introduction by the editor

Economic Semantics,
Fritz Machlup. With an introduction by Mark Perlman

Economists and the Economy, Second Edition
Roger Backhouse.

Economists and the Public,
William Harold Hutt. With an introduction by Warren J. Samuels

The Economy as a System of Power
Edited by Marc R. Tool and Warren J. Samuels

Epistemics and Economics,
G.L.S. Shackle. With a new introduction by the author

Essays on Entrepreneurs, Innovations, Business Cycles and the Evolution of Capitalism,
Joseph A. Schumpeter. With an introduction by Richard Swedberg

Evolutionary Economics,
David Hamilton. With a new introduction by the author

The Future of Economics,
Edited by Alexander J. Field. With a new introduction by the editor

Institutional Economics,
John Commons. With an introduction by Malcolm Rutherford

Inventors and Moneymakers,
Frank W. Taussig. With an introduction by Warren J. Samuels

Main Currents in Modern Economics,
Ben Seligman. With an introduction by E. Ray Canterbery

Methodology of Economic Thought,
Edited by Marc R. Tool and Warren J. Samuels

Philosophy and Political Economy,
James Bonar. With an introduction by Warren J. Samuels

Political Elements in Development of Economic Theory,
Gunnar Myrdal. With an introduction by Richard Swedberg

Production and Distribution Theories,
George J. Stigler. With a new introduction by Douglas Irwin

State, Society, and Corporation Power
Edited by Marc R. Tool and Warren J. Samuels

The Future of Economics

edited by Alexander J. Field

with a new introduction by the editor

Routledge
Taylor & Francis Group
NEW YORK AND LONDON

Originally published in 1987 by Kluwer Nijhoff Publishing.
Published 1995 by Transaction Publishers

Published 2020 by Routledge
605 Third Avenue, New York, NY 10158

and by Routledge
4 Park Square, Milton Park, Abingdon, Oxon OX14 4RN

First issued in hardback 2020

Routledge is an imprint of the Taylor & Francis Group, an informa business

Library of Congress Catalog Number: 94-15741

Library of Congress Cataloging-in-Publication Data

The Future of economics/edited by Alexander J. Field; with a new introduction by the editor.
p. cm. — (Classics in economics series)
Rev. ed. of: The future of economic history. 1987.
Includes bibliographical references and index.
ISBN 1-56000-765-6
1. Economics—History. 2. Economic history. I. Field, Alexander J. II. Future of economic history. III. Series: Classics in economics.
HB75.F88 1994
330'.09—dc20 94-15741
CIP

ISBN 13: 978-1-138-53579-4 (hbk)
ISBN 13: 978-1-56000-765-4 (pbk)

Contents

INTRODUCTION TO THE TRANSACTION EDITION

This book was originally published in 1987 under the title *The Future of Economic History*. It has been out of print for several years and it was welcome news when I heard that Transaction Publishers was interested in reissuing it with a new introduction and a slightly modified title. Is the title change warranted? In other words is this book as much about the future of economics as it is about the future of economic history? A very good case can be made affirmatively. A central theme of my essay—the first in this collection—is that economics has as much to learn from the practice of economic history as vice versa. My proclamation that the Cliometric revolution was dead—rhetorical indulgence intended to attract the somnolent browser—I explained to mean that new economic historians were no longer, could no longer, and did no longer consider themselves insurgents. The revolution may be over, of course, but quantitative economic history, informed by explicit economic theory and employing the latest statistical techniques, continues to display an unmistakable heartbeat. As one of its practitioners, and a card carrying economist to boot, I wish it, and economics, a long life. My larger theme about the ways in which economic history and economics ought to interact was concerned with fostering that longevity. What preventive steps might we now take to reduce the danger of intellectual hardening of the arteries? My recommendations on diet and exercise (or their equivalents) seem as valid today as they did several years ago.

If economics is to retain (some would say reattain) a sense of intellectual vibrancy, we need a continuing recognition of the limited explanatory powers of "pure theory" in all its axiomatic deductive grandeur. This is not a brief against the rigorous thinking that distinguishes economic argument at its best. It is a claim that as one of the social sciences, and one concerned with outcomes at the macro or aggregated level as well as at the individual or household level, economics requires an empirical foundation, one that has roots in both the historical and behavioral sciences. Intellectual specialization is inevitable and to a large degree desirable, but the walls separating those collecting and analyzing quantitative and qualitative data, and theorists developing the interconnections of conceptual categories and their implications, ought to be thin and ultimately permeable. If economics is to remain a social science, theoretical enterprise cannot become completely untethered from empirical moorings.

Within economics departments there have traditionally been two historically oriented subdisciplines. One, the history of economic thought, is a branch of intellectual history or the history of ideas. Although the study of history of thought can enrich our understanding of current theoretical concepts, and expose us to an inventory of ideas and formulations not all of which have necessarily outlived their usefulness, it is not ultimately an empirical practice. Although familiarity with the development of thought provides a "historical perspective," it does not necessarily provide insurance against the uncoupling of theoretical work from contact with data.

It falls to economic history, the history of economic development, a discipline at once both historical and empirical, to provide that insurance. From the standpoint of both methodology and subject matter, a vibrant practice of economics very much depends on a continuing healthy level of activity in economic history, pursued in a balanced fashion that blends the use of statistical techniques and the logic of economic theory with an understanding of the importance of institutions and legal traditions. In these ways and others, this collection of essays about the future of economic history is very much and directly about the future of economics.

My essay included data, up through and including the 1980-81 academic year, on trends in degrees awarded in economics and history at both the bachelor's and doctoral level. A new introduction provides an opportunity to update these numbers. The latest available at the time of this writing show that for the 1989-90 academic year, 23,899 bachelors' degrees in economics were awarded vs. 22,232 first degrees in history. Economics' slight edge over history, which appeared initially in 1981, has been sustained, although the margin did not grow substantially because the downward trends in history first degrees reversed itself. and both disciplines participated in a growth of overall undergraduate enrollments slightly faster in the 1980s than was true in the 1970s.

At the doctoral level, an economics edge over history also first appeared in 1980-81, but the margin widened substantially during the 1980s. In 1989-90 822 economics doctorates were awarded as compared with 570 in history. Because of the strength of undergraduate enrollments and growing replacement demand, production of history doctorates will likely increase somewhat faster in the next decade. For reasons noted in my essay, however, it remains likely that economic history will, at least in the United States, continue to be practiced predominantly within economics departments. If we adopt the right regimen, this symbiotic relationship should continue to prove mutually beneficial.

Alexander J. Field
Santa Clara University

PREFACE

This collection represents a modest attempt to chart a new course for the intellectual discipline known as economic history. (The book is not about productivity growth in the 1990s, lest the title give rise to any confusion.) As a group, these essays suggest new and potentially fruitful areas or approaches for research and at the same time address weaknesses in past efforts.

One important audience will be graduate students attempting to decide whether to write a dissertation in economic history, or trying to select or refine dissertation topics in the area, and determine how to approach them. Some of the essays will most certainly be appropriate additions to the quarter or semester courses in economic history that remain a fixture in graduate economics training programs.

A second audience should be established scholars who are now or have in the past done research in economic history and are interested in the perspectives of a relatively younger group of scholars. The term "younger" is used here advisedly to describe a group of scholars born between 1943 and 1954. Nevertheless, the authors of these essays can on at least one dimension be distinguished from the pathbreaking new economic historians who established their academic reputations in the early 1960s. Indeed, the contributors to this volume include students of such pioneers as Richard Easterlin, Albert Fishlow, William Parker, and Jeffrey Williamson.

Finally, and this is likely to be the largest audience numerically, the book is aimed at the broader group of economists and other social scientists who have not done much research in economic history but who coexist with economic historians in economics departments and universities, and wish to learn more about the past and potential contribution of research in economic history to the scholarly enterprise. All of the chapters are written primarily from the perspective of scholars trained in economics—six of the seven contributors currently teach in economics departments—but there should be material here of interest for students and scholars in history departments as well. The essays, both directly and by example, make a case for a continuing and expanded role for economic history in the graduate research and instructional programs in economics.

Having described the intended audience for the book, and what it hopes to accomplish, it is important to indicate what it is not. The essays do not attempt, either individually or collectively, to be comprehensive. The topical coverage is selective, and most of the contributions deal with European and U.S. materials (an exception is David Feeny's, which covers topics in Asian economic history). The essays were not written collaboratively, although I have commented on each of them, and—in my own essay—benefitted from the advice of several of the other contributors. As is only natural in a collection written by a group of independent thinkers, the essays reflect differences of opinion and approach, although they also display commonalities which give the collection a certain cohesiveness. My remaining remarks in this preface touch on some of these commonalities, while giving readers a rough idea of what they can expect to find here.

My own essay, somewhat broader in scope than those that follow, argues that the future of economic history depends, as in the past, not only on the success of economic historians in defining a mission within economics departments, but also on the external macroacademic environment. The unlikely return of the favorable macroacademic conditions prevailing between 1957 and 1969 (the years in which the Cliometrics revolution enjoyed such astonishing success) reinforces a case for reexamining the relations between economic history and the two traditions it links. I argue, inter alia, that economic historians need to avoid the vices of a priorism and thoughtless empiricism—the "data-set-without-a-problem" syndrome—at the same time they make their peace with the older descriptive tradition against which new economic historians rebelled so strongly.

Barry Eichengreen's essay surveys in short compass a wide range of research in the area of macroeconomic history. Almost half the paper deals with studies of the tumultuous interwar period in both Europe and the United States. Other topics covered include the debates about the causes and consequences of the inflow of bullion from the New World to Spain and Europe in the sixteenth century, crowding out during the Napoleonic Wars, and the operation of the Classical gold standard during the nineteenth century.

Economic history in one sense is the history of economic development, and David Feeny emphasizes that inductive generalizations from the economic history of different nations and regions have provided the building blocks for general theories of economic development. At the same time, such data have been used to challenge or test theoretical propositions with claims to generality. Feeny is optimistic that the methods and data of economic history can contribute to a better understanding of a wide range of institutional and demographic phenomena, and of their roles in developing economies.

The following two essays, by Michael Haines and Mark Thomas, are the most detailed in their descriptions of methodological tools and in their suggestions of areas for future research. They will be especially valuable for students gravitating toward dissertation topics in these areas.

Mark Thomas brings together in one place a treatment of a range of general equilibrium modeling techniques, including Leontief models, social accounting matrix models, (which close the Leontief models with Keynesian income-expenditure relations in the household sector), and neoclassical general equilibrium models. Thomas emphasizes not only what has been accomplished with these methods, but also a variety of issues which invite further analysis.

Michael Haines surveys some of the methods and results of demographic history, an area that has attracted considerable interest among economics historians in recent years. Haines' lengthy and up-to-date bibliography will be an especially valuable reference tool for those trying to learn more about research in this area.

Finally, both William Lazonick and Gavin Wright address, from different perspectives, the potential for research in economic history to illuminate our understanding of the operation of labor markets. Lazonick argues that Marx's writings offer useful general approaches to the study of economic history, even though much of his specific analysis of the development of British industrial capitalism needs to be discarded or revised. Lazonick illustrates these points with reference to his own research and that of others.

Gavin Wright, emphasizing American materials (particularly from the South) more than the British materials referenced by Lazonick, argues that labor history would benefit from more (labor) economic history. Wright reinforces arguments developed in the first essay, in particular the idea that economists and economic historians need to recognize their dependence on the work of traditional historians, even as they argue that traditional history could benefit from an infusion of economics.

1 THE FUTURE OF ECONOMIC HISTORY

Alexander J. Field

The Cliometrics revolution is dead. By this I mean that the banners under which new economic historians organized and made common cause with technically oriented theorists, econometricians, and other applied economists no longer have the ability to inspire revolutionary fervor (especially among younger recruits) within economics departments. (The situation in history departments is somewhat different, as detailed below.) The Cliometrics revolution was part of a more general struggle against a more institutional/descriptive, less technically oriented old guard. The revolution is over because that battle was won—not only by new economic historians, but also by a new generation of applied mathematicians and theoretical statisticians working in economics departments.

The reason Cliometric banners have relatively little motivational impact today is that new economic historians are no longer under pressure from an older guard who are long on description and perhaps shorter on analytical techniques (few remain), but rather from their own technically oriented colleagues. If technical competence in statistics and economic theory were the criteria whereby new economic historians measured their superiority vis-à-vis older economic historians, some economic theorists

Special thanks to Barry Eichengreen, David Feeny, Bill Lazonick and Gavin Wright for their comments on earlier versions of this chapter. Responsibility for the argument remains, of course, my own.

now question what lies behind the special claim of economic historians for departmental resources, since on purely technical grounds there may be other economists who (unburdened by the need to study and absorb historical detail) have superior backgrounds in mathematics and statistics. The banners under which new economic historians marched in the late 1950s and 1960s are of little use in responding to these queries.

Why should economic history continue to occupy an important role in instructional and research programs in economic departments? In past years, the answers to this question apparently seemed so obvious that it was seldom asked. Yet in an era in which resources are at best growing slowly, the question has and is being asked, and is not always answered in a manner that does justice to what economic history has to offer. To answer the question more effectively, economic historians in economics departments need first to recognize that current controversies surrounding the future of economic history are different from those of a quarter-century past, and are taking place within a different historical context. Secondly, they need to articulate more clearly what differentiates them from—and what they can offer to—economic historians with history Ph.D.s on the one hand, and more theoretically minded colleagues, on the other hand. Finally, if economic history is to fulfill its promise, it will need not only to inform the study of history in ways that complement the work of—and are comprehensible to—traditional historians, but also to play an active role in the development and refinement of modern economic theory.

Nevertheless, one must be careful in justifying a continuing or expanded mission for economic history on these latter grounds—that research in economic history can and should play a role in fostering theoretical advancement. The development of theory cannot, implicitly or explicitly, be an end in itself. Economic theory is a means to an end—a conceptual framework for analyzing contemporary and historical phenomena, but not something whose advancement can be evaluated without reference to such phenomena. Put another way, economics is ultimately a social rather than a mathematical science. Economic historians need to lean against the undercurrent of a priorism that underlies much of modern economic theory, and at the same time, make their peace, in both practical and philosophical terms, with the legal and traditional historical approaches against which Cliometrics rebelled so strongly.

"Old" vs. "New" Economic History

"Old" economic history, with strong links to traditional historical and legal scholarship, viewed as its primary task the description of the changing legal, geographical, and technological environment within which individuals pursued material gain. Traditional narrative was the preferred vehicle for communicating research results. New economic historians advocated replacing imprecise qualitative judgments common in narrative history with more precise quantitative estimates.[1] They also tried, where possible, to move beyond simple description and informal explanation in historical scholarship to the investigation of causal relationships linking exogenous and endogenous variables. Cliometricians shifted attention from documentary to statistical primary source material, and emphasized the use of techniques of statistical inference to infer population characteristics from small samples and to test or estimate posited relationships among variables. In 1965 Fritz Redlich offered a concise statement of the contrast between the respective approaches of new and old economic history:

> Traditional economic history deals primarily with the development of economic institutions and secondarily with processes taking place therein. The new approaches tend to deal primarily and directly with economic processes while more or less neglecting economic institutions. (Redlich 1965, p. 482)

New economic historians were part of a self-conscious intellectual movement whose identity was reinforced through common conference participation and publication outlets. Attendance at the annual Cliometrics meetings beginning at Purdue University in December 1960 and continuing at the University of Wisconsin and elsewhere in the Midwest after 1969 has been one indication of membership in the fraternity. So too has been publication in the *Journal of Economic History* and *Explorations in Economic History*,[2] whose pages, during the 1960s, became increasingly dominated by the research of new economic historians.

Reference to statistical as well as documentary materials in narrative economic history was not new in the late 1950s. But Cliometrics used statistics in new ways to address different kinds of questions. Cliometrics also either presumed or denigrated the importance of knowledge of the changing legal and institutional environment that traditional economic history took such pains to describe. The result was a literature that differed markedly in style and content from what had gone before. The spirit of the older tradition, at least as it applied to American economic history, can be appreciated by examining older textbooks, as well as several multivolumed series whose publication spans the half-century from 1910 to 1962, and comparing these works with representative publications of the new economic history.

Consider first the ambitious *Economic History of the United States* (published by Harper & Brothers), a planned ten volumes, eight of which eventually appeared between 1945 and 1962. Several of these volumes, in particular those dealing with nineteenth-century antebellum topics—e.g., the volumes by Paul Gates (1960) and George Rogers Taylor (1951)—stand the test of time well, and remain worthwhile introductions to the material covered. Although publication of this series extended into the early years of the Cliometric revolution, its volumes represented the fruition of careers in economic history built, in the older tradition, on detailed specialized knowledge of the documentary and statistical materials pertaining to a particular region or time period. Whereas each of these volumes ran several hundred pages, the Lance Davis, Richard Easterlin, William Parker treatise (1972), published only a decade after the last of this series appeared, covered essentially the same territory in 17 chapters and less than 700 pages.

Tracing the lineage of old economic history further, going back in time, one can point to a series published under the auspices of the Carnegie Institution. Originally projected in 1904, seven "Contributions to American Economic History" appeared between 1916 and 1933, including classic works by Percy Bidwell and John Falconer (1925) on northern and Lewis C. Gray (1933) on southern agriculture, as well as volumes on transportation, trade, and labor. Victor Clark's 1929 multivolume work on manufactures was also part of this series.[3]

Finally, those still puzzled about what the new economic historians rebelled against should consult the 10-volume *A Documentary History of American Industrial Society*, published in 1910–1911, edited by John R. Commons and Ulrich B. Philips, among others, with a preface by Richard T. Ely and an introduction by John B. Clark. Traditional economic historians and, indeed, the founding fathers of the American Economic Association took the history of agricultural and industrial labor very seriously; they believed that the documentary record provided the foundation for its study. These 10 volumes consisted of a compendium of documentary source materials, presented entirely without commentary.

The descriptive, document-based tradition of older economic history is also reflected in one-volume treatments of American economic development, such as Harold U. Faulkner's *American Economic History*, which went through eight editions between 1924 and 1960 with remarkably little revision.[4] Faulkner's text ran over 700 pages in the first edition, and just over 800 in the eighth. In contrast, in 1966 the first edition of Douglass North's *Growth and Welfare in the American Past* covered roughly the same ground in under 200 pages.

The new economic history promised to overturn and supplant the older intellectual tradition. The decade of the 1960s was the heyday of Cliometrics, a period marked by a sense of ongoing cumulative progress and methodological unity. *The Reinterpretation of Economic History*, a set of papers edited by Robert Fogel and Stanley Engerman (1971), and the Davis, Easterlin, Parker et al "textbook" *American Economic Growth* (1972), already mentioned, reflect the optimism and shared sense of purpose of that period.

The publication of *Time on the Cross* (Fogel and Engerman 1974) and the acrimonious debate that followed form a watershed marking the beginning of the end of Cliometrics as an intellectual movement promising a revolution in methods and results.[5] Regardless of where they stood on the points at issue in this debate, many economic historians, once sympathetic to the iconoclastic goals of the new economic history, came, in the decade that followed, to doubt whether some or all of these goals were as attainable or desirable as once had been thought.

One might counter that the annual Cliometrics meetings recently celebrated their twenty-fifth anniversary (1960–1985) under the auspices of a newly formed Cliometrics society. But in spite of the self-congratulations characterizing that event, the tenor is different today. In contrast to the immodest and controversial statements of new economic history pioneers, the organizational statement of the Cliometrics society lacks any reference to furthering the application of economic theory and/or statistical methods to economic history. Rather, the *primary* purpose of the organization is to be the maintenance and circulation of a mailing list; the secondary objective is to secure a reduced subscription rate to *Explorations in Economic History*.[6] Worthy objectives, to be sure, but scarcely those of an organization spearheading a continuing intellectual revolution.

Economists frequently view ideas as competing in an intellectual marketplace, and ascribe significance to those ideas that survive and persist. What then explains the extraordinary success of Cliometrics in the 1960s? Was it simply the emphasis on number crunching in an era when costs of data processing were declining dramatically? Or its concentration on slavery and development topics that capitalized on interest in the Civil Rights movement on the one hand and concern with poverty in the developing world on the other? While these factors undoubtedly played a role, they did so against a backdrop of economic and demographic developments that created an extremely favorable environment for Cliometrics in particular and academics in general. That reality needs to be kept in mind in reflecting on Cliometrics' golden years, because these conditions did not obtain for more than a decade-and-a-half thereafter—and are unlikely to return, at least with quite the same force, in the foreseeable future.

The positive elements of the Cliometric research program—the emphasis on statistical sources and on causal explanation rather than simple description—maintain considerable appeal among a broad range of economic historians, including this author. But the absence today of a revolutionary attitude among proponents reflects an implicit recognition of the limitations of the new economic history—as practiced and marketed in the 1960s and early 1970s. The most serious liabilities in that program included tendencies first to downplay dependence on the older descriptive tradition, and second, to embrace too enthusiastically received economic theory as a source of hypotheses to be investigated. These liabilities have been recognized periodically by new economic historians (including some suffering from their influence), but that recognition has had an uneven impact on the conduct of research and teaching. It is more urgent today that weaknesses be recognized and addressed, because the academic and economic environment following the boom years of the 1960s has been less favorable to holders of doctorates.[7]

The vitality of economic history has in the past and will in the future depend partly on macroeconomic and demographic conditions influencing the expansion rates of economics departments in which it is principally practiced, and partly on success in defining a mission within those departments. The latter effort depends on tight thinking and coherent argument, the character of which becomes more critical when the academic sector as a whole is contracting, or in a slow-growth mode. The correlation —spurious or not—between the rise of the new economic history and the years of academic boom reinforces a case (which can be made on purely substantive grounds) for reexamining the relations between economic history and economic theory, on the one hand, and traditional history, on the other.

The evidence of Cliometric "success" in the 1960s does not necessarily imply that these relations were adequately worked out during that decade. In a boom environment, incomplete or deficient intellectual merchandise may for a time survive a market test, yet such success does not necessarily speak to survivability in less favorable environments. Most people understand the qualitative point that macroacademic conditions have changed since the 1960s, but fewer are aware of just how exceptional that decade was. Examination of the economic history of the profession itself can complement consideration of substantive issues in helping us understand the rapid diffusion of a new set of ideas and attitudes, and their deficiencies and strengths. Intellectual trends develop in part according to their own dynamic, but they do not do so in a vacuum.

The Cliometric Revolution and the Golden Age of Academics

Individuals completing their graduate work in economics (and other disciplines) between 1957 and 1969, including the new generation of economic historians priding themselves on their training in formal economic theory and statistics, experienced a demand for their services the strength of which had not been seen before and was not to be seen again, at least through the early 1980s. Demographic factors were partly responsible. Like a large rat being slowly swallowed by a mongoose, the children of the postwar baby boom moved through the educational system, producing cramped facilities and excess demands for personnel as they progressed from one level to the next. Elementary and secondary school teachers benefited initially as districts ran double and triple sessions. Rising income levels and the correct perception that a college education had traditionally been a worthwhile investment based on economic and other criteria fueled high levels of college aspiration among parents and children. These factors combined with the high post-World War II birthrate caused large cohorts of students to enroll in the nation's institutions of higher learning in the mid-nineteen sixties, creating a very strong demand for instructional personnel at the college and university level.

Macroeconomic and political developments reinforced these demographic trends during the decade of the 1960s. Defense research and various Great Society programs—liberally funded—released time at research universities (further increasing the demand for academic personnel) at the same time federal spending on research and development increased the demand for nonacademically employed economists in the public and private sectors. These trends in turn complemented increases in the relative demand for doctorates originating in the private sector as the result of shifts in organizational and production technologies within and between sectors. In calendar year 1957, prior to the impact of Sputnik and the influences outlined above, the wages of all Ph.D.s relative to manufacturing workers reversed a long-term downward trend, and began to increase (Freeman 1971, p. 80).

Finally, the creation of new Ph.D.s involves a human-capital formation process with a gestation period of several years. Responding to the excess demand for doctorates, many state and some private universities opened new Ph.D. programs and struggled to attract faculty to staff them, causing demand for new Ph.D.s in industry, government, and education to feed upon itself, in a manner captured in a traditional capital stock adjustment model.

Both old and new doctoral programs scrambled to attract students, who traditionally had viewed academics (correctly) as a relatively unlucrative profession. Incentives included generous fellowship support; several loan programs offered full or partial forgiveness of loans if students went into college teaching. Contrary to the situation in the 1970s, a Ph.D. in hand was not a virtual prerequisite for embarking on an academic career. Promotion and tenure came relatively quickly; and the salary structure itself moved up steadily in real terms. Economic historians, like other economists, knew that if they tired of one institution, there were others eager for their services.

The relative wages and the employment of economists both rose—the hallmark of a demand-driven employment expansion—and within this context new economic historians found a ready market for their services. The extraordinarily rapid success of the Cliometric movement coincides closely with this boom, and is attributable partly to these powerful demographic and economic forces influencing the academic labor market. From the standpoint of financial rewards and job security, it was a golden age for economic historians and academics in general.

The Cliometric revolution represented a successful campaign begun in the late 1950s against a previous generation of less empirically and analytically oriented economic historians. The struggle paralleled the broader effort by younger economic theorists to gain wider acceptance of the use of mathematical and statistical techniques in economic research. By the late 1960s, having triumphed over their intellectual elders by stressing the superiority of research that made greater use of theoretical analysis and econometric techniques, new economic historians inhabited economic departments where these values were no longer matters of serious controversy.

Then, beginning in the academic year 1969–70, the supply/demand imbalance in economics and other disciplines began to turn around. On the supply side, the high relative wages prevailing in the 1960s when career decisions were being made had been reinforced by recruiting efforts, high levels of fellowship support, and the nonpecuniary benefits that made the ivory tower seem an attractive refuge from the turbulence of the era—a career relatively insulated from the hierarchical relations, lack of autonomy, and competitive pressures of nonacademic employment. The consequence was a huge wave of highly qualified baby boomers, now through college, entering graduate school and eventually emerging in the 1970s with doctorates.

At the start of the academic boom in 1957, fewer than 9,000 doctorates were granted annually in the United States (this was, however, double the level a decade earlier). With the onset of boom conditions (as evidenced by shortages and rapid absolute and relative wage growth), the number of doctorates awarded rose, first slowly and then, after a lag, rapidly. By 1965–66, degrees awarded had risen to 18,237, and with the award of 29,866 doctorates four years later in 1969–70, the shortages ended and relative wage growth ceased. Doctorates awarded in economics jumped from 458 in 1965–66 to 794 in 1969–70, a 73 percent increase, and in history from 527 to 1,038, a 97 percent increase over the same period, with the largest absolute and percentage increases in both disciplines occuring between 1968–69 and 1969–70 (see table 1.1). The 25-percent one-year jump in new awards at the end of the 1960s, the largest annual percentage increase in the past two decades in either discipline, was the result of a supply response to the favorable economic signals prevailing four or five years earlier, and coincided with the end of the academic

Table 1.1. Doctorates Granted, Economics, and History, 1965–81

Academic Year	*Economics*	*Increase (%)*	*History*	*Increase (%)*	*Economics / History*
1964–65	410		576	−9	.71
1965–66	458	+12	527		.87
1966–67[a]					
1967–68	600	+15[b]	688	+15[b]	.87
1968–69	634	+6	826	+20	.77
1969–70	794	+25	1,038	+26	.76
1970–71	721	−9	991	−5	.73
1971–72	794	+10	1,133	+14	.70
1972–73	845	+6	1,140	+1	.74
1973–74	788	−7	1,114	−2	.71
1974–75	815	+3	1,117	+0	.72
1975–76	763	−6	1,014	−9	.75
1976–77	758	−1	921	−9	.82
1977–78	706	−7	813	−12	.87
1978–79	712	+1	756	−7	.94
1979–80	677	−5	712	−6	.95
1980–81	727	+7	643	−10	1.13

Sources: U.S. Department of Education, National Center for Education Statistics, *Digest of Education Statistics* (various years).

[a] Data unavilable for 1966–67.

[b] Interpolated from two-year rate of growth.

boom in economics, history, and the academic market in general in the United States.

In subsequent years the overall number of doctorates awarded continued to grow, although the rate of increase slowed dramatically. Economics and history doctorates awarded both peaked in 1972–73, economics at 845 and history at 1,140.[8] The series for all doctorates awarded in the U.S. has the same turning point, peaking at 34,777 degrees granted in the year 1972–73.[9] In spite of the slowing down and slight decline, overall degrees granted remained at historically high levels throughout the 1970s. Indeed, although as measured by wage data and reports of shortages, the academic boom ended in 1969–70. During the 11-year period beginning in July of 1970, over 360,000 new doctorates were granted, more than one out of every two doctorate degrees ever granted in the U.S. through June of 1980 (U.S. Department of Education, National Center for Education Statistics 1982, pp. 130–131).

Years of Feast; Years of Famine

Shortages ended in the 1970s not only because of the supply response to previous boom conditions, but also because, on the demand side, the numbers of potential students in the prime college-going age groups ceased to rise at the same rate. Bachelor's degrees awarded more than doubled between 1961–62 and 1971–72, growing from 417,846 to 887,273 over that decade (a 112 percent increase). Between 1971–72 and 1981–82 an additional increase of only 7.4 percent occurred, to 952,998 in the latter year (U.S. Department of Education 1982).[10] Some disillusionment also set in with regard to the benefits of an increasingly expensive college degree, as some studies—based in part on end-period data for the early 1970s—prematurely reported that demand for college graduates had finally ceased to outrun supply, and the rate of return to college education had fallen (Freeman 1976). While benefits were being called into question, college costs rose faster than general price indexes, not because relative faculty wages continued to accelerate, but because of slow productivity growth in comparison with other sectors such as manufacturing (Baumol 1967).

The Vietnam war wound down; defense expenditures fell as a share of GNP; administrations on average were less disposed to expand or even maintain existing social programs. Total R&D spending, an important determinant of demand for Ph.D.s in the private sector, peaked in 1968 at $29,833 billion (1972 dollars), not attaining the same level again until 1977 (National Science Foundation 1983, appendix table 2.2). New

Ph.D. programs came onstream and contributed to the rapid expansion of doctorates during the 1970s at about the same time that their staffing requirements ceased adding to the demand for new doctorates.

In spite of increased female participation in the labor force, real output grew at a significantly slower rate during the 1970s, as compared with the 1960s, the consequence of relatively slow growth in person hour productivity. The 1974–1975 recession was deeper than any experienced in the previous two decades. Negative supply shocks interacted with high rates of monetary growth to produce an unsettled macroeconomic environment characterized by high and variable inflation and interest rates, and volatile asset markets. Academic institutions became more cautious in granting appointments without limits of time, a caution reinforced by the relative youth of the tenured professoriate as universities and colleges entered the 1970s.

These developments impinged directly on all economic historians and economists, especially those receiving their doctorates in the 1970s. With some exceptions, promotions have been slower and tenure rates lower. Relative wages declined and real wage growth was slow. In response to a deteriorating supply/demand imbalance, many of the nation's top economics departments cut the size of their incoming Ph.D. programs, some universities eliminated their programs altogether, and many bright students who might in the previous decade have pursued doctorates in economics went on to law or business school. This supply response does not show up completely in the aggregate date because it is counterbalanced by the increased flow from new and generally lesser-known programs. The drastic decline in federal doctoral support added to the negative signals emanating from the academic marketplace. The number of graduate students supported on federal fellowships and traineeships rose from 11,591 in FY1961 to 51,446 in FY1968, and then dropped to under 7,000 in 1974 (Freeman and Breneman 1974, p. 13).

Because of long doctoral gestation periods, the supply response reflected in new history doctorates did not occur until the second half of the 1970s. History Ph.D.s awarded fell from 1,117 in 1974–75 to 643 in 1981, a 42 percent drop in 7 years. The response in economics was more modest, partly because demand conditions did not deteriorate as badly. Still, such data understate the supply response among U.S. nationals alone, since a larger fraction of Ph.D. awards in the 1970s went to foreign nationals returning to their country of origin after completion of training. Finally, this discussion of supply response in academic labor markets ignores the role of attrition within the existing stocks (particularly important in history) and reduced inflows of foreign-trained doctorates (relatively more important in economics).

Eventually, after almost a decade in the doldrums, total R&D spending again rose rapidly after 1977 (approximately 25 percent in real terms between 1977 and 1983), a rise associated with the revolution in semiconductors and bioengineering, and the pick up in the rate of growth of military spending (National Science Foundation 1983, appendix 2.2). Taking trends on both the supply and demand side into consideration, the overall outlook for holders of doctorates has improved modestly in the mid-1980s. Economics departments in particular have been able to maintain their graduate enrollments by admitting larger numbers of foreign students. In addition, the expansion of business schools has created a growing market for economics Ph.D.s, since business schools have not been able to satisfy internally (through their own Ph.D. programs) the increased demand for faculty resulting from surging enrollements.[11] But if economics graduates have been able to maintain a relatively successful position in the academic marketplace, the demand/supply balance as reflected in real and relative wage growth is still a far cry from what it was during the period between 1957 and 1969.

The fluctuating fortunes of the academic enterprise as a whole underly the importance to economic historians of adequately defining a mission within economics departments. Cliometrics developed during a period of rapid growth and great intellectual flux, and never adequately addressed (because it took for granted) the role of economic history in economics departments. Today, as before, the future of economic history depends not only on how fast economics departments are expanding, but also on the centrality—or lack thereof—of economic history in the research and teaching programs of such departments. A coherent and intellectually defensible case for such centrality is therefore essential, even if the macro-academic environment should continue to improve during the remainder of the 1980s.

The Outlook Within History Departments

As part of their definition of mission, economist economic historians need to acknowledge their dependence on the methods and results of traditional history in a manner anathema in the early years of Clio. But even though joint appointments in economics and history (among the tenured professoriate) became more fashionable in the latter half of the 1970s, we should be clear that most research in economic history will continue to be done, as it is today, in economics rather than history departments. The reasons for this are partly intellectual and partly demographic.

Even more so than is the case in economics, demand for history doctorates is driven by undergraduate enrollments. Although the demand/supply balance for all doctorates deteriorated after 1969, the deterioration was relatively worse in history because of a collapse in undergraduate enrollments. For reasons having to do with the greater geographical specificity of skills taught and lower overall foreign demand, history departments in America have not been able to tap into overseas markets for graduate education as successfully as have economics departments in the 1970s and early 1980s. Finally, the strength of nonacademic demand for historians is lower than it is for economists.

The rise and collapse of undergraduate enrollments in history is truly astonishing. Undergraduate degrees in history soared during the 1960s, rising from 25,854 in 1964–65 to a peak of 44,663 in 1970–71, an increase of 73 percent.[12] In the next decade, the number of undergraduate history degrees awarded plunged 59 percent, to 18,301 in 1980–81 (see table 1.2). In 1970–71, history departments produced 2.8 times as many first degrees as economics departments. In 1980–81—the latest year for which data are available, economics bachelor's degrees outnumbered those awarded in history for the first time, even though the absolute number of economics

Table 1.2. B.A.s Granted: Economics and History

Year	*Econ B.A.*	*Hist B.A.*
1964–65	10,875	25,854
1965–66	11,585	28,770
1966–67	n.a.	n.a.
1967–68	15,193	35,291
1968–69	16,867	40,939
1969–70	17,197	43,386
1970–71	15,758	44,663
1971–72	15,231	43,695
1972–73	14,770	40,943
1973–74	14,285	37,049
1974–75	14,046	31,470
1975–76	14,741	28,400
1976–77	15,296	25,433
1977–78	15,661	23,004
1978–79	16,409	21,019
1979–80	17,863	19,301
1980–81	18,753	18,301

Sources: See table 1.1. n.a. = not available.

B.A.s grew only slightly during the 1970s. With a substantial lag, the collapse in demand for historians has had a dramatic effect on the number of new doctorates granted. 1980–81 also marks the first year in which such degree grants fell below those in economics (see table 1.1). Many economists do not realize that throughout the 1960s and 1970s, substantially more history than economics doctorates were granted—in some years more than 40 percent more.

Even if there were a major turnaround in undergraduate history enrollments, there are reasons having to do with the structure of the history profession which help explain both why Cliometrics had so little impact in history departments during the boom years—and why it is unlikely to have a major impact now, when the demographics are worse. First of all, there is no comparable contemporaneous revolution introducing higher-level mathematics and statistics into historical theory. Indeed, there is no comparable distinction between theoretical and applied fields within history departments, which are segmented along different lines. Secondly, opposition to the encroachment of social science methods, or the definition of history as a social science, has been vigorous and imaginative, if at times polemical. The revived defense of narrative history is one example.

The growth of the Social Science History Association and the establishment of courses in quantitative methods within history departments indicate that within history departments the Cliometric revolution still has some life. This is particularly so within the area of demographic history (see Haines 1986). Such trends will no doubt continue (although some of those staffing economics or social science history positions are and will continue to be trained in economics departments). But Cliometric methodology is unlikely to revolutionize history departments in the current state of contraction much more than it did during the boom period of the 1960s, and will never overwhelm entire history departments the way it did the teaching of economic history within economics departments. Traditional history is too firmly entrenched, and, as I shall argue later, Cliometric, economic, or social science history is ultimately too dependent on the work of traditional historians for such an outcome even to be desirable.

The Challenge Within Economics Departments

But if the bulk of research in economic history will continue to be performed in economics departments, the place of economic history in research and instructional programs of such departments cannot be taken for granted. In the slower growth atmosphere of the 1970s and early 1980s, that role came under increased scrutiny, especially from other economists. With technically oriented faculty recruiting technically oriented students for Ph.D. programs, the justification for required courses in economic history and the need for faculty to teach them has in some instances been seriously questioned by students and faculty. In some cases the economic history requirement had been eliminated or weakened, going the route of foreign language requirements.

It would be tempting to see the current developments as recapitulating the debates and soul searching of the late 1950s associated with the opening shots in the Cliometric revolution: the repetition of an intellectual cycle with a periodicity of a quarter century. But doing so would obscure an important point. The debates a quarter century ago, at least in the United States, concerned the methods and the content of economic history research and training. The persistence of economic history as a major element in the research and training programs of economics departments was not directly at issue. One can argue that it would have been had the Cliometric revolution not been successful. Still, the persistence issue lies much closer to the surface today.

These concerns need to be kept in perspective. If economic history has withered on the vine at some institutions, it remains vigorous at others, though numbers be small.[13] Scholarship remains active, and economic history course offerings remain popular at the undergraduate level. In calling attention to the uncertain future of economic history, one must recognize that participants in other fields within economics departments are also capable, if so inclined, of perceiving their future in cloudy terms, perhaps with justification. Still, there is an asymmetry, for example, between the situations faced by economist historians and economic theorists, an asymmetry that goes beyond the obvious differences in stocks of employed and flows of new doctorates in the two specializations. The role of economic history in graduate training programs has been questioned at some institutions; that is not the case for courses in micro- and macroeconomic theory.

Are these trends cause for pessimism? On their face they are as sobering as the demographic trends discussed earlier. But they are also less preordained and therefore more subject to alteration. Therein lies cause for some optimism about a future in which economic history plays a larger role in economics departments, to the benefit of theorists and historians alike. Whether that optimism will turn out to be justified depends in part on how adequately economic historians respond to current challenges. The persistence issue *is* surfacing directly in hiring, retention, and curriculum discussions. Perhaps it deserves to, given that Cliometric statements of the 1960s did not adequately address the issue.

What we need are better statements of what distinguishes economic history from—and what we have to offer to—practitioners of "traditional history" on the one hand, and members of our departments on the other. Remarks to the effect that economic history is what economic historians do in other epochs may have successfully avoided lengthy discussion that detracted from time available for research. Such discussions are unavoidable, however, when the resources and commitments necessary to insure the continued viability of the enterprise may be in jeopardy.

Economic Theory and Economic History

Can a history Ph.D. with several courses in quantitative methods generally perform the same kinds of research as an economic historian trained in an economics department? To answer this question affirmatively is to leave open the question of why a Ph.D. in economics is necessary or even desirable for an economic historian and, derivatively, why economic history should be an integral part of training in economics. Moreover, if it is true that economic historians with economics Ph.D.s are no better prepared for their research than history Ph.D.s with quantitative methods training, it is hard to defend the former against the charge of being both second-rate economists and second-rate historians—the precious years of graduate study squandered in the contemplation of bordered Hessians and other esoterica unrecognizable to traditional historians, even of a military inclination.

To begin with, economist economic historians need to recognize more than they sometimes do that the typical history Ph.D. does bring special strengths to his or her research. In addition to more experience and superior skills in archival work—in particular, in the interpretation and evaluation of documentary records (see Chandler 1973)—the history Ph.D. is likely to have a better awareness of the historiography or intellectual topography of an era or topic under investigation. Overall, in comparison with the economics doctorate, the historian is likely to have a broader knowledge of the cultural and intellectual traditions relevant to the topic under study (Wright 1986).

The economics doctorate is likely to be less experienced in archival work or the interpretation of documents. Less specialized with respect to the historical period or topic, he or she is also likely to be less knowledgeable as to its historiography, at least in the initial stages of a project. Finally, the economist economic historian, torn between the historian's love of data and the economic theorists' disdain for "mere facts"—may suffer from an ambivalent and at times schizophrenic attitude toward primary source materials.

But there are compensations, important ones. In addition to greater expertise in the use of multivariate techniques for estimation and hypothesis testing, the economic historian trained in an economics department also brings to the study of history a better understanding of the concepts and structure of economic theory, and knowledge of how it can be used to inform the study of real-world problems. A basic inventory of such tools might include (1) an understanding of the use of demand and supply analysis within a partial equilibrium context, in particular an awareness of how these tools are used to investigate the impact of shifts in exogenous factors, such as technological change or taxes, on endogenous variables such as price and quantity; (2) a grasp of the basic structure of general equilibrium theory as a conceptual apparatus for interrelating propositions about the relation between levels and changes in technology, preferences, institutions, and endowments on the one hand, and prices and quantities on the other (Thomas 1986); (3) an understanding of the categories and concepts of modern aggregate economics—in particular how markets in labor, goods, and assets interact, as manifested in a comprehension of the subtleties of the IS/LM variant of general equilibrium analysis (Eichengreen 1986); and (4) a grasp of the rudiments of international economics, in particular the categories and concepts related to current and capital account flows and their determinants.

Complementing basic statistical and theoretical knowledge, an economist economic historian may also bring to the study of history specialized skills involving the empirical implementation of some of the theoretical tools outlined above. Examples include experience in estimating money demand functions, or demand or supply schedules in a single market; construction and use of general equilibrium models; or experience running simulations with multiequation macroeconomic models.

By and large, new economic historians have been too uncritically accepting of received economic theory, and have not adequately accepted the challenge of contributing to its development and refinement. Still, familiarity brings with it the danger of underestimating the importance of exposure to economic theory, which at its best represents the distillation of decades of conceptual and empirical research. Relative to the history doctorate, familiarity with theory as a means of modeling complex and sometimes nonintuitive relationships between exogenous and endogenous variables compensates in varying amounts for economists' generally lower level of specialization and sophistication in the sources and historiography of topics under study. The apparent consensus, at least in history departments, that the chief difference between the economics and history doctorate working in economic history is the economist's knowledge of statistics and econometrics needs to be rejected.

Some observers still argue that the key distinction between the historian and the economist is that the former is concerned with the particular, whereas the latter is concerned with the particular only as an example of a more general category of phenomena (Arrow 1985, p. 320). Although the majority of historians continue to be concerned with the particular, the profession seems to have accepted the desirability of symbiosis with those whose interests are more far reaching; the tolerance of at least some "social science historians" within history departments evidences this. But the complexity of the questions an economist economic historian is prepared to ask (and answer), given the right data and the reasonableness of making the necessary assumptions, goes considerably beyond the complexity of questions that might suggest themselves to a traditional historian exposed to an introductory course in quantitative methods alone.

On the other hand, the ultimate goal of research in history and economics should be to advance our understanding of historical and contemporary social phenomena. Many research projects of interest to economic historians simply do not require very sophisticated analytical or econometric skills. And research projects that do require such analysis or techniques are dependent on preparatory ground work—done by economists, historians, or others—which may again place little demand on the skills just inventoried. Primary source materials, be they documents or statistics, are the bedrock of historical analysis. Their collection, interpretation, and initial evaluation are preconditions for more virtuoso exercises to be undertaken by economists.

Because they stand astride the disciplines of history and economics, economic historians have the opportunity to draw on the strengths of both traditions. But they are also susceptible to weaknesses particular to each. Indeed, at its most polemical, Cliometric methodology opened the way to dazzling combinations or iterations between (what one can call) the vices of the theorist and those of the historian. In an era of academic expansion, these issues received relatively little attention, at least among the victorious Cliometricians, but in the context of the lean years that followed, the excesses associated with diffusion of the new economic history methodology need to be identified and better understood, if only to avoid them. In attempting to chart a new course, economic historians need to steer clear of two distinguishable syndromes, susceptibility to which they inherit from the different traditions they link.

Occupational Hazards: 1. The Theorist's Vice

In 1965 Alexander Gerschenkron observed that "until recently the field of economic history was *dominated* not by economists, but by lawyers and historians" (Fishlow 1965, p. vii). Gerschenkron's workshop at Harvard produced many of the contributors to the new economic history revolution, a revolution that made formal training in economic theory and statistics a prerequisite for teaching economic history in an economics department. But because the methodological program of the new economic history was directed so polemically at the older tradition described by Gerschenkron, it has had the unfortunate consequence of perpetuating a misapprehension about the analytical structure of economic theory; a misapprehesion that, if left uncorrected, will continue to vitiate the practice of economic history. (It also threatens the progress of pure theory, but that is not the central matter at issue here.) This misapprehension involves the role of initial conditions in economic theory as well as applied economics, including economic history. If an understanding of basic economic theory is a strength of economist economic historians, it brings with it exposure to a potentially debilitating syndrome: the disease of *a priorism*.

The traditional domination of economic history by historians and lawyers reflected an implicit understanding that *purely descriptive* knowledge of exogenous (and endogenous) variables was a foundation for meaningful economic analysis. Yet many economic theorists today look down on *mere facts* just as they look down on *mere description*. Economic theory does permit us to do better than simply describe prices and quantities: using economic theory, we can explain them—link their variation to variation in other exogenous variables. But since specification of exogenous and endogenous variables remains central to the explanatory enterprise, economic theorists are not justified in disdaining the descriptive foundations for their work. The new economic historians' at times uncritical embracing of economic theory has exposed them to this disdain, a prejudice fundamentally at variance with the inductive and particularistic traditions of historical scholarship.

As illustration of the deleterious consequences of this misapprehension, consider the tendency in economic discourse to dismiss analyses on the grounds that they are ad hoc. Without some relative judgment comparing what is ad hoc in one model with what is ad hoc in another (preferred) model, such criticism is specious. It is specious because all scientific explanation by its nature depends on ad hoc elements, and is therefore partly conditional on variables whose levels or changes are themselves unexplained. We call these ad hoc elements exogenous variables. What is exogenous in one model might be made endogenous in a more complex model, but ultimately any explanation must have some initial conditions that are simply described. To say a model is ad hoc without comparing it to some preferred alternative is not in itself a justifiable criticism. Identifying the ad hoc elements in an analysis is the beginning, not the conclusion of an evaluation of its merits.

The bread and butter of economic analysis consists of comparative statics exercises in which an economic model is constructed, initial equilibrium values for endogenous variables are determined, an exogenous variable or parameter is altered, and a new equilibrium is calculated and compared with the original. Exogenous variables may be altered hypothetically for a variety of exploratory purposes, ranging from (a) predicting the impact of a policy change under consideration to (b) estimating the influence of a particular (actual) historical development or policy change on endogenous variables by positing a world, similar in other respects, in which this development was absent. But whether the exogenous variable(s) altered are tax schedules; the rate of growth of the money supply; government spending; transfer entitlements; tariffs; work/leisure preferences; land endowments; oil cartels; climate; agricultural, transportation, industrial, or communication technology; or rules governing the holding, registration, conveyance, inheritance, and bequest of real or personal property, the basic framework of positive economic analysis is designed to investigate the *consequences* of such changes, not their causes. By definition, the values of exogenous variables are unexplained within the context of an economic model.

The art in economic model building consists in *choosing* the unexplained starting points, not in trying to eliminate them entirely. Economic historians ought to be in a position actively to advance this perspective within economics departments. Sadly, by distancing themselves so much from the older tradition of historical and legal scholarship, some new economic historians have not been well situated to do so.

The prior development of economic theory does provide a general starting framework as one moves beyond simple description of endogenous variables such as relative prices, quantities, or the rate of inflation, and attempts to link variation in such variables to variation in exogenous variables of the sort listed above. Elaboration of the basic framework of economic analysis represents a major intellectual and scientific achievement of the nineteenth and twentieth centuries. But in any specific application, such explanatory efforts remain dependent on the groundwork of traditional historians and government statisticians for measurements of the objects of explanation, for accurate characterization of variation in the exogenous variables, and for guidance on the reasonableness of the simplifications and abstractions involved in building an economic model.

Applied econometricians are urged from time to time to take a more active role in developing the data with which they work (see Griliches 1985). Such efforts would of course be desirable in economic history, for they would make users more aware of the potentialities as well as limitations of their quantitative sources. But if economic historians wish to develop better explanatory models in their research they also need to pay more attention to qualitative sources. Without some familiarity with these sources, acquired either directly or indirectly through secondary treatments, it is difficult to make informed decisions regarding what to include and what to leave out of the simplified mechanisms captured in an economic model. It is better that such decisions be made from positions of knowledge than ignorance.[14]

The consequences of this prejudice against "mere facts" need to be recognized. (Indeed, it would be desirable if economic historians took a more active role in combatting its influence within the economics profession at large.) The idea that economists can somehow do useful research in economic history with only the sketchiest knowledge of the particularities of the topic or era they are studying is symptomatic of a trend within economic theory that has attempted to make it a purely axiomatic deductive science.

But if economic theory is to have applications, can it claim to be a purely axiomatic science? It would be silly to maintain that differences in preference orderings across individuals can be derived axiomatically. In most economic analysis, preference orderings are exogenous, i.e., merely described or specified. Nor is it reasonable to maintain that climate, technological availabilities at a moment in time, or natural resource endowments can be axiomatically derived. They too are generally specified as exogenous. Finally, the attempt to construct economic models without appeal to exogenous basic rules is likewise a chimera (Field, 1979b, 1981, 1984c).[15]

Because theoretical work has become so specialized, a considerable number of theorists operate with ambivalent attitudes toward the empirical "facts" they attempt to explain and those they adduce to explain them with. The use of "stylized facts" both to justify behavioral assumptions and to characterize exogenous and endogenous variables is common in economic model building. The practice is tolerable with respect to assumptions and exogenous variables, since the "reasonableness" of such abstractions usually influences how accurately a model will explain or predict. If the stylized facts bear little relation to empirical reality, the model will typically perform poorly when subject to empirical test: that is, it will neither explain nor predict well.[16]

The use of stylized facts as explanations in theoretical work is considerably more dangerous because it attenuates, to the point of breaking, the link between model building and model verification. If exogenous variables, behavioral assumptions, and endogenous variables are *all* justified with reference to stylized facts, there is precious little opportunity for empirical reality to intrude on the theoretical enterprise. Theorists are often not well equipped to make judgments with respect to the accuracy and reasonableness of their stylized facts, and in their eagerness to proceed, may minimize their dependence on others for such judgments. The result is that theoretical "advance" has a tendency periodically to lose contact with the empirical phenomena it is supposed to account for.

Economic historians need therefore to become more discriminating users of "new" theoretical developments. The belief that successful careers in economic history should involve a one-way arbitrage from new theoretical ideas to old data tends to produce an arid and unilluminating literature in economic history and contributes indirectly to a barrenness in the theoretical literature. It reinforces tendencies of the theoretical enterprise to cut itself loose from applied empirical work. It produces work that is of little interest to traditional historians. Initially, it may be applauded by theorists, flattered by the uncritical acceptance of theoretical tools about whose applicability they may in fact have grave doubts. But eventually, if the arbitrage is only in one direction, theorists will ask why they really need economic historians at all in an economics department, given the opportunity to hire another applied mathematician. The appropriate communication between history and theory needs to be two way.

In defense of pure theory, it is indeed sometimes the case that significant contributions to economic theory can be made by individuals with no sensitivity whatsoever to institutional, technological, or geographical variation. If the groundwork has been done by others, a brilliant applied mathematician may produce results that counter our initial intuition, but offer powerful insights in understanding the links between exogenous and endogenous variables. But the contribution of such a theorist to the progress of economics is dependent on his or her being fed a diet of interesting and relevant puzzles or problems by those with more empirical or historical sensitivities. The belief that proficiency in axiomatic or deductive reasoning can substitute for such knowledge is a delusion. Ultimately pure theorists must look to research in economic history and other empirical fields for validation of the significance of their research, rather than vice versa.

Exposure to research in economic history should offer the aspiring theorist a window into the art of developing useful simplifications (abstractions) used in economic model building.[17] At the same time, coursework in economic history should offer the aspiring theorist—and empirical economist—the motivation and sensitivities to evaluate theoretical models on criteria above and beyond logical coherence. If the dependence of new economic history on the concerns and methods of the older tradition is rejected or downplayed, as one tendency within the new economic history has in polemical moments counselled, the justification for retaining economic history courses in graduate curricula becomes indeed problematic.

Contributions of the New Economic History to Historical Understanding

A consideration of some of the major areas to which the new economic history has claimed significant contributions over the past quarter-century can illustrate some of the points developed above. Two areas of research stand out in many lists of Cliometric "successes"—cases where careful research apparently overturned what Gerschenkron described as "uncertain hypotheses [tending] to gain wide acceptance as well established propositions."

The first concerns the impact of the railroad on levels and growth rates of nineteenth-century American GNP; the second has to do with the profitability and viability of slavery. Impressed by the dynamism of railway machinery, and the vast (absolute) amount of resources devoted to railway construction, traditional historians and indeed some economic historians (Rostow 1961) had maintained in qualitative terms that railroads were in some sense indispensable to American development (Fogel 1964, pp. 11–13). The research of Fogel (1964) and Fishlow (1965) attempted to quantify the concept of indispensability, by positing a world without the railroad and asking how much it would have cost to provide transport services using alternate transport modes (canal, river, turnpike). Although the precise numerical estimate of the social saving of the railroad differed, depending on the year for which the calculation was made and the attributes of the assumed counterfactual world, the range of estimates was considerably smaller than many felt had been implied by the qualitative term "indispensable."

Similarly, research on the economics of slavery, beginning with the work of Conrad and Meyer (1958), made it difficult to argue, based on selected qualitative evidence that slavery was doomed to break down because of its unprofitability to the landowner or its internal contradictions, or that it was fundamentally antithetical to capitalist rationality, any more than one could so argue for apartheid today. Using concepts drawn from the finance and accounting literature, Conrad and Meyer argued that the rate of return to holding slave capital did not differ significantly from that obtainable through holding other forms of capital. Gavin Wright has argued persuasively that this work demolished not the typical views of contemporary (antebellum) commentators, but those of historians of the 1920s and 1930s, and that the analytical tools used were available in the nineteenth century (Wright 1973, p. 453). The contribution of Conrad and Meyer, and the work that followed in its wake, has nevertheless served as a corrective to entrenched views, be they of relatively recent vintage. Wright's point does nonetheless underline how desirable it would be for new economic historians to gain more detailed awareness of the historiography of the topics they study.

The significant commonality in these two research programs is that both involve investigations of the *consequences* of the level or change in one of the variables typically taken as exogenous in a general equilibrium model—in the former case a technical innovation; in the latter a social and legal institution. In the former instance an explanation for why the railroad was invented is not offered or attempted. What is under study is the consequences of this change in available transport technologies. In the latter instance, the origins of slavery, or even the causes of its demise, are not directly at issue. Rather, what is under study are the consequences of this institution for economic growth, industrialization, and income distribution.

It is not as easy to reach a consensus on what have been the less successful enterprises of the new economic history. But I believe one of the more compelling examples is the North and Thomas attempt to make endogenous institutional variation in Europe over an 800-year period (North and Thomas 1973; Field 1981). Fogel, writing in 1971, suggested two important future avenues of research: first, the greater use of multisector general equilibrium models, and second, models involving "interrelationships among economic, political, and social variables"

(Fishlow and Fogel 1971, p. 32). Although in the past 15 years, Fogel himself has followed up neither suggestion, others have, in the first case with some success. (M. Thomas 1986); and in the second case without a great deal of success, for reasons Fogel himself pointed out at the end of his essay. It is true nevertheless that the second line of inquiry, examining "the reverse line of causation—the effect of economic variables on political and social behavior...falls within the tradition of our discipline" (Fishlow and Fogel 1971, p. 38). It is a tradition that has a Marxian, a structural-functional, and a neoclassical/economic variant, all of which lead the unwary to minimize the independent causal role of variation in basic rules.[18]

Fogel's second suggestion is a siren call to theoretically minded scholars that is best resisted by ambitious economic historians and other social scientists. After all, if there is general agreement that traditional economic history was concerned simply with the description of institutional environments (Redlich 1965, p. 482), one must ask why scholars were willing to devote lifetimes to this task. They were willing to do so because of an implicit recognition that institutional variation exercised an important determining influence on economic outcomes in their own right; that scientific explanation required adequate *descriptions* of initial conditions, and that economic historians could make a useful contribution by accurately characterizing these conditions and their changes over time. The North and Thomas enterprise illustrates the danger of the a priorism implicit in the theorist's vice. What is notable in this work is a reluctance to accept the proposition that some basic rules in economic analysis must be treated exogenously. There are other approaches to the problem, an example of which is Hughes' treatment of the defining influence of English land law on the pattern of land settlement and economic development in the American colonies (Hughes 1983, pp. 11–18).[19]

Not every economic or social scientific model need treat all rules as exogenous. Some rules, especially those designed to solve coordination problems (which typically require no or little enforcement), have a natural efficiency interpretation (Field 1984c, pp. 692–694). And given a basic legal structure providing for the enforcement of contracts over time, we may be able to explain (make endogenous) selection from a book of subsidiary contractual forms, much as we would account for choice of technology from a book of available blueprints. Such explanations may be cast in terms of relative prices (endogenous to the model as a whole, but parametric to individuals), or, more directly, in terms of relative scarcity of endowments or technological availabilities (which along with other givens influence prices) and/or in terms of different attitudes toward risk among the contracting parties in an uncertain world, where such differences were again exogenously given.

But the need for ad hoc unexplained description is not avoided by endogenizing rule structures in this manner—it is merely pushed back to prior levels. The recognition of the necessity of describing exogenous variables, of couching every explanation in terms of variables themselves unexplained, provides a key to understanding why a knowledge of history and historical research is an essential aspect of the training of a good economist—an economist who is able to make judgments as to what makes a model a good explanatory model, as opposed to one that is simply logically consistent. Economic historians should be extremely suspicious of research that is quick to stigmatize other work as "ad hoc" and is not open about the exogenous unexplained elements in its own analysis. Such elements are always present.

Although the new economic history has had some success in correcting misconceptions or errors in the traditional story, it has been less successful in substituting a basic text of its own. That is because the new economic history at its best represented an extension built on the descriptive foundations of the old economic history, an extension that corrected and modified some of the primitive attempts at explanation implicit in older writings. But the new economic history cannot live without that older tradition, any more than economic theory can survive well without continuing exposure to the findings and methods used in research in economic history and other applied fields.

Economic History and History of Economic Thought

How can economic historians become more discriminating users of economic theory? One means of doing so would be to obtain more direct familiarity with the historical development of economic theory. The evolution of economic theory is not simply a unilateral progression toward received wisdom, but includes a number of lines of inquiry that have previously been dismissed as dead ends. A knowledge of the history of economic ideas can help distinguish between genuinely new theoretical contributions—and those that represent an attempt to resurrect old and long-rejected ideas, perhaps in new packaging. On the other hand, past judgments do sometimes need to be reexamined. Dead ends may be worth a second look, especially when new or less-expensive data processing techniques have become available in the interim.

My own research on the influence of stock trading on the transactions demand for money during the 1920s involved the resurrection of an idea that had been bruited theoretically in the interwar years, then rejected on grounds of casual empiricism. I first encountered the key proposition in a close reading of Keynes' *Treatise on Money* (1930), although it could have been found elsewhere. In the last half-century, the cost of running multiple regressions has dropped dramatically. Using such techniques I was able to estimate the influence of fluctuations in transactions in secondary asset markets on the demand to hold cash balances, and in a manner that has offered new insights into the onset of the great depression and suggests a reconsideration of our standard theoretical specification of the transactions demand for money (Field 1984a, b).

Similarly, it was a close reading of Ricardo (1817) that set me to reconsidering the links between land abundance (or scarcity) and technical choice in Britain and the United States in the nineteenth-century, research which casts serious doubt on the stylized fact that has been the object of explanation in so much of the Habakkuk debate (Field 1983, 1985a).[20] Still, the point is not that all wisdom resides in the unread texts of the classics. Ricardo and Marx are as much at fault as modern economists in causing us to devote such disproportionate attention to the machinery proportion of our national capital stocks (Field 1985a). And much of what lies in the history of economic thought record is not worth rehashing; the advance of modern mathematical and theoretical techniques has incorporated and transcended many nineteenth-century contributions (Baumol 1985).

But as theorists become more specialized, they also become more dependent on a fresh supply of problems, the significance of which they can count on others to have verified. Greater specialization brings with it a greater probability that skills in judging the significance or lack thereof of a theoretical advance become too far removed from those actually doing the work. A knowledge of the history of thought, including some of the abandoned lines of inquiry, can be especially valuable to economic historians in developing a critical perspective on received theory and in insuring that the influences linking economic theory and economic history are not uniformly from the former to the latter. Such efforts can greatly illuminate research in economic history, even when the specific conclusions of the economist under study may be rejected (Lazonick 1986).

The cessation of research and teaching of economic history within graduate programs, even if teaching at the undergraduate level continued, would be equivalent to the intellectual decapitation of the field. One can get some idea of the consequences of such a development by observing that something comparable has already happened in history of economic thought. Very few Ph.D.s in this area have been generated at major research universities in the past two decades. History of economic thought, which used to be a central part of the graduate curriculum, no longer is so. A specialized journal in the area (*History of Political Economy*) does continue to publish, and related articles do from time to time appear in the general interest economics journals. But the discipline seems torn between those who view themselves as upholding high standards of exegetical scholarship (see, e.g., Hollander 1979) and the sometimes more lively contributions of theorists such as Samuelson (1971), who are not specialists in doctrinal scholarship. Neither type of contribution, regretably, is actively linked to any program of empirical research.

In contrast with history of economic thought, economic history has had close links, at least in the last three decades, with development economics—an applied empirical field. Indeed, from a subject matter standpoint, economic history can be viewed as the history of economic development (Feeny 1986). A concern with developmental issues has always been the hallmark of economic history, but the centrality of the developmental concerns—at the partial expense of a concern with distribution (Fishlow and Fogel 1971, p. 18)—seems to have been reinforced by the methodological revolution associated with the new economic history.

History of economic thought, in contrast, is the history of economic theory. Since it is inconceivable that economic theory will be eliminated from the core curricula, there will always be a supply of economic theorists with some interest in their predecessors to inject some life and controversy into studies of the evolution of doctrine. Were economic development so centrally situated in economics curricula, one could count on a similar mechanism operating in economic history. But it is not and one cannot. Thus, the downgrading of economic history to the position of history of economic thought in the curriculum would likely have even graver consequences than it has in history of thought.

Occupational Hazards: 2. The Historian's Vice

In order to survive and prosper, economist historians need to avoid the theorist's vice—the conceit that a purely axiomatic deductive science of society is possible. But they also must steer clear of a vice that has its origins in association with the historical tradition. This vice rarely influences economic historians' teaching in economics departments, but it can and does affect research.

Like most historians, the economist economic historian is, in general, strongly committed to the analysis of source material. There may be on balance a preference for numbers over documents, but with the diffusion of quantitative methods courses and a social science history presence in history departments, these differences between historian and economist economic historians have narrowed. In addition to its stress on the use of economic theory to investigate historical connections that had not previously been studied, the new economic history placed a high premium on the testing and measurement of theoretically predicted linkages through the systematic analysis of quantitative data.

Pressures to complete dissertations and research projects being what they are, some researchers have taken to searching first for a data set, and worrying later about what (presumably interesting) questions it might answer. Sometimes, regretably, no satisfactory resolution to this issue is reached. A second occupational hazard, then, of economist economic historians, is the "data-set-without-a-question" disease. The spectacle of an economic historian deeply immersed in the analysis of a rich data set, uncertain as to what questions are being asked of it—like a masterless samurai roaming the landscape of feudal Japan—can only inspire feelings of fear, sympathy, and pathos. Rich, unexploited data sets are, of course, difficult to come by, and it is only natural for an economic historian, stumbling on one, to ask what more general issues it might illuminate. Sometimes the answer is obvious, sometimes an answer occurs in a short while. Some preliminary analysis may be helpful in surfacing appropriate questions.

But if the researcher intends to "apply the tools of economic theory to historical data," decisions need to be reached at some point—certainly before the writing up of "results" begins—regarding the question of what relationships are being estimated, or what previously posited relationships are being rejected. The longer the "exploratory" process continues without closure on these matters, the more likely is it to produce multitabled output, the presentation of which lacks focus and organization, and the publication of which fuels the objections of the most vociferous opponents of "quantitative history."[21]

Although traditional historians are quick to heap scorn on this kind of work, it should be noted that they are also at risk with respect to this syndrome, although the data set at issue is more frequently archival as opposed to statistical. Economist economic historians, however, are under stronger pressure to go beyond simple descriptions of numerical sources and use data to estimate or test relationships established or predicted by prior research. Costly investments in economic theory and econometric methodology cry out for amortization.

But the successful integration of theory, econometric techniques, and historical data depends partly on fortuitous circumstance. Economic research is by and large a nonexperimental science, and we must take the experiments of history as we find them, and as their data have been collected and preserved for us. The successful use of historical data for sophisticated economic analysis requires ascertaining not only what theoretical variables the data may proxy (Kuznets 1941), but what experiments have in fact been run. When an economic historian plunges ahead with the econometric machinery associated with estimation and/or hypothesis testing "as if" he or she had an interesting problem, the "results" typically lack focus or coherence.

Since a central theme of this essay has been that research in economic history should actively contribute to the advance of economic theory, rather than simply the reverse, it would be contradictory to insist that all data analysis begin with a well established economic model in which the variables to be included, and their coefficient signs, were known in advance or a priori, and all that needed to be done was to estimate parameter values. If that position were strictly adopted, data could never contravene or modify prior maintained hypotheses. There is, however, a difference between the data set without a problem syndrome, and the use of relatively simple statistical techniques for "exploratory data analysis" (Tukey 1977). The economic historian's version of the historian's vice involves trying to force what have, in fact, been—for want of better terminology—forays of exploratory data analysis onto a Procrustean bed of classical hypothesis testing or formal estimation which presupposes well-worked-out maintained hypotheses. It is perhaps some consolation that economic historians are not the only applied econometricians who are, from time to time, subject to this affliction.

Sometimes it is neither the serendipitous discovery of a data set, nor concern with a more general issue that drives the research program; it may be that prior interest in a new econometric or demographic technique guides the search for the data base. It may happen that the marriage of technique and data produces useful historical insight as an unintended by-product. Moreover, the development and application of new techniques may make it possible to ask questions that were previously, for practical purposes, unanswerable. There is a danger, however, that these justifications can become rationalizations, and when interest in illuminating the historical record wanes, as concern with the means begins to overshadows the end, we had best beware.

The Search for Balance

The need to search for balance between the theoretical and historical traditions, and to avoid the occupational hazards associated with each, requires that scholars preparing for careers in economic history, or continuing in them, must make hard decisions regarding the areas or skills in which they invest. Gerschenkron's objection to the older legal or historical tradition in economic history, a tradition marked by relative ignorance of economic theory, was that "very uncertain hypotheses tended to gain acceptance as well established propositions," while many potentially fruitful areas of research remained unexplored (Fishlow 1965, p. vii).

The revolution to which Gerschenkron made such a contribution, through his students, if not his own work, has drastically altered the training of economic historians, especially in economics departments, and what gains have been achieved have naturally had associated with them opportunity costs. On the average, coursework in economic theory and statistics has substituted for time that might have been spent absorbing details of historiography; legal, cultural, or political history; or foreign languages. This loss was less evident in the first and second generations of students who, in reacting to an older tradition, by necessity also absorbed its strengths. Secondly, motivated by revolutionary ardor, the pioneers may simply have worked harder on *adding* more extensive training in economic theory and statistics to the traditional preparatory work for a career in economic history.

For better or for worse, economic theory has become increasingly more abstract over time, and understanding its logic has come to demand more preparatory work in mathematics. Econometric techniques also have increased in their sophistication, although this has been partially compensated for by dramatic drops in the time required to perform them, with continued declines in the cost of computing. Aspiring economic historians have to ask themselves how much time they should spend studying the details of legal, institutional, technological, diplomatic, political, or cultural history, let alone geography.

The Cliometric revolution emphasized both the use of economic theory to address historical problems, and the use of quantitative data to estimate and test relationships suggested by prior research. Since the art of actually conducting empirical research is not easily communicated in lecture format, and tends to be learned in research apprenticeships, the emphasis on applying theory has had the greater influence on graduate instruction as the Cliometric revolution progressed. Inspired by a belief in the universality of the organizing principles being taught, economic history courses taught at the graduate level in economics departments have, in the last two decades, frequently reflected a topical orientation—the objective being to illustrate how the application of economic theory could illuminate problems of historical research. In such courses, knowledge of the details of the period or region under study was either presumed or, by implication, treated as of secondary importance compared with the theoretical propositions being illustrated. History department courses, in contrast, typically have a temporal or regional demarcation.

Except in the hands of very skilled instructors, or among students with strong preparation in traditional history, the topical approach ran the risk of sending mixed signals to students about the importance of historical detail. The principle message was that economic theory could illuminate historical problems. Relatively little emphasis was placed on the reverse potential for research in economic history to contribute to or modify the development of economic theory. Since the "facts" of the historical record were frequently alluded to only indirectly, the student might reasonably conclude that the study of economic history was merely an arena for applying theory—wherein the historical examples illustrate and reinforce theoretical verities treated more formally and comprehensively in theory courses.

If a student rejected this conclusion, he or she was then hit with the apparent presumption of a solid grounding in the history of all these widely varied topics. As the 1970s progressed, the reasonableness of this presumption declined. The number of B.A.s awarded each year in history has dropped precipitously (table 1.2), and few of the recipients have gone on to pursue doctorates in economics. The share of foreign students in doctoral programs has increased. Where was this background to come from? Can it reasonably be presumed? And if not, are current methods of graduate instruction, which emphasize the topical approach, really appropriate?

In order to absorb all the "necessary" theory and econometrics, study of history and historiography, and experience with archival materials frequently take a back seat. In making these difficult compromises, aspiring economic historians run the risk of striking a Faustian bargain: preparing themselves for careers in which they perform research in economic history with only the sketchiest knowledge of the details of what they are studying or its previous historiography. Cynics may remark that it is only when relieved of such burdens that economists can do their best work in the historical arena or elsewhere.

As in much humor, there is an element of truth here: many economic historians trained in economics departments are autodidacts when it comes to their history. Autodidactism can have its advantages—ignorance of the historiography of a topic may open the way to fresh insights. But autodidactism has its downside—a susceptibility to the most egregious errors, and the repetition of past mistakes.

A commitment to analyzing quantitative data sets, although admirable in itself, is not a substitute for knowledge of the qualitative sources. And ignorance of the historiography of a topic deprives economic historians of access to the prior work of historical scholars. At best, it opens the way to repeated reinventions of the wheel, retracing the steps and repeating the basic conclusions of those who have worked earlier. While there is nothing wrong with replication of results, it is important that such efforts be distinguished from novel interpretations which appear novel only because past work has been overlooked. Economists who see no dangers in their status as self-taught historians should recognize how they react to self-taught economists—who are likely to ask probing, often profound, questions one's own professional training has caused one to cease asking—at the same time persisting in the most embarrassing errors, repetitions, and misunderstandings.

The search for balance is not however simply a question of avoiding "tilting too far in the direction of theory." Economic theory as it has developed in the United States in the postwar period contains a powerful current of a priorism that continually threatens to tear the enterprise loose from the social phenomena it is supposed to illuminate. Economic history, which ought to have strong ties to the older traditions of historical and legal scholarship should be one influence helping to apply empirical discipline to the evolution of theory, at the same time opening new areas of historical inquiry to its application and evaluating the "very uncertain hypotheses [which have gained] acceptance as well established propositions." Thus it is not simply a question of altering allocations of intellectual investments between history and theory, and continuing in a passive fashion to "consume" theory, perhaps at lower intake levels. Rather, economic historians should use the strategic position of economic history to direct and influence developments in both directions.

This chapter has called on economist economic historians to develop greater familiarity with the qualitative sources and historiography of the topics they study. One might reasonably ask whether this can be done, given the number of hours in a day, while maintaining skills in economic theory and econometrics. The suggested development of a more critical perspective on theoretical advance by studying more history of theory seems only to compound the problem by adding yet another item to an already crowded agenda. The trick lies in a changed perception of the relation between economic theory and economic history: in redefining economic history as an active contributor to the development of economic theory, not a passive consumer of it.

Standing astride the traditions of history and theory, economic historians need to adopt a posture of critical respect toward both, a posture that recognizes weaknesses as well as strengths in each tradition and avoids excesses of enthusiasm in either direction. In particular, it means developing a better statement of the relationships between traditional history, economic history, and economic theory to supplant that offered by the new economic history. And it means encouraging those who have come to view economic history as another branch of "applied" economics to rethink the very usage of the terms "theoretical" and "applied," which have come to imply a hierarchical and asymmetrical influence from the former to the latter. In reexamining these issues, much of the leadership will come and is coming from younger scholars.

Conclusions

The young Turks of the Cliometrics revolution are now established scholars. Somewhat surprisingly, the generation that now attempts to chart a new course for economic history is less likely to meet outright opposition from their elders as it is to meet indifference. Two decades ago, one might have predicted otherwise. In his presidential address to the Economic History Association in 1966, an address he himself referred to as rambling (p. 458), Alexander Gerschenkron finally turned from answering critics of his own research, to a defense of his seminar students and others like them, pioneers of the new economic history. Here his remarks rose to the level of eloquence as he defended new economic historians against their critics:

> Periods like this are the star hours in the history of a discipline, and no dogmatic criticism, sometimes stemming from inadequate comprehension of the nature of the tools used, should be allowed to interfere with the work and to dim its promise. Nothing, of course, lasts forever. After a decade or so of assiduous work, diminishing returns will set in, and the lure of new problems and new methods will lead economic historians to other yet undiscernible tasks. The innovators of today may well become the conservators of tomorrow. But this is their day, and its splendor should be neither beclouded nor begrudged. (Gerschenkron 1967, p. 458)

Two decades have now past, but at least one of Gerschenkron's predictions has not been realized. Rather than a conservative elite dominating the subdiscipline, and demanding allegiance to the methodological tenets of the new economic history as the price for advancement, many of the pioneering new economic historians have shifted their main research efforts to other fields, and are not overly energized by the issues addressed in this essay or debated so strenuously in the initial days of the Cliometrics revolution. The December 1984 meetings of the American Economic Association in Dallas, Texas, included a session on "Economic Histroy: A Necessary Though Not Sufficient Condition for an Economist." The session, whose title promised explorations of what economic history had to offer economic theory, and vice versa, included papers by two prominent theorists (Professors Arrow and Solow) and two prominent economic historians (Professor David and Temin). The two economic historians avoided directly addressing the issues in the session title, instead presenting papers which, although they had indirect implications for the issues at hand, could easily have been presented in a number of other forums. This left it to Professors Kenneth Arrow and Robert Solow, effectively, to carry the ball.

By their choice of articles, the economic historians revealed a preference not to address directly the issues tackled by Professors Arrow and Solow. Their decisions were disappointing to those in the audience anticipating more reflective presentations. The relation between economic history and economic theory is too important to be left to theorists, even sympathetic theorists. It is certainly better that energies be spent in productive research in economic history or elsewhere than in conservative defense of some of the extreme positions of the Cliometric revolution which are, in the long run, not defensible. Still, the contributions to this forum underlie the extent to which leadership in charting a new course for economic history will, as was the case a quarter-century ago, likely come from newer entrants, rather than more established participants.

At its best the new economic history promised a successful integration of theorist virtues with those of the historian: a creative tension in which the strong points of each tradition would operate as a check on the potential excesses of the other. The theorist's willingness to abstract, and move beyond "mere" description to causal models that link levels and changes in exogenous variables to levels and changes in endogenous variables would serve as a challenge to the particularistic traditions of historical scholarship. At the same time, the historian's concern with and knowledge of primary source materials and the particularities of economic and social phenomena would operate as a counterbalance to the a priori deductivism of economic theory, which in its search for the general can develop great—perhaps excessive—tolerance for inability to account for or illuminate the particular.

If at times the new economic history veered off course and brought us the worst of each world, rather than the best of both, this was perhaps only to be expected from an intellectual movement born in such propitious and unconstraining times. Cliometrics flourished in an extraordinarily favorable academic climate, and as a result exhibited tendencies to excess in certain directions. These tendencies need to be checked if economic history is to define a continuing, or indeed growing, mission within economics departments.

What qualities are desirable in future work? Most importantly, we need to recognize explicitly the limited explanatory objectives of social science—or science in general. One consequence of the new economic history revolution has been an ambivalence toward the descriptive tradition embodied in old economic history. That ambivalence needs to be resolved. If stylized facts are wrong (i.e., bad abstractions), or if theorists cease caring whether they are reasonable abstractions, theoretical research proceeds adrift from empirical moorings. Without some concern for realism or relevance, the most elegant theoretical model becomes so much wasted intellectual effort, inasmuch as economics is to remain a social science. The ultimate test of economic theory is its ability to illuminate aspects of the real world, and that is an evaluation the economic historian may be in a better position to provide than the theorist.

Explanation will always and inevitably be in terms of variables whose levels or changes are themselves unexplained. However, although some events or initial conditions must necessarily be described, we need not be limited in our research to narrative history, since other phenomena may be deducible (explained) with reference to these initial conditions. Such deductions may be quite complex and sometimes lead to nonintuitive conclusions. Mathematical methods in economic theory do have a role to play here, and are instrumental in integrating specific research into a more general and, where possible, cumulative research enterprise.

Notes

1. The terms Cliometrics (from the Latin: *Clio*, the muse of history; *metrics* meaning measurement) and new economic history are used interchangeably here. Both refer to a self-conscious movement, principally among economist economic historians, that began in the late 1950s.

2. Known, before 1969, as *Explorations in Entrepreneurial History*.

3. The 1929 edition published by Macmillan included a 1916 volume on manufactures from 1607 to 1860, and a 1928 volume on manufactures from 1860 to 1914, along with two additional chapters.

4. A 1976 text by Harry Scheiber and Harold G. Vatter is based in part on Faulkner's 8th edition, and attempts to extend this tradition.

5. Debate on the book broke out at a famous Rochester conference in October 1975, and was reflected in print in the 1976 collection *Reckoning with Slavery* (David 1976).

6. See the *Newsletter of the Cliometrics Society* 1 (September 1985):1.

7. See Hughes 1966; Davis 1968; or McCloskey 1976, for recognition of some of the problems addressed in this essay.

8. Economics awards have probably surpassed that level in the middle 1980s, but history awards surely have not.

9. The latest available data, for 1982–83, show 32,775 total doctorates awarded.

10. This doubling of annual B.A. awards in less than a decade makes understandable the successful opening of new colleges and universities during the period.

11. This expanded role for economics doctorates has been especially evident, not only in economics instruction, but also in finance, decision sciences, and accounting; much less so in marketing and management. In the late 1980s and early 1990s, holders of doctorates across the board are likely to experience rising relative wages, due to the large number of anticipated retirements and the relative paucity of new entrants. But this boom will not be associated with a major surge in the number of faculty slots, in contrast with what took place during the 1960s.

12. In contrast, economics B.A.s increased 58 percent: from 10,875 in 1964–65 to a peak–one year earlier than in history—of 17,197 economics B.A.s awarded in 1969–70.

13. A high percentage of recent economics doctorates has been exposed to reseach in economic history, and has written papers in the area as graduate students. A much lower percentage has gone on to write dissertations and continue to do research in the field. I estimate conservatively that economic historians have comprised less than 2 percent of economics Ph.D. output in the last decade in the United States. Between 1975 and 1981, 4,343 doctorates were awarded in the United States, an average of 724 a year (see table 1.1). If we assume an average of 800 over the next four years (1981–1985), we reach a decadal total of just over 7,500. An examination of the annual Ph.D. degree lists in December issues of the *American Economic Review* indicates that an average of somewhere in the range of 4–9 doctorates in the field of economic history were generated in recent years in the United States. The estimate is conservative because the lists are incomplete, and because some dissertations are not obviously classifiable. When a macroeconomist writes a paper on the gold standard, should he or she then also be counted as an economic historian? By classifying more liberally, one can push the cumulative total above 75 (1 percent)—but not, I think, above 150 (2 percent)—over the last ten years.

14. This recommendation is easy to make, but since it entails additional background work, it runs up against a research and training agenda already crammed with other items. The problem is addressed in more detail below.

15. For examples of how this insight can aid in the interpretation of empirical/historical material see Field (1976a,b,; 1979a,c). The first three of these papers explore the relationships between economic and educational change in nineteenth-century Massachusetts; the fourth focuses on nineteenth-century Lancashire.

16. Although even here there is a problem. By redefining upward the generality of a model, a theorist can always reduce the unexplained variance in any particular empirical test to relative unimportance.

17. Useful in the sense that they produce models with good predictive or explanatory power.

18. In this regard, see also Lazonick 1986.

19. Basic rules are of course not the only exogenous variables in economic analysis. Other

examples might include major technological innovations discovered by accident, Supreme Court decisions, and waves of cultural or religious enthusiasm that may alter preferences and influence behavior. Such events or developments need to be treated individually on a case-by-case basis. A descriptive knowledge of the evolution of Supreme Court decisions, for example, is extremely useful in studying and explaining American economic, political, and social development, Ex post, a determined economist may attempt to provide an "efficiency" interpretation of such decisions. But ex ante, conflicting principles or precedents may provide a rationalization for several possible outcomes. This is one explanation for the close relationship between legal scholarship and traditional economic history.

20. I argue in this work, inter alia, that capital/labor and capital/output ratios in the United States economy (and its component sectors) were lower, not higher, than comparable ratios in Britain in 1860.

21. Of course the practice of running hundreds of regressions, and then reporting the "best" results as if they offered parameter estimates for a model known or deduced in advance makes a mockery of significance tests (see Denton 1985).

References

Arrow, Kenneth. 1985. Maine and Texas. *American Economic Review* 75: 320–323.

Baumol, William. 1967. Macroeconomics of unbalanced growth. *American Economic Review* 57:415–426.

Baumol, William. 1985. On method in economics a century earlier. *American Economic Review* 75:1–12.

Bidwell, P.W. and J.I. Falconer. 1925. *History of Agriculture in the Northern United States, 1620–1860*. Washington: Carnegie Institution.

Chandler, Alfred. 1973. Decision making and modern institutional change. *Journal of Economic History* 33:1–15.

Commons, J.R., et al. 1910–1911. *Documentary History of American Industrial Society*. 10 vols. Cleveland: Arthur H. Clark.

Conrad, Alfred, and John Meyer. 1958. The economics of slavery in the antebellum South. *Journal of Political Economy* 66:95–130.

David, Paul. 1985. Clio and the economics of QWERTY. *American Economic Review* 75 (May):332–37.

David, Paul, et al. 1976. *Reckoning with Slavery*. New York: Oxford University Press.

Davis, Lance. 1968. And it will never be literature. *Explorations in Entrepreneurial History* 2nd ser. 6:75–92.

Davis, Lance, and Douglass C. North. 1971. *Institutional Change and American Economic Growth*. Cambridge: Cambridge University Press.

Davis, Lance, et al. 1972. *American Economic Growth*. New York: Harper & Row.

Denton, Frank. 1985. Data mining as an industry. *Review of Economics and Statistics* 67:124–127.

Eichengreen, Barry. 1986. Macroeconomics and history. In Alexander J. Field

(ed.), *The Future of Economic History*. Boston: Kluwer-Nijhoff.
Faulkner, Harold U. 1924. *American Economic History*, 1st ed. New York: Harper & Row; 8th ed. 1960.
Feeny, David. 1986. The exploration of economic change: The contribution of economic history to development economics. In Alexander J. Field (ed.), *The Future of Economic History*. Boston: Kluwer-Nijhoff.
Field, A.J. 1976a. Educational reform and manufacturing development in mid-nineteenth century Massachusetts. *Journal of Economic History* 36:263–266.
Field, A.J. 1976b. Educational expansion in mid-nineteenth century Massachusetts: Human capital fomation or structural reinforcement? *Harvard Educational Review* 46:521–552.
Field, A.J. 1979a. Occupational structure, dissent and educational commitment, Lancashire, 1841. *Research in Economic History* 4:235–287.
Field, A.J. 1979b. On the explanation of rules using rational choice models. *Journal of Economic Issues* 13:49–72.
Field, A.J. 1979c. Economic and demographic determinants of educational commitment, Massachusetts, 1855. *Journal of Economic History* 39:435–459.
Field, A.J. 1981. The problem with neoclassical institutional economics: A critique with special reference to the North-Thomas model of pre-1500 Europe. *Explorations in Economic History* 18:174–198.
Field, A.J. 1983. Land abundance, interest-profit rates and nineteenth century American and British technology. *Journal of Economic History* 43:405–431.
Field, A.J. 1984a. Asset exchanges and the transactions demand for money, 1919–1929. *American Economic Review* 74:43–59.
Field, A.J. 1984b. A new interpretation of the onset of the great depression. *Journal of Economic History* 44:489–498.
Field, A.J. 1984c. Microeconomics, norms and rationality. *Economic Development and Cultural Change* 32:683–711.
Field, A.J. 1985a. On the unimportance of machinery. *Explorations in Economic History* 22:378–401.
Field, A.J. 1985b. Modern business enterprise as a capital saving innovation. Paper presented at the 1986 Economic History Association meetings, Hartford, Conn.
Fishlow, Albert. 1965. *American Railroads and the Transformation of the Antebellum Economy*. Cambridge: Harvard University Press.
Fishlow, Albert, and Robert Fogel. 1971. Quantitative economic history: An interim evaluation: Past trends and present tendencies. *Journal of Economic History* 31:15–42.
Fogel, Robert. 1964. *Railroads and American Economic Growth: Essays in Econometric History*. Baltimore: Johns Hopkins University Press.
Fogel, Robert, and Stanley Engerman, (eds.) 1971. *The Reinterpretation of American Economic History*. New York: Harper & Row.
Fogel, Robert, and Stanley Engerman. 1974. *Time on the Cross: The Economics of American Negro Slavery*. Boston: Little, Brown.
Freeman, Richard. 1971. *The Market for College Trained Manpower*. Cambridge: Harvard Unviersity Press.

Freeman, Richard. 1976. *The Overeducated American*. New York: Academic Press.

Freeman, Richard, and David W. Breneman. 1974. Forecasting the Ph.D. labor market: Pitfalls for policy. *Technical Report* no. 2. Washington: National Board on Graduate Education.

Gerschenkron, Alexander. 1967. The discipline and I. *Journal of Economic History* 27:443–459.

Gray, L.C. 1933. *History of Agriculture in the Southern United States to 1860*, 2 vols. Washington: Carnegie Institution.

Griliches, Zvi. 1985. Data and econometricians—The uneasy alliance. *American Economic Review* 75:196–200.

Hacker, Louis. 1940. *The Triumph of American Capitalism*. New York: Simon and Schuster.

Haines, Michael. 1986. Economic history and historical demography: Past, present and future. In Alexander J. Field (ed.), *The Future of Economic History*. Boston: Kluwer-Nijhoff.

Hollander, Samuel. 1979. *The Economics of David Ricardo*. Toronto: University of Toronto Press.

Hughes, Jonathan. 1966. Fact and theory in economic history. *Explorations in Economic History* 2nd ser. 3:75–100.

Hughes, Jonathan. 1983. *American Economic History*. Glenview, Ill.: Scott Foresman.

Keynes, J.M. 1930. *A Treatise on Money*. 2. vols. London: Macmillan.

Kirkland, E. 1933. *History of American Economic Life*. New York: F.S. Crofts.

Kuznets, Simon. 1941. Statistics and economic history. *Journal of Economic History* 1:26–41.

Kuznets, Simon. 1966. *Modern Economic Growth*. New Haven: Yale University Press.

Landes, David. 1978. On avoiding Babel. *Journal of Economic History* 38:3–12.

Lazonick, William. 1986. Theory and history in Marxian economics. In A.J. Field (ed.), *The Future of Economic History*. Boston: Kluwer-Nijhoff.

McCloskey, Donald. 1976. Does the past have useful economics? *Journal of Economic Literature* 14:434–461.

McCloskey, Donald. 1978. The achievements of the Cliometric school. *Journal of Economic History* 38:13–28.

National Science Foundation. 1983. National Science Board, *Science Indicators, 1982: An Analysis of the State of U.S. Science, Engineering and Technology*.

North, Douglass. 1966. *Growth and Welfare in the American Past*. Englewood Cliffs, NJ: Prentice-Hall.

North, Douglass C., and R.P. Thomas. 1973. *The Rise of the Western World*. Cambridge: Cambridge University Press.

Parker, William. 1968. American economic growth: Its historiography in the twentieth century. *Ventures: The Magazine of the Yale Graduate School*, (Fall):71–82.

Redlich, Fritz. 1965. New and traditional approaches to economic history and their independence. *Journal of Economic History* 25:480–495.

Ricardo, David. 1817. *Principles of Political Economy and Taxation*. Ed. P. Sraffa (1951). Cambridge: Cambridge University Press.

Rostow, W.W. 1961. *The Stages of Economic Growth: A Non-Communist Manifesto*. Cambridge: Cambridge University Press.

Samuelson, Paul. 1971. Understanding the Marxian notion of exploitation: A summary of the so-called transformation problem between Marxian values and competitive prices. *Journal of Economic Literature* 9:399–431.

Scheiber, Harry N., Richard G. Vatter, and Harold Faulkner. 1976. *American Economic History*. New York: Harper & Row.

Solow, Robert. 1985. Economic history and economics. *American Economic Review* 75:328–31.

Temin, Peter, and Geoffrey Peters. 1985. Is history stranger than theory? The origins of telephone separations. *American Economic Review* 75:324–327.

Thomas, Mark. 1986. General equilibrium models and research in economic history. In A.J. Field (ed.), *The Future of Economic History*. Boston: Kluwer-Nijhoff.

Tukey, John W. 1977. *Exploratory Data Analysis*. Reading MA: Addison Wesley.

U.S. Department of Education. (1965–1984). National Center for Education Statistics, *Digest of Education Statistics*. Washington: Government Printing Office.

Usher, A.P. 1949. The significance of modern empiricism for history and economics. *Journal of Economic History* 9:137–155.

Wright, Gavin. 1973. New and old views on the economics of slavery. *Journal of Economic History* 33:452–466.

2 MACROECONOMICS AND HISTORY

Barry Eichengreen

The modern subdiscipline of macroeconomics can trace its origins to the profound economic and intellectual disturbance occasioned by the Great Depression. This is not to say that political economists had previously ignored the fluctuation of such economic aggregates as prices, interest rates, and production. What for example was the Bullionist Controversy at the beginning of the nineteenth-century if not a debate over the relationship of different measures of money supply to the general level of prices? By the end of that century, analyses of fluctuations in the level of prices and economic activity had achieved considerable sophistication, in Great Britain under the aegis of trade cycle analysis and in the United States in connection with the study of financial crises.

Yet modern macroeconomics as I define it—the study of not just the determination of general levels of prices and interest rates but also of wage and employment dynamics in a framework that admits the possibility that the market's self-equilibrating forces are weak and slowly operating—

With apologies to Sims (1980) for the title. Work on this essay was completed during a visit to the Department of Economic History of the Research School for Social Sciences, Australian National University, whose hospitality is acknowledged with thanks. I am grateful to Tim Hatton and Ian McLean for discussions and insistence on blunt answers to hard questions. I also appreciate the comments of Michael Bordo, Stanley Engerman, Alex Field, Charles Kindleberger, William Parker, and Jeffrey Williamson.

is unique to the post-Depression era. The very fact that it draws upon and speaks to a subdiscipline with an intellectual lifespan of just 50 years indicates how recent an innovation is the adoption by economic history of a macroeconomic perspective ("macroeconomic history" for want of a better term).

The interplay between macroeconomics and economic history takes place simultaneously on several planes. To some economists, macroeconomic history amounts to little more than the use of exceptionally long time series to test popular models. Enthusiasm for this enterprise is contingent upon the topic considered, if not the results. The problem is one of confronting on a daily basis the reaction William Parker encountered upon announcing to his Harvard advisors his decision to write a dissertation in economic history. "Professor Mason thought history was fine since it dealt with industrial organization. Professor Leontief thought history was fine since it could be tackled with an input-output model. Professor Isard...assured me that historical study of the influence of energy sources on industrial location would be a valuable contribution" (Parker 1984, p. 239). In the same vein, macroeconomists value historical studies of the stability of money demand functions if such stability is a fundamental plank of their monetarist platform. If Keynesian by persuasion they respond enthusiastically to historical evidence of the effectiveness of fiscal policy. If their rational-expectations orientation predicts shifts in the covariation of macroeconomic time series with changes in policy regime, they encourage historical analyses of the process by which policy is formulated. That examples of this approach to macroeconomic history have been drawn from three competing schools should make clear that its practice is not confined to economists of a particular stripe.

To other macroeconomists, economic history offers more than case studies or degrees of feedom, for they view their discipline as fundamentally historical. Every discipline has a few central questions that are universally acknowledged to be situated at its core. In macroeconomics, nearly all such questions relate to the issue of how pronounced fluctuations in output and employment at the aggregate level can be reconciled with intelligent (in strong form, optimizing) behavior by individuals. If any generally recognized advance in a field must pass the test of providing a superior answer to its central questions, in macroeconomics the ultimate test is historical: to explain satisfactorily the fluctuations in output and prices and the dramatic rise in unemployment associated with the Great Depression—the historical episode providing impetus for the development of the field. In this view, macroeconomic history is still empirical macroeconomics, but an essential sort.

For the historian, the relationship of economic history to macroeconomics is both more subtle and more complex than this. That relationship must be at the same time intimate—as when historians draw (as they should) both technique and topic from current macroeconomics—and distant, for the economic historian's approach to macroeconomic problems should differ fundamentally from the economist's. The argument is that macroeconomic history is a distinct—in ways to be specified—but by no means independent discipline from macroeconomics. In what follows, I will attempt to develop this argument by example rather than discourse on methodology, although there will be points, notably in the conclusion, where the methodological points are explicit. Since the application of macroeconomic theory to economic history is a recent innovation, the relevant literature is not as extensive as in other subfields of economic history. The point must be made as much by indicating directions in which research is headed as in describing terrain already covered. This chapter is therefore very much concerned with the future of economic history.

I

Events possessing a macroeconomic component are found in every historical era. Harvest failures, natural resource discoveries, and military conflicts, to take three examples, affect not only relative prices of different commodities and relative returns to different factors of production but also such macroeconomic variables as national income, the price level, and the rate of population growth. Thus, the range of questions that could be surveyed is virtually limitless. I will concentrate here on topics that are clearly macroeconomic by virtue of (1) their association with changes in the level of prices or resource utilization in the economy as a whole and (2) propagation of their effects through labor, commodity, and asset markets.[1]

A danger with applying modern macroeconomic analysis to temporally distant eras is that its central concepts may be predicated on market structures or institutions absent in those times. Many Keynesian models, for example, rely on certain sometimes implicit assumptions about the role of money as a medium of exchange or about the nature of employment contracts. Such assumptions may be inappropriate and cause misunderstanding if carelessly applied to historical questions.

The literature on the sixteenth-century Price Revolution is a case in point. The problem of the Price Revolution is macroeconomic because it requires an explanation for both the rise in Spanish prices after 1519—the year the first Aztez spoils arrived from Mexico—and the apparent changes in real returns and rates of growth that accompanied that inflation. Although a variety of explanations have been advanced for the inflation, the two dominant hypotheses are based, respectively, on monetary and demographic factors. The argument that the Price Revolution resulted from the hugh influx of precious metal from the New World, persuasively developed by Hamilton (1934), as a straightforward application of the quantity theory of money requires no elaboration. The alternative, that population pressure was responsible for sixteenth-century inflation, derives from the difficulty of extracting from the monetary hypothesis an explanation for concurrent movements in relative prices (notably the substantial rise in the relative price of agricultural goods).[2] Most economists' initial reaction to this literature is that the demographic hypothesis is based on an elementary confusion between changes in relative prices, which reflect microeconomic factors, and movements in the overall price level, which when persisting for a period of decades are necessarily a monetary phenomenon. (See Brown and Hopkins 1957; or, more recently, Flynn 1978.)

Since Hamilton's time, the historian's response has been that the two hypotheses are related. Postan (1959, p. 178), for one, described himself as "emphasizing the primary role of secular changes in demand [but] always assum[ing] that demand would not influence prices except insofar as it was 'effective,' i.e., accompanied by corresponding adjustments in the supply of money." The term "effective demand" is revealing. Writing in England at the end of the decade when Keynesian macroeconomics was at the height of its influence, Postan adopted from that literature the Keynesian distinction between notional and effective demand and the attendant skepticism that money growth alone would necessarily alter spending and prices. The Keynesian notion of effective demand derives in this context from the concept of the liquidity trap: a monetary expansion unaccompanied by direct stimulus to spending has no effects because the demand for money is infinitely elastic at prevailing interest rates. The demographic argument thus reformulated is that New World treasure would have disappeared into hoards in the absence of pressure to spend it on food. There are clear problems with the analogy. The concept of the liquidity trap is based on a modern fractional reserve banking system's elastic demand for excess reserves at low interest rates. Banks willingly hold the incremental base money because, given the low level of interest rates relative to transactions costs, the risks of lending are scarcely justified by the returns. That the Spanish Crown and others to whom New World treasure accrued were similarly without incentive to spend or invest is implausible. The Crown experienced no difficulty in finding immediate use for that quarter of the American treasure that accrued to it directly or for the remainder, which it either taxed, sequestered, or borrowed from private parties in connection with war finance. Even had the Crown simply hoarded its growing stock of precious metal, the rich would have surely maintained if not increased their expenditure out of hoards.

Population growth still could have raised the rate of inflation associated with the specie inflow had it reduced per capita incomes and had the demand for money fallen sufficiently to increase the velocity of circulation. If the demand for money depends solely on per capita real income, then for population growth to be inflationary, the product of two variables—the absolute value of the elasticity of per capita income with respect to population growth and the income elasticity of per capita money demand—must exceed unity.[3] Given that the first of these variables is likely to be considerably less than unity and the second is usually found to be close to that value, this case would seem difficult to prove. If both logical and internally consistent when viewed in this way, demographic factors emerge neither as a necessary condition for the Price Revolution nor as of obvious first-order importance.

The macroeconomic character of the Price Revolution is nowhere more apparent than in the debate over its real effects. Keynes himself thought to have adduced evidence of nonneutrality. (Keynes 1930, vol. 2, pp. 152–161). The mechanism through which Spanish inflation supposedly was expansionary was wage lag, or "profit inflation" in the parlance of the *Treatise on Money*. Between 1519 and 1588 when, according to Hamilton, the rate of Spanish inflation was highest, wages rose steeply but continued to lag behind prices. From a base of 100 in 1500–1520, Keynes calculated on the basis of Hamilton's figures that the real wage fell to 90 in the 1520s, 82 in the 1530s, 80 in the 1540s, and 79 in the 1550s, before finally beginning to recover and regaining its 1500–1520 level at the turn of the century (Keynes 1930, vol. 2, pp. 160–161). The period from 1520 to 1560 is characterized as a great boom when "the conditions were set in Spain for the very rapid accumulation of wealth"; but after that point, with the rise in costs and decline in profitability, "there was no money to be made there" (Keynes 1930, vol. 2, p. 155). During the boom, some portion of increased profits was ploughed back into capital formation, accelerating growth; in subsequent decades, the opposite was true.

If in the short run wages may lag behind prices under a variety of plausible circumstances, it is difficult to envisage conditions under which individuals fail to adapt for a period of decades to a monetary disturbance that erodes their real incomes. Keynes acknowledged the paradox, noting that the short run, "it would seem, thinks nothing of living longer than a man" (Keynes 1930, vol. 2, p. 159). But he made no effort to examine the dynamics of labor supply and demand achieving this result. In a criticism of Keynes' view, Felix (1956) noted that the growth of mortmain and latifundium in Spain was extending the purview of custom and reducing the importance of wage labor precisely when imperfections in the wage labor market supposedly came into play. He attempted to undermine further the wage-lag hypothesis by noting that expulsion of the Moriscos, expansion of military and colonial service, and opening of the clerical ranks to lower-class recruits had all but eliminated unemployment and underemployment, which serve as a necessary condition for wage lag in most Keynesian models. But Felix' suggestions remain merely that. No one has as yet provided a satisfying macroeconomic explanation for sixteenth-century real wage and relative price trends.

II

"Economic history," Eric Jones has observed, "is a supply side subject" (Jones 1973). Economic historians were thus less startled than reassured by macroeconomists' rediscovery in the 1970s of the supply side: of the importance of supply shocks, productivity growth, and investment. The longer the perspective, the greater the emphasis typically placed on additions to the stock of productive resources and on improvements in technologies and organizational forms relative to fluctuations in the intensity with which those resources are used. Yet there exist issues in economic history whose duration is longer than the harvest cycle but shorter than the economist's "long run" to which both supply- and demand-side considerations apply. The historian's problem is to disentangle their effects. The literature on the British Industrial Revolution during the half-century characterized by "trend acceleration" illustrates both the insight and the confusion that result from attempts to cut into an historical problem with both blades of Marshall's scissors.

It seems logical in retrospect that Elizabeth Gilboy's plea for viewing demand as an equal partner to supply in any explanation for the Industrial Revolution should have appeared in 1932 at the very time events provoked Keynes and his compatriots to develop a theory of effective demand (see Gilboy 1932). It follows that the Gilboy thesis should have experienced its greatest popularity in the 1960s during the heyday of Keynesian economics, before being questioned in the mid-seventies.[4] Although there are various interpretations of the Gilboy thesis, the most appealing has her suggesting that the Industrial Revolution had a macroeconomic component. She portrays the growth of British industrial production in the decades after 1780 as resulting from a combination of three factors: (1) outward shifts in the demand curves for manufactured goods both at home and abroad, (2) the technological and organizational capacity to produce at least some manufactured goods (in other words, the existence of an industrial supply curve), and (3) the availability of additional resources to the industrial sector (or the existence of a positive elasticity of supply). Only the potential for industrialization arises when technological advance causes the supply of industrial goods to shift out and become more elastic. The actuality requires that demand be found corresponding to the increased capacity to supply.

That both demand and supply must rise for output to increase is uncontroversial. Controversy arises once it is argued that demand deserves a place of equality if not primacy relative to supply in explanations for economic growth during the Industrial Revolution. The extreme position that aggregate demand was solely responsible for economic growth during the British Industrial Revolution can be dismissed. Assume, following Harley (1982), that income per capita grew between 1770 and 1841 at 0.5 percent per year.[5] Assume, following Crafts (1981), that the elasticity of output with respect to labor was 0.5 over the period. Then for demand to account for the observed rise in GNP, employment would have had to rise by 1 percent per annum over seven decades, implying an implausibly large shift to labor from leisure or incredible rates of underutilized productive capacity at the beginning of the period.[6]

Disposing of the argument that demand was mainly responsible for the observed rise in industrial production appears to require three things: (1) a model of the British economy, complete with price and income elasticities; (2) estimates of rates of growth of British and foreign incomes; and (3) a definition of "mainly." The last requirement turns out to be superfluous. Using a simple model from the neoclassical theory of international trade and economic growth, Findlay (1983) calculates that the outward shift in the supply curve of manufactures more than fully accounts for the expansion of British industry over the last two decades of the eighteenth-century. While the particulars of his exercise can be disputed, it leaves little doubt that the macroeconomics of the first industrial revolution are macroeconomics of saving, investment, labor supply, and productivity growth.

These macroeconomics have recently been analyzed by Williamson (1984) in the context of neoclassical models of growth. His hypothesis is that British economic growth during the Industrial Revolution compares unfavorably with growth in other industrializing countries because "Britain tried to do two things at once—industrialize and fight expensive wars" (Williamson 1984, p. 689). Government borrowing to finance military expenditures competed with industry for the scarce funds of British savers, resulting in rates of investment and growth considerably below those that would have obtained in the absence of debt finance. This conclusion derives from a model featuring three critical assumptions. First, government bonds satisfy the private sector's demand for wealth and are substitutes for industrial bonds and shares. Individuals do not offset them against the future taxes required for debt service.[7] Second, to a first approximation, productive resources are fully employed. Thus, deficit spending does not have multiplier effects which ameliorate the crowding out of investment. Third, the marginal propensity to save is independent of the real interest rate. Any increase in the supply of government bonds implies a fall in other claims because the aggregate savings schedule is inelastic.

Most historians would consider uncontroversial the assumption that government bonds of the late eighteenth and early nineteenth century were net wealth. Similarly, the constant-employment assumption is unobjectionable given the long horizon relevant to studies of industrialization. The controversial assumption will undoubtedly be the interest inelasticity of the savings schedule. Prospects for empirical work on this question are not promising. The dispute surrounding Boskin's (1978) efforts to identify such a savings relationship for the twentieth-century indicates the sensitivity of estimates of the interest elasticity given even relatively reliable data.

In view of the quality of the income estimates available for the beginning of the nineteenth-century, a more realistic alternative to structural estimation would be to assume various interest elasticities for the aggregate investment schedule and then to see what the observed movement in interest rates, in conjunction with the assumed interest elasticity of investment, implies for the interest elasticity of saving. The larger the rise in interest rate, the less elastic the aggregate savings schedule.[8] A problem with even this conservative approach is that the appropriate interest rate measure can be obtained but only with difficulty. Although Gayer, Rostow, and Schwartz (1953) and others provide time series on nominal interest rates, a measure of the real interest rate is still required. One possibility would be to estimate a price forecasting equation and to use the difference between the nominal interest rate and the inflation forecast as measure of the real rate. Such an approach has been applied by Mishkin (1981) and others to the postwar period.

Similar themes have been taken up by economic historians in a variety of different contexts. James and Sylla (1980) suggest that the rapid expansion of state debt in the United States after 1820 may have crowded out investment by the private sector. Williamson (1974) ascribes half the observed increase in the rate of American capital formation between the 1850s and 1870s to the federal government's policy of debt retirement. In a recent study buttressed by econometric estimates of the critical parameters, James (1984) calculates that the United Stated capital stock would have been 8 percent lower and real income 3 percent lower by 1900 had the postbellum policy of debt retirement not been pursued.[9]

III

Crowding out of investment by debt finance of military expenditures is only one of several macroeconomic dimensions of war that have been considered by economic historians. War, along with harvest failures and natural resource discoveries, is to earlier periods in history what oil shocks are to the 1970s and 1980s. As a supply and demand disturbance of unparalleled severity, it places in relief an economy's capacity to adjust.

One way to conceptualize the macroeconomic effects of these disturbances is as an export-market shock to a trading economy. Consider a country that trades internationally and produces two categories of goods: importables and exportables. A deterioration in its terms of trade due to the outbreak of hostilities (in extreme form, an embargo precluding trade altogether) reduces real incomes given initial patterns of output and employment. Over time, this decline in real incomes can be moderated by reallocating resources from the exportables to the importables sector. However, there may be costs of adjustment associated with this process of reallocation whose macroeconomic correlates are unemployment and foregone output. The path from one point to another on the production possibilities frontier may lie inside it.

Although these dynamics are recognized as important by historians of the Napoleonic and American Civil Wars, and while similar concerns are shared by macroeconomists and trade theorists drawing inspiration from recent experience, neither group has made much progress in quantifying adjustment costs.[10] Frankel (1982) has considered the costs to Britain and the United States of the 1807–1809 embargo, inferring the success with which resources were reallocated from the extent of changes in relative prices in the two countries. Since his model assumes, however, that adjustment occurs along the production possibilities frontier, macroeconomic costs are not addressed. Goldin and Lewis (1980) take three approaches to analyzing the export-market impact on the United States of the Napoleonic Wars: a first which considers terms of trade effects in isolation by taking the employment of resources as fixed; a second which allows movements along the production possibilities frontier linking the importables and exportables sectors; and a third which allows activity in both sectors to adjust but assumes resources utilized in each to be without alternative uses. The third approach, by introducing changes in the general level of employment, comes closest to a macroeconomic analysis. Yet even this approach is too simple to shed much light on the macroeconomics of foreign shocks. Goldin and Lewis make no attempt to model the forces encouraging the reemployment of temporarily idle resources. Macroeconomics is, after all, the study of dynamics of adjustment at the aggregate level. It is extreme to assume that resources thrown out of employment by an export shock remain unemployed over the entirety of the 1793–1807 period. Thus, Goldin and Lewis's third approach provides at best an upper-bound estimate of macroeconomic costs.

One study that considers the labor market's adjustment to wartime dislocations in a macroeconomic rather than in a comparative statics framework is DeCanio and Mokyr's (1977) analysis of the American Civil War. They adopt the Keynesian wage-lag hypothesis, anticipated in this context by Mitchell (1903). The traditional approach to the labor market response to wartime inflation is to assume that real wages adjust with a lag to their market-clearing level but that, since workers negotiate over nominal and not real wages, adaptively formed price expectations influence the money wages demanded. Responding to previous work which cast doubt on the wage-lag hypothesis, DeCanio and Mokyr add to the standard formulation proxies for a number of real variables, notably the international terms of trade, whose movements alter the market-clearing real wage. With this amendment the wage-lag hypothesis is rehabilitated.

This finding has implications for the weight that should be attached to the results of related analyses of "crowding out." In the case of the American Civil War, monetization succeeded in reducing the burden of debt finance not just via the inflation tax but also by redistributing income away from wage earners and freeing resources previously devoted to labor's consumption for governmental use. The possibility that wage lag during the Napoleonic Wars may have similarly reduced the extent of crowding out in Britain, as suggested in a previous generation of textbooks, has not yet been integrated into the recent generation of studies on the First Industrial Revolution.[11]

IV

Compared to the dramatic war-time disruption of normal trade patterns, peace-time fluctuations in the nineteenth-century have attracted less attention. The recent neglect of cyclical fluctuations in what is conventionally denoted the Atlantic Economy is all the more surprising given the attention such fluctuations are paid in the older literature on long swings and Kuznets Cycles.[12] Historians may have been discouraged from pursuing issues raised by Kondratieff and Kuznets by the difficulty of reconciling the existence of medium- and long-term cycles with mainstream macroeconomics. Whether fluctuations are of the equilibrium business cycle variety, in which cycles result from price surprises and persist only because certain forms of adjustment take time (for example, "time to build" in the case of investment), or of the Keynesian variety, in which demand and supply shocks—anticipated or unanticipated—are propagated over time by nominal wage and price inertia, modern macroeconomics has difficulty explaining fluctuations with a periodicity longer than the Kitchin Cycle of three to five years. Left without modern theoretical underpinnings and discouraged by the statistical work of Howrey (1968) and others who undermined the empirical basis for the cycles Kuznets thought he observed, long swings have fallen from fashion. Yet with the transformation in outlook that followed the first OPEC price shock, economists have again begun to entertain the notion that economies pass through distinct phases lasting perhaps a generation. There are parallels between (a) the long-swing paradigm that has for many years informed the work of economic historians and (b) the comparisons now made between the golden era of postwar reconstruction and prosperity—extending roughly from 1948 to 1972—and the difficult period of slower growth and higher unemployment that has prevailed since that time. Still, it has not been established that recent developments satisfy the necessary conditions for a cycle, notably an endogenous recurrence mechanism and a stable periodicity.

It is on the trade cycle or conventional business cycle that recent work has concentrated. Where earlier investigators scrutinized time series of real and financial variables in the attempt to discern cycles and inflection points, recent studies have employed formal macroeconomic models and time-series econometrics.[13] The time-series approach as utilized in Eichengreen (1983) is not far removed from the analyses of Burns and Mitchell.[14] As in Burns and Mitchell (1946), a set of economically interrelated variables is selected a priori, and the timing of their co-movements is studied. Statistical results on timing and on the speed with which particular variables respond to innovations in others indicate whether one variable's evolution helps to explain another's subsequent path. If one variable's evolution does help to explain another's subsequent movement, then an appropriate historical model must include links through which the first variable is permitted to influence the second. Thus, these time-series methods help to narrow the range of plausible models consistent with the observed time-series properties of the data, and provide guidance on the appropriate way to structure further investigation.[15]

Much recent work using these and similar techniques focuses on the role of real and monetary factors in price and output fluctuations. Lewis (1978) and Rostow (1978) have both argued the importance of real forces in the determination of price and output fluctuations, Rostow for the century 1797–1914 and Lewis for the final four decades of the period. The forces on which they concentrate include the growth of industrial and agricultural production, export demand, and residential construction. In contrast, Bordo and Schwartz (1980a, 1980b) argue the modern quantity theory or monetarist position, which attaches special weight to money supply and demand.[16] Lewis (1978) and Bordo and Schwartz (1980b) both run regressions of various price variables against gold stocks, national income measures, and proxies for real disturbances—in Lewis' case, outputs of primary commodities and in Bordo and Schwartz' case, the international terms of trade. In each set of results, both gold stocks and proxies for real factors have a statistically significant impact on the level of prices, judged at standard confidence levels. The problem with such econometric tests is that, in the absence of a clearly specified model, the results can be interpreted variously. Lewis discerns support for real determinants of prices in the finding that, in addition to the positive impact of gold stocks on prices, primary commodity supplies have negative effects. Bordo and Schwartz argue that Lewis's commodity variable is likely to be correlated with national income, a determinant of money demand, and that his results therefore support the quantity theory. In their own results, not just gold stocks but also the international terms of trade influence the level of prices, although Bordo and Schwartz dismiss this result on grounds of the variable's small coefficient. The problem with this interpretation is that the terms of trade may be a poor proxy for any real shock which drives prices; and if it measures that shock with error, its estimated coefficient will be biased toward zero.

Further progress in identifying the forces underlying nineteenth-century business cycles requires testing more rigorously specified versions of both the real and monetary hypotheses, embedding those that survive in macroeconomic models, and comparing the success with which dynamic simulations of the competing models track the cycles considered. The work of Bourguignon and Lévy-Leboyer (1984) on France and of Dwyer (1985) on Britain suggests the practicality of this approach. Unfortunately, true believers typically object to the way in which their favored hypothesis is represented by investigators who approach the problem with different priors. This should be taken as an argument for collaboration rather than evidence of malice or proof that it is unrealistic to hope for mutually acceptable specifications upon which tests of historical questions might be based. In the case discussed, where the distinction between real and monetary factors is clear, investigators predisposed toward the two positions could easily collaborate in the specification, estimation, and simulation of otherwise comparable models embodying their preferred hypotheses.

V

Studies of macroeconomic fluctuations in the second half of the nineteenth-century can be distinguished by whether the assumptions upon which they are based are institutional or behavioral. For those adopting the first approach, the critical institutions whose macroeconomic effects must be considered are international: the classical gold standard and free trade.

Building on an older but still influential generation of studies, research on the classical gold standard centers on three traditional themes.[17] The first is the question of how the gold standard worked. Narrowly defined, the problem is to account for the successful maintenance of fixed exchange rates over a period of decades by explaining why the balance-of-payments adjustment process worked so smoothly before World War I. The popular research strategy is to formulate models of the adjustment mechanism and subject them to test. A glance at the literature appears to reveal many competing models of the adjustment process. In competition with the price-specie-flow mechanism of Hume (1752), there are accounts of the adjustment process that emphasize spending or absorption (Whale 1937; Ford 1960), stabilizing capital flows (Scammell 1965), wealth or real balance effects (McCloskey and Zecher 1976, 1984), and the differential impact of credit conditions on markets for primary and manufactured goods (Triffin 1964). The contrast among models is especially emphasized by McCloskey and Zecher, who characterize the monetary approach and the price-specie-flow mechanism as incompatible alternatives. The debate as they portray it pits those who believe international equilibrium was maintained by the impact of changing relative commodity prices on international flows of goods against those who see relative price changes as negligible in magnitude and effect and instead emphasize changes in the level of spending.

In their 1976 article, McCloskey and Zecher estimate money demand functions for Britain and the United States and show how well the excess of predicted money demand over actual supply tracks the inflow of gold. In their 1984 article, they regress changes in the U.S.-U.K. trade balance on changes in relative national price levels and show how poorly the latter predict the former. Those who view the competing hypotheses not as incompatible alternatives but as elements of a larger general equilibrium model—not to mention true believers in the price-specie-flow mechanism—are unlikely to be converted by these results. Convincing tests would have to be derived from a more general specification, preferably model-based, which incorporates the possible influences of both real-balance and relative-price effects and acknowledges the endogeneity of many of the important variables.

Given the attention the adjustment mechanism has long attracted and the stark manner in which the question is posed, it is remarkable that McCloskey and Zecher's hypothesis has not elicited more empirical work. The only recent empirical study addressing the issues they raise is Fratianni and Spinelli's (1984) analysis of Italian experience. Regressing a proxy for the excess demand for goods (their dependent variable) on a proxy for the excess demand for money and a measure of relative prices yields coefficients on both independent variables that are statistically significant at standard confidence levels. They interpret this result as providing support for both the monetary model and the price-specie-flow mechanism. While a useful start, some readers will question the regression results because the specification is not model-based. Others will question whether the proxy for goods-market disequilibrium, the deviation of real output from trend, is an appropriate measure of external imbalance. Still others will object that the ability of regressors to satisfy conventional tests of statistical significance does not reveal how much the different factors contribute to fluctuation of the dependent variable; for this, simulations are required. Finally, others will wish that the authors had incorporated into their specification alternative views of the adjustment process, such as Triffin's hypothesis that a gold outflow which leads a central bank to tighten credit conditions will be accompanied by an improvement rather than a deterioration in the terms of trade of countries exporting manufactures and financial services due to the exceptional sensitivity of primary commodity prices to the cost and availability of credit.

The second traditional theme providing a focal point for research is the popular association of the gold standard with price and income stability. Bordo (1981) and Cooper (1982) compare rates of inflation, unemployment and income growth in the United States and United Kingdom under the classical gold standard and in other periods. They find the average rate of change of wholesale prices to have been more moderate under the gold standard than in recent years. In contrast, comparisons of per capita income growth and unemployment indicate no superiority over recent monetary arrangements; if anything, the opposite is true. Even the relatively low inflation rates under the classical gold standard can be questioned, since they are the product of averaging together two decades of deflation prior to 1893 with two subsequent decades of inflation.

In much of this literature nothing is said of the mechanism through which the gold standard tends to exert a stabilizing tendency over the level of prices. The mechanism offered in the few studies which treat the matter explicitly is the mining industry's response to changes in the price of gold. Barro (1979) has provided a theoretical analysis of the behavior of prices when the flow supply of new gold is an increasing function of its relative price. In his model, the impact on the price level of real disturbances is moderated but not eliminated by the response of the mining industry. Rush (1978) has attempted to provide empirical support for this mechanism by regressing gold production on the reciprocal of a wholesale price deflator (the purchasing power of gold when the nominal gold price is fixed). Although he finds some evidence of a positive supply elasticity, his results have been questioned, for different reasons, by Rockoff (1984) and by Eichengreen and McLean (1986). Rockoff identifies the proximate sources of changing gold production in the nineteenth-century not as changing rates of exploitation of known reserves using known technology, but as technological change (notably the cyanide process) and discovery and development of a few great gold fields. The critical question is whether gold discoveries and technological change were price induced or coincidental. To get at this question, Eichengreen and McLean draw on the literature on the history of mineral-rich regions, in which various non-price determinants of gold discovery and extraction are suggested. On the basis of their analysis of state-level data for the United States at the turn of the century, they find some evidence of an induced response in a small but positive price elasticity of supply, but conclude that the magnitude of the response was heavily conditioned by the region's recent economic history and pattern of economic development. The implication is that the tendency, if any, of new gold supply to stabilize the level of prices will vary with historical conditions, a conclusion that casts doubt on any sweeping generalization about price stability under the gold standard.

If it is the variability, either total or unpredictable, rather than the average rate of inflation or income growth that interferes with the efficiency of resource allocation, then evidence of the gold standard's operation is more difficult to assess. Bordo (1981) computes various measures of inflation and income growth variability, on whose basis he finds it difficult to rank the performance of alternative monetary standards. He finds for Britain that the standard deviation of prices was somewhat lower during the four decades of the classical gold standard than during the post-1913 period; for the United States, it was slightly higher. In both countries, rates of real income growth were more variable under the gold standard. The problem with comparisons conducted for such long periods is one of data compatability. For the United States, Romer (1986) has shown that what appears to be greater income stability in the postwar economy is largely an artifact of the way the historical statistics are constructed. When the methods used to construct the historical index of industrial production are applied to the modern era, much of the difference between periods is eliminated.[18]

If efficiency losses result only from price fluctuations that cannot be anticipated, then evidence is still more difficult to obtain. Price predictability under alternative regimes could be evaluated by constructing price forecasts for different periods and comparing their mean squared errors. The results of such exercises remain open to question, given the innumerable forms a forecasting equation might take. In one such study, Callahan (1984) has derived a price forecasting equation from a New Classical model of the United States. Not only is this a very special way of modeling the United States economy, but the weight we attach to her results hinges crucially on the credibility we invest in her model. We could be convinced in two ways: by being shown that her preferred reduced-form specification for prices was supported by econometric estimates of the structural equations of the underlying model, or by being shown that model choice did not matter since alternative specifications yielded the same conclusions.

The third traditional theme on which research on the gold standard centers concerns central banks and the "rules of the game." For some, the question is whether the gold standard was a managed system; for others, it is how that standard was managed. The popular test for adherence to rules of the game as formulated by Nurkse (1944) and Bloomfield (1959) is that the central bank's internal and external assets fluctuate in the same direction, or at least that they do not offset one another. The historically relevant question is not, however, whether central banks completely disregarded external balance, but the extent to which they were influenced, at least for short periods, by other considerations. Hence recent work, like that of Goodhart (1972), Pippinger (1984), and Dutton (1984) on the Bank of England, has moved from simple correlation to multiple regression. Using the reaction function framework familiar from modern studies of monetary policy, the central bank's domestic assets or discount rate is regressed on variables proxying for the authorities' possible concerns. It is revealing of the methodology that the two most recent studies, by Dutton and Pippinger, reach opposing conclusions, Dutton concluding that the rules of the game were violated, Pippinger that they were obeyed. The inconclusiveness of these studies of Britain sugggests conducting similar analyses for several gold standard countries to increase the power of the test. But the greatest gains may lie not in additional case studies but in better grounding the econometrics in the historical literature. If the classic studies of central banking lack formal hypotheses and tests, they provide a rich lode of information on the mechanics of decision making, the information available to decision makers, and the political pressures brought to bear, much of which has been neglected by those who have relied on an econometric methodology.

While these three traditional themes do in fact encompass most of what is important and controversial about the gold standard's operation, other aspects of the mechanism are equally deserving of attention. One is asymmetries in the impact of the adjustment process on countries at different stages of economic development. In much of the historical literature it is argued that such asymmetries were pervasive: capital importers and exporters, financial centers and financially underdeveloped regions, producers of primary products and of manufactured goods, each are said to have been affected in different ways by the gold standard's operation. If so, there is no canonical model of the international gold standard applicable to all times and places. Work in structural macroeconomics, notably by Taylor (1983), has suggested that external shocks can affect an economy in very different ways depending on, for example, whether a domestic financial market is present or absent or on whether or not export supplies are elastic. Application of a similar framework to gold standard experience might prove illuminating.

VI

Compared to the classical gold standard, the impact of foreign trade on the domestic economy has attracted much attention but been subjected to little formal analysis. In part, this reflects the problem's difficult nature. The impact of trade on an industrializing economy is a general equilibrium problem of great complexity; few of the variables normally held constant in positive analyses of trade policy can properly be held exogenous. The question therefore provides a litmus test of investigators' methodological preferences. The alternatives are spanned by simple two-sector Heckscher-Ohlin models as adopted by McCloskey (1980a), and computational general equilibrium models as constructed by Thomas (1984). McCloskey reminds the reader that in a world that is otherwise distortion free, international trade is superior to no trade, but an optimal tariff which exploits a country's market power is superior to free trade. Given his assumptions about supply and demand elasticities, the costs to Britain of adhering to free trade, which show up as potential terms of trade improvements foregone, are impressively if not overwhelmingly large.

Cain (1982) has objected to the static nature of McCloskey's model and to the assumption that other distortions are absent. He cites full employment and the absence of such dynamic effects as learning-by-doing and productivity spillovers as assumptions that should be relaxed. McCloskey dismisses Cain's objection to the full-employment assumption on the grounds of his long-run perspective. As in the literature on industrialization, it is difficult to sustain the argument that changes in aggregate demand, in this case induced by a tariff, account for secular trends in growth. While he also dismisses as dead ends the dynamic possibilities raised by Cain, neither the theoretical nor the empirical bases for so doing seem particularly compelling (McCloskey 1982, p. 210).[19] A number of studies have documented the presence of dynamic effects such as learning-by-doing for the nineteenth-century.[20] But before they can provide the basis for a reinterpretation of the costs and benefits of free trade, the empirical importance of these effects needs to be established, as does the extent to which productivity improvements attributable to learning were external to the firm.[21]

An attempt to proceed along these lines is provided by Bairoch (1972), who compares the pace of productivity improvement, inventiveness, and output growth under free trade and protection in nineteenth-century Europe. He computes annual rates of change of various indices of progressiveness, such as output per worker and patents registered, separately for periods when tariffs were in place and for the free trade era, reaching the surprising conclusion that economic expansion proceeded most rapidly under protection and that trade liberalization hindered growth.

One objection to Bairoch's results is that he makes no effort to measure the height of tariff barriers, instead simply categorizing Britain as free trade after 1840, France from 1860 to 1890, Germany from 1862 to 1879, and Italy from 1863 to 1887. Nor does he consider the significance of the differences he detects. Thus, Capie (1983) has cast doubt on Bairoch's conclusions by econometrically analyzing British, Italian, German, and Russian data for the four decades prior to World War I. Regressing the growth of industrial production on various measures of the stringency of commercial policy, he fails to identify statistically significant effects. The fundamental problem with Bairoch's analysis is not, however, its lack of formal tests but its ceteris paribus nature. For example, Bairoch's indicators suggest that Britain grew most quickly before 1840 when the Corn Laws were in place. But these years of the Industrial Revolution were unique in numerous respects that cannot be attributed to commercial policy. Similarly, Germany and Italy grew more quickly after 1880 than before for reasons presumably having less to do with tariff protection than with political and economic unification and the diffusion of new technologies.

The effects of trade and protection can only be convincingly assessed once they are embedded in a structural model of economic growth. Measures of import taxation could be entered as additional policy variables in a model like that of Bourgugnon and Lévy-Leboyer (1984). It seems unlikely, however, that such an aggregated approach will yield much insight into the long-run effects of commercial policy. Levels of protection whether calculated as nominal or effective rates differed greatly across industries. Moreover, the same level of protection could have very different effects depending on the degree of competition in product markets, the market power of workers and their ability to capture rents, capital intensity, and extent of scale economies in production. Aggregative analyses are unlikely to provide an adequate substitute for industrial case studies along the lines of Toniolo (1977) and Webb (1980).

This skepticism concerning the benefits of a macroeconomic analysis may seem misplaced in an essay on macroeconomic history. The point is that macroeconomic analysis sheds light only on problems that can be approached at high levels of aggregation. When the disturbance considered, or the response it elicits, varies considerably across sectors, there may be no adequate substitute for detailed studies at a disaggregated level.

VII

The Great Depression rightly serves as the focal point for economic histories of the interwar years. Yet if it is not to be portrayed as Paul

Samuelson once described it—as a series of historical accidents (as cited in Kindleberger 1973, pp. 19–20)—this Depression experience must be placed in the context of the macroeconomic developments of the surrounding decades. Unfortunately, only a minority of recent studies relate their analyses of the Depression to long-term developments in the world economy.

An integrated view of the period's macroeconomic fluctuations might start by characterizing the extent of structural disequilibrium following World War I and continue by tracing the connection between structural difficulties and the various economies' susceptibility to macroeconomic shocks.[22] The war had been responsible for extensive dislocation, including the loss of up to 3 percent of total population in Germany and France, and for extensive destruction of productive capacity. At the same time, it provided considerable stimulus to industry and agriculture in North America and in regions on the periphery of the industrial world, creating structural difficulties for the advanced economies as they attempted to restore productive capacity and regain customary shares of newly contested markets. These difficulties provide the backdrop against which historical studies of the Great Depression must be placed.

The most infamous economic consequences of World War I were those emphasized by Keynes: war debts and reparations. The war debts and reparations questions continue to preoccupy social, political, and diplomatic historians, including recently Maier (1975), Schuker (1976), Trachtenberg (1980), and Silverman (1982). Explicitly economic analyses have been provided, in addition, by contributors to the theoretical literature on the transfer problem, although much of this literature is far removed from the underlying historical issues. The basic issue addressed by this literature is the issue originally dividing Keynes (1929) and Bertil Ohlin (1929): viz, whether a country required to pay reparations, for example in the form of a fixed transfer of purchasing power, will suffer a secondary burden in the form of a terms-of-trade deterioration. While Keynes argued that this secondary burden might be substantial, Ohlin suggested that a secondary benefit in the form of a terms-of-trade improvement was as likely to occur. Many of the highly abstract theoretical analyses that take this dispute as their point of departure have focused on the special case where the terms of trade of the transfer-receiving country deteriorate to the point where its welfare is reduced. It was long presumed that domestic distortions were required for this special case to obtain, but recent analyses have shown that immiserizing transfers can arise without such distortions once a third country is introduced into the analysis. However, given the extreme assumptions needed to generate this result, this and similar theoretical work is likely to remain tangential to the historical debate.

The extent to which modern international trade theory of the Heckscher-Ohlin-Samuelson variety can shed light on the transfer problem was indicated by Jones (1975) a decade ago. In a Heckscher-Ohlin (two-country, two-factor, two-commodity) world with incomplete specialization in production, in which countries differ only in terms of consumers' preferences and in the extent to which each country has a comparative advantage in the production of its exportable good, a transfer-making country's terms of trade will worsen (or improve) if the tastes of consumers are more (or less) heavily biased toward their country's exportable good than the bias on the supply side due to comparative advantage in production.[23] The model's implementation would appear straightforward. The slopes of production possibilities frontiers and demand curves could be estimated and used to calibrate a general equilibrium model of the type advanced by Jones. Given the heart generated by the debate and the straightforward nature of the exercise, it is remarkable that the German transfer problem has not yet attracted empirical work along these lines.

The most dramatic of the reparations question's immediate macroeconomic consequences were hyperinflation in Germany and budgetary difficulties in France. Despite the attention devoted to the German hyperinflation, social scientists have not yet developed an integrated understanding of the episode. Existing studies tend to focus narrowly on either the political economy and social origins of hyperinflation, its transmission, or its economic and social effects.[24] Following Cagan (1956), most econometric studies focus on an equation in which prices adjust to equate money supply and demand. Since money demand is a function of nominal interest rates, which are dominated by expectations of inflation, assumptions about expectations formation play a crucial role in all such analyses. Under extreme conditions like hyperinflation, it is plausible that agents devote significant resources to forecasting future conditions; not surprisingly, recent investigators get mileage from the rational expectations assumption. Flood and Garber (1980a), for example, impose restrictions under which they are able to separate the component of hyperinflation associated with market fundamentals from any component attributable to "bubbles," or the temporarily self-fulfilling expectation that prices will simply move off in a particular direction. With further assumptions about structure, Flood and Garber (1980b) are able to extract from prices an estimate of the implicit probabilities attached by the public to future monetary reform. While the issues if not the methodology are likely to be of considerable interest to historians, given the extremity of the simplifying assumptions required for tractability, none of the historical issues can be considered resolved.

Another intriguing aspect of hyperinflation is the light it sheds on the real effects of stabilization. Motivation for most economists' studies of price stabilization derives from the postwar debate over the optimal speed with which to terminate inflation. The conventional view is that stabilization costs are substantial since nominal variables are slow to adapt—if, for example, wages continue to rise after inflation decelerates, a sizeable recession could be induced by the rise in real labor costs. In contrast, Sargent (1982) invoked interwar evidence that stabilization-induced recessions in Central Europe were both shallow and short lived in support of the rational-expectations position that the costs of credible stabilization are low. That position is that both expectations and the nominal variables they influence are quick to adapt to credible changes in policy. Hence Sargent places great weight on the highly visible institutional reforms that accompanied stabilization in the 1920s, on the fact that the announcement of reform was often sufficient to induce a change in price behavior even before the monetary authority's printing presses began to slow, and on historical evidence that the inflation-unemployment trade-off at these junctures was very different than in periods in which no regime change took place.

While the rational-expectations assumption provides a useful perspective on certain historical episodes, objections have been raised in connection with this application to interwar experience. The least substantial objection is that such an exceptional phenomenon as hyperinflation contains few valid implications for periods of moderate inflation. In response, Sargent (1983) has presented an historical analysis of Poincaré's stabilization of the relatively moderate French inflation in the summer of 1926. A more serious reservation is that the evidence simply does not support the conclusion that the costs of stabilization were low. Dornbusch (1981, 1985), Garber (1982), and Spechler (1982) all have questioned Sargent's evidence, but none has presented a definitive accounting of the costs of interwar stabilizations.

The fundamental objection to historical analyses adopting the rational-expectations view is that they rest on the nebulous and unobservable concept of credibility. Proponents of the rational-expectations paradigm argue that the costs of credible stabilization are low. Shown that the costs of stabilization were high in a particular historical episode, they respond that this indicates not that their paradigm is invalid but that the policy changes were not sufficiently credible. The difficulty of testing separately two distinct propositions—that credible policy changes rapidly alter behavior, and that particular policy changes are credible—is the inevitable limitation of historical applications of the rational-expectations assumption to the analysis of economic policy.

VIII

Excepting the 1927–1929 stock market boom in the United States, the origins of which remain shrouded in mystery, the macroeconomic difficulties of the remainder of the 1920s were all connected with the resurrection of the international gold standard.[25] Historical research has concentrated more on the formulation of this policy than on its effects. In a series of studies which exercised considerable influence over subsequent British research in twentieth-century economic history, Moggridge (1969, 1972) made use of the public records to analyze the British decision to return to gold in 1925. (See also Pressnell 1978.) Previously, Britain's return to gold had been characterized as a grave mistake made by the Chancellor of the Exchequer, Winston Churchill, who was viewed as having been misled by his advisors. It had been suggested that those who recognized the policy's costs willingly sacrificed the interests of industry to those of British finance. While concurring that the return to gold was a mistake, Moggridge shows that Keynes and others who argued against it in fact had access to the Chancellor and other policymakers, who simply found their arguments unpersuasive. He indicates the difficulties with the argument that the interests of industry were sacrificed to those of finance.

The work of Moggridge and of those who till the same fields relies primarily on qualitative evidence drawn from government records.[26] The acceptance it has met may reflect prevailing British skepticism of the merits of quantitative, model-based economic history. Relying heavily on archival evidence and emphasizing the personalities of the individuals involved, these studies go so far as to report time series for economic variables of interest, interpreting their behavior as contemporaries may have done and then reinterpreting them, usually in Keynesian fashion. But the framework underlying that reinterpretation is frequently left implicit. Admittedly, policy decisions like the return to gold are exceptionally difficult to model formally. But this is at best an argument for analyzing the formulation of policy using traditional historical methods and its impact using formal economic analysis. As yet, there are few studies that combine qualitative evidence on policy formulation with quantitative evidence on its effects.[27]

Studies of the economic policy-making process often lean heavily on peculiarly British features of the civil service and the political environment. It remains to be established that valid generalizations regarding the formulation of economic policy in the pre-Keynesian era can be based on British experience. Whether such generalizations can in fact be drawn will turn upon the outcome of research on other countries. For example, France and Italy both entered the 1920s with equally strong commitments to resurrection of their prewar gold standard parities, but unlike Britain their efforts to do so ended in failure. While French and Italian decisions about the parity at which to stabilize have been studied by Schmid (1974) and Cohen (1976), no one has yet attempted a synthesis of the various national case studies.

The decision to stabilize the exchange rate and return to gold was part of a policy package whose elements included balancing the government budget and consolidating the public debt. The recent controversy surrounding budget deficits in the United States has encouraged the reorientation of historical interest toward the issue of fiscal policy. The dominant paradigm for organizing historical analyses of fiscal policy remains the constant-employment budget balance framework developed by Brown (1956).[28] Given Keynesian assumptions, these measures can be used to characterize the macroeconomic impact of taxation and public spending. The limitation of such studies is that they rarely scrutinize the Keynesian assumptions upon which they are based or ask whether fiscal policy might have worked through different channels than those posited in textbooks. (For further discussion, see Pincus 1985.)

A related aspect of interwar experience to which recent developments direct attention is exchange rate management. The interwar period provides evidence on every modern exchange rate regime: clean floating in the early 1920s and a gold-exchange standard thereafter, followed by dirty floating and exchange control in the 1930s. Positions on many of the central issues in the current debate over the efficacy of floating rates, for example, can be traced to the impression that the 1920s was the only previous period in contemporary history when exchange rates floated freely. Questions such as whether floating rates are subject to destabilizing speculative influences or whether they effectively insulate an economy from foreign shocks can be examined using historical evidence from this era. Frenkel and Clements (1981), Grissa (1981), and Eichengreen (1982) all have attempted to understand movements of the exchange rate during the 1920s through the application of modern models of exchange-rate determination. Unfortunately, the explanatory power of these models is less than impressive when applied to data from the 1970s, and their performance in the 1920s is little better. Thus, they fail to provide a totally satisfactory explanation for the fluctuation of exchange rates in this historical era. What these studies provide is a contrast in the approach of economists and historians, with the former attempting to confirm the power of a preferred theory using historical data, and the latter modifying and adapting theory in the attempt to understand historical experience.

The consensus in existing studies is increasingly that exchange rate management exercised a powerful influence over interwar economic performance. Choudri and Kochin (1980) compare Spain's experience under a floating exchange rate after 1929 with that of countries on the gold standard. While arguing that the relative stability of prices and production in Spain is evidence of the insulation properties of floating rates, they neither specify the channels through which foreign disturbances were transmitted nor explore the mechanism by which exchange rate adjustments provided insulation.[29] The findings of Eichengreen and Sachs (1985) are consistent with those of Choudri and Kochin, but besides considering a larger cross-section of countries they analyze both the supply- and demand-side channels through which exchange rates made their influence felt.[30]

Finally, the interwar gold-exchange standard is studied for the contrast it provides with both floating exchange rates in the twenties and thirties and the classical gold standard of prewar years. It is tempting to dismiss the interwar system as neither fish nor fowl—as neither a true gold standard on the nineteenth-century model nor a conventional fixed exchange rate regime a la Bretton Woods. Yet Lindert's (1969) work suggests that the differences between the interwar and prewar gold standard are more quantitative differences in the value of foreign reserve holdings than qualitative differences in behavior, and that the quantitative differences are small at that.

Some, such as Cooper (1982), have questioned whether useful generalizations can be based on the performance of a short-lived regime whose lifetime is conventionally demarcated by Britain's return to gold in 1925 and her devaluation in 1931. Clearly, valid generalizations would have considerable value; since interwar market structures more closely resemble modern conditions than do their nineteenth-century precedessors, interwar experience should have greater ability to shed light on the operation of a prospective gold standard. Moreover, even those who now urge a return to gold recognize the reluctance of governments to tie their own hands and the likelihood—or danger—that any future gold standard would closely resemble the interwar system in which discretion played a central role.

The interwar gold standard shared few of the virtues popularly attributed to its nineteenth-century predecessor. It lent little stability to the international monetary system, as its early demise clearly indicated.

It was far from conducive to price and income stability, as dramatically illustrated by the Great Depression. The principal explanations for its malfunctioning include:

1. Sterilization operations by central banks unwilling to play by the rules of the gold standard game;
2. The absence of a dominant central bank willing and able to exercise leadership in managing the system, and in lieu of such leadership the failure of cooperation among the competing financial centers (Clarke 1967; Kindleberger 1973; Moggridge 1981; Eichengreen 1984, 1985);
3. Inadequate world stocks of monetary gold and their uneven international distribution;
4. The increasingly inflexible structure of domestic and international markets, as reflected in growing wage and price rigidities and the rise of tariff barriers to international trade.

Hesitancy to analyze the operation of the interwar gold standard can be attributed to a degrees-of-freedom problem—viz, relevant dimensions of the system are many compared to the information contained in less than a decade of historical data. This problem is surmountable, however, by additional data and more sophisticated quantitative methods. Eichengreen, Watson, and Grossman (1985) have, for example, considered the determinants of Bank of England policy during the period of the interwar gold standard using weekly data and econometric techniques explicitly designed to take into account the small number of changes in the stance of monetary policy. They find that the Bank of England responded quite differently to gold inflows and outflows, in sharp contrast to the so-called rules of the game, and that in addition to external pressures the Bank was responsive to a limited extent to internal factors.[31]

IX

Nowhere is the symbiotic relationship of economic history and macroeconomics more evident than in the literature on the causes of the Great Depression. Proponents of Classical, New Classical, Keynesian, and Monetarist theories of macroeconomic fluctuations, while far from notorious for the range of issues on which they concur, agree that their preferred interpretation should provide a satisfactory explanation for the onset, depth, and duration of the Depression. The vigor with which rival interpretations of the Depression have been advanced and the sustained attention devoted by macroeconomists to this juncture in twentieth-century history raise questions about the role of the economic historian in the analysis of such episodes. Should historians permit their investigations to be organized around the competing paradigms of the economics profession? Or is there a distinctly historical approach to the analysis of such events that transcends doctrinal disputes among economists?

Much recent historical research, particularly on the United States, has simply engaged economists on their own turf. The leading example is the dispute between advocates of Keynesian and Monetarist interpretations of the Depression. Interest was stimulated by the exchange between Friedman and Schwartz (1963), who argued that the Depression was attributable to monetary forces, and Temin (1976), who argued that it originated instead with shocks to the level of spending.[32] The spending hypothesis is the older of these interpretations: the Keynesian presumption that macroeconomic fluctuations are driven by the instability of investment spending for many years predisposed readers in its favor. Empirical macromodels of the interwar economy, such as that of Bolch and Pilgrim (1973), generated evidence that was at least superficially consistent with the spending hypothesis. They indicated that the path of the Depression could be mimicked by a set of simple Keynesian relationships, with much of the action provided by consumption and investment functions.

The limitations of such models is that they take as exogenous the critical variables whose behavior most requires explanation. Thus, they fail ultimately to provide a satisfying explanation for the onset of the Depression. For example, while proponents of the spending hypothesis have identified components of spending that declined after the summer of 1929, they are unable to provide a satisfying explanation for the initiation of this movement. The traditional Keynesian interpretation is that investment spending was depressed by the wave of pessimism set off by the 1929 stock market crash; Temin shows, however, that the exceptional feature of the fall in investment spending was its composition, not its magnitude. He attributes the fall in spending to an unusually low level of consumption but provides only hints about why consumption spending was depressed.[33]

Recently, Field (1984, 1984b) has argued that the decline in both consumption and investment was initiated by monetary forces different from those emphasized by Friedman and Schwartz. He shows first that the demand for money depended not only on its conventional determinants but also on the volume of transactions in security markets. He argues next that this additional source of transactions demand was overlooked by policymakers who maintained their tight antispeculative policy stance. He concludes that money market stringency elevated real interest rates, ultimately depressing investment spending in such sectors as construction and consumer spending on automobiles and other durable goods. The final links involving real interest rates and their effects on spending are the most speculative part of the argument, to which we return below.[34]

Exponents of the monetary interpretation of the Great Depression tend to pass quickly over the causes of the 1929 downturn, emphasizing the depth of the contraction and its persistence after 1930, which they attribute to banking panics and policy mistakes by the Federal Reserve, which led to a contraction of the money supply and a decline in economic activity.[35] While the contraction of the money supply is an indisputable fact, the question is whether it was a cause or a consequence of the concomitant decline in income. One approach to sorting out cause and effect considers evidence on timing—the "causality tests" referred to above. Both Schwartz (1981) and Gordon and Wilcox (1981) run bivariate autoregressions of money and economic activity in attempts to determine whether innovations in one of these variables preceded innovations in the others. Ironically, this is precisely the context in which the limitations of this methodology were anticipated by Tobin (1970). For example, if soon after the 1929 downturn a further decline in real incomes was anticipated, individuals' demands for money could have fallen due to downward revisions in their estimates of permanent income. Evidence on timing yields little useful information on cause and effect; in this example the fall in money precedes the fall in income despite the fact that the latter is responsible for the former.

Again, there is no substitute for specifying the mechanism linking cause and effect and subjecting it to tests of a priori plausibility and conformance with historical evidence. The frustrating aspect of the literature is precisely the principals' inability to engage in constructive debate along these lines. Temin's (1981) efforts to formulate the two hypotheses in IS-LM terms is one of the few attempts to provide a basis for communication. Extending his approach, a simple model can serve to illustrate the central points in dispute. We take aggregate supply as a function of the ratio of product prices to costs. Assuming that costs are the slower moving of these two variables, we can simplify by making supply an increasing function of price alone, $y = y\,(p)$. (Lower-case letters denote logs.) Demand depends on income and on the interest rate relevant to spending decisions R. Equating supply and demand gives us the IS curve

$$y(p) = \theta y(p) - \gamma R \qquad (2.1)$$

The demand for real-money balances $(m - p)$ is a function of income and possibly also the interest rate relevant to money market decisions I.

$$m - p = \phi y - \lambda I \tag{2.2}$$

Dispute can be characterized as centering on the specification of interest rate effects. One question is the magnitude of the interest semielasticity of money demand λ, with Temin inclined toward larger values than Friedman and Schwartz (see Temin, 1981, figs. 1–2). The major dispute concerns, however, the definition of the relevant interest rates. Much of Temin's (1981) discussion proceeds on the assumption that the nominal interest rate is the appropriate proxy for both R and I. Mayer (1978), Schwartz (1981), and Gandolfi and Lothian (1977) all suggest that the ex ante real interest rate, not the nominal rate, should appear in the IS curve. In other words:

$$R = I - fE\dot{p} \tag{2.3}$$

where now I is the nominal interest rate, E is the expectations operator, $\dot{p}$ denotes the percentage change in prices, and f is a (nonnegative) parameter. The two interpretations can be distinguished by whether f equals zero—the Temin (1981) case—or one—the Schwartz (1981) case. In the second case, an additional assumption about expectations formation is needed to close the model.

If $f = 0$, then an implication of the model is that a downturn initiated by a decline in m should have been accompanied by higher nominal interest rates. Thus, Temin finds evidence inconsistent with the monetary hypothesis in the decline in nominal interest rates after the summer of 1929. The monetarist objection to this inference is that real rather than nominal interest rates may be the more important determinant of economic decisions, especially in commodity markets. A depression initiated by a decline in m could have been accompanied by lower nominal interest rates if those rates reflected expectations of deflation.

Resolving this dispute, which requires only measures of ex ante real interest rates, would appear straightforward. For constructing ex ante real rates, Mishkin (1981) and others have developed an empirical methodology which involves specifying an information set and estimating forecasting equations for prices under the assumption that agents make efficient use of that information. Combining price forecasts with nominal interest rates, ex ante real rates can be constructed. These real interest rate measures could be used along with various nominal interest rates to test the sensitivity of commodity and asset demands to the alternative rates of return. Contingent upon these assumptions, the empirical implications of the monetary and spending hypotheses could be accepted or rejected.[36]

X

If assumptions about the expectations of asset-market participants play a critical role in distinguishing the Keynesian and Monetarist interpretations of the Great Depression, the role of expectations is even more central to the literature on the labor market in the Depression. The Keynesian and New Classical interpretations of unemployment in the Depression differ primarily by the weight they attach to institutions and expectations, respectively, in wage determination. The characterization of the labor market associated with Keynes (1936) is that workers' concern with relative wages, defined both over time and across individuals, together with the institutions that mediate those concerns, impart inertia to the movement of nominal wages.[37] In the Keynesian model, when prices declined due to deficient demand at the outset of the Depression, institutional and social determinants of labor-market outcomes caused money wages to lag behind, leading real wages to rise and employment to fall. The unemployment that resulted was Keynesian insofar as stimulus to aggregate demand, by raising prices, could have reduced the real wage and unemployment, but in its absence unemployment persisted into the 1930s. This vision of the labor market continues to inform the work of, among others, Hatton (1983), Broadberry (1984b) and Eichengreen and Sachs (1985).

The alternative to the Keynesian framework is the expectations-driven model of Lucas and Rapping (1969, 1972), who attempt to determine whether a neoclassical model of a smoothly functioning labor market can account for the observed fluctuation of unemployment. The distinguishing feature of their model is that labor supply is determined by expected real wages and real interest rates, while labor demand is determined by realized values. Forecast errors can therefore give rise to unemployment. Assuming, following Lucas and Rapping, that price expectations are formed adaptively, much of the price decline after 1929 can be taken as unanticipated. Consequently, most of the subsequent increase in unemployment is predicted by their model: while the United States unemployment rate actually rose by 22 percentage points between 1929 and 1932, the predicted rise is 17 points. Where the model collapses is in failing to capture the persistence of unemployment after 1932. It predicts that unemployment should have returned to normal levels once price expectations were appropriately revised; but whereas the actual rate never fell below 14 per cent of the labor force over the remainder of the 1930s, after 1932 the model predicts single-digit unemployment. This suggests that institutional rigidities contributing inertia to nominal wages must provide part of the explanation for interwar unemployment. The work of Weinstein (1980) on New Deal NIRA codes and of Darby (1976) and Wallis and Benjamin (1981) on public employment suggests likely factors to consider.

A possible defense of the model is that the adaptive expectations mechanism inadequately captures agents' forecasts of wages, interest rates, and prices. Altonji (1982) has shown, however, that the alternative of rational expectations is decisively rejected by the data. Moreover, if expectations are permitted to adjust more quickly under the assumption of rationality, the intertemporal substitution model's capacity to explain the initial rise in unemployment will be severely diminished.

An attempt has been made recently by Beenstock, Capie, and Griffiths (1984) to apply a variant of this same intertemporal substitution model to interwar Britain. They attribute the speed and strength of Britain's recovery after 1931 to the stability of real wages during expansion, and interpret the failure of real wages to rise during recovery in terms of a smoothly functioning neoclassical labor market characterized by temporary excess supply in which wages are quick to adjust to market-clearing levels. But if the smooth functioning of the labor market holds the key to Britain's successful recovery, the authors are in a bind when it comes to explaining how Britain got into this mess in the first place. The only explanation consistent with a flexible labor market is the notion, drawn from the intertemporal substitution model, that real wages were only temporarily above market-clearing levels due to a negative price shock in 1929. One must embrace the assumption that most of the decline in prices starting in 1929 could not be predicted by workers until at least 1931.[38] While the plausibility of this assumption can be argued on a priori grounds, it would again be more fruitful to construct empirical measures of price expectations in order to subject the hypothesis to test.[39]

In Britain as in America, unemployment remained persistently high after 1932. In explanation Beenstock, Capie, and Griffiths invoke the work of Benjamin and Kochin (1979) on the incentive effects of unemployment insurance. Unfortunately, the jury is still out on the statistical significance and economic importance of these effects. Those predisposed toward them conclude that their influence has been convincingly documented on the basis of precisely the same assertions and evidence that have led those predisposed toward skepticism to conclude that this hypothesis has been decisively rejected. One suspects that existing evidence is, in fact, less than conclusive.

There are at least three approaches to be taken in future research designed to better identify the effects of interwar unemployment insurance. The first is to consider the influence of benefits at a less aggregate level. Since 19 annual macroeconomic observations contain a limited amount of statistical information, moving to monthly or quarterly data as in Hatton (1985) is a step in the right direction. Considering the effects of benefits in a variety of industries, as in Collins (1982), is also helpful. But since benefits are thought to influence decisions made at the individual or household level, microeconomic evidence may ultimately be required.

The second approach to better identifying the effects of benefits is to model explicitly those aspects of individual behavior most likely to be influenced by an insurance scheme. Advocates of the insurance hypothesis argue that unemployment benefits subsidize search activity; the logical approach is therefore to specify and estimate a model of search for the interwar years. This is the tack Hatton (1985) has taken. It is noteworthy that his results provide little support for the insurance hypothesis.

A third approach to better identifying the effects of unemployment benefits is to embed their effects in a structural model which attempts to capture the influence of labor market institutions. The institutional arrangements whose impact on wages most need to be distinguished from that of benefits are trade unionism and the minimum wages mandated by the provisions of the British Trade Boards Act.

XI

To this point, discussion of the Great Depression has focused on events in the United Kingdom and United States. Despite some recent work on the German (Temin 1971; Overy 1975; Falkus 1975; Neal 1979; Balderston 1983), French (Kemp 1971), Swedish (Jonung 1981, 1983), Czechoslovak (Pryor 1979), Australian (Eichengreen 1985c), and Latin American (Diaz-Alejandro 1983; Thorp 1984; Eichengreen and Portes 1986) cases, this is where the bulk of the literature lies. International comparisons and extensions are an obvious avenue for research. For example, hypotheses about the channels of transmission by which the Great Depression was propagated internationally can most effectively be tested with evidence from a variety of countries. Questions about the role of economic institutions in conditioning responses to the Depression can best be addressed by comparing the reaction in several countries where different institutional arrangements prevailed. Some investigators attach considerable weight, for example, to the provisions of unemployment insurance and public assistance systems in influencing the behavior of the unemployed. Comparisons of Britain and France, where the provisions of such schemes differed in some respects but bore a family resemblance in others, might shed new light on the implications of such institutions for the operation of the labor market.

Another application of comparative macroeconomic history is to the formulation of economic policy. Much of the work by economists on the Depression takes policy as exogenous or at least temporally prior to the market adjustments under consideration. Where the studies of economists and economic historians differ, therefore, is in the extent to which they treat the stance of policy, its determinants, and its effects together in a unified analytical framework. Historical analyses are infused with the notion that the very attitudes and expectations that condition agents' response to macroeconomic shocks influence equally the responses of policymakers. For instance, after 1931 the British and French attached very different weights to continued maintenance of the gold standard, with British allegiance to gold and any impulse to return quickly dissolving after devaluation, while France continued to adhere to the gold-based regime until the bitter end in 1936. One factor contributing to these different national attitudes was the belief in France that devaluation would unleash inflation, a fear attributable to the nation's experience with inflation in the previous decade. At the same time, the response of French financial markets to new information on monetary trends differed from that of British markets because of precisely the same heightened sensitivity in France to prospects for inflation. In this instance, the same historical preconditions influenced both policy's formulation and its effects.

In a sense, the challenge confronting historians who wish to consider both the formulation of policy and its effects in a unified analytical framework is what econometricians call an "identification problem." A logically consistent model of economic behavior requires the inclusion of a certain number of exogenous factors to explain the behavior of the endogenous variables. Economists satisfy these requirements by imposing exclusion restrictions and exogeneity assumptions. Their analyses of the effects of economic policy take the formulation of policy as exogenous. Their analyses of policy formulation take the behavior of the variables of concern to policymakers as predetermined at the time of decision. Placing either the determinants or the effects of policy outside the scope of the analysis permits their use to pin down the effects of their counterparts. But to endogenize both policy's formulation and effects in a meaningful way, some other underlying determinant of these two aspects of the political economy is needed to account for their evolution. The public and policymakers' past experience, their collective memories, and the market structures and social institutions they develop in response—in other words, economic history—is the ingredient needed to implement this type of integrated analysis. In the comparison of Britain and France just mentioned, for example, differences across countries in the historical experience of the 1920s is the predetermined variable required to pin down differences in both policy's formulation and effects in the 1930s. But the use of history to facilitate integrated analyses of economic policy is a general proposition whose relevance extends well beyond this example and examples that resemble it. If macroeconomists are to move beyond partial equilibrium treatments of their subject which take the most interesting aspects of the problem as given, they must develop an historical perspective that extends beyond the merits of long time series to include the role of historical experience as an influence on the characteristics of institutions and the attitudes of individuals in both the private and public sectors.

XII

What then does this survey of the state of research suggest the relationship of economic history to macroeconomics should be? It suggests no cause for alarm over the fact that research in economic history is responsive to current issues in macroeconomics, any more than there is reason to bemoan, for example, the inspiration social historians draw from current social trends. Responsiveness to events is a healthy sign insofar as one function of historical scholarship is to lend a long-run perspective to the discussion of current developments. The contribution is equally valuable whether it is the generality or specificity of contemporary events which is established. Yet there are dangers, both substantive and methodological, when this relationship becomes too intimate. The usefulness of economic theory and econometrics is one of the lessons to be derived from the turmoil and intellectual ferment that have characterized research in economic history for the last 25 years. Another lesson is acknowledgement of the strength of the temptation to limit oneself to the models, methods, and issues currently fashionable in economics. Both the integrity of research in economic history and its value to related disciplines are threatened when economic historians confine themselves to aspects of historical issues that can be neatly addressed with these tools and fail to provide a bridge to the perspectives and methodologies of other historical specialties. To do so is to lose sight of economic history's equally intimate connection to the discipline of history. The historian's perspective encompasses aspects of economic problems whose importance is typically minimized by economists, sometimes because of the inability of conventional economic analysis to address them. Thus, the strength of economic history, in relation to economics, is that its perspective is not just longer but also wider. That strength is undermined when it too closely emulates *either* of the disciplines to which it is connected.

Notes

1. The survey strays into fields such as International Trade and Development where macroeconomic aspects of the problems they consider are prominent.
2. See for example Elsas (1935).
3. Let $m - p = n(\phi y - \lambda r)$, where all variables are in logs and m is money, p is prices, n is population, r is the interest rate (held constant throughout), and y is per capita income. Assume $y = y(n)$, $y' < 0$. Then $dp/dn = -\phi\partial y/\partial n - 1 \lesseqgtr 0$. Note that this condition for pouplation growth to be inflationary takes the supply of money as exogenous.
4. An example of the extensive literature from the 1960s building on Gilboy's work is Eversley (1967). Criticism of the thesis then appears in Rostow (1975) and Mokyr (1977), after which it falls from favor. See however Crouzet (1980), Cole (1981), and Hatton et al. (1983).
5. Harley's precise estimate is 0.52.
6. Recall that the only reason a given supply curve is elastic is that varying amounts of labor can be combined with fixed factors of production.
7. "Shares" should be understood broadly to mean ownership in one form or another of claims to a share of an enterprise's future profits. In other words, the Ricardian Equivalence Theorem does not hold. (See Barro 1974.)
8. Assume $S(r) = I(r) + \theta$, where S is private saving, I is private investment, r is the interest rate, and θ is government absorption of private saving. Then $(\partial S/\partial r - \partial I/\partial r)\, dr = d\theta$. With observed values of dr and $d\theta$ and an assumed value of $\partial I/\partial r$, a value of $\partial S/\partial r$ can be derived.
9. These estimates are drawn from James' table 4 simulations in which it is assumed that government spending in adjusted along with counterfactual changes in debt, respecting the government budget constraint. It is hard to meaningfully interpret the alternative—money finance of deficits—under the gold standard.
10. Trade theorists such as Lapan (1976), Neary (1982), and Mussa (1982) have studied dynamics of adjustment to export and import market shocks at the theoretical level. Yet little if any progress has been made in empirically implementing their theories. Some recent work on the macroeconomics of labor market adjustment provides promising suggestions of how the relationship of structural shifts to aggregate unemployment might be quantified. See Lilien (1982).
11. On the previous generation of studies, see, for example, Deane (1969 p. 245) or Mathias (1969, p. 46). For recent hints along these lines, see Williamson (1985).
12. See, however, Ford (1981) for a notable exception.
13. An example of a structural model is Bourguignon and Lévy-Leboyer (1984). An example of the time series approach is Eichengreen (1983). Both approaches are put to work by Edelstein (1982) and Eichengreen (1982b).
14. Two of the seminal articles on this methodology are Sims (1972) and Sims (1980).
15. Unfortunately, so much has been claimed for these techniques—by macroeconomists

and statisticians, it should be noted, rather than historians—that they have fallen into disrepute. Time-series analyses have been misleadingly referred to as "causality tests" and offered as alternatives to models, theories, and economic reasoning. While causality has unambiguous meanings in logic with direct applications to problems in history, it is unlikely in practice that historical debates over causation can be resolved through observation of comovements of variables in the time domain. The problem of shifts in critical parameters accompanying changes in policy regime (the "Lucas Critique") that in principle plagues structural macroeconomic models and initially motivated the development of the time-series approach can be equally problematic in time-series analysis. It should be no surprise to the historian that only an analysis alert to the possibility of changes in structure can shed light on the question of whether such shifts are important in practice. Time-series analysis is, unsurprisingly, incapable of freeing the historian from the need to specify the model he or she has in mind and to marshal the evidence for and against it. It is useful only as a systematic approach to the specification of such tests. For further discussion, see Eichengreen (1983, p. 154).

16. A related study which considers evidence from both the United States and Britain is Friedman and Schwartz (1982). See also Bessler (1984). For evidence on France, see also Saint Marc (1983).

17. Recent contributions are presented or discussed in Bordo and Schwartz (1984) and Eichengreen (1985d).

18. This excess volatility in the historical data seems to be due to the over-representation of metals and intermediate goods in early indexes of industrial production. Again, see Romer (1984).

19. Moreover, the Theory of the Second Best suggests that, in the presence of such externalities, not only may the sign of a tariff's effects be reversed but magnitudes may be greatly enhanced.

20. For a review of the literature, see David (1975).

21. Even if learning-by-doing is shown to have been important in the nineteenth-century and to have exercised a critical influence on the pattern of growth, it represents a distortion and provides a rationale for intervention only if firms were unable to capture the benefits themselves.

22. See Svennilson (1953), Kindleberger (1973), and Sauvy (1984) for suggestions along these lines.

23. Jones (1975) makes precise what is meant by "difference."

24. A selection of the more eclectic contributions to this literature includes Webb (1984), Holtfrerich (1982), and the articles collected in Feldman et al. (1982).

25. A notable attempt to explain the Wall Street boom and crash is however provided by Minsky (1982).

26. See for example Booth (1983), Eichengreen (1981), Howson (1975), Howson and Winch (1977), and Peden (1984). Booth and Glynn (1979) provide a review of this literature.

27. Two examples are Middleton (1981) and Cairncross and Eichengreen (1983).

28. See for example Peppers (1973), Thomas (1981), Middleton (1981, 1984), Broadberry (1984), and Maddock (1985).

29. A study by Harrison (1983) suggests, however, that it may not be appropriate to treat Spain symmetrically with industrial Europe.

30. See also Dimsdale (1981), Wright (1981), and Cairncross and Eichengreen (1983) for further evidence on the British case.

31. In related work, Eichengreen (1986) has considered the operations of the Bank of France and the allegation that France's accumulation of vast amounts of gold between 1926

and 1932 contributed to the demise of the interwar gold standard. He concludes that, contrary to common impression, the Bank of France had no choice, given the statutes under which it operated, but to passively accumulate gold. If France's acquisition of gold in fact contributed to the demise of the interwar gold standard, then responsibility should be deflected from the central bankers to the politicians responsible for passage of the statutes under which the Bank of France operated.

32. The ramifications of the debate can be found in Brunner (1981). For a review of the relevent literature, see Barber (1978).

33. The conclusion that consumption was exceptionally depressed in 1929 is based on the residuals from an estimated consumption function. Mayer (1978) has shown that the evidence from interwar consumption functions may be more ambiguous than Temin suggests. Two interesting approaches to explaining the behavior of consumption are taken by Green (1971) and Mishkin (1978).

34. A final explanation with persistent popularity is the Smoot-Hawley tariff imposed by the United States in the first half of 1930. While the Smoot-Hawley tariff has been blamed for a variety of ills (Saint Etienne, 1984), the most influential accounts, by Meltzer (1976) and Gordon and Wilcox (1981), blame it not for the onset of the Depression but for the unusual severity of the subsequent contraction. A critique of these arguments appears in Eichengreen (1985b).

35. The causes of banking panics are considered by Temin (1976), White (1984), and Wicker (1980). Their consequences for money supply are examined by Boughton and Wicker (1979), Wicker (1984), and Trescott (1982).

36. Precisely the same methodology can be used to test Field's explanation for the Depression's onset. Field's hypothesis is that high real interest rates were associated with the high nominal interest rates caused by the exceptional volume of stock exchange transactions in the last years of the 1920s, and that these high real rates depressed expenditure on consumer durables and investment in construction. Testing this hypothesis requires a measure of the ex ante real interest rate, which in turn requires an empirical proxy for price expectations.

37. An excellent description of Keynesian labor market assumptions as applied to this period appears in Baily (1982). It is contrasted with classical labor market assumptions by Casson (1983).

38. Other criticisms of their interpretation are provided by Worswick (1984) and Dimsdale (1984).

39. Similarly, estimates of the ex ante real interest rate could be used to test the hypothesis advanced by Capie et al. (1983) that the 1932 war loan conversion had no noticeable impact on real variables.

References

Altonji, Joseph. 1982. The intertemporal substitution model of labor market fluctuations: An empirical analysis. *Review of Economic Studies* 49:783–824.

Baily, Martin. 1982. The labor market in the 1930s. In James Tobin (ed.), *Macroeconomics, Prices and Quantities*. Washington, DC: Brookings Institution. pp. 21–62.

Bairoch, Paul 1972. Free trade and European economic development in the 19th century. *European Economic Review* 3:211–245.

Balderston, T. 1983. The beginning of the depression in Germany, 1927–30: Investment and the capital market. *Economic History Review* 36:395–415.

Barker, Clarence L. 1978. On the origins of the Great Depression. *Southern Economic Journal* 44:432–456.

Barro, Robert. 1974. Are government bonds net wealth? *Journal of Political Economy* 82:1095–1117.

Barro, Robert. 1979. Money and the price level under the gold standard. *Economic Journal* 89:13–33.

Beenstock, M., F. Capie, and B. Griffiths. 1984. Economic recovery in the United Kingdom in the 1930s. Bank of England Panel of Academic Consultants Paper No. 23 (April).

Benjamin, Daniel, and Levis Kochin. 1979. Searching for an explanation of unemployment in interwar Britain. *Journal of Political Economy* 87:441–478.

Bessler, David A. 1984. Additional evidence on money and prices: U.S. data, 1870–1919. *Explorations in Economic History* 21:125–132.

Bloomfield, Arthur. 1959. *Monetary policy under the international gold standard.* New York: Federal Reserve Bank of New York.

Bolch, Ben W., and John D. Pilgrim. 1973. A reappraisal of some factors associated with fluctuations in the United States in the interwar period. *Southern Economic Journal* 39:327–344.

Booth Alan. 1983. The "Keynesian Revolution" in economic policy-making. *Economic History Review* 36:103–124.

Booth, Alan, and S. Glynn. 1979. The public records and recent British economic historiography. *Economic History Review* 32:303–315.

Bordo, Michael. 1981. The classical gold standard: Some lessons for today. *Federal Reserve Bank of St. Louis Review* 63:1–17.

Bordo, Michael D., and Anna Schwartz. 1980. Money and prices in the 19th century: An old debate rejoined. *Journal of Economic History* 40:61–67.

Bordo, Michael D., and Anna Schwartz. 1980b. Money and prices in the 19th century: Was Thomas Tooke Right? *Explorations in Economic History* 18:97–127.

Bordo, Michael D., and Anna Schwartz. 1984. *A Retrospective on the Classical Gold Standard.* Chicago: University of Chicago Press.

Boskin, Michael J. 1978. Taxation, saving and the rate of interest. *Journal of Political Economy* 86:S3–S27.

Boughton, James M., and Elmus R. Wicker. 1979. The behavior of the currency-deposit ratio during the Great Depression. *Journal of Money, Credit and Banking* 11:405–418.

Bourguignon, F., and M. Lévy-Leboyer. 1984. An econometric model of France during the 19th century, *European Economic Review* 25:107–142.

Broadberry, S.N. 1983. Unemployment in interwar Britain: A disequilibrium approach. *Oxford Economic Papers* 35:463–485.

Broadberry, S.N. 1984. Fiscal policy in Britain during the 1930s. *Economic History Review* 37:95–107.

Broadberry, S.N. 1984b. Wages and prices in interwar Britain. Unpublished,

University College, Cardiff.
Brown, E. Cary. 1956. Fiscal policy in the thirties: A reappraisal. *American Economic Review* 46:857–879.
Brown, E. H. P., and S. V. Hopkins. 1957. Wage rates and prices: Evidence for population pressure in the 16th century. *Economica* 24:289–306.
Brunner, Karl, ed. 1981. *The Great Depression Revisited*, Boston: Kluwer-Nijhoff.
Burns, Arthur, and W. C. Mitchell. 1946. *Measuring Business Cycles*. New York: National Bureau of Economic Research.
Cagan, Philip. 1956. The monetary dynamics of hyperinflation. In M. Friedman (ed.), *Studies in the Quantity Theory of Money*. Chicago: University of Chicago Press.
Cain, P. J. 1982. Professor McCloskey on British free trade, 1841–1881: Some comments. *Explorations in Economic History* 19:201–207.
Cairncross, Alec, and Barry Eichengreen. 1983. *Sterling in Decline: The Devaluations of 1931, 1949 and 1967*. Oxford: Blackwell.
Callahan, C. 1984. Movements in aggregate price uncertainty in the United States. Unpublished, University of North Carolina.
Capie, F. 1983. Tariff protection and economic performance in the 19th century. In John Black and L. A. Winters (eds.), *Policy and Performance in International Trade*. London: Macmillan. Pp. 1–24.
Capie, F., T. C. Mills, M. J. Thomas, and G. E. Wood. 1983. Was the war loan conversion a success? City University Monetary History Discussion Paper No. 5.
Casson, Mark. 1983. *The Economics of Unemployment: An Historical Perspective*. Oxford: Martin Robertson.
Choudri, E. J., and L. A. Kochin. 1980. The exchange rate and international business cycle disturbances: Some evidence from the Great Depression. *Journal of Money, Credit and Banking* 12:565–574.
Clarke, S. V. O. 1967. *Central Bank Cooperation, 1924–1931*. New York: Federal Reserve Bank of New York.
Cohen, Jon S. 1976. The 1927 revaluation of the lira: A study in political economy. *Economic History Review* 29:642–654.
Cole, W. A. 1981. Factors in demand, 1700–80. In Roderick Floud and Donald McCloskey, eds. *The Economic History of Britain Since 1700*. Cambridge: Cambridge University Press, v.1, pp. 36–65.
Collins, Michael. 1982. Unemployment in interwar Britain: Still searching for an explanation. *Journal of Political Economy* 90:369–379.
Cooper, Richard. 1982. The gold standard: Historical facts and future prospects. *Brookings Papers on Economic Activity* 1:1–45.
Crafts, N. F. R. 1981. The eighteenth century: A survey. In R. Floud and D. McCloskey (eds.), *The Economic History of Britain Since 1700*. Cambridge: Cambridge University Press, 1, pp. 1–17.
Cross, Rodney. 1982. How much voluntary unemployment in interwar Britain? *Journal of Political Economy* 90:380–385.
Crouzet, Francois. 1980. Toward an export economy: British exports during the

industrial revolution. *Explorations in Economic History* 17:48–93.

Darby, Michael. 1976. Three-and-a-half million U.S. employees have been mislaid; or, an explanation of unemployment 1934–1941. *Journal of Political Economy* 84:1–16.

David, Paul. 1975. *Technical Choice, Innovation and Economic Growth*. New York: Cambridge University Press.

Deane, P. 1969. *The First Industrial Revolution*. Cambridge: Cambridge University Press.

DeCanio, Stephen J., and Joel Mokyr. 1977. Inflation and wage lag during the American Civil War. *Explorations in Economic History* 14:331–336.

Diaz-Alejandro, Carlos A. 1983. Stories of the 1930s for the 1980s. In P.A. Armella, R. Dornbusch, and M. Obstfeld (eds.), *Financial Policies and the World Capital Market: The Problem of Latin American Countries*. Chicago: University of Chicago Press.

Dimsdale, N.H. 1981. British monetary policy and the exchange rate, 1920–38. In W.A. Eltis and P.J.N. Sinclair (eds.), *The Money Supply and the Exchange Rate*. Oxford: Clarendon Press.

Dimsdale, N.H. 1984. Employment and real wages in the interwar period. *National Institute Economic Review* 110:94–103.

Dornbusch, Rudiger. 1981. Some comments on Thomas Sargent's Stopping Moderate Inflation. Unpublished, MIT.

Dornbusch, Rudiger. 1985. Stopping Hyperinflation: Lessons from the German inflation experience of the 1920s. NBER Working Paper No. 1675.

Dowie, J.A. 1975. 1919–20 is in need of attention. *Economic History Review* 28:429–450.

Dutton, John, 1984. The Bank of England and the rules of the game under the international gold standard. In M. Bordo and A. Schwartz (eds.), *A Retrospective on the Classical Gold Standard*. Chicago: University of Chicago Press. Pp. 173–207.

Dwyer, Gerald P., Jr. 1985. Money, Income and Prices in the United Kingdom, 1870–1913. *Economic Inquiry* XXIII:415–436.

Edelstein, Michael. 1982. *Overseas Investment in the Age of High Imperialism*. New York: Columbia University Press.

Eichengreen, Barry. 1981. Sterling and the tariff, 1929–32. *Princeton Studies in International Finance* 48. Princeton: Princeton University Press.

Eichengreen, Barry. 1982. Did speculation destabilize the French franc in the 1920s? *Explorations in Economic History* 19:71–100.

Eichengreen, Barry. 1982b. Asset markets and investment fluctuations in late Victorian Britain. *Research in Economic History* 8:145–179.

Eichengreen, Barry. 1983. The causes of British business cycles, 1833–1913. *Journal of European Economic History* 12:145–161.

Eichengreen, Barry. 1984. Central bank cooperation under the interwar gold standard. *Explorations in Economic History* 21:64–87.

Eichengreen, Barry. 1985. International policy coordination in historical perspective: A view from the interwar years. In Willem Buiter and Richard Marston (eds.), *International Economic Policy Coordination*. Cambridge: Cambridge University Press. Pp. 139–177.

Eichengreen, Barry. 1985b. The political economy of the Smoot-Hawley Tariff. *Research in Economic History* (forthcoming).

Eichengreen, Barry. 1985c. The Australian economic recovery of the 1930s in international comparative perspective. Australian National University Working Paper in Economic History No. 36. (Forthcoming in N.G. Butlin and R. Gregory (eds.), *Economic Recovery in Australia in the 1930s*, Cambridge: Cambridge University Press.

Eichengreen, Barry, ed. 1985d. *The Gold Standard in Theory and History*, London: Methuen.

Eichengreen, Barry. 1986. The Bank of France and the sterilization of gold, 1926–1932. *Explorations in Economic History*. 23:56–84.

Eichengreen, Barry, and Ian McLean. 1986. The Midas touch: The supply of gold under the pre-1914 gold standard. Unpublished.

Eichengreen, Barry, and Richard Portes. 1986. Debt and default in the 1930s: Causes and consequences. *European Economic Review* 30:599–640.

Eichengreen, Barry, and Jeffrey Sachs. 1985. Exchange rates and economic recovery in the 1930s. *Journal of Economic History* 45: 925–946.

Eichengreen, Barry, Mark Watson, and Richard Grossman. 1985. Bank rate policy under the interwar gold standard: a dynamic probit model. *Economic Journal* 95:725–745.

Elsas, M.J. 1935. Price data from Munich 1500–1700. *Economic Journal Supplement* 3:63–78.

Eversley, D. 1967. The home market and economic growth in England 1750–1780. In E.L. Jones and G.E. Mingay (eds.), *Land, Labour and Population in the Industrial Revolution*. London: Edward Arnold pp. 206–259.

Falkus, Malcum E. 1975. The German business cycle in the 1920s. *Economic History Review* 28:451–465.

Feldman, Gerald D., C-L. Holtfrerich, G.A. Ritter, and P-C. Witt. 1982. *The German Inflation Reconsidered*. Berlin and New York: Walter de Gruyter.

Felix, David. 1956. Profit inflation and industrial growth: The historic record and contemporary analogies. *Quarterly Journal of Economics* 70:441–463.

Field, Alexander J. 1984. Asset exchanges and the transactions demand for money, 1919–29. *American Economic Review* 74:43–59.

Field, Alexander J. 1984b. A new interpretation of the onset of the Great Depression. *Journal of Economic History* 44:489–498.

Findlay, Ronald. 1983. Trade and growth in the Industrial Revolution. In C. Kindleberger and G. di Tella (eds.), *Economics in the Long View: Essays in Honor of W. W. Rostow*. London: Macmillan.

Flood, Robert, and Peter Garber. 1980a. Market fundamentals versus price level bubbles: The first tests. *Journal of Political Economy* 88:745–770.

Flood, Robert, and Peter Garber. 1980b. An economic theory of monetary reform. *Journal of Political Economy* 88:24–59.

Flynn, Dennis O. 1978. A new perspective on the Spanish Price Revolution: The monetary approach to the balance of payments. *Explorations in Economic History* 15:388–406.

Ford, Alec. 1960. Notes on the working of the gold standard before 1914. *Oxford Economic Papers* 12:52–76.

Ford, Alec. 1981. The trade cycle in Britain 1860–1914. In R. Floud and D. McCloskey (eds.), *The Economic History of Britain Since 1700*. Cambridge: Cambridge University Press, v.2, pp. 27–49.

Frankel, Jeffrey A. 1982. The 1807–1809 embargo against Great Britain. *Journal of Economic History* 42:291–308.

Fratianni, M., and F. Spinelli. 1984. Italy in the gold standard period, 1861–1914. In Michael D. Bordo and Anna Schwartz (eds.), *A Retrospective on the Classical Gold Standard*. Chicago: University of Chicago Press. Pp. 405–454.

Frenkel. J.A., and K. Clements. 1981. Exchange rates in the 1920s: A monetary approach. In M.J. Flanders and A. Razin (eds.), *Development in an Inflationary World*. New York: Academic Press. Pp. 283–318.

Friedman, Milton, and Anna Schwartz. 1963. *A Monetary History of the United States, 1867–1960*. Princeton: Princeton University Press.

Friedman, Milton, and Anna Schwartz. 1982. *Monetary Trends in the United States and the United Kingdom*. Chicago: University of Chicago Press.

Gandolfi, A., and J. Lothian. 1977. Did monetary forces cause the Great Depression? A review article. *Journal of Money, Credit and Banking* 9:679–691.

Garber, Peter. 1982. Transition from inflation to price stability. *Carnegie Rochester Conference Series on Public Policy* 16:11–42.

Garside, W.R. 1977. Juvenile unemployment and public policy between the wars. *Economic History Review* 30:322–339.

Gayer, A., W.W. Rostow and A.J. Schwartz. 1953. *The Growth and Fluctuation of the British Economy, 1790–1850*. Oxford: The Clarendon Press.

Gilboy, E.W. 1932. Demand as a factor in the Industrial Revoultion. Reprinted in R.M. Hartwell, (ed.), *The Causes of the Industrial Revolution in England*. London: Methuen, 1967.

Glynn, Sean, and Alan Booth. 1983. Unemployment in interwar Britain: A case for relearning the lessons of the 1930s? *Economic History Review* 36:329–348.

Goldin, Claudia D., and Frank D. Lewis. 1980. The role of exports in American economic growth during the Napoleonic wars, 1793–1807. *Explorations in Economic History* 17:6–25.

Goodhart, Charles. 1972. *The Business of Banking*. London: Weidenfield and Nicolson.

Gordon, Robert, and James Wilcox. 1981. Monetarist interpretations of the Great Depression: Evaluation and critique. In Karl Brunner (ed.), *The Great Depression Revisted*. Boston: Kluwer-Nijhoff.

Green, G.D. 1971. The economic impact of the stock market boom and crash of 1929. In Federal Reserve Bank of Boston, *Consumer Spending and Monetary Policy*. Boston: Federal Reserve.

Grissa, A. 1981. The French monetary and exchange rate experience in the 1920s. Unpublished.

Hamilton, E.J. 1934. *American Treasure and the Price Revolution in Spain, 1501–1650.* Cambridge: Harvard University Press.

Harley, C. Knick. 1982. British industrialization before 1841: Evidence of slower growth during the Industrial Revolution. *Journal of Economic History* 42: 267–289.

Harrison, J. 1983. The interwar depression and the Spanish economy. *Journal of European Economic History* 12:295–322.

Hatton, T.J. 1983. Unemployment benefits and the macroeconomics of the inter-war labour market: A further analysis. *Oxford Economic Papers* 35: 486–505.

Hatton, T.J. 1985. The British labor market in the 1920s: A test of the search-turnover approach. *Explorations in Economic History* 22:257–270.

Hatton, T.J., John S. Lyons, and S.E. Satchell. 1983. Eighteenth-century British trade: Homespun or empire made? *Explorations in Economic History* 20: 163–182.

Holt, Charles. 1977. Who benefitted from the prosperity of the twenties? *Explorations in Economic History* 14:227–289.

Holtfrerich, Carl-Ludwig. 1982. *Die Deutsche Inflation, 1914–1923.* Berlin and New York: de Gruyter.

Howrey, E. 1968. A spectrum analysis of the long swing hypothesis. *International Economic Review* 9:228–252.

Howson, Susan. 1975. *Domestic Monetary Management in Britain, 1919–38.* Cambridge: Cambridge University Press.

Howson, Susan, and Donald Winch. 1977. *The Economic Advisory Council, 1930–1939.* Cambridge: Cambridge University Press.

Hume, David. 1752. *Essays, Moral, Political and Literary.* London: Longmans, Green. (1898 edition.)

James, John. 1984. Public debt management and nineteenth-century American economic growth. *Explorations in Economic History* 21:192–217.

James, John, and Richard Sylla. 1980. The changing nature of American public debt, 1690–1835. In *La Dette Publique aux XVIIIe et XIXe Siècles.* Brussels, Credit Communal de Belgique.

Jones, Eric L. 1973. The fashion manipulators: Consumer tastes and British industries, 1660–1800. In Louis P. Cain and Paul J. Uselding (eds.), *Business Enterprise and Economic Change.* Kent, OH: Kent State University Press. Pp. 198–228.

Jones, Ronald. 1975. Presumption and the transfer problem. *Journal of International Economics* 5:263–274.

Jonung, Lars. 1981. The Depression in Sweden and the United States: A comparison. In Karl Brunner (ed.), *The Great Depression Revisited.* Boston: Kluwer-Nijhoff. Pp. 286–315.

Jonung, Lars. 1983. Monetization and the behavior of velocity in Sweden, 1871–1913. *Explorations in Economic History* 20:418–439.

Kemp, Tom. 1971. The French economy under the Franc Poincaré. *Economic History Review* 24:82–99.

Keynes, J.M. 1929. The German transfer problem. *Economic Journal* 39:1–7.

Keynes, J.M. 1930. *A Treatise on Money*. London: Macmillan.

Keynes, J.M. 1931. *Essays in Persuasion*. London: Macmillan.

Keynes, J.M. 1936. *The General Theory of Employment, Interest and Money*. London: Macmillan.

Kindleberger, Charles P. 1973. *The World in Depression, 1929–1939*. Berkeley: University of California Press.

Lapan, H. 1976. International trade, factor market distortions, and the optimal dynamic subsidy. *American Economic Review* 66:335–346.

Lewis, W.A. 1978. *Growth and Fluctuations, 1880–1914*. London: Allen and Unwin.

Lilien, David M. 1982. Sectoral shifts and cyclical unemployment. *Journal of Political Economy* 90:777–793.

Lindert, Peter H. 1969. Key currencies and gold, 1900–1913. *Princeton Studies in International Finance* 24. Princeton: Princeton University Press.

Lucas, Robert, and L.A. Rapping. 1969. Real wages, employment and inflation. *Journal of Political Economy* 77:721–754.

Lucas, Robert, and L.A. Rapping. 1972. Unemployment in the Great Depression: Is there a full explanation? *Journal of Political Economy* 80:186–191.

Maddock, Rod. 1985. Australian fiscal policy in the 1930s. Australian National University Working Paper in Economic History no. 50 (August).

Maier, Charles. 1975. *Recasting Bourgeois Europe*. Princeton: Princeton University Press.

Mathias, P. 1969. *The First Industrial Nation*. London: Methuen.

Mayer, Thomas. 1978. Money and the Great Depression: A critique of Professor Temin's thesis. *Explorations in Economic History* 15:127–145.

McCloskey, D.N. 1980a. Magnanimous Albion: Free trade and British national income, 1841–1881. *Explorations in Economic History* 17:302–320.

Mcloskey, D.N. 1980b. A preliminary note on the anomalous price rise of 1933–34. Unpublished.

McCloskey, D.N. 1982. Reply to Peter Cain. *Explorations in Economic History* 19:208–210.

McCloskey, D.N. and J.R. Zecher. 1976. How the gold standard worked, 1880–1913. In J.A. Frenkel and H.G. Johnson (eds.), *The Monetary Approach to the Balance of Payments*. London: Allen & Unwin. Pp. 357–385.

McCloskey, D.N., and J.R. Zecher. 1984. The success of purchasing-power parity: Historical evidence and its implications for macroeconomics. In Michael D. Bordo and Anna Schwartz (eds.), *A Retrospective on the Classical Gold Standard*. Chicago: University of Chicago Press. Pp. 121–172.

Meltzer, Alan H. 1976. Monetary and other explanations for the start of the Great Depression. *Journal of Monetary Economics* 2:455–472.

Middleton, Roger. 1981. The constant employment budget balance and British budgetary policy, 1929–39. *Economic History Review* 34:287–300.

Middleton, Roger. 1984. The measurement of fiscal influence in Britain in the 1930s. *Economic History Review* 37:103–106.

Minsky, Hyman P. 1982. The financial instability hypothesis: Capitalist processes

and the behavior of the economy. In C.P. Kindleberger and J.-P. Laffarge (eds.), *Financial Crises*. Cambridge: Cambridge University Press. Pp. 13–47.
Mishkin, F.S. 1978. The household balance sheet and the Great Depression. *Journal of Economic History* 38:918–937.
Mishkin, F.S. 1981. The real interest rate: An empirical investigation. In K. Brunner and A.H. Meltzer (eds.), *The Costs and Consequences of Inflation*, Carnegie Rochester Conference Series on Public Policy 15:151–200.
Mitchell, W.C. 1903. *A History of the Greenbacks*. Chicago: University of Chicago Press.
Moggridge, D.E. 1969. *The Return to Gold, 1925*. Cambridge: Cambridge University Press.
Moggridge, D.E. 1972. *British Monetary Policy, 1924–1931*. Cambridge: Cambridge University Press.
Moggridge, D.E. 1981. Financial crises and lenders of last resort in the crises of 1920 and 1929. *Journal of European Economic History* 10:47–70.
Mokyr, Joel. 1977. Supply and demand in the Industrial Revolution. *Journal of Economic History* 37:981–1000.
Mokyr, Joel, and N.E. Savin. 1976. Stagflation in historical perspective: The Napoleonic Wars revisited. *Research in Economic History* 1:198–259.
Mussa, Michael. 1982. Government policy and the adjustment process. In J.N. Bhagwati, *Import Competition and Response*. Chicago: University of Chicago Press. Pp. 73–122.
Neal, Larry. 1979. The economics and finance of bilateral clearing agreements: Germany, 1934–8. *Economic History Review* 32:391–404.
Neary, J. Peter. 1982. Intersectoral capital mobility, wage stickiness, and the case for adjustment assistance. In J.N. Bhagwati (ed.), *Import Competition and Response*. Chicago: University of Chicago Press. Pp. 39–72.
Nurkse, Ragnar. 1944. *International Currency Experience*. Geneva: League of Nations.
Ohlin, Bertil. 1929. The reparation problem: A discussion. *Economic Journal* 39:172–173.
Overy, R.J. 1975. Cars, roads and economic recovery in Germany, 1932–38. *Economic History Review* 28:466–483.
Parker, William N. 1984. *Europe, America and the Wider World*. Cambridge: Cambridge University Press.
Peden, G.C. 1984. The Treasury view on public works and employment in the interwar period. *Economic History Review* 37:167–181.
Peppers, Larry. 1973. Full-employment surplus analysis and structural change: The 1930s. *Explorations in Economic History* 10:177–196.
Pincus, J. 1985. Public enterprise in Australia in the 1930s. Australian National University Working Paper in Economic History No. 53 (August).
Pippenger, John. 1984. Bank of England operations 1893–1913. In Michael D. Bordo and Anna Schwartz (eds.), *A Retrospective on the Classical Gold Standard*. Chicago: University of Chicago Press. Pp. 203–232.
Postan, M.M. 1959. Note. *Economic History Review* 12:77–82.

Pressnell, L.S. 1978. 1925: The burden of sterling. *Economic History Review* 31:67–88.

Pryor, Zora P. 1979. Czechoslovak fiscal policies in the Great Depression. *Economic History Review* 32:228–240.

Rockoff, Hugh. 1984. Some evidence on the real price of gold, its cost of production, and commodity prices. In Michael D. Bordo and Anna Schwartz (eds.), *A Retrospective on the Classical Gold Standard*. Chicago: University of Chicago Press. Pp. 613–650.

Romer, C. 1986. Spurious Volatility in Historical Unemployment Data. *Journal of Political Economy* 94:1–37.

Rostow, W.W. 1975. *How It All Began*. New York: McGraw-Hill.

Rostow, W.W. 1978. *The World Economy: History and Prospect*. Austin: University of Texas Press.

Rush, M. 1978. Money, output and unemployment in the United States under the gold standard. Unpublished, University of Rochester.

Saint Marc, Michele. 1983. *Histoire Monétaire de la France, 1800–1980*. Paris: PUF.

Saint-Etienne, Christian. 1984. *The Great Depression 1919–1939: Lessons for the 1980s*. Stanford: Hoover Institution Press.

Sargent, Thomas. 1982. The end of four big inflations. In Robert E. Hall (ed.), *Inflation*. Chicago: University of Chicago Press. Pp. 41–98.

Sargent, Thomas. 1983. Stopping moderate inflations: The methods of Poincaré and Thatcher. In R. Dornbusch and M.H. Simonsen (eds.), *Inflation, Debt and Indexation*. Cambridge: MIT Press. Pp. 54–98.

Sauvy, Alfred. 1984. *Histoire Économique de la France entre les Deux Guerres*. 2nd ed. Paris: PUF.

Scammell, W.M. 1965. The working of the gold standard. *Yorkshire Bulletin of Economic and Social Research*, special number, pp. 31–45.

Schmid, G.C. 1974. The politics of currency stabilization: The French franc, 1926. *Journal of European Economic History* 3:359–377.

Schuker, Stephen. 1976. *The End of French Predominance in Europe*. Chapel Hill: University of North Carolina Press.

Schwartz, Anna 1981. Understanding 1929–1931. In Karl Brunner (ed.), *The Great Depression Revisited*. Boston: Kluwer-Nijhoff. Pp. 5–48.

Silverman, Dan. 1982. *Reconstructing Europe After the Great War*. Cambridge: Harvard University Press.

Sims, Christopher. 1972. Money, income and causality. *American Economic Review* 62:540–552.

Sims, Christopher. 1980. Macroeconomics and reality. *Econometrica* 48:1–48.

Spechler, Martin. 1982. Ending big inflations: Lessons from comparative European economic history. Unpublished.

Svennilson, Ingmar. 1953. *Growth and Transformation of the European economy*. Geneva: United Nations.

Taylor, Lance. 1983. *Structuralist Macroeconomics*. New York: Basic Books.

Temin, Peter. 1971. The beginning of the Depression in Germany. *Economic History Review* 24:240–248.
Temin, Peter. 1976. *Did Monetary Forces Cause the Great Depression*? New York: Norton.
Temin, Peter. 1981. Notes on the causes of the Great Depression. In Karl Brunner (ed.), *The Great Depression Revisited*. Boston: Kluwer-Nijhoff. Pp. 108–125.
Thomas, Mark. 1983. Rearmament and economic recovery in the late 1930s. *Economic History Review* 36:552–579.
Thomas, Mark. 1984. An input-output approach to the Edwardian economy. D. Phil. thesis, Oxford University.
Thomas, T. 1981. Aggregate demand in the United Kingdom, 1918–45. In R. Floud and D. McCloskey (eds.), *The Economic History of Britain Since 1700*, vol. 2. Cambridge: Cambridge University Press. Pp. 332–346.
Thorp, R., ed. 1984. *Latin America in the 1930s*. London: Macmillan.
Tobin, J. 1970. "Money and Prices: Post hoc ergo propter hoc?" *Quarterly Journal of Economics* 84:301–317.
Toniolo, G. 1977. Effective protection and industrial growth: The case of Italian engineering, 1898–1913. *Journal of European Economic History* 6:659–674.
Trachtenberg, Marc. 1980. *Reparations in World Politics*. New York: Columbia University Press.
Trescott, Paul B. 1982. Federal Reserve policy in the Great Contraction: A counterfactual assessment. *Explorations in Economic History* 19:211–220.
Triffin, Robert. 1964. The myth and realities of the so-called gold standard. In *Our International Monetary System: Yesterday, Today, and Tomorrow*. New York: Random House.
Wallis, John Joseph, and Daniel K. Benjamin. 1981. Public relief and private employment in the Great Depression. *Journal of Economic History* 41:97–102.
Webb, Stephen B. 1980. Tariffs, cartels, technology and growth in the German steel industry, 1879–1914. *Journal of Economic History* 40:309–330.
Webb, Stephen B. 1984. The supply of money and Reichsbank financing of government and corporate debt in Germany, 1919–1923. *Journal of Economic History* 44:499–508.
Weinstein, M. M. 1980. *Recovery and Redistribution under the NIRA*. Amsterdam: North-Holland.
Weir, M., and T. Skocpol. 1985. State structures and the possibilities for "Keynesian" responses to the Great Depression in Sweden, Britain and the United States. In P. Evans et al., (eds.) *Bringing the State Back In*. Cambridge: Cambridge University Press. Pp. 107–168.
Whale, P. B. 1937. The working of the pre-war gold standard. *Economica* 4:18–32.
White, Eugene Nelson. 1984. A reinterpretation of the banking crisis of 1930. *Journal of Economic History* 44:119–138.
Wicker, Elmus. 1980. A reconsideration of the causes of the banking panic of 1930. *Journal of Economic History* 40:571–584.
Wicker, Elmus. 1982. Interest rate and expenditure effects of the banking panic of

1930. *Explorations in Economic History* 19:435–445.

Williamson, Jeffrey G. 1974. Watersheds and turning points: Conjectures on the long-term impact of Civil War financing. *Journal of Economic History* 34:636–661

Williamson, Jeffrey G. 1984. Why was British economic growth so slow during the Industrial Revolution? *Journal of Economic History* 44:687–712.

Williamson, Jeffrey G. 1985. The historical context of the classical labor surplus model. *Population and Development Review* 11:171–191.

Worswick, G.D.N. 1984. The sources of recovery in UK in the 1930s. *National Institute Economic Review* 110:85–93.

Wright, J.F. 1981. Britain's inter-war experience. In W.A. Eltis and P.J.N. Sinclair (eds.), *The Money Supply and the Exchange Rate*. Oxford: Clarendon Press. Pp. 282–305.

3 THE EXPLORATION OF ECONOMIC CHANGE: THE CONTRIBUTION OF ECONOMIC HISTORY TO DEVELOPMENT ECONOMICS

David Feeny

Introduction

Although the potential of economic history in the discipline of economics has generally not been realized, economic history has made important contributions to the literature on economic development. Key development hypotheses have been tested on historical samples. Much of the best work in agricultural development, trade and development, demography, income distribution, and institutional change has come from economic history. In turn, issues in the development literature have often motivated historical studies.

Two sorts of studies in economic history have affected the literature of development economics: (1) studies of the trends in the now developed countries during development, and (2) economic histories of less developed countries. Given the focus of economic historians on measuring and

---

The author acknowledges the helpful comments of Philip D. Curtin, Alexander J. Field, George Grantham, John R. Hanson, II, Yujiro Hayami, Donald N. McCloskey, Stuart Mestelman, Alan Richards, Theodore W. Schultz, Jeffrey G. Williamson, and Gavin Wright on an earlier version. This chapter is not meant to be an exhaustive or comprehensive survey of the literature. Although major works on the economic history of now developed countries will be discussed, the focus is on the often neglected literature on the economic history of less developed countries.

explaining the development experience in the United States, United Kingdom, Europe, Japan, and Oceania it is not surprising that the first category has provided a richer harvest. There is, however, a growing literature in the second category.

The classification of a study as economic history is somewhat arbitrary. Several criteria could be used. The approach taken here to select the works to be discussed is to focus on pastness with a bias toward works done by economists.

It is also appropriate to consider briefly what is meant by development economics. For our purposes here, development economics refers to the literature that utilizes modes of economic analysis and measurement to study the growth and development of less developed countries. Thus development economics is an applied field in economics in which the sample is taken from poor countries. Tools of analysis are drawn from a variety of subdisciplines in economics, including labor and demography, health, agricultural economics, public finance, monetary economics, international trade and finance, macroeconomic theory, and microeconomic theory. Much the same can be said about economic history: the application of tools of economic analysis to historical samples. Thus both the economic historian and the development economist are cursed and blessed by being generalists.

It is also relevant to consider what we mean by development. The usual definitions reflect enduring truths, prevailing conventional wisdoms, and prevailing moral concerns. At present many definitions of development explicitly include equity, in part confusing the goal of policy with the subject. Here, a somewhat old-fashioned definition will be used: viz, economic development is a process characterized by sustained growth in per capita income accompanied by structural change. As will be clarified below, this definition draws on the inductive insights of Simon Kuznets.

Inductive Generalizations

Economics as a discipline is dominated by the deductive approach in which assumptions are made, and testable implications are derived from them; the inductive approach has made only modest contributions. Given the nonexperimental character of most economics scholarship, this is far from surprising. Yet stylized facts about reality affect the abstract modeler as well as the process by which economists think, argue, and convince each other (see, for instance, McCloskey 1983).

A major exception to the generalization is the work of economic historians, in which inductive generalizations have been important. Perhaps the best example is Simon Kuznets' seminal work on long-term trends, as reflected in *Modern Economic Growth*. Kuznets (1966) examined the long-term trends experienced by the now developed countries and the characteristics of the economics of contemporary less developed countries, within the framework of national income accounting, a tool he developed.

Much of what we know about development was first gleaned from the growth record of the now developed countries. Cross-sectional studies among contemporary less developed countries at various levels of development have corroborated these inductive generalizations (see, for example, Chenery and Syrquin 1975 and Chenery 1979).

Kuznets defined the economic epoch during which the now rich countries developed as the period of modern economic growth. The distinguishing feature of the epoch was the application of science to the problems of production. Modern economic growth was accompanied by the rise of secularism, egalitarianism, and nationalism. It was characterized by a rapid growth in population, even more rapid growth in output, and thus a substantial growth in per capita income—on the order of magnitude of 10–20 percent per decade. The relatively high and sustained rate of growth in the economy was not the single distinguishing feature. Growth was accompanied by a fundamental change in the structure of the economy and society. At first, agriculture accounted for approximately 50 percent of value added in the economy (and perhaps 80 percent of employment); by the end, it accounted for 20 percent or less. The relative decline of agriculture was mirrored in the relative rise of industry from 20–30 percent to 40–50 percent (the share of total output accounted for by services showed no strong secular trend). That development means a growth in per capita income over a sustained period of time accompanied by structural change in the economy—i.e., it is both a quantitative and qualitative process—is a feature in virtually all definitions of development. Our way of thinking about development is derived from Kuznet's inductions.

During development the economy was transformed from a rural-based one in which self-employment dominated into an industrial urban-based one in which most people are employees. More complex forms of business organization emerged and large transportation, distribution, and financial sectors grew up to facilitate the coordination of production and consumption which increasingly no longer took place within the same household or locality. International interdependence also rose. Again, the historical record has provided the basic description of development.

Kuznets brought together evidence demonstrating that the growth in per capita inputs could "account" for only a small proportion of the growth in per capita output. Development was not merely a quantitative change.

He also examined the trends in income distribution. The result was the Kuznet's U-shaped hypothesis of falling and then rising equality in the distribution of income. Cross-sectional contemporary studies among less developed countries reveal a similar pattern (see, for example, Ahluwalia 1976 and Chenery 1979).[1] Kuznets anticipated the concerns with equity that were to become fashionable in the 1970s.

The Use of Economic History as a Laboratory

Among the recent developments in economics is the rise of experimental methods. Although the trend is exciting and holds great promise, especially in microeconomics, the size and scope of application of experimental methods in economics is still relatively minor. There have been a few major large-scale field experiments in income maintenance and health insurance programs; there is a rapidly growing literature based on laboratory experiments. In addition, sophisticated longitudinal data have been developed. Yet, for the most part, hypothesis testing in economics has relied upon and will continue to rely upon the interpretation of natural experiments.

The dominance of the non experimental approach within economics is reflected in the two core elements found in virtually all economics curricula—theory and statistics (mainly statistical inference). The University of Chicago oral tradition (according to second-hand reports) extends the argument, maintaining that every economist should know theory, statistics, and history.[2] History is added as a core subject because it is the repository of natural experiments. It permits the scholar at least partially to escape from the confines of contemporary studies in which he can observe only a certain range of variation in the variables of interest conditioned by an existing set of institutions and prior events. Thus history can powerfully serve as a testing ground for theory (see Arrow 1985; McCloskey 1976; North 1978; Schultz 1977; Solow 1985; and Wright 1986). Although the use of economic history as a laboratory has been underutilized to the detriment of economic theory, the development literature provides a number of examples revealing its advantages.

Agricultural Development

A striking and simple example is provided in Theodore W. Schultz's seminal work, *Transforming Traditional Agriculture* (Schultz 1964).

During the 1950s and early 1960s the classical dual economy model was the leading development paradigm. It was based on writings of the classical economists and the seminal application of their ideas to development by Lewis in 1954 (with subsequent elaboration by Fei and Ranis in 1964). It was alleged that in some poor economies population pressure was so high that the marginal product of rural labor was zero. Schultz searched for a natural experiment with which to test the assertion. He found it in the effects of the great influenza epidemic of 1918–1919 in India (Schultz 1964, pp. 63–70), a country typically classified as a surplus-labor economy. Schultz argued that the epidemic had a disproportionate impact on members of the adult labor force; did not affect livestock or other factors of production; that the course of the disease was short, resulting in either death or quick recovery; and that its usefulness as a natural experiment was enhanced by the fact that its incidence varied geographically. Area sown and agricultural output, of course, respond to more than the size of the agricultural labor force and in the Indian subcontinent are particularly sensitive to variations in rainfall. Schultz therefore argued that 1917–18, during which India experienced a bumper crop, would serve poorly as a base year and instead chose 1916–17. The rainfall in the crop year after the epidemic, 1919–20, was similar to that in 1916–17 making it an appropriate year for comparison. Relying on Kingsley Davis's estimates of the mortality due to the epidemic, (20 million people or 6.2 percent of the population) and an estimate that the mortality rate among members of the agricultural labor force exceeded the overall rate for the population by one third, Schultz calculated an 8.3 percent decline in the agricultural labor force. Because the area-sown data are more reliable than output data, he then compared on a province-by-province basis the decline in labor input to the decline in the total area sown between 1916–17 and 1919–20. In aggregate, the area sown declined by 3.8 percent. In general, the provinces with the highest death rates also had the largest percentage reductions in the area sown. Schultz concluded that the evidence is sharply inconsistent with an hypothesis of zero marginal product of labor. In one form, the surplus-labor stylized fact was clearly rejected.[3]

Although refinements to the procedures used and further sensitivity tests can readily be imagined, Schultz's exercise represented one plank in a competing edifice Schultz was constructing with which to analyze rural development.[4] Schultz argued that in the context of traditional agriculture, farmers were poor but efficient. They were seen as rational decision makers who were not unduly limited by custom and were in fact responsive to price incentives. Yet productivity was low. In order to transform traditional agriculture—a state of long-run equilibrium in which technology and tastes had been stable for a length of time of sufficient duration that most opportunities had already been exploited—what was needed was investments in new high-pay-off inputs (technical change) and in rural human capital. Improvements in health and education would enhance the ability of agents to exploit the new opportunities and the disequilibria they created. Schultz's 1964 volume has had a powerful influence on development economics.

Trade and Development

The use of history to refute assertions about the facts and to test propositions is not confined to the literature on agricultural development. Much contemporary commentary on development presumes that in contrast to the nineteenth-century, today less developed countries face less favorable opportunities to grow through exporting. In contrast to the nineteenth-century exports as the engine of growth period, the barriers to export-led growth are said to include greater instability in export revenues, less favorable growth in the demand for exports of countries in the periphery, and less price-elastic demand for those exports. These and other propositions about the relationships between trade and development and how the relationships have changed over time have been examined by Kravis, Hanson, Williamson, and others (see Kravis 1970; Hanson 1977a. 1977b, 1977c, 1980, 1983; McCloskey 1981; Murray 1978; Williamson 1980; and Feeny 1982a; also Eichengreen 1986).

One approach taken by Kravis was to compare the performance of the United States in the nineteenth-century with that of other primary-product exporters who were less successful. Kravis found that the size of the export stimulus in the United States did not differ significantly from the stimulus afforded to India and Sri Lanka in the same period. The magnitude of the stimulus does not differentiate success from failure.

In reaching this conclusion Kravis examined evidence for a number of countries in the periphery in the nineteenth-century period. Hanson (1977b) provides a more formal test. Using the constant-market-shares analysis technique Hanson decomposes the growth in export earnings from 1860 to 1900 for a group of less developed countries into the growth in export earnings that could be explained by the growth in world demand, a competitiveness factor which measures the growth in exports that could be explained by the change in the country's share of the world market for its export commodities, and a diversification factor reflecting the country's ability to increase its exports through diversification of the commodities exported. The first factor, the world market factor, is a proxy for demand—the size of the export stimulus. The latter two factors are proxies for the supply side, reflecting conditions internal to the economy. Hanson finds that the ranking of countries by overall export performance and by the competitiveness factor are highly correlated; the rankings by overall performance and world market factor are only weakly related. The result is corroborated in a study of the post-World War II period reported in Kravis (1970). Again, internal or supply-side factors appear to distinguish successful exporters from less successful ones.

Kravis (1970) argues that the size of the stimulus available to poor countries today exceeds that available to countries in the periphery in the nineteenth-century, including the countries said to have developed through exporting such as the United States, Canada, Australia, and New Zealand. In the nineteenth-century the gross national products of the center were approximately twice the level of the GNPs of the periphery; today the ratio is approximately 4.5 to 1. In addition, post-World War II growth rates have exceeded those experienced in the nineteenth-century. Again, when assertions about the relatively unfavorable opportunities for contemporary less developed countries were compared to economic history, little evidence in support of the assertions was found.

In order to investigate the proposition that contemporary less developed countries experience greater instability in export earnings than the non-European now-developed countries did in the nineteenth-century, Hanson (1977c) constructs estimates of instability for the now-developed countries for the 1850–1906 period and compares them to estimates for less developed countries for the 1950–1969 period. He finds that the level of instability experienced by poor countries today does not substantially differ from the level experienced by yesterday's developing countries. Hanson (1980) goes on to show that the degree of price instability experienced by the now-developed countries in the 1850–1899 period was roughly comparable to the level experienced by less developed countries in the same period.

Once again, the assertions used to justify the promotion of inward-working import-substitution development policies appear to fail a simple test. External conditions—the degree of export stimulus or the level of instability—do not appear to be factors that distinguish development exporters from nondeveloping exporters.

The discussion points to several important cases in which facts appear to refute the conventional wisdom. More important are attempts to explore and test causal mechanisms. Kravis (1970) argues that Nurkse based his generalizations about the nineteenth-century as a period in which exports served as the engine of growth on the experience of the regions of recent settlement: Agrentina, Australia, Canada, New Zealand, South Africa, the United States, and Uruguay. He then argues that if Nurkse was right we might expect to observe at least some of the following features: (1) a large or growing share of exports in the overall economy, (2) changes in exports leading changes in GNP, (3) a concentration of exports in sectors that were growing relatively rapidly, and (4) a concentration of foreign capital in export industries or industries closely linked to them. Kravis (1972) concludes that for the United States these implications of the exports as the engine of growth are not systematically observed. He concludes that although trade expansion may facilitate growth, internal factors are more important. Trade is the handmaiden rather than the engine of growth.

The tests provided by Kravis are crude and involve neither necessary nor sufficient conditions for growth to be export-led. In the context of the Midwestern grain export boom of the late nineteenth-century, Williamson (1980) provides a more rigorous general equilibrium model with which to test a number of export-led growth hypotheses.[5] The model is comprised of two regions, the Northeast and the Midwest, and two sectors, manufacturing and agriculture, with the Northeast specialized in manufacturing. Capital and labor are inputs in the industrial and agricultural production functions; land is specific to agriculture. The domestic interregional transport cost is treated exogenously as a tariff rate. The external terms of trade are exogenously determined, as are the limits on the degree of labor and capital mobility, the rates of sectoral total factor-productivity growth, the savings rates, and the growth in the stock of land in improved acres. The model allows for both short-run disequilibrium and the dynamic effects of export booms on savings, accumulation, and domestic and international migration.

Williamson (1980) first demonstrates that the international terms of trade for wheat may reasonably be treated as exogenous—that the United States was a price taker on the world market. Then using initial values from one full-employment period, 1870, the model is simulated over the 1870–1892 period. Its ability to track the performance of the 1892 economy is impressive.

Although the model is admirably constructed to decompose the Midwestern wheat boom into the impact of railroads, the impact of world markets, and the impact of Midwest supply forces, the exogeneity of the land stock and its growth is a feature which weakens the model's ability to capture important ideas in the export-led growth literature. Although allowance for several key dynamic effects is made, including induced migration and savings, the influence of the agricultural export boom on land clearing, an important component of nineteenth-century United States capital formation, is not accomodated endogenously.

Nevertheless, Williamson's counterfactuals provide important tests of the hypothesis. He examines the impact of world markets by holding constant the 1870 east-coast terms of trade rather than allowing them to decline as in the actual case. Both Midwest farm income and national per capita income would have been higher in this counterfactual world. Capital accumulation would also have been higher. Thus external forces matter.

If the external markets could have been more favorable to United States development but the export boom occurred anyway, is there not an inconsistency? The explanation is that while the terms of trade declined in the east in the actual case, they rose in the Midwest as a result of the sharp decline in interregional transportation costs. Williamson assesses the impact of the transportation cost revolution by simulating the 1870–1892 period as if transport costs had been frozen at their 1870 level. The result is a much lower than actually observed level of income and growth. Thus the gains of domestic productivity within the transportation sector were an important source of growth.

Williamson then combines the two counterfactuals to assess the relative importance of the domestic decline in transport costs and the external decline in the terms of trade. On net, with 1870 terms of trade *and* transport costs, the 1892 economy would have been worse off. In the actual case trade appears to have made an important contribution to United States development in spite of the declining world terms of trade. (It is likely that a similar investigation of the Canadian wheat boom would reveal an even greater role for trade.) As in the arguments put forth by Kravis, the ability of the United States economy to exploit the opportunities for exporting and the ability to generate productivity growth (in the transport sector in the counterfactuals discussed above) appear to be important in accounting for development through trade.

The Economics of Imperialism

Issues involving economic and political relationships between colonial powers and their colonies have also featured prominently in the literature on economic development and history. Critics have held that successful development in the center came at the expense of development in the periphery. Furthermore it was alleged that high economic returns on empire investments greatly influenced patterns of investment and served to postpone the decline in ailing capitalist economies. In a major study of the British Empire, Davis and Huttenback address the traditional empirical assertions and analyze and quantify some of the effects of imperialism on the interactions between the colonial and home country economies (for an interim report on the project see Davis and Huttenback, 1982).

Davis and Huttenback (1982) examine British financial markets in the mid-nineteenth-century-to-1914 period. They find that, contrary to the qualitative descriptive literature, the domestic economy received a large proportion of the long-term finance and that foreign investments (non-Empire) as opposed to Empire (colonial) investments played the dominant role in the market.

They compare the rates of return on equity for a sample of 447 firms. They find that while initially (1860–1880) the rate of return on foreign and Empire investments exceeded the rate on domestic firms, by the early twentieth-century the rates of return on foreign and especially Empire investments had fallen to a level only slightly in excess of the rates earned on domestic firms. Financial firms involved in the foreign and Empire sectors continued, however, to earn rates of return in excess of the rates earned in the domestic sector. Thus it would appear that Empire investments lacked the aggregate importance accorded them in much of the literature.

When Davis and Huttenback compare the returns from imperial investments in excess of the domestic rate of return to the financial burdens of the Empire (mainly defense and other public goods), they find that on net (in these terms) the Empire represented a burden to Britain. They why did Britain maintain its empire? An examination of the stockholders in 271 firms sheds some light. Ownership of firms with Empire investments was concentrated among financiers, large banks, and the gentry. Ownership of firms whose primary business was domestic was concentrated in the middle class, the class Davis and Huttenback identify as bearing the taxes for the support of the Empire. So although Britain in these narrow terms was a net loser on its investment in the Empire, an elite class, that was well represented in government, was a net gainer.

The work of Davis and Huttenback addresses only some of the issues involved in interpreting imperialism. (Other studies dealing with these issues include Feeny 1979; McAlpin 1983; and Birnberg and Resnick 1973, 1975.) As Edelstein (1982) points out, their estimates ignore the gains to the United Kingdom through a lack of barriers to United Kingdom exports in the Empire and in the informal empire of noncolonies who nevertheless were influenced by British policies (for instance China, Argentina, and Thailand). The impact of external forces on the internal structure of less developed countries is an important issue not fully addressed by their study. Yet the use of careful quantitative analysis challenges the conventional wisdoms about colonial economic relations and development. Such studies have the potential to greatly elevate the level of debate and scholarship on issues of historical development.

Contributions of Economic History to Development Economic: Testing Dual Economy Models

Major programs of research in development economics were built around attempts to construct models capable of generating the stylized facts of development exposed by Kuznets. One example is the literature on the dual economy. The models made the processes of accumulation and structural change endogenous. In the classical dual economy model framework of Lewis (1954) or Ranis and Fei (1961) and Fei and Ranis (1964), wages were institutionally set above the marginal product of labor in the taditional (rural, agricultural) sector. When this assumption is coupled with the classical saving-function assumption of savings out of profits, the transfer of labor from the traditional sector to the modern capitalist industrial one (in which labor is paid the value of its marginal product) generates increased profits, savings, investment, and growth. The process will continue until the pool of surplus labor is exhausted, at which point the industrial sector begins to face an upward-sloping supply curve to labor.

It is important to explore several economic-history-based tests of the Lewis-Fei-Ranis approach. Naturally the notion of surplus labor and of an institutionally determined wage in the traditional or agricultural sector drew criticism, especially from neoclassical economists. The crude test of one implication of one definition of surplus labor by Schultz (1964) has already been described. Furthermore, analytical critiques demonstrated that if one assumed that agents were utility maximizers, even if labor was redundant, it did not necessarily follow that the supply curve of labor to the industrial sector would be infinitely elastic at the institutionally determined wage.

Neoclassical dual economy models were constructed in direct competition with the classical ones. Like their ancestors the models endogenously determined the overall rate of growth and accumulation as well as structural change. Unlike their predecessors the models did not depart from marginal-product pricing.

In a major test of the neoclassical approach, Kelley and Williamson

(1974), building on the earlier work of Kelley, Willliamson, and Cheetham (1972) and Jorgenson (1961, 1969), built a model of Meiji Japan. The case is important because of its intrinsic interest, because Japan is one of the few non-Western developed countries, and because Fei and Ranis specifically argued that the stability of real wages in Japanese development was evidence in favor of the classical dual-economy model.

Kelley and Williamson (1974) constructed a general equilibrium model with two sectors—agriculture and industry—and three factors—mobile labor and capital and land specific to agriculture. A multidimensional concept of dualism is employed in which the rates and biases of technical change, factor intensities, and elasticities of substitution between the two sectors differ (production dualism). There is also dualism on the demand side in that preferences vary across sectors. Comparative static exercises generate ambiguous results in a number of important cases. Yet Kelley and Williamson are often able to bring evidence to bear to constrain parameter values into ranges in which determinate results may be obtained.

Another important feature of the approach is the focus on dynamic simulation in which the initial solution of the model together with endogenous saving and investment are used to construct a path of change over time. Because we are interested in the path of development and because of limitations in the evaluation of models in terms of their steady-state properties, the approach is valuable.

Once the model has been validated against the historical path of the Meiji economy from 1887 to 1915, Kelley and Williamson perform a number of counterfactual simulations. They use classical saving functions in which landlords and capitalists save and workers do not. This introduces a mechanism through which trends in the functional distribution of income can affect the rate of capital accumulation. But the quantitatively important feature of the Meiji economy, which accounted for the rise in the rate of capital accumulation, was the secular decline in the relative price of capital goods. The decline in that relative price in turn reflected the importance of technical change, especially in the agricultural sector from which the bulk of the savings were generated. Thus savings were generated in the agricultural sector not through the release of surplus labor but through productivity growth.

A second set of results concern the importance of demographic factors in explaining Japanese success. While less developed countries today are experiencing rates of population growth in excess of 2 and even 3 percent per annum, Meiji Japan's population grew at 0.9 percent per year. A moment's casual reflection deeply rooted in partial-equilibrium neo-Malthusian reasoning might lead one to reject the relevance of the

Japanese experience. Kelley and Williamson provide a more rigorous test. They simulate the Meiji period as if the rate of growth of population had been three times as large—as rapid as in less developed countries today. The resulting path and performance differ little from the baseline simulation—Japan's unique demographic experience does not appear to have been crucial to its success.[6] The reason that the more rapid population growth only slightly depresses the growth in real per capita income is that the decline in real wages accompanying the more rapid growth of the labor force induces a decline in the relative price of agricultural goods. This in turn shifts the income distribution to profits and higher marginal-saving-rate income recipients so that higher rates of accumualtion compensate for the rapid population growth. The result demonstrates a major advantage of the general equilibrium approach.

Demographic experience was not all that was unique in the Japanese case. Industrialization in Japan was more rapid that either the rates experienced in other now-developed countries or in today's less developed countries. The counterfactuals performed by Kelley and Williamson indicate that the low income elasticity of demand (given the level of per capita income) for agricultural products in Japan played an important role in promoting the rapid rate of industrialization.

A third set of simulations demonstrates the importance of the Tokugawa heritage to Meiji development. High rates of total factor-productivity growth experienced by the agricultural sector in the pre-World War I period, and in particular the rapid labor-augmenting technical change, served to generate stable real wages, increasing labor earnings, and capital accumulation. Much of the success within the agriculture sector was associated with the rapid diffusion of improved technologies. Had slower rates of agricultural total factor-productivity growth been experienced, the rate of industrialization would have been higher, not lower as in the Fei-Ranis model. The stability of real wages (and growth in labor earnings) in the neoclassical model of Kelley and Williamson is accounted for by the rapid rate of labor-augmenting technical change, not by assuming an institutionally determined real wage as in the classical approach.[7]

Overall the results of the Kelley-Williamson study point to the importance of technical change in accounting for the patterns observed. The results also point to the importance of general equilibrium approaches capable of incorporating complicated interactions and feedbacks. Finally the importance of economic history as a testing ground is underscored. For development issues the path of change of the economy is what we are often most interested in. If quantitative tests are to be performed, of necessity the record provided in economic history is likely to be among the few in which time series of sufficient duration are available with which to perform meaningful comparisons.[8]

Induced Technical Change

The work of Kuznets and others who studied the economic history of the developed countries indicates that only a small portion of the rise in per capita output can be accounted for by increases in per capita inputs. Changes in input quality, organization, institutions, and technology may then be fundamental to development. Kelley and Williamson also point to the importance of technical change and imbalances in sectoral rates of growth of total factor productivity and factor-saving biases in influencing economic performance and structural change.

Although the role of technical change is underscored in neoclassical dual economy models, technical change is taken as exogenous. In seminal work on the role of technical change in agricultural development, Hayami and Ruttan (1971, 1985) construct a model in which the rate and direction of technical change is endogenous. The apparent importance of technical change in development implies high potential returns to uncovering the underlying causal mechanisms that generate technical change. Within the agricultural development literature the arguments of Schultz (1964) further underscore the importance of making technical change endogenous. Schultz had argued that agriculture could be a potent source of growth if investment were made in rural human capital and in developing new high pay-off technologies. Schultz did discuss the reasons for market failure in agricultural research—economies of scale and a lack of apropriability of the returns, especially for disembodied technical change. He went on to examine socialized agricultural research as an institutional response to this market failure. Yet the mechanisms by which the new high pay-off inputs were to be developed were left largely unspecified. The work of Hayami, Ruttan, Evenson, Feeny, and others can be seen as an elaboration and generation of testable hypotheses concerning those mechanisms.

Hayami and Ruttan base their model of agricultural development on the notion of induced technical change derived from the seminal work of Hicks's 1932 *Theory of Wages* (see Hicks 1963). In that approach it is postulated that a rise in the relative price of a factor of production not only induces a substitution of the relatively cheaper factor for the more expensive one within the constraints imposed by the existing set of production possibilities, but in the longer run, also induces a search for new technologies to facilitiate further substitutions. Thus the path of technical change responds to the trends in relative factor prices. Clearly the process is a long-run one; thus economic history affords a unique opportunity for the testing of such hypotheses.

Hayami and Ruttan extend the argument in two important ways. First, because socialized agricultural research, development, and extension have been so important in the agricultural sector they include induced public *and* private sector behavior in their model. Second, building on the work of Schultz, North, Davis, and Thomas (see for instance Davis and North 1971; North 1981; North and Thomas 1973; Schultz 1968), they hypothesize that institutional change may also be examined within an induced model in which trends in relative prices and technology generate the incentives for altering institutional arrangements.

They marshall an array of cross-sectional contemporary and historical evidence in order to test their hypotheses. The agricultural histories of Japan, as a land-scarce labor-abundant economy, and the United States, as a labor-scarce land-abundant economy, are fruitfully exploited. The United States adopted a mechanical path of technical change which permitted the substitution of capital and land (as the source of crops to fuel animal-powered mechanization) for increasingly expensive labor. In Japan a biological path of technical change emerged in which new fertilizer-responsive varieties were developed, permitting the substitution of labor for increasingly expensive land. Technical change was complemented by investments in irrigation systems and their management to further increase land productivity. The impressive gains in land and total factor productivity had a substantial effect on economic development in Japan, as the discussion on Meiji development indicated.

Hayami and Ruttan also examine an earlier "green revolution"—the transfer of Japanese rice technology to the then Japanese colonies of Korea and Taiwan. Meiji development was fueled in part by the growth in agricultural productivity. By the end of World War I the gains from diffusing previous Tokugawa-period innovations in agricultural technology had been largely exhausted. The rate of growth of productivity slowed. Investments in modern rice-breeding and socialized agricultural research were not to bear fruit until the 1930s. The Japanese government decided to turn to its colonies as a source of cheap rice and in the 1920s embarked on vigorous programs to increase rice exports from the colonies, eventually with considerable success.

The problems encountered in transferring Japanese rice technology in each case are illustrative. In the Korean case geoclimatic conditions did not present a formidable barrier to the adaptation of Japanese rice varieties to

Korean conditions, since they were sufficiently close to those in Japan. The lack of a complementary input—water control—did however. The widespread diffusion of the new varieties was delayed pending the extension of an irrigation system.

In Taiwan the existing infrastructure included, courtesy of the sugarcane industry, an adequate irrigation system. The formidable problem in this case was adapting the short-straw fertilizer-responsive *Japonica* temperate-zone varieties for cultivation under tropical and semi-tropical conditions. The resulting cross, the Ponlai varieties, exhibited superior yields and underwrote an impressive growth in the interwar period in fertilizer usage, rice yields, rice production, rice exports, and total factor productivity in the rice sector (see Ho 1966; Lee and Chen 1979).

Several key lessons emerge from this earlier green revolution experience. First, agricultural technologies tend to be location specific and the transfer of such technologies, especially biological ones, requires local adaptation. Thus an indigenous capacity to do some research and development is important (see Evenson and Kislev 1975). Second, the returns obtained from investing in the development of new technologies will in part depend on the complementary infrastructure investments; in this case the new varieties demanded a fairly well-developed system of water control. Finally, induced institutional change (the creation of agricultural research and irrigation agencies in the colonial government of Korea and Taiwan) and induced public investment (the level of support for those agencies) do not depend only on demand-side factors—the potential social benefits of the investments—but on supply-side factors—in this case the return to the Japanese government in terms of the economic and political gains it perceived from importing cheap rice. The rising price of food induced a search for technical and institutional changes to increase land productivity. It also lessened the opposition of industrial interests to increased government expenditures on agricultural research and infrastructure, thus lowering the political cost. Socialized agricultural research systems and public irrigation authorities in Korea and Taiwan were created in response to the demands generated by the trends in relative factor prices and by the potential returns to the suppliers of new institutional arrangements, the elite decision makers of government.[9]

Induced Institutional Change

If economic history is well suited to the examination of evidence with respect to induced technical change, it may be an even more fertile ground on which to base studies of institutional change. Institutional arrangements confer benefits by virture of their power to assure agents about the likelihood of their receiving the flows resulting from the actions they take. Thus frequent changes in institutional arrangements may reduce their value; on the other hand inflexibility will leave potential gains uncaptured or inefficiently captured. This tension greatly complicates attempts to make institutional change endogenous—and to explain the direction, nature, and extent of change in institutional arrangements over time. Nevertheless important advances have been made.

The work of Hayami and Ruttan provides one important example of this approach in the development economics literature. In the Japanese case it concerned the rise of new institutions (and investments) to increase the productivity of land through technical change and irrigation. The rise in real land rents associated with the growth of world trade and appreciation of the agricultural terms of trade in the nineteenth-century, however, served to focus attention on more than new seeds and irrigation. The growth of commercialized agriculture and the rise of land rents relative to other factor returns also induced fundamental changes in the systems of property rights in South and Southeast Asian economies.

The case of Thailand provides an illustration. Over the 1865 to 1912 period the agricultural terms of trade (measured as the ratio of the rice export price to the import price of cloth) appreciated by approximately 1.5 percent per year (Feeny 1982b, pp. 127–131; 1984). Not surprisingly the cultivation and exporting of rice increased rapidly (the quantity of rice exports increased by 4.4 percent per year from 1864 to 1910). Qualitative reports and scanty quantitative evidence all point to a substantial rise in real land rents during the period.[10]

The increased attractiveness of rice farming led to a rapid extension of the area under cultivation as new lands were cleared within the existing usufruct system of land rights. Traditionally vacant lands, land which no one had been using in the previous three years or which had never been cleared, became the usufruct property of the developer as long as taxes were paid and the land was not left idle for more than three consecutive years. With the appreciation of land prices, land disputes became frequent. In response to the demands for more secure property rights in land, new title documents obtainable by presenting tax receipts for the previous ten years were issued. The persistence of land disputes led the government in the 1880s to issue standard forms and prescribe standardized procedures. When the administrative solutions proved to be inadequate a new comprehensive land law was passed in 1892 with provisions for transferable title deeds and the use of land as collateral. Yet the lack of a central land titles office, a means by which the land referred to in the title could be unambiguously identified, and other administrative deficiencies continued to plague the system. Thus in 1896 the government began a cadastral survey in Rangsit, the site of some of the most bitter land disputes and an area in which many government officials were landowners. In 1901 the government formally adopted a Torrens land titling system with central provincial land record offices.[11]

In the Thai case the appreciation in land prices led to an increase in the demand for institutional arrangements to more securely define property rights in land. The government responded with a series of changes utlimately culminating in the development of a full cadastral survey system. Institutional change appears to have been induced by the change in relative factor prices. As landowners themselves, the suppliers of the new institutional arrangements—government officials—also found it to be in their interests to respond to the demand shift. Thus change was forthcoming.

In contrast, in the cases of irrigation and socialized agricultural research investments in Thailand, the supply of institutional change was not forthcoming in the pre-World War II period. The rise in land rents did focus attention on the development of new seeds and irrigation as means of increasing land productivity. Proposals for agricultural research and irrigation projects were articulated but major investments were not made until the post-World War II period because even though such investments would have been in the social interest, they were not in the interests of elite decision makers (see Feeny 1982a, 1982b, 1983a).

Because of the long time frame needed to analyze institutional change, economic history inherently has a special contribution to make in this area. Its comparative advantage rests, however, on more than the duration of the sample upon which it is based. Like the historian, the economic historian is caught in the sometimes tedious and sometimes delightful process of describing the environment in which behavior takes place and in particular the existing array of institutional arrangements. Although economists traditionally assert that preferences, technology, and endowments are all that need to be specified (for criticisms of this approach see Arrow 1985; Field 1984; Solow 1985; and Wright 1986), the economic historian has generally implicitly or explicitly recognized that the existing set of institutional arrangements also deserves attention. At a trivial level, how can the initial distribution of endowments be separated from some form of social arrangements which recognizes and enforces some form of property rights?

The literature on induced institutional change takes as given a fundamental set of institutions (such as a "constitution") which specifies rules on how to make rules; these are taken as exogenous. The tools of economic analysis are then applied to make specific institutional arrangements and operational rules endogenous. Thus in the Thai property rights case cited above the form of govenment and basic distibution of political power are taken as given and used to explain the innovation of new forms of property rights and the specific operational rules adopted.

Because the existing institutional arrangements affect the path of subsequent change it is necessary that such arrangements be carefully specified and described. Thus this literature is inherently less elegant than much of economic theory. Because measures for this institutional variety are likely to remain crude and imprecise, refinement and testing are likely to proceed slowly. Yet if the intellectual costs of such research are high, so are the potential benefits. The work of North, Thomas, Hayami, and Ruttan cited earlier focuses attention on the role of institutional change in accounting for successful economic performance.

But in view of the difficulties involved in this line of research, it is natural to ask what can be achieved? Are the best results of such studies (or economic history in general) sophisticated and rigorous storytelling (see Field 1984; McCloskey 1986), or are we really constructing explanatory models that can be used to predict?

The answer depends in part on the level of explanation required. The literature on institutional change takes some set of institutions as given. It implicitly argues that economists in general should postulate four pillars upon which their equilibria rest: preferences, technology, endowments, and institutions. Thus I am not claiming that all institutions are endogenous.

With that major caveat in mind, however, story telling versus explanation still remains as a real issue. Clearly much of the existing literature can best be characterized as good storytelling. I would argue, however, that the combination of economic history to delineate the relevant variables, and economics and economic history to suggest the relationships among them, when combined with experimental methodologies (both laboratory experiments and larger-scale field experiments) should permit the economist/social scientist to go beyond storytelling and into prediction. Prediction, however, is not necessarily explanation.

An example may clarify. Economic analysis concerning the free-rider problem and casual empiricism indicates that difficulties will be encountered in organizing the socially optimal exploitation of a common-pool resource. Economic history and contemporary studies of the management of such resources in successful and unsuccessful cases generate important stories, interpreted through economic theory, about the range and nature of institutional arrangements relevant to the amelioration of such problems. An understanding of how institutional arrangements affect performance, derived from both contemporary and historical studies, can be used to suggest hypotheses for further testing in small laboratory experiments. Institutional arrangements which improve the ability of the system to achieve a stated set of objectives in these simplified settings can be further tested in the real world through field experiments. Thus even if explanation is not obtained, social science in general and economics in particular can contribute to more effective institutional design—thus substituting experimental design for the costly trial and error associated with a reliance on natural experiments. Such methods of analysis are underutilized. The role of economic history in such an intellectual enterprise is substantial.

The studies described above focus on the use of economic history studies to generate or test important hypotheses about the development experience, Numerous other examples could be provided. Fishlow's 1965 work on United States railroads provided a direct test of Rostow's take-off hypothesis (Rostow 1960), challenging a then influential development hypothesis concerning the crucial role of leading sectors. The literature on economic history and development has also valuably interacted to advance our understanding of the effects of risk, the economics of contract choice, and institutional forms for organizing agricultural production. (See, for example, Bardhan 1977; Cheung 1969; Feeny 1983b; Hallagan 1980; Higgs 1974; McAlpin 1983; Ransom and Sutch 1977; Reid 1979; Roumasset 1978; and Winters 1978. For more exclusively analytical studies see Braverman and Stiglitz 1982; Newbery 1977; Newbery and Stiglitz 1979; Reid 1976; and Stiglitz 1974.) Similarly our understanding of the causes and effects of both modern and premodern famine has been largely based on the work of economic historians (e.g., McAlpin 1983).

For development specialists who find it important to understand the functioning of a particular economy, economic history studies have made important contributions to the productivity of subsequent research work. By establishing the economic history narrative and insights into the conditioning effects of institutions on the functioning of a particular economy, such economic histories of less developed countries provide valuable, if underutilized, resources for the contemporary development specialist.

An example of such a study is the pioneering work of Ingram (1971) on the economy of Thailand. Although the economic literature on Thailand has grown considerably since the 1955 publication of Ingram's first edition (see Feeny 1978a), it is difficult to find an issue that is not dealt with in a thoughtful and insightful way in Ingram's work. Undoubtedly, similar examples could be readily produced for the economies of other less developed countries. (For instance, for the important case of India see Kumar and Desai 1983 and McAlpin 1983; for Egypt see Richards 1978, 1982; for West Africa, see Curtin 1975; for Brazil, see Leff 1982).

There is, of course, a tension between the use of economic history to provide a narrative of events in a particular economy in a particular period—the approach often taken by the traditional historian—and the use of economic history as a laboratory with which to test economic theory—the approach frequently taken by the economist/economic historian. In part the tension hinges on the difference between internal and external validity—the difference between constructing an internally consistent account and being able to generalize outside the scope of the specific study. By suppressing detail, the latter is less accurate but also potentially more powerful. The art arises in the choice of simplification and identification of the salient features that drive the economic outcomes. The whole enterprise of constructing economic theory, of course, shares this problem.

Directions for Future Research in Economic Development and History

It is useful to speculate on fruitful areas for new investigations. Some hypotheses require a long time span in order to be meaningfully tested. Such studies lie in the sphere of the comparative advantage of economic history. A number of the research areas fit this category.

Among the important developments in economics in recent decades has been human capital and the complementary development of the new household economics. The application of economic analysis to household decisions about the allocation of time, division of labor, investments in child schooling and nutrition, family size, and investments in health has broadened the scope and relevance of development economics. Although consumption behavior for nondurable goods and services may often be successfully analyzed using data for relatively short periods of time, investments in children (the "ultimate" consumer durable) and child quality (schooling, nutrition, health services, and other forms of human capital) of necessity involve behavior over time. Although contemporary longitudinal data sets are being developed, much of the rigorous testing and development of hypotheses in this area will rely upon historical samples.

The interwar period should provide fruitful ground for an examination of the causes and effects of default and other issues concerning international finance, economic stability, and development (see Eichengreen 1986). Stylized facts which inform both the current policy debate and analytical frameworks may be tested through historical studies.

The issues surrounding environmental problems in development settings are becoming an increasingly popular and important topic for research (see, for instance, Richards and Tucker 1983). Among the concerns are deforestation, the degradation of water resources, destruction of range lands, reduction in biological diversity, changes in climate, desertification, and increases in the frequency and severity of flooding.

Several implications for the research agenda emerge. First, such problems do not arise overnight. The methods of economic history should be applied to the growing body of environmental history in less developed countries. Second, because the issues involve some form of externalities and the potential for market failure, the area is a fruitful one for research on the evolution of institutions to ameliorate such problems. The interactions among market forces, property institutions, and environmental concerns should provide important data for the further development and testing of models of institutional change. In a broader context this is another example of the potential power of economic history to explore the extent to which economic behavior is affected by and affects the array of institutions within which the economy operates.

Similarly, the evolution of a wide variety of institutions in credit markets, labor markets, agricultural research systems, educational systems, health care systems, and industrial organization should provide opportunities for the testing of models and enhancement of our understanding of economic development. The change in institutional arrangements within and among firms, including the nature of labor markets and contractual relationships, is an important area for research in which important propositions in microeconomic theory may be tested. As a by-product, the almost totally undeveloped literature on economic history in the manufacturing sector in less developed countries could be augmented. Such studies will be valuable in two ways. First they will help to extend economics by refining our understanding of the interactions between the institutional context and analytical models. Second, economic history can serve as a laboratory of natural experiments with which to test theory. Such tests are somewhat asymmetric; models that explain what we know has already happened may still not fail to predict the future. Models that fail the test of explaining the past are, however, even poorer candidates. The latter assertion is implicit in the approach taken within economics and economic history. Although methodologists need to test the assertion, it appears reasonable to assume that in general we are less concerned with Type II errors of rejecting a true hypothesis than with Type I errors of failing to reject a false one.

Because economic history is almost uniquely able to address issues concerning long-run household behavior, technological change, institutional change, and structural change, it has and will continue to play an important role in development economics. Many of the most intriguing issues in development involve behavior over time. It is unfortunate that the techniques of economic history have been underutilized in development economics. Although there are impediments to doing economic history studies in less developed country settings, posed by the linguistic demands of foreign and often non-European languages and often lower quality data stocks, the richness of the economic history studies of less developed countries mentioned above demonstrates that the barriers are not insurmountable and that the intellectual rewards are substantial.

Notes

1. For examples of models in which the trends in U.S. income distribution are endogenous see Williamson (1979) and Williamson and Lindert (1980); similar approaches to documenting and explaining British income and wealth distribution trends during development can be found in Lindert and Williamson (1983) and Williamson (1985a, 1985b). For a good general review of the issues see Lindert and Williamson (1985).

2. Ironically, economic history is not a requirement in the graduate program at Chicago, unlike the practice at Harvard, Stanford, Yale, and a number of other universities.

3. While not specifically designed to address the same issue, the evidence presented in McAlpin (1983, pp. 74–83, 230–231) on weather conditions in the crop seasons in question tends to indicate that Schultz's choice of the 1919–20 crop year as the basis for comparison did not bias the results in his favor.

4. In an interchange concerning this test (see Sen 1967a, 1967b; Schultz 1967), Sen points out that Schultz confined his test to 10 provinces when data were available for 13. Schultz suggested that the tests could be refined by weighting the provincial observations on mortality and the declines in the area sown. (Sen also corrected population figures used by Schultz to reflect population growth between 1916–17 and 1919–20). Schultz and Sen investigated both the correlation between provincial mortality and the decline in the area sown and the coefficient on labor input implied by the relationship between the drop in output and the drop in labor input. Because the output data are less reliable than the area-sown data (see Heston 1973), the focus here will be on the simple correlation exercise. Data on the percentage change in total area sown for each of the 13 provinces identified by Sen are taken from India (1922, pp. 135–139). Data on the deaths per 100 in the population due to the epidemic are taken from Sen (1967a; p. 160, col. 3). The observations on the percentage change in area sown were weighted by the share in the total area sown in 1916–17 for the 13 provinces

accounted for by that province. The provincial mortality rates were weighted by the province's share of the total population for the 13 provinces in 1941. Data on 1941 provincial populations are taken from Davis (1951, p. 21; except the figure for Burma, taken from Andrus 1948, p. 24). (An unkind interlibrary loan department mandated the use of 1941 rather than 1921 population weights.) When the weighted percentage change in total area sown was regressed on the weighted deaths per 100 in the population, the coefficient on the latter was −0.006 (t statistic, 8.8; $R^{-2} = 0.87$). Using the weighted data, the coefficient was −0.013 (t statistic, 3.18; $R^{-2} = 0.43$). With 11 degrees of freedom, the t statistics are significant at the 1 percent level; in both cases the coefficient on the intercept was insignificant. As Schultz had predicted, the sensitivity tests did not affect his conclusions. The weighting of the provincial observations in fact improved the results.

5. For more on the use of general equilibrium analysis in economic history, see Eichengreen (ch. 2 of this volume), James (1984), and Thomas (ch. 4 of this volume). For a review of the application of macroeconomic models to less developed countries, see Taylor (1979). The application of computable general equilibrium models in development studies is illustrated by Adelman and Robinson (1978), and Dervis, DeMelo, and Robinson (1982).

6. The counterfactual performed by Kelley and Williamson tests the effects of more rapid population growth during the Meiji era and thus the effects of Japan's unusual demographic experience. It does not, however, test the effects of Japan's slow rate of population growth in the preceding Tokugawa period on subsequent development in the Meiji era. How different would performance have been if the Meiji economy had started with an even higher man-land ratio? This question is left unanswered. I owe this point in large part to Professor Margaret A. McKean, Duke University.

7. Williamson (1985b) reaches similar conclusions in his investigation of real-wage stability during the early industrial revolution in Britain. The classical economists whose work formed the basis for Lewis's famous 1954 paper based their model of development on the observed stability in real wages. On the basis of recent quantitative research Williamson (1985b) concludes that in fact real wages were stable until the 1820s. He then shows that the stability in real wages can better be explained by a neoclassical than a labor surplus model. Sluggish growth and accumulation generated by the crowding out effects of public expenditures on the Napoleonic Wars, rather than surplus labor, appear to account for the stability in real wages.

8. General equilibrium models in which urbanization during development is made endogenous are tested in a similar fashion in Kelley and Williamson (1984a, 1984b).

9. For an elaboration on the importance of the supply of institutional change see Feeny (1978b, 1982b, 1983a), Hayami and Kikuchi (1981), Hayami and Ruttan (1985), Kikuchi and Hayami (1978), North (1978, 1981), and Ruttan and Hayami (1984).

10. A simple Jones (1965) type general equilibrium model in which there are two sectors, agriculture and manufacturing, and three factors, mobile labor and capital and land specific to agriculture, underscores the sensitivity of real land rents to trends in the terms of trade and aids in the corroboration of the scanty evidence of the appreciation of real land rents (see Feeny 1982b, 1984).

11. The Torrens system embodied in the 1901 legislation created an elaborate administrative structure which did not readily accomodate traditional land clearing and development practices in Thailand. Subsequent legislation in the 1930s and the revised land code of 1954 created a hierarchy of land documents, each providing greater security, each obtained at greater transaction cost, with a cadastral survey based land title as the most secure form of property rights; see Feeny (1982b, 1984).

References

Adelman, I., and S. Robinson. 1978. *Income Distribution Policies in Developing Countries: A Case Study of Korea*. Stanford: Stanford University Press.

Ahluwalia, M.S. 1976. Inequality, poverty, and development. *Journal of Development Economics* 3:307–342.

Andrus, J.R. 1948. *Burmese Economic Life*. Stanford: Stanford University Press.

Arrow, K. 1985. Maine and Texas. *American Economic Review* 75:320–323.

Bardhan, P.K. 1977. Variations in forms of tenancy in a peasant economy. *Journal of Development Economics* 4:105–118.

Birnberg, T., and S.A. Resnick. 1973. A model of the trade and government sectors in colonial economies. *American Economic Review* 63:572–587.

Birnberg, T., and S.A. Resnick. 1975. *Colonial Development: An Econometric Study*. New Haven: Yale University Press.

Braverman, A., and J.E. Stiglitz. 1982. Sharecropping and the interlinking of agrarian markets. *American Economic Review* 72:695–715.

Chenery, H. 1979. *Structural Change and Development Policy*. New York: Oxford University Press.

Chenery, H., and J. Syrquin. 1975. *Patterns of Development, 1950–1970*. London: Oxford University Press.

Cheung, S.N.S. 1969. *The Theory of Share Tenancy: With Special Application to Asian Agriculture and the First Phase of Taiwan Land Reform*. Chicago: University of Chicago Press.

Curtin, P.D. 1975. *Economic Change in Precolonial Africa: Senegambia in the Era of the Slave Trade*, 2 vols. Madison: University of Wisconsin Press.

Davis, K. 1951. *The Population of India and Pakistan*. Princeton: Princeton University Press.

Davis, L.E., and R.A. Huttenback. 1982. The political economy of British imperialism: Measures of benefits and support. *Journal of Economic History* 42:119–130.

Davis, L.E., and D.C. North. 1971. *Institutional Change and American Economic Growth*. London: Cambridge University Press.

Dervis, K., J., DeMelo, and S. Robinson. 1982. *General Equilibrium Models for Development Policy*. Cambridge: Cambridge University Press.

Edelstein, M. 1982. Discussion. *Journal of Economic History* 42:131–132.

Evenson, R.E., and Y. Kislev. 1975. *Agricultural Research and Productivity*. New Haven: Yale University Press.

Feeny, D. 1978a. Economic studies of Thailand. In E.B. Ayal (ed.), *The Study of Thailand*. Athens: Ohio University Center for International Studies. Pp. 118–153.

Feeny, D. 1978b. Induced technical and institutional change: A Thai case study. In G. Means (ed.), *The Past in Southeast Asia's Present*. Ottawa: Canadian Society for Asian Studies. Pp. 56–69.

Feeny, D. 1979. Competing hypotheses of underdevelopment: A Thai case study. *Journal of Economic History* 39:113–127.

Feeny, D. 1982a. Infrastructure linkages and trade performance: Thailand, 1900–1940. *Exploration in Economic History* 19:1–27.

Feeny, D. 1982b. *The Political Economy of Productivity: Thai Agricultural Development 1880–1975*. Vancouver: University of British Columbia Press.

Feeny D. 1983a. Extensive versus intensive agricultural development: Induced public investment in southeast Asia, 1900–1940. *Journal of Economic History* 43:687–704.

Feeny, D. 1983b. The moral or the rational peasant? Competing hypotheses of collective action. *Journal of Asian Studies* 42:769–789.

Feeny, D. 1984. The development of property rights in land: A comparative study. Yale University Economic Growth Center Discussion Paper No. 459.

Fei, J.C.H., and G. Ranis. 1964. *Development of the Labor Surplus Economy: Theory and Policy*. Homewood, Ill: Irwin.

Field, A.J. 1984. Microeconomics, norms, and rationality. *Economic Development and Cultural Change* 32:683–711.

Fishlow, A. 1965. *American railroads and the transformation of the antebellum economy*. Cambridge, MA: Harvard University Press.

Hallagan, W.S. 1980. Labor contracting in turn-of-the-century California agriculture. *Journal of Economic History* 40:757–776.

Hanson, J.R., II. 1977a. Diversification and concentration of LDC exports: Victorian trends. *Explorations in Economic History* 14:44–69.

Hanson, J.R., II. 1977b. More on trade as a handmaiden of growth. *Economic Journal* 87:554–557.

Hanson, J.R., II. 1977c. Export instability in historical perspective. *Explorations in Economic History* 14:293–310.

Hanson, J.R., II. 1980. Export instability in historical perspective: Further results. *Journal of Economic History* 40:17–23.

Hanson, J.R., II. 1983. Export earnings instability before World War II: Price, quantity, supply, demand? *Economic Development and Cultural Change* 31:621–637.

Hayami, Y., and M. Kikuchi. 1981. *Asian Village Economy at the Crossroads: An Economic Approach to Institutional Change*. Tokyo: University of Tokyo Press.

Hayami, Y., and V.W. Ruttan. 1971. *Agricultural Development: An International Perspective*. Baltimore: Johns Hopkins University Press.

Hayami, Y., and V.W. Ruttan. 1985. *Agricultural Development: An International Perspective, Revised Edition*. Baltimore: Johns Hopkins University Press.

Heston, A. 1973. Official yields per acre in India, 1886–1947; Some questions of interpretation. *Indian Social and Economic History Review* 10:303–332.

Hicks, J.R. 1963. *The Theory of Wages, Second Edition*. London: St. Martin's Press.

Higgs, R. 1974. Patterns of farm rental in the Georgia Cotton Belt, 1880–1900. *Journal of Economic History* 34:468–482.

Ho, Y.M. 1966. *Agricultural Development of Taiwan 1903–1960*. Nashville: Vanderbilt University Press.

India, Department of Statistics. 1922. *Agricultural Statistics of India 1920–21*, vol. 1. Calcutta: Superintendent of Government Printing.

Ingram, J.C. 1971. *Economic Change in Thailand, 1850–1970, Second Edition*. Stanford: Stanford University Press.

James, J.A. 1984. The use of general equilibrium analysis in economic history. *Explorations in Economic History* 21:231–253.

Jones, R.W. 1965. The structure of simple general equilibrium models. *Journal of Political Economy* 73:557–572.

Jorgenson, D.W. 1961. The development of a dual economy. *Economic Journal* 71:309–334.

Jorgenson, D.W. 1969. The role of agriculture in economic development: Classical versus neoclassical models of growth. In C.R. Wharton (ed.), *Subsistence Agriculture and Economic Development*. Chicago: Aldine Publishing. Pp. 320–348.

Kelley, A.C., and J.G. Williamson. 1974. *Lessons from Japanese Development: An Analytical Economic History*. Chicago: University of Chicago Press.

Kelley, A.C., and J.G. Williamson. 1984a. Population growth, industrial revolutions, and the urban transition. *Population and Development Review* 10:419–441.

Kelley, A.C., and J.G. Williamson. 1984b. *What Drives Third World City Growth?*. Princeton: Princeton University Press.

Kelley, A.C., J.G. Williamson, and R.J. Cheethem. 1972. *Dualistic Economic Development: Theory and History*. Chicago: University of Chicago Press.

Kikuchi, M., and Y. Hayami. 1978. Agricultural growth against a land resource constraint: A comparative history of Japan, Taiwan, Korea, and the Philippines. *Journal of Economic History* 38:839–864.

Kravis, I.B. 1970. Trade as a handmaiden of growth: Similarities between the nineteenth and twentieth centuries. *Economic Journal* 80:850–872.

Kravis, I.B. 1972. The role of exports in nineteenth-century United States growth. *Economic Development and Cultural Change* 20:387–405.

Kumar, D., and M. Desai, eds. 1983. *The Cambridge Economic History of India, vol. 2: c. 1757–c. 1970*. Cambridge: Cambridge University Press.

Kuznets, S. 1966. *Modern Economic Growth: Rate, Structure, and Spread*. New Haven: Yale University Press.

Lee, T., and Y. Chen. 1979. Agricultural growth in Taiwan, 1911–1972. In Y. Hayami, V.W. Ruttan, and H.M. Southworth (eds.), *Agricultural Growth in Japan, Taiwan, Korea, and the Philippines*. Honolulu: East-West Center. Pp. 59–89.

Leff, N.H. 1982. *Underdevelopment and Development in Brazil*, 2 vols. Boston: Allen & Unwin.

Lewis, W.A. 1954. Economic development with unlimited supplies of labour. *Manchester School of Economic and Social Studies* 22:139–191.

Lindert, P.H., and J.G. Williamson. 1983. English workers' living standards during the Industrial Revolution: A new look. *Economic History Review 2nd ser.* 36:1–25.

Lindert, P.H., and J.G. Williamson. 1985. Growth, equality, and history. *Explorations in Economic History* 22:341–377.

McAlpin, M.B. 1983. *Subject to Famine: Food Crises and Economic Change in Western India, 1860–1920*. Princeton: Princeton University Press.

McCloskey, D.N. 1976. Does the past have useful economics? *Journal of Economic Literature* 14:434–461.

McCloskey, D.N. 1981. *Enterprise and Trade in Victorian Britain: Essays in Historical Economics*. London: Allen & Unwin.

McCloskey, D.N. 1983. The rhetoric of economics. *Journal of Economic Literature* 21:481–517.

McCloskey, D.N. 1986. Economics as a historical science. In W.N. Parker (ed.), *Economic History and the Modern Economist*, New York: Blackwell.

Murray, D. 1978. Export earnings instability: Price, quantity, supply, demand? *Economic Development and Cultural Change* 28:61–73.

Newbery, D.M.G. 1977. Risk sharing, sharecropping and uncertain labour markets. *Review of Economic Studies* 44:585–594.

Newbery, D.M.G., and J.E. Stiglitz. 1979. Sharecropping, risk sharing and the importance of imperfect information. In J.A. Roumasset, J. Boussard, and I.J. Singh (eds.), *Risk Uncertainty and Agricultural Development*. Laguna: Agricultural Development Council. Pp. 311–339.

North, D.C. 1978. Structure and performance: The task of economic history. *Journal Economic Literature* 16:963–978.

North, D.C. 1981. *Structure and Change in Economic History*. New York: Norton.

North, D.C., and R.P. Thomas. 1973. *The Rise of the Western World: A New Economic History*. London: Cambridge University Press.

Ranis, G., and J.C.H. Fei. 1961. A theory of economic development. *American Economic Review* 51:533–564.

Ransom, R.L., and R. Sutch. 1977. *One Kind of Freedom: The Economic Consequences of Emancipation*. Cambridge: Cambridge University Press.

Reid, J.D. 1976. Sharecropping and agricultural uncertainty. *Economic Development and Cultural Change* 24:549–576.

Reid, J.D. 1979. Sharecropping and tenancy in American history. In J.A. Roumasset, J. Boussard, and I.J. Singh (eds.), *Risk, Uncertainty and Agricultural Development*. Laguna: Agricultural Development Council. Pp. 283–309.

Richards, A. 1978. Technical and social change in Egyptian agriculture: 1890–1914. *Economic Development and Cultural Change* 26:725–745.

Richards, A. 1982. *Egypt's Agricultural Development, 1800–1980: Technical and Social Change*. Boulder: Westview Press.

Richards, J.F., and R.P. Tucker. 1983. *Deforestation and the Nineteenth Century World Economy*. Durham: Duke University Press.

Rostow, W.W. 1960. *The Stages of Economic Growth: A Non-Communist Manifesto*. Cambridge: Cambridge University Press.

Roumasset, J.A. 1978. The new Institutional economics and agricultural organization. *Philippine Economic Journal* 17:331–348.

Ruttan, V.W., and Y. Hayami. 1984. Toward a theory of induced institutional innovation. *Journal of Development Studies* 20:203–223.

Schultz, T.W. 1964. *Transforming Traditional Agriculture*. New Haven: Yale University Press.

Schultz, T.W. 1967. Significance of India's 1918–19 losses of agricultural labour—A reply. *Economic Journal* 77:161–163.

Schultz, T.W. 1968. Institutions and the rising economic value of man. *American Journal of Agricultural Economics* 50:1113–1122.

Schultz. T.W. 1977. On economic history in extending economics. In M. Nash (ed.), *Essays on Economic Development and Cultural Change in Honor of Bert F. Hoselitz*. Supplement to *Economic Development and Cultural Change* 25:245–253.

Sen, A.K. 1967a. Surplus labour in India: A critique of Schultz's statistical test. *Economic Journal* 77:154–161.

Sen, A. 1967b. Surplus labour in India: A rejoinder. *Economic Journal* 77: 163–165.

Solow, R.M. 1985. Economic history and economics. *American Economic Review* 75:328–331.

Stiglitz, J.E. 1974. Incentives and risk sharing in sharecropping. *Review of Economic Studies* 41:219–255.

Taylor, L. 1979. *Macro Models for Developing Countries*. New York: McGraw-Hill.

Williamson, J.G. 1979. Inequality, accumulation, and technological imbalances: A growth-equity conflict in American history? *Economic Development and Cultural Change* 27:231–253.

Williamson, J.G. 1980. Greasing the wheels of sputtering export engines: Midwestern grains and American growth. *Explorations in Economic History* 17:189–217.

Williamson, J.G. 1985a. *Did British Capitalism Breed Inequality*? London: Allen & Unwin.

Williamson, J.G. 1985b. The historical content of the classical labor surplus model. *Population and Development Review* 11:171–191.

Williamson, J.G., and P.H. Lindert. 1980. *American Inequality: A Macroeconomic History*. New York: Academic Press.

Winters, D.L. 1978. *Farmers without Farms: Agricultural Tenancy in Nineteenth-Century Iowa*. Westport, CT: Greenwood Press.

Wright, G. 1986. History and the future of economics: Comments. In W.N. Parker (ed.), *Economic History and the Modern Economist*. New York: Blackwell.

4 GENERAL EQUILIBRIUM MODELS AND RESEARCH IN ECONOMIC HISTORY

Mark Thomas

General equilibrium models have become an integral part of the literature of the "new economic history." They reflect many of the central concerns of the methodological revolution of the cliometricians. General equilibrium (GE) models operate within an explicit theoretical structure, are quantitative in orientation, and posit counterfactual analysis as the best way to understand the importance of particular events to historical developments. They are ideal for dealing with the "big issues" of economic history, because of their formal recognition of second-, third-, and n-th round effects in historical developments, and are therefore superior to partial equilibrium analysis for any questions in which these effects are believed to be important. Such questions as the impact of technical improvements in transportation on economic development, the impact of tariffs on resource allocation, the sources of changes in the distribution of incomes, and the contribution of war to industrialization have all benefited from analysis within the GE framework. In these and other cases, applied GE analysis has clearly made more sense of the impact of these factors. Yet only a handful of economic historians have responded to Temin's

---

I have had useful discussions on the content of this chapter in its various incarnations with John James, N.F.R. Crafts, Alan Powell, Jonathan Pincus, Barry Eichengreen, and Alex Field. I should like to thank them all, without retracting the standard author's caveat.

(1971a) plea for increased application of GE models to improve our understanding of the process of economic growth and its implications. This chapter suggests that there is still a significant role that GE analysis can play in economic history, and that Temin's suggestion is all the more attractive given recent developments in the theory and practice of applied models.

The chapter is organized thematically around a number of central concerns to GE modelers: theory, data, computation, application, and interpretation. The purpose is not to provide a survey of previous applications of GE techniques to historical questions. There is an excellent recent review article available (James 1984), and there have been too few developments in this field in the two years since to require another essay written from this perspective.[1] Although references to the established literature will be made where appropriate, this chapter may best be described as an introduction for prospective users of GE models. Our purpose is to review the range of modeling procedures currently available; to discuss the theoretical and computational demands of particular model formulations; and to analyze the range of historical problems for which GE models may be suitable. We shall also examine the data requirements for models of this sort; methods for developing estimates for missing parameter values, and for improving the quality of the available data; methods of calibration; solution algorithms; and procedures for evaluating the success of a model application.

What is a general equilibrium model? In the crudest terms, GE models depict quantitatively the relationships underlying the simple circular flow diagrams of basic macroeconomic texts. Neoclassical GE models attempt additionally to model these economic interrelationships in accordance with certain behavioral standards. Thus, consumers are assumed to organize their consumption and their allocation of time between labor and leisure in order to maximize their utility; producers are assumed to be motivated by profit maximization. The methodology of applied GE analysis is to model these behavioral standards in a consistent fashion, developing them in the context of the economy-wide structure of economic relationships. The resulting models may then be used in the pursuit of comparative statics analysis, whereby the effect on economic phenomena within the model (the endogenous variables) of a change in a factor outside the model (the exogenous variable) is measured. They may also be used, as we shall see below, to explore and explain the dynamics of growth in an economy.

The purpose and style of GE modeling can be contrasted with the dominant form of economy-wide modeling in both contemporary and historical literatures: the macroeconomic tradition of the Klein-Keynes models.[2] These too depict quantitatively the circular flow of incomes, and have been most often used for comparative statics analysis and the simulation of business cycle fluctations through time. Large-scale econometric models can be summarized as modeling from the top down, operating at the level of the national income aggregates, with relatively few attempts to disagregate.[3] The model formulations are set in discrete time with lag structures employed to capture disequilibrium dynamics. Macroeconometric exercises generally concentrate attention on activity variables (income, employment) to the exclusion of relative price variables, and have often been modeled with little or no attention paid to microtheoretic foundations.

"Walras rather than Keynes is the patron saint of multisectoral analysis" in the GE mold (Dervis, Melo, and Robinson 1982, p. 6). In contrast to the Klein-Keynes tradition, GE models make a virtue of disaggregation, and multisectoral models with many production activities and consumers disaggregated by characteristics are common. GE models postulate neoclassical production (supply) functions and price sensitive demand functions, linked in a Walrasian general equilibrium framework that endogenously determines both prices and quantities. Given the greater emphasis on the microeconomics of decision making, they are more firmly grounded in optimization theory than their macro cousins. This should not suggest, however, that the models are textbook irrelevancies, unable to assume the realities of historical institutions and nonmarket mechanisms. The GE system is, at best, flexible enough to handle a range of issues on a pragmatic basis.

In what follows, we shall employ a distinction between two categories of GE modeling, which we shall label analytical (AGE) and computable (CGE) respectively. These variants differ in their approach to solving the general equilibrium system, the key to which lies in the way the supply and demand equations are structured. Analytical methods organize the GE model as a linear system of simultaneous equations and employ related solution techniques. For smaller GE models of this sort, solutions can be determined by hand. This was the approach of Jones (1965, 1971) and of the first economic historians to work with numerical GE models (e.g., Passell and Schmundt 1971). For larger models, the basic solution method is that of matrix inversion. This, as we shall see below, can be applied to both price sensitive and fixed price models. Computable techniques, in contrast, follow the solution path implicit to the Walrasian system. Equilibrium in the competitive Walrasian model is a function of the vector of relative prices. Disequilibrium in any sector will disturb the price vector. If demands exceed supply, prices will be forced up; if there is excess supply, prices will fall to clear the market. CGE methods work from this basic insight. Starting with the original equilibrium vector of prices, they follow the effects of a shock to the system in search of the new set of relative prices that will force all excess demands to zero, and thereby re-establish equilibrium. Analytical methods, then, use the mathematical properties of the system to determine a solution, while CGE methods explore the structure of factor and commodity markets to solve the model, working through the disequilibrium dynamics as the system moves from one general equilibrium to another.

II

The pioneer in the field of empirical general equilibrium modeling was certainly Leontief, and his work on input-output economics serves as the earliest example of an attempt to quantify the interrelationships of producers and households in an explicitly general equilibrium framework.[4] The purpose of input-output analysis is captured in the name itself. The output of most industries serves not only as finished product for consumption by domestic or foreign households, but also as intermediate goods purchased by other producers as raw materials for their production, or as semimanufactured commodities for further working up before final sale. Thus, for example, nineteenth-century coal mines not only provided fuel for the domestic hearths of households, but also for the open hearths of blast furnaces and the furnaces of the merchant marine. The interrelationships are not, however, restricted to transactions between firms in different industries: specialization within particular subsectors of industry is also of consequence in the developed markets of a modern economy. The extent of such intraindustry transactions depends, of course, on the definition of an industry and also on the way in which transactions are measured. These technicalities aside, the input-output table presents transactions within and between industries in a symmetric accounting framework.

The input-output table is in the first instance an accounting mechanism, a system of double-entry bookkeeping; it consists of a square matrix of *n* rows and columns, each representing a sector of the economy; each figure in a table represents the value of goods and services originating in the sector specified by the row and directed (sold) to the sector specified by the column. Figures in a row, then, show the distribution of the output of one sector between the other sectors of the economy, and those in a column show the cost pattern of a sector in terms of goods and services flowing from other sectors. The row shows the distribution of output from a sector; the column the distribution of input into a sector. The input-output table thus captures the interdependence of producers within an economy in a compact and elegant manner.

The interdependence of production activities in any economy ensures that the effects of an increase in output of a single sector will not simply generate direct demands on the production of other industries, but will also provide indirect stimuli on total output, working through the repercussions of direct effects on other sectors. Thus, increased demand for the output of the iron and steel industry requires, among other materials, the input of coal and coke. This demand for coke brings forth an additional demand for coal, working indirectly from the original increase in iron and steel production. The interpendence ensures that an increased demand for the products of any single sector will reverberate through the system of production and have repercussions on the output demands of all other sectors. The technical coefficients of the input-output model, calculated as the value of inputs of row sectors per unit of output of each column sector, provide a general equilibrium framework for capturing the supply responses to an increase in demand for the output of a particular industrial sector. The reverberation of the interindustry transactions continues through the system until the production sector has moved back into equilibrium. The system is restrained from exploding because of the leakages out of the production system—some of the additional demand for commodities will be met by imports, in which case the reverberations are exported to the supplier nation, while a significant proportion of the value of additional output escapes the production chain through payments to factors of production in the form of wages, salaries, profits, and dividends. The increase in household income generated by the increase in demand for output is considered as a leakage from the system in the basic open Leontief model. We shall return to this unattractive proposition later.

The input-output approach, then, traces the total effect on output of an increase in the demand for a particular sector's output. Clearly we need a method of calculating the total effect of these production responses that avoids the tedious task of pursuing each path separately. The general approach is to create what has become known as the Leontief inverse. The first step in the solution of the production system by this method is the presentation of the input-output table as a system of simultaneous equations. By noting that each row of the input-output table may be interpreted such that total gross output of sector i is distributed as output to final consumers or as intermediate inputs to other sectors, we may write the supply and demand balance for this sector as:

$$x_i = w_{i1} + w_{i2} + \cdots + w_{in} + f_i \tag{4.1}$$

where f_i is the total final demands for sector i's output, and w_{ij} is the absorption of sector i's output by sector j, where $j = 1,\ldots,n$. The total input-output table is, therefore,

$$\begin{aligned} x_1 &\equiv w_{11} + w_{12} + \cdots + w_{1n} + f_1 \\ x_2 &\equiv w_{21} + w_{22} + \cdots + w_{2n} + f_2 \\ &\vdots \\ x_n &\equiv w_{n1} + w_{n2} + \cdots + w_{nn} + f_n \end{aligned} \tag{4.2}$$

which is the supply-demand balance equations for the entire production system. This is written as a system of identities because of the equilibrium nature of the economy: expenditures and outputs must, by definition, be equal, even if this condition is satisfied by unintended stock accumulation or depletion. This system can be transformed by recognizing the functional relationship between total output and intermediate inputs. This relationship may be expressed as either:

$$w_{ij} = a_{ij}x_j \tag{4.3}$$

or

$$w_{ij} = b_{ij} + m_{ij}x_j \tag{4.3'}$$

By substituting either of these equations into the input-output system, we arrive at a system of simultaneous equations which can be solved with relative ease. The choice between these two linear functional forms depends in part upon theoretical expectations and, in larger part, upon empircal constraints. In the first equation, a_{ij} is the average input-output coefficient, derived via $a_{ij} = w_{ij}/x_j$ where

$$x_j = \sum_{i=1}^{n} w_{ij} + v_j$$

with v_j being value-added to factor inputs into sector j. This solution procedure assumes constant returns to scale in production, such that a scalar change in inputs results in a scalar change in outputs. The second equation assumes nonproportionality in the impact of input increases on output: m_{ij} is the marginal input-output coefficient, and increases in inputs of the output of sector j can result in a greater- or less-than-proportionate increase in the value of w_{ij}. For most analyses, data for the construction of marginal input-output coefficients are not available, forcing the acceptance of average input-output coefficients as the transformation variable. Thus,

$$\begin{aligned} x_1 &= a_{11}x_1 + a_{12}x_2 + \cdots + a_{1n}x_n + f_1 \\ x_2 &= a_{21}x_1 + a_{22}x_2 + \cdots + a_{2n}x_n + f_2 \\ &\vdots \\ x_n &= a_{n1}x_1 + a_{n2}x_2 + \cdots + a_{nn}x_n + f_n \end{aligned} \tag{4.4}$$

This system may be more simply written in matrix form:

$$x = Ax + f \tag{4.5}$$

where A is the $(n \times n)$ matrix of a_{ij} coefficients and x and f are vectors of gross outputs and final demands respectively. This may be rewritten

$$[I - A]x = f \tag{4.6}$$

where I is the identity (unit matrix). By matrix manipulation of equation 4.6, we produce

$$x = [I - A]^{-1}f \tag{4.7}$$

where $[I - A]^{-1}$ is the Leontief inverse. Knowledge of this inverse, itself requiring only the input-output coefficients, and of the vector of final demands is enough to solve the general equilibrium system.

Input-output methods are principally an agent for short-run comparative statics analysis. They may be used to test for the total effects on employment and output of changes in the structure of final demands, whether these originate from tariff changes oveseas or government policies at home. The methodology employed is much the same as for all GE analysis: what are the effects on those variables deemed endogenous of changes in the vector of exogenous factors? The virtues of the input-output approach are to be found in its operational simplicity and the high level of disaggregation it makes possible in the analysis of any issue.

Despite these benefits, input-output analysis has held limited appeal for economic historians. There are only a few historical input-output tables available, chief among them being Leontief's original matrixes for the United States for 1919, 1929, and 1939. Further tables exist for the United States in 1899 (Whitney 1968), and Britain in 1907 (Thomas 1984) and 1935 (Barna 1952). It is not in itself surprising that such few tables exist. They require a great deal of statistical information at the industry level, and are severely labor-intensive in their construction if the end product is to reach the degree of accuracy and internal consistency necessary to make the matrix operationally effective.

Those matrixes that do exist have found little favor with economic historians. Virtually none of the historical applications, moreover, use the GE aspects of interindustry methods. The only GE use of the U.S. tables is Whitney's thesis, which analyzes the sectoral effects of changes in the structure of demand, as well as the relations between international trade and domestic production. The 1899 table was also employed by Hawke (1975) in his calculation of the effective rate of protection provided by the McKinley tariff. Barna's table for Britain in 1935 has received more attention. This is due in part to the perceived importance of structural change and the "new industries" in British developments of the 1930s. Hence, H.W. Richardson (1962) cites Barna in his analysis of the over-commitment of the British economy to traditional staples, although it was left to G.N. von Tunzelmann (1982), in a valuable contribution to the debate on interwar structural change, to use the 1935 matrix effectively to analyze the extent to which the new industries of the 1930s provided a development block that promoted economic recovery. The Barna matrix has also been used by Capie (1978) in his measurement of sectoral effective protection rates in the mid-1930s. Finally, mention should be made of Harley's (1974) use of input-output methods to explore the factor endowments of the Edwardian economy as a means of testing for the existence of a Leontief paradox in British trading patterns.

The one historical application of input-output methods for GE purposes to the British economy is that of Meyer (1955). He used a Leontief inverse constructed from the Census of Production of 1907 to measure the effects of the slowing down of British export expansion between 1872 and 1907 on domestic growth and performance. Meyer concluded that the source of the British climacteric could indeed be found in overseas markets. However, it has been argued that by using Leontief methods, Meyer only paid attention to demand-side influences, never asking whether the reason for the decline in export growth might best be found in the inhibiting effects of factor supply. Also, Meyer used comparative statics methods to address an issue relating to the dynamics of growth. The striking theoretical criticisms by McCloskey (1970) and Kindleberger (1964) of this particular input-output exercise may have led some economic historians to eschew the method. Nevertheless, the problems with Meyer's paper are not endemic to input-output methods in historical economics, but rather indicate that the limitations of the approach should be recognized and respected.[5]

The principal criticism of input-output modeling is that it hinges upon the assumption that the a_{ij} of the input coefficient matrix can be taken as constant throughout the analysis. This assumption is sometimes taken to mean that the input-output coefficients are held fixed over *time*; this is a mistaken critique. The point is rather that the coefficients are taken to be invariant to changes in either endogenous or exogenous variables. This follows from the joint assumption that each sector's output is produced under conditions of constant returns to scale, using a fixed technological relationship between inputs and outputs. Under these conditions, average input coefficients will be reproduced at the margin. In the open Leontief model, the fixed technology assumption in essence argues that the elasticity of substitution between intermediate inputs in response to relative price changes is zero.[6] In the closed model, this assertion is extended to embrace substitution between intermediate goods and primary factors. This need not be a totally damning indictment of the Leontief treatment. Klein (1953) has suggested that the a_{ij} be interpreted as deriving from a Cobb-Douglas production function, in which case the coefficients should be regarded as constant when applied to value as opposed to volume data. This interpretation has become a standard assumption in the construction of multisectoral models of the Johansen type (see below).

Finally, the assumption of fixed coefficients has another implication. The method of input-output takes each sector of the economy to be producing a single homogenous good, which can be used interchangeably for consumption, investment, export, or as an input into other sectors. If this assumption is relaxed, changes in the structure of demands may well result in changes in the input coefficients. If homogeneity of sectoral output is not assumed (and it is difficult to see how it can be, in practice), the use of fixed coefficients must imply the additional assumption that the structure of production within a sector is invariant to changes in final demands. This should be more troubling to GE modelers than the issue of fixed coefficients and technology.

Comparative statics exercises that use input-output methods should be reserved for the short run within which technology may be assumed fixed.[7] This judgment may suggest that input-output methods have nothing to offer the economic historian interested in long-run issues of growth and development. This is not so. Economic growth necessarily involves technical and structural change in production and resource allocation, and shifts in the pattern of demand. By comparison of input-output relations through time, the contribution of technology to growth through factor and input saving may be analyzed. The use of a succession of snapshots of static structural relationships within a particular economy would surely provide an interesting and valid perspective on the growth process, and one that has not been used often enough by historians (cf. Carter 1970).

The major issue, however, is not that of hindsight analysis, but that of building simulation models of the past (present, or future) around fixed coefficient matrixes. Many of the suggested ways of relaxing the assumption of constant returns in short-run models (e.g., marginal coefficients or fixed relations in value terms) are applicable here. The real difficulty, however, extends to knowing the direction of technical change. Historians can embed known changes in input-output coefficients into a multisectoral model. In the absence of a unified theory of technical progress, there seems to be little else to do. Technology is invariably treated as exogenous in model building by historians and contemporary economists. At least the historian has some idea of the form taken by technological developments over the course of analysis.[8] The issue of technology and GE modeling is one to which we return below.

One disadvantage of input-output methods not yet considered is that the Leontief model concentrates on a limited depiction of general equilibrium, there being no thorough analysis of the demand side of the economy. The open system excludes households from the circular flow, their purchases entering exogenously through forecasts of total final demand and their incomes treated as leakages. Yet, realistic modeling of the economy requires that consumer behavior not be treated as exogenous. The simplest method of closing the circular flow on the demand side treats households as an additional industry, which sells labor output to other producing sectors and purchases food, shelter, and consumer goods as inputs into a domestic production function necessary to sustain output. This method was introduced by Leontief in his early work. The treatment of the relationship between production, income generation, and consumption on a fixed coefficients basis is, however, likely to give misleading results. The standard input-output assumption, that technical relationships are invariant with respect to the scale of operations, which implies constant coefficients, cannot easily be applied to the household sector. This would require a unitary income elasticity of demand for commodities by households; to the extent that the income elasticity is less than one, the revised input-output model will overestimate the total effects on the economy of increasing the exogenous vector of final demands. This is because part of the value added created in production will be devoted to additional savings and should be considered a leakage out of the system, rather than recycled into the flow of expenditures. The difficulty here is enhanced when it is realized that income elasticities vary by product and that the bias in the recorded sectoral multipliers will not be uniform, either in size or, indeed, given that income elasticities can be greater than one, in direction.

The introduction of income elasticities of demand suggests a further problem with this naive and restrictive closure procedure. Nonunitary income elasticities imply that savings rates will tend to vary across households according to their income levels. The variation in income elasticities by commodity suggests not only that the average propensity to consume will vary across income groups, but that so too will the composition of the basket of goods purchased. This observation, when coupled with the propositions that income levels by household reflect their factor endowments and that each sectoral production technology employs factors in different combinations, suggests a more sophisticated and robust method of integrating the demand side with the general equilibrium production framework of input-output analysis.

This method is the Social Accounting Matrix (hereafter SAM), pioneered by Sir Richard Stone and recently developed in a series of studies by Pyatt, Thorbecke et al. (Cambridge 1962–1974; Pyatt and Roe 1977). Thorbecke has described the model as "a modular analytical framework specifying, for a set of interconnected subsystems, the major relationships among variables within and between the subsystems" (Thorbecke 1978, p.4). The structure of production activities (as mapped out in an input-output table of interindustry demands) generates a specific pattern of value added which accrues to the various factors of production and, pari passu, to the individuals, households, and other institutions that embody those factors (primarily labor and capital); when transfers between institutions (including taxes and subsidies) are allocated, the income distribution across institutions is determined; the pattern of expenditure is in turn derived from this distribution, and, assuming a closed economy, provides the vector of final demands that faces industry, agriculture, and the service sector; when this vector is integrated with the production activities submatrix, it serves to complete the circle, thereby describing an internally consistent model of the economy. Necessarily, any attempt to capture the interdependent and simultaneous determination of economic variables for an economy-wide system must aim to chart the complex of relationships in as complete, explicit, and realistic manner as theory and data allow. The simple approach outlined above should be extended to take account of such realities as the openness of the economy, the direct and indirect contribution of government, the dynamics of savings and investment, and so on.

An essential principle of economic modeling is that every model must have either an implicit or explicit accounting framework. If we turn to table

4.1, we can see how the circular flow is mapped out in the data framework of a Social Accounting Matrix. The SAM is essentially a form of double-entry bookkeeping: for every outgoing expenditure, there must be an incoming receipt. The matrix consists of an (equal) number of rows and columns each representing a sector of the economy; following convention, the columns show expenditure of the sector specified by the column head on the products of the sector specified by the row heading. In this particular example we have modeled the economy incorporating accounts for capital and the rest of the world, thus making the description of the circular flow more realistic.

The net result of organizing microeconomic data in this fashion is to produce an internally consistent snapshot of the structural relations of production, income generation and expenditure in a particular economy. The system so constructed can be analyzed as a strictly linear model of economic activity, integrating institutions, commodities, and factors into the matrix arrangement of input-output analysis. Typically, as in table 4.1, government, the capital account, and the international sector are distinguished as exogenous sectors, on the grounds that their behavior does not follow automatically from the receipt of incomes. Each of these accounts requires either information or modeling procedure independent of the SAM. Exogenous expenditures (government outlays, investment, and exports) generate direct and indirect production demands and, working through the demand for factors and, in turn, commodities, induced (endogenous) demands. The total effect of these chain reactions can be captured in an extended multiplier. In general, the integration of households into the input-output system will considerably increase the measured impact of any exogenous change.

These structural accounting multipliers are generated by assuming strict linearity and fixed coefficients in all accounts. These cannot easily be defended as predictive tools. Comparative statics analysis of particular counterfactuals requires us to focus on marginal rather than average behavior. We have argued in our discussion of input-output analysis that the assumption of fixed coefficients in the production system is not inappropriate for short-run impact analysis. No such assumption can be justified for the coefficients in the demand subsystem. As with the simple Leontief closure method, the use of fixed coefficients derived from a single SAM has an implicit assumption that average and marginal propensities to consume are the same. This is equivalent to asserting that the income elasticity of each class of consumption is unity. As with the simple one-sector Keynesian model, we should employ marginal propensities to

Table 4.1. Simplified Social Accounting Matrix

		Expenditures				
	1	2	3	4		
				Other Accounts		
	Factors	Institutions Including Households	Production Activities	Combined Capital	Rest of World	Totals
Receipts 1 Factors			Factorial Income Distribution			Income of Factors
Receipts 2 Institutions Including Households	Income Distribution to Households and Other Institutions	Transfers, Taxes and Subsidies		1	2 •	Income of Institutions
Receipts 3 Production Activities		Inst. Demand (Households & Others) for Goods/ Services	Interindustry Demand	3	4	Gross Demand Equals Gross Output
Receipts 4 Others: Combined Capital		5			6	Aggregate Savings
Receipts 4 Others: Rest of World		7	8			Total Foreign Exchange Outflow
Totals	Outlay (= Income) of Factors	Expenditures of Institutions	Gross Output	Aggregate Investment	Total Foreign Exchange Inflow	

Notes: 1. Government receipt from combined capital account
2. Institutions (i.e., government) receipts from rest of world
3. Gross capital formation
4. Exports
5. Savings by institutions
6. Deficit in current account of balance of payments
7. Imports of competitive goods
8. Imports of non-competitive goods

consume when using the SAM as a means of assessing the effects on income and output of changes in exogenous variables. These marginal propensities require no additional information beyond what is already necessary for the construction of a SAM, being calculated as the product of the average coefficients and the income elasticity of demand for the product. The multipliers produced by inverting the amended SAM are generally referred to as *fixed-price multipliers*. They retain the fundamental assumption of Leontief models in the absence of modeling price endogeneity, namely that prices are assumed fixed during the period of analysis.

The analytical methods of the SAM are among the simplest versions of GE modeling. They are suitable for short-run analysis when it can be assumed that there is little or no tendency for factor or input substitution in production or commodity substitution in consumption due to price effects. They would, for example, be perfectly appropriate for analysis of an economy in which there is Leontief technology for intermediate inputs (fixed coefficients), and Cobb-Douglas production functions with cost-minimizing behavior by firms and product price-setting on a strict principle of markup over normal costs. If wages are set to clear the labor market, and there is, in turn, some underemployment of labor and spare capacity of production facilities, factor prices may be assumed insensitive to changes in the structure of demand. The relative price of capital and labor inputs remains constant under such circumstances, and there is no tendency for factor substitution in the production function.

This perspective was taken in my work on the impact of rearmament expenditures on British economic recovery in the late 1930s (Thomas 1983b). Fixed price modeling is appropriate for interwar Britain, with an economic environment characterized by dramatic underemployment of all factors of production. A 62 × 62 sector SAM was set up for 1935 following the organization of table 4.1. A major advantage of the SAM methodology in this case was that it allowed the formal introduction of institutions into the model. We were able to incorporate into our analysis the role of transfers between institutions, in particular between households and government. It was therefore possible to calculate the deflationary effect of paying for increased defense expenditures through increased tax burdens. As well as measuring the impact of defense expenditures on output and employment, the SAM was used to estimate the impact of a counterfactual public works program, working through the construction sector, on economic activity.

Indeed, one of the strengths of the SAM is its flexibility. One SAM can be redesigned to focus on particular issues. Thus, the 1935 matrix could have been used to determine the implications for balance of payments of different government policies, or the effects on the British economy of a decline in export orders due to an overseas tariff. Other problems may require a data matrix organized differently; thus, for example, regional location, ethnic or racial origin, religious affiliation, and occupational or socioeconomic status could be integrated into the schema of the system if it was felt that additional insights into the organization of the economy and society would be so provided. In a society where the ownership and control of income-generating assets is ethnically determined (such as contemporary Malaysia), disaggregating the household accounts to incorporate such information would be of value. In a SAM for interwar Britain or nineteenth-century America, there would be strong grounds for including a regional element in organizing the table. These example emphasize the striking data requirements of developing even a fixed-price SAM: for example, the construction of regional social accounts requires data on regional income patterns, regional consumption behavior. and, ideally, a regional input-output table. In the end, the dual considerations of research agenda and data availability, tempered by the principle of parsimony, will determine the exact specifications of any particular matrix.[9]

III

The general equilibrium framework implicit in the input-output strategy and its SAM derivative is essentially Keynesian. The interdependence between sectors results from relationships between incomes and expenditures, and is not influenced by relative price changes as determined by supplies and demands in individual markets. The second class of general equilibrium models is more microeconomic in orientation, in that these incorporate relative price adjustments and factor and input substitution. These models owe their origin to an extension of input-output methodology proposed by Johansen (1960), and their popularity in economic history to two seminal articles by Ronald W. Jones (1965, 1971).

In their simplest form these models operate by reproducing the dynamics of the exchange mechanisms that underlie the standard Edgeworth box diagrams of intermediate microeconomics texts (Bator 1957). As an application of the simple analytics of general equilibrium analysis, we use a currently popular diagrammatic version as applied to "Booming Sector and Dutch Disease" economics. This analysis is particularly directed to the experience of structural change in contemporary economies, whereby extractive industries have undergone expansion at the expense of resources previously devoted to the manufacturing sector. The context of the following, then, is an attempt to understand the process of deindustrialization in response to developments in oil (e.g., United Kingdom, Norway, Nigeria), natural gas (Netherlands), and metallic minerals (Australia). Nevertheless, as we shall note, this approach has certain historical parallels. The virtue of the booming sector literature for our purposes is that it provides a simple diagrammatic exposition of the issues involved in more complex numerical general equilibrium modeling without recourse to the often impenetrable algebra in which such models are couched. The core of the argument is presented in Corden and Neary (1982) and Corden (1984), upon which much of the following is based.

Booming sector models generally posit three sectors, of which two (manufacturing and mining) produce final goods which are traded at exogenously determined world prices, while the third produces nontraded services. The framework is that of a small open economy. In addition, it is assumed that there are no distortions in product or factor markets, and in particular that prices move to clear all markets, leading to full employment of all factors and zero profits in production. There is no money in this model, a feature common to almost all GE exercises, such that the solution is expressed in relative rather than absolute prices. Finally, the standard working assumption of Jones-type models is made: each of the three sectors employs a single specific factor (capital) as well as a factor (labor) that is perfectly mobile between sectors. This particular version of the booming sector model, then, concentrates on the short to medium term, although different degrees of capital mobility can be introduced to shift focus to longer-run questions.[10] It should be noted, however, that models with no specific factors are more complex and more vulnerable to parameter dependent results.

Let us assume that the extractive industry in our example experiences a Hicks-neutral improvement in technology. The increase in the size of the mining sector can be related to other developments, such as an exogenous increase in demand due to the development of new processes overseas, or a windfall discovery of new resources at home; each of these can easily be built into the framework of the basic model. The effects of a boom in mining can be illustrated diagrammatically.

Figure 4.1 shows the goods market from the production side. Since the structure of relative prices between manufactures and mining products is given by the small-country assumption, we can aggregate these into one traded goods sector. The preboom equilibrium in the goods market is given by point *A* on the original production possibilities frontier, *ST*, where the marginal rates of transformation and substitution are equalized. Technical progress in mining increases the maximum feasible amount of traded goods production, leaving the output potential in services unaltered. The effect is to rotate the production possibilities frontier (PPF) upwards to *ST′*, a new equilibrium being established at the tangency point *D*. The shift from *A* to *D* can be separated into the spending and the resource movement effects respectively. The comparative strength of the two effects will determine

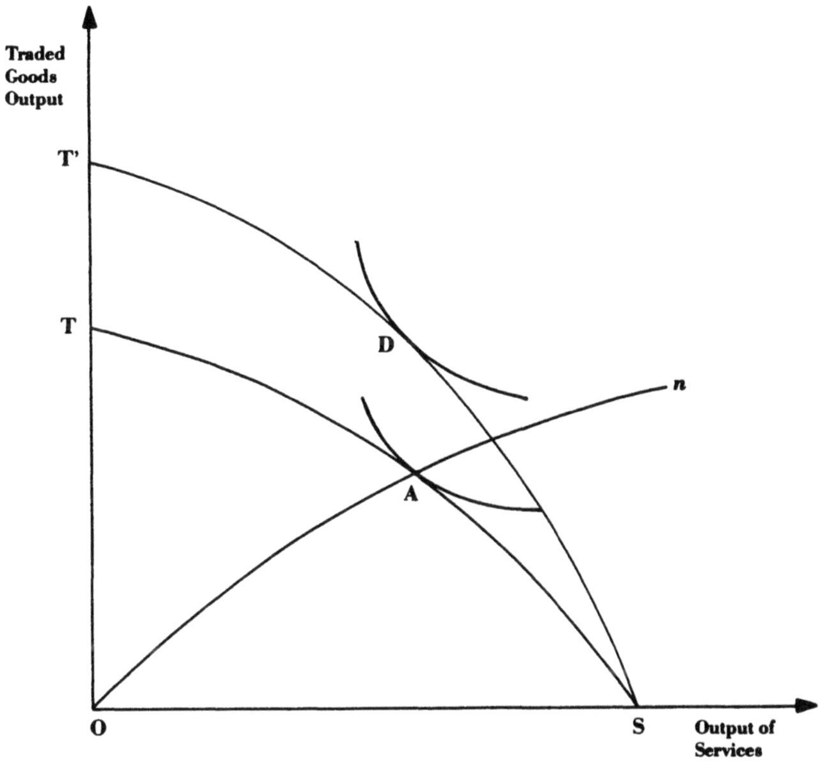

Figure 4.1. Effect of boom on commodity market.

the position of *D* relative to *A*; it is clear that the mining boom could lead to either more or less output in services than in the original equilibrium. We can analyze the spending and resource movement effects in turn by invoking ceteris paribus assumptions. These may be best understood with reference to figure 4.2.

In figure 4.2, the horizontal axis shows the output (and employment) of services, and the vertical axis displays the price of services relative to that of tradeables (*Ps*/*Pt*). A boom in the extractive sector has the initial effect of raising incomes of the factors that are employed there. The spending effect refers to the increased expenditure arising from the additional income, whether spent by factor owners or by the government after taxation of the windfall gains. Provided that the income elasticity of demand for the nontraded good is positive, this will lead to an upward shift in the market demand curve, from *DD* to *D*′*D*′, causing the relative price,

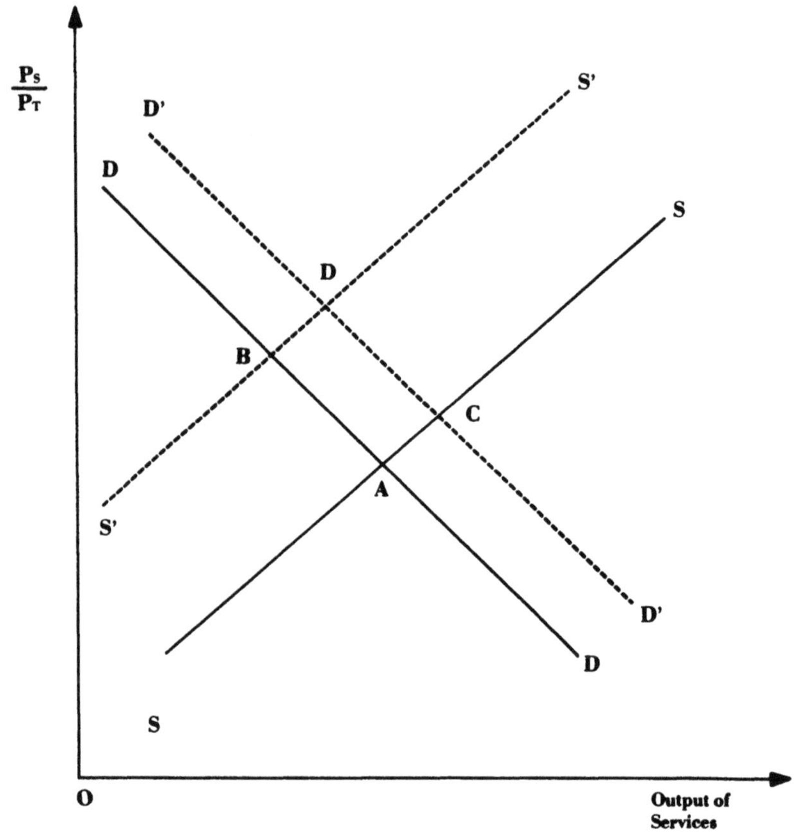

Figure 4.2. Commodity market—spending and resource movement effects.

Ps/Pt, to rise. Corden and Neary refer to this as a real appreciation. The rise in the relative price of services will create the resource movement effect, whereby resources shift out of the nontraded goods sector into the booming industry (with its exogenously determined prices) in order to reap their share of the increased rents in that sector and thereby compete them away. This will have the effect of shifting the supply curve from *SS* to *S′S′*. The net effect on output and employment in the service sector can be either positive or negative, depending on the relative magnitudes of the two effects.[11] The price movement is, however, unambiguous: services become more expensive relative to traded goods.

Diagrammatic representation of GE factors is clearly very valuable in articulating a story about the effects of a sector-specific resource boom. Nevertheless, the telling of that story soon becomes very complicated as more realistic aspects of the economy are integrated. Cook and Sieper (1984) show that, for example, the addition of a third factor of production (say, by distinguishing skilled and unskilled labor) can lead to ambiguity about the direction in which the supply curve in figure 4.2 shifts. "With more than two sectors and more than one mobile factor, supply complementarities are possible and thus a wide range of results emerge as theoretical possibilities." (p. 105). As a general proposition, diagrammatic representation of GE models rapidly becomes completely intractable as the sophistication of the model assumptions increases, and as the number of factors and commodities in the model expands.

Nevertheless, despite their lack of quantitative precision, booming sector models are useful to historians. They provide an explanatory framework for understanding historical developments in cases where formal modeling procedures may be unnecessary or infeasible. Maddock and McLean (1984) have recently dealt with the impact of the gold rush of the 1850s on the economies of two of Britain's Australian colonies, New South Wales and Victoria, using the Corden-Neary approach. A variant of the simple model was used in which the standard assumption of fixed factor endowments was relaxed to incorporate the massive inflow of labor from overseas in response to perceived real wage increases. Maddock and McLean conclude that this modified booming sector model provides a valuable framework for understanding developments in Australia in the 1850s. It appears that the spending effect dominated the resource movement effect in this case, leading to an expansion of services and mining production at the expense of wool and other agricultural production. International movement of labor ensured that living standards in the new equilibrium were little higher than in the preboom era, population in the colonies almost trebling in the ten years after 1850. Clearly, analysis of the Californian and Yukon gold rushes could be undertaken in a similar spirit. Forsyth and Nicholas (1983) have analyzed the decline of Spanish industry in the second half of the sixteenth-century as a further example of minerals-induced structural change, in this case in response to the inflow of gold and silver from the New World.

Use of such simple models need not, however, be restricted to analyses of structural change in production and consumption arising from developments in the extractive sector. For example, the rise of manufacturing behind increased tariff barriers in economies such as Australia, Argentina, and Ireland in the interwar years would be amenable to treatment in this framework. O'Grada and Neary (1985) have adapted figure 4.2 to the Eire of the 1930s. Unlike our paradigm case, however, or the examples of Australia and California in gold rush times, the interwar period was one marked not by resource scarcity, but by large-scale factor underemployment. Therefore, the (working) assumption of O'Grada and Neary of perfectly flexible wages and full employment of all factors seems untenable. Nevertheless, our attention need not be limited to full-employment economies. Although the original models were framed in a market-clearing context, it is perfectly possible to adapt them to circumstances of classical or Keynesian unemployment, where these are defined as resulting from rigid real and nominal wages, respectively.

If we take the labor market analogue to the treatment of the commodity market in figure 4.2 and introduce wage rigidities, we can derive some useful results. This approach suggests that the impact of a sectoral expansion in a Keynesian world of fixed nominal wages depends on the exchange rate regime. If the exchange rate is fixed, the Keynesian multiplier is positive; it will be zero if there is a float and the money supply is fixed. In cases of real wage resistance, the results will be qualitatively similar to those occurring in a flexible wage model with full employment. It is therefore possible for a sector specific boom to lead to higher or lower unemployment. In situations where the real wage would have risen in the flexible-factor price case, then the boom would lead to a reduction of unemployment. If the net effect is to raise prices relative to wages in the flex-price system, rigid wages would create more unemployment (Corden 1984, pp. 369–371). Once again, the requirement is for a fully specified numerical model to determine the comparative statics of the resource boom. As the model becomes more complex, we move rapidly beyond the scope of diagrammatic analysis. It is necessary to turn instead to algebra. This provides a more powerful framework for dealing with model complications and also a base for numerical calculation. We can give a broadly complete structure of a neoclassical economy in a few equations.

The core equations of an applied GE model refer to production and consumption. The simplest form of price sensitive GE models assumes constant returns to scale in production and additively separable utility functions governing consumption. As a simple example, we consider a closed economy with n production sectors and 2 factors. Output is given by Cobb-Douglas production functions,

$$X_i = A_i L_i^{\alpha_i} K_i^{\beta_i} \qquad i = 1, 2, \ldots, n \tag{4.8}$$

where L_i and K_i are labor capital inputs into sector i, α_i, and β_i are distribution parameters (which sum to unity), and A_i is a constant sector-specific efficiency scalar. The demand for these homogenous and perfectly mobile factors is determined by each sector minimizing production costs with regard to factor price. The factor demand equations are

$$L_i = \alpha_i P_i(X_i/w) \qquad i = 1, 2, \ldots, n \tag{4.9}$$

$$K_i = \beta_i P_i(X_i/r) \qquad i = 1, 2, \ldots, n \tag{4.10}$$

The factor price frontier in this example is given by

$$P_i = (\alpha_i^{\alpha_i}\beta_i^{\beta_i})^{-1} w^{\alpha_i} r^{\beta_i} \qquad i = 1, 2, \ldots, n \tag{4.11}$$

If we assume fixed economy-wide stocks of labor and capital, then aggregate income in the economy is equal to

$$Y = w\bar{L} + r\bar{K} \tag{4.12}$$

Given our assumption of additively separable utility functions, the economy can be treated as a single household. The demand functions for sectoral output will depend on relative prices and aggregate income,

$$D_i = D_i(P_1, P_2, \cdots, P_n, Y) \qquad i = 1, 2, \ldots, n \tag{4.13}$$

where $\Sigma_i P_i D_i \equiv Y$. In this system, we have a simple algebraic redefinition of the welfare maximization geometry of figure 4.1. Any particular combination of w and r will determine commodity prices, as well as the level of total income. Sectoral output prices and total income will in turn set the level of aggregate demand.

The allocation of aggregate demand between sectoral outputs will establish sectoral factor demands for any given ratio of factor and goods prices. In equilibrium, the demand for factors will exhaust the (inelastic) supply,

$$\Sigma_i L_i^d - L^s = 0 \tag{4.14}$$

$$\Sigma_i K_i^d - K^s = 0$$

The stability of the factor-price ratio (w/r) will clearly depend on the fulfillment of the factor market equilibrium condition. If the original factor-price ratio implies, for example, an excess supply of labor (unemployment) and an excess demand for capital, then the wage rate may be expected to fall and the user cost of capital to rise. The disturbance in the factor price ratio will set in train a readjustment of output prices, of total income and demand, which in turn establish the aggregate levels of factor demand. Continued factor market disequilibrium will result in further shifts in the factor-price ratio.

The development of price endogenous systems of this type invariably leads to a highly nonlinear set of relationships, which cannot be solved using the simultaneous equation techniques of the Leontief inverse. Some alternative has to be found. There are three standard solution procedures available: linearize the equations and solve analytically using matrix methods (the Jones-Johansen procedure); employ computational techniques that concentrate on the excess demand nature of the implicit solution in the Walrasian model; develop progamming algorithms that set up the GE system as a constrained optimization problem.[12]

There are two dominant computable GE techniques in common usage that utilize the excess demand properties of the Walrasian system. The first applies a *tâtonnement* procedure to drive the excess demands to zero. The second uses an algorithm similar to the simplex method of linear programming to find equilibrium price vector(s) (Scarf 1969, 1984; Scarf and Hansen 1973; Todd 1984). This can be done by searching for a point in which both factor and product excess demands are zero, or searching only in factor price space. A major advantage of fixed point methods is that a solution is assured, although it is necessary to experiment with different starting points within the price space to ensure that a global rather than local solution has been found.

It is generally helpful to consider solution algorithms using the flow chart of the solution strategy. The solution strategy for the excess demand algorithm has already been discussed above. We can get a better understanding by considering a model of a small open economy in which sectoral capital stocks are fixed. The process can be summarized briefly. Start with an initial guess at the product prices and the wage rate. Profit maximization gives the labor demands consistent with the given technology and the sectoral stock of capital. The aggregate labor demand is then compared with the labor supply, and the wage rate adjusted until the labor market clears. Given the level of employment of factors in each sector, the total output of each sector can be calculated from the sectoral production functions. Given the factor prices, factor incomes can be calculated. From this, the total product demand can be generated. This demand will be compared with product supplies. Excess demands suggest that the initial guess at the product price was too low, and excess supplies the opposite. The system is then set to a new vector of product prices and the experiment run again. Prices will continue to be changed until all excess demands fall to zero, and the model will converge iteratively toward equilibrium. The solution strategy is complicated in this instance by the assumption of sector-specific capital, which makes it impossible to separate the factor and product markets in the process. Nevertheless, the *tâtonnement* process implicit in this solution strategy should be clear.

The choice of the solution algorithm will determine just how rapidly the system as a whole will converge. Clearly the most efficient algorithm (for a given expenditure of computational effort) is one that forces convergence in the least number of iterations. To this end, Kimbell and Harrison (1983) have suggested a factor price revision rule (FPRR) that uses known production function parameters to increase the efficiency of the *tâtonnement* search. The rule, simply stated, is that the higher the elasticity of substitution between capital and labor, the smaller should be each factor price change in the convergence process.[13]

Although the fixed-point methods of the Scarf algorithm are generally recognized as providing a most elegant solution to the problem of nonlinearities in a general equilibrium system, the only historical application is James' (1981) exploration of the optimal tariff in the antebellum United States. It is quite clear why such little use has been made of the Scarf technique: elegant in theory, in practice it is computationally complex, requiring significant programming abilities. Further, it turns out to be a relatively expensive solution method when applied to models with more than a score or so excess demand equations (Dervis, Melo, and Robinson 1982, p. 492.). There are simpler solution methods available that pose less formidable issues of theory and programming. Those algorithms that rely upon iterative factor price revisions to solve out factor and product market excess demand functions are likely to have more appeal to historians. The number of investigations proceeding along this route has nevertheless been limited, one of the few examples being that of James and Skinner (1985) in their resolution of the labor scarcity paradox.[14] The fact is that an even more straightforward method of solving the excess demand equations exists, a method that is sufficient for almost all applications of GE modeling to historical issues.

This method was first derived by Leif Johansen. It proceeds by logarithmically differentiating the equations characterizing a Walrasian competitive equilibrium with regard to time, thereby producing a simultaneous system of equations which are linear in all growth rates. A set of growth rates is then specified exogenously and a matrix inversion is sufficient to arrive at all of the other growth rates in the system. This is essentially the same methodology as that developed by Jones in the characterization of general equilibrium in simple economies (i.e., with only a limited amount of disaggregation).[15]

The Jones-type model is predicated on the assumption of perfect competition, in which firms maximize profits, which are driven to zero in equilibrium.[16] Technology is of the constant-returns type, and all factors are fully employed. In the simplest form, there are two factors (labor, L, and capital, K) and two products (manufactures, M, and foodstuffs, A).

The economy is closed to international transactions. In this model, we are trying to explain eight unknowns: the two factor prices, the two commodity outputs, and the factor allocations to each sector (four). We require eight equations to solve for the unknowns.

In equilibrium, prices are set equal to average costs. This yields cost equations of the form

$$a_{lm}w + a_{km}r = p_m \tag{4.15}$$

$$a_{la}w + a_{ka}r = p_a \tag{4.16}$$

The a_{ij} represent the quantity of factor i required to make a single unit of output j; p_j are the output prices; and and w and r are the factor prices of labor and capital respectively. Full-employment equilibrium conditions in each factor market are set by the following conditions:

$$a_{lm}M + a_{la}A = L \tag{4.17}$$

$$a_{km}K + a_{ka}A = K \tag{4.18}$$

The model can be closed by invoking the cost minimizing requirement that each a_{ij} relies solely upon the ratio of factor prices.

The comparative statics properties of this model can be analyzed by restating the level form of equilibrium in rate of change form. This proceeds by logarithmic differentiation of the core equations of the model. Thus, equations 4.15 through 4.18 can be rewritten as

$$\overset{*}{p}_m = \theta_{lm}\overset{*}{w} + \theta_{km}\overset{*}{r} + \overset{*}{a}_{lm}\theta_{lm} + \overset{*}{a}_{km}\theta_{km} \tag{4.19}$$

$$\overset{*}{p}_a = \theta_{la}\overset{*}{w} + \theta_{ka}\overset{*}{r} + \overset{*}{a}_{la}\theta_{la} + \overset{*}{a}_{ka}\theta_{ka} \tag{4.20}$$

where $\overset{*}{a}_{lm}\theta_{lm} + \overset{*}{a}_{km}\theta_{km} = (1 - \overset{*}{T}_m)$, where T is total factor productivity growth,

$$\overset{*}{L} = \lambda_{la}(\overset{*}{A} + \overset{*}{a}_{la}) + \lambda_{lm}(\overset{*}{M} + \overset{*}{a}_{lm}) \tag{4.21}$$

$$\overset{*}{K} = \lambda_{ka}(\overset{*}{A} + \overset{*}{a}_{ka}) + \lambda_{km}(\overset{*}{M} + \overset{*}{a}_{km}) \tag{4.22}$$

In these equations, θ_{ij} represents the sectoral factor cost share for the ith factor in the jth sector, and λ_{ij} is the share of the ith factor used in the jth sector.

The model is closed by determining the sources of changes in the factor-output ratios in each sector. The relevant equations can be shown to be

$$\overset{*}{a}_{lj} = -\theta_{kj}\sigma_j(\overset{*}{w} - \overset{*}{r}) \qquad j = A,M \tag{4.23}$$

$$\overset{*}{a}_{kj} = \theta_{lj}\sigma_j(\overset{*}{w} - \overset{*}{r}) \qquad j = A,M \tag{4.24}$$

The additional parameter, σ_j, is the elasticity of substitution between capital and labor in the two sectors. With the addition of these four equations, the general equilibrium model is now identified: eight equations to explain eight unknowns. The solution of the model will depend on the choice of exogenous parameters.

In this simple model, a GE solution can be calculated by manipulating the simultaneous equations by hand. However, as soon as realistic extensions to the model are made, the system rapidly becomes too complex for simple substitution techniques. In such cases, the system of simultaneous equations can be organized such that endogenous variables are placed on the right, and exogenous, independent variables on the left side of the equation set. By analogy with input-output analysis, this gives a matrix (A) of endogenous elements in the system in relation to the vector (B) of exogenous parameters. The inverse of A measures the elasticity of the endogenous variables to unit changes in the exogenous factors. The system can then be solved by post multiplying this inverse by the vector of exogenous elements.

Jones-type models provide a flexible form for GE analysis. They can be made into more realistic characterizations of the circular flow in an economy by postulating, for example, consumers with demand behavior predicated on identical homothetic preference functions for each individual. The relevant equations would be equivalent to the log-linearized versions of equations 4.12 and 4.13. Similarly, the assumption of a closed economy can be relaxed, with exports and imports entering the relevant economy-wide demand equations.

The inherent problem with Jones-type models in open economies is shown by the Stolper-Samuelson theorem. In a two-factor, two-good world, this theorem states that an increase in the price of one commodity will lead to an increase in the rate of return to the factor used more intensively in the production of that commodity, and a decrease in the price of the other factor. In a small open economy, the relative commodity price structure is set by world demand and supply condition. Provided there are as many internationally traded goods as there are factors of production, the equilibrium factor prices correspond uniquely to the exogenously determined commodity price ratio. The only possible benefits of GE modeling of this sort would be to estimate the allocation of factors between sectors. The Stolper-Samuelson theorem also implies that any small open economy in which goods outnumber factors will be unstable in the short run, with the long-run equilibrium established by the removal of excess production sectors until the equality of factors and goods is affected. To escape this unfortunate and restrictive result, Jones (1971) and Samuelson (1971) developed a model in which factors were specific to a particular production sector. Thus, agricultural capital would not be transferable into manufacturing over the period of analysis. This escapes the assumption of perfectly mobile factors which underlies the discussion above.[17] It is this breed of GE models that has been most often implemented by economic historians.

Many of the most important and puzzling issues in American economic history of the nineteenth-century are amenable to general equilibrium analysis at the level of simple Jones-style models requiring only two or three sectors and two or three factors. Furthermore, for most situations the United States economy could be treated as closed. The models developed and the themes explored by economic historians within this GE framework have mostly examined elements of the transfer of productive resources from agriculture to industry during the process of industrialization. Thus Pope's work on the impact of the antebellum tariff (Pope 1972); the work of Passel and Schmundt (1971) on antebellum land policy; Lewis' (1979) contribution to understanding the shift of labor to manufacturing industry; and Wlliamson's treatment of, among other issues, railroad, immigration, the rate of land settlement, and capital market imperfections in his monumental study of *Late Nineteenth-Century American Development* (Willimson 1974) all focus on aspects of this central question. All operate within the framework established by Jones.[18]

Johansen's work (1960), in contrast, has had little impact on GE work in economic history. The Johansen model is multisectoral by scope, neoclassical by orientation, and linear in computational form. It takes the simple GE system outlined here on pages 140–141 and increases the number of production sectors, linking these by an input-output matrix. The model is something of a cross between the extended Leontief system of the social accounting matrix and the Jones class of models. It may best be characterized as a flexi-price SAM, in which elements are modeled behaviorally to solve prices endogenously. As in the Jones model, the system is solved by restating the (nonlinear) set of equations in growth rate form and inverting the matrix of endogenous variables. The most sophisticated development of Johansen-type models is the ORANI model for contemporary Australia (Dixon, Parmenter, Sutton, and Vincent 1982). One of the spin-offs from this large-scale project has been the work of Siriwardana (1985) on a multisectoral GE model of the colony of Victoria in 1880. Siriwardana has used this to examine the relationship of protection to the economic development of the colony in the late nineteenth-century. The primary disadvantage of the Johansen model is its formidable data requirements. Nevertheless, there will be many issues for which the degree of sectoral disaggregation it makes available will be of interest. Where structural change at the industry level provides an important part of the historical narrative, as in Britain after 1870, the disaggregation of the Johansen model will be advantageous. The greater the degree of emphasis on resource reallocation between sectors as a source of economic growth in a particular economy, the more useful will be the Johansen approach.

Why have most historians favored analytical over computable methods of GE modeling? The major reason for preferring the linear formulation of the Jones-Johansen framework for the majority of historical applications may be summarized as simplicity and computational cheapness. If we share Whalley's judgment that "computational experience...appears to indicate that solution method, per se, is not a major issue with applied models in current use" (in Scarf and Shoven 1984, p. 533), there seems little reason to pursue more complex solution methods than is necessary. A further motivation lies in the numerical form of AGE and CGE solutions to the Walrasian system. The Scarf-Newton and Kimbell-Harrison approaches solve the system in level terms; the Johansen-Jones methodology provides a solution in growth rate format. The growth rate form is clearly very attractive to the historian interested in long-run developments and their explanation. The former approach is of more consequence in analyzing issues of short-run incidence or measuring the welfare effects of changes in a particular exogenous factor.

AGE models also provide a flexible framework for integrating complicating factors in the depiction of economies. It is relatively straightforward to incorporate price distortions into these models, such as tariffs and subsidies, institutionally fixed "exogenous" wage rates, and so on. Once these are built into any model, however, proceeding by Walras' Law (or perhaps by the slackness conditions of linear programming), a counterbalancing arrangement needs to be made. Thus, if a sectoral wage rate is fixed, then the amount of unemployment in that sector becomes endogenous. Also, it should be stated that many of the deviations from the perfectly competitive norm can only be introduced in an ad hoc fashion; although there has been a gradual move toward the development of noncompetitive GE models at various levels of departure from the perfectly competitive paradigm, these have not yet reached the sophistication of the pure Walrasian GE models (e.g., Staelin, 1976). For relatively large-scale modeling, moreover, Powell (1981) argues that the flexibility and tractability of the Johansen system provides distinct advantages over the nonlinear methodologies of the Scarf-Newton methods. Nevertheless, there are disadvantages of the Jones-Johansen procedure that need to be mentioned.

The major problems arise from the linear nature of the approach. As we have seen, almost all of the GE models used in historical research are linear by orientation. The log-linear derivation of Jones-Johansen models provides a close approximation to nonlinear reality only for small changes in the structure of the system. The matrix inversion framework of this class of models should, therefore, be limited to marginal changes in the exogenous factors. To the extent that economic historians are interested in large-scale structural changes in institutional arrangements and market relationships, the local linearity assumption may not hold and use of Jones-type models may give seriously distorted results. There are two responses to this question: use nonlinear methods, such as the fixed-point Scarf system, or break down the large change into a number of smaller ones, for which the local linearity conditions may be assumed to hold (Dixon, Parmenter, and Powell 1984; Dixon, Parmenter, Sutton, and Vincent 1982; Bovenberg and Keller 1983). The advantage of the latter is that it is computationally straightforward, whereas the Scarf algorithm tends to become both expensive and complex to handle as model size increases.

This leads to consideration of a related problem. Some exercises in historical simulation use a single matrix of relationships to make counterfactual predictions for periods as long as fifty years. Yet practitioners working with GE models of contemporary economies argue that such forecasting procedures should only be used for periods of three to five years, beyond which they rapidly decline in reliability.[19] The way to finesse this problem for longer-run simulation studies is to derive a moving escalator of benchmark equilibrium estimates, each one serving as the starting point for the calculation of the next equilibrium. This method was introduced by Johansen in his multisectoral forecasting model of the Norwegian economy (1968) and was later implemented by Taylor and Cardoso in their identity based model of Brazil (Taylor, Bacha, Cardoso, and Lysy 1980). It should be said that there is a difference here between the experiences of small Jones-class models, and the larger multisectoral exercises of the Johansen type. It is particularly in the latter models, with their high degree of interdependence between production sectors, that the issue of coefficient stability is likely to be most troublesome.

Jones-Johansen models are not immune to more general difficulties with GE technology. The most general criticism of GE exercises is one directed at all model-building exercises, namely that they are based on an artificial distinction between exogenous and endogenous elements. The "public choice" critique is that institutional developments (normally treated in GE models as exogenous) reflect the activities of economic agents in response to certain market signals. Thus, it is argued, the political process of elections, of coalition formation within and beyond the parliamentary and congressional frameworks, the direction and extent of rent-seeking activities, none of which are usually modeled in general equilibrium or econometric exercises, may well be within the schedule of likely responses to policy initiatives or other structural changes. Moreover, policy making is not independent of changes in endogenous variables nor of other policy decisions. As an example, consider a GE model of the Great Depression in Britain in the 1930s. It has long been debated whether devaluation, the tariff, or cheap money was a more significant influence on the pattern of the recovery in Britain after 1932. A possible treatment of this issue would be to simulate the British economy after 1932 incorporating each of these policies, and then to conduct a series of counterfactual experiments in which each policy was voided in turn with the others remaining in place. The problem here is that it may not be legitimate to treat each policy as exogenous and independent. A case can be made that the introduction of cheap money was contingent on the devaluation of sterling to relax foreign exchange constraints (see Cairncross and Eichengreen 1983). If this were true, it would not only be misleading to conduct counterfactual experiments of cheap money without devaluation, but the original simulation would also give misleading indicators of the contributory role of each factor in promoting recovery. Thus, a 1 percent reduction in the interest rate may not have been feasible (in reality or in the minds of the policy makers, it matters not) without a 5 percent devaluation in sterling. Ceteris paribus analysis in the counterfactual comparative statics tradition, without recognition of the jointness of the policy measures, would be misleading.

The historical record alerts us in this case to the jointness of policy decisions. Not always can the policy (or political) response to a particular counterfactual be gauged as readily. As a second example, let us assume that we are trying to measure the optimum tariff for Britain in 1932. There are two potential difficulties here: the rent-seeking activities of domestic producers that will help set the structure of the tariff, and the reaction of overseas governments to the new tariff level. In a model of the optimum tariff, the possibility of retaliatory tariffs would not normally be accommodated in a GE exercise, since the reaction functions of foregin governments do not normally fall within the rubric of endogenous elements within the model. Nevertheless, the true optimum tariff (that which maximizes domestic welfare) should take into consideration the potential effects on export performance.[20] A multisectoral model will also need to take into account the structure of the tariff and its determinants.

The public choice critique is directed both at the interpretation of the results of GE modeling and at its theoretical foundations. The current literature on GE analysis focuses its debates and disagreements on precisely these two considerations. As in the above paragraphs, it is hard to treat these independently. A central concern in recent GE modeling has been model specification, and in particular the issue of model closure. Ginsburgh and Robinson (1984, pp. 432–433) have analyzed the structure of a GE model under a number of heads: agents, behavioral rules, institutional structure, signals, and system constraints. Thus, a perfectly competitive Walrasian model is modeled around firms and households (the agents), operating according to profit and utility maximization (the rules) under conditions of fully flexible price with atomistic competition and fully mobile factors (the structure), their decisions about production and consumption solely determined by relative prices (the signals). The full determination of the general equilibrium is established not only by the actions of these agents, but also by the constraints of the entire system. The conditions of equilibrium may be formally defined as a set of signals such that the decisions of all agents jointly satisfy the system constraints. In a competitive model, the system constraints is provided by the assumption that all markets clear with zero excess demands.

Considerable attention has been paid in the recent literature on GE modeling, particularly with regard to developing economies, to the way in which the system constraints operate. Sen (1965) may have been the first to point out explicitly that a model's predictions about growth and distribution may depend crucially on how the system is made algebraically determinate, or closed. In this context, closure refers to the way in which the model achieves balance between savings and investment.[21] The main advocate of examining closure rules has been Lance Taylor (1979), who has suggested that different closure rules are likely to imply very different model paths. Thus, in a neoclassical model, investment is set by the supply of loanable funds, such that productivity and thrift determine the level of investment in the short run and the growth path of the economy in the long run. In a neo-Keynesian model, incorporating the parable of the widow's cruse, investment is determined by animal spirits tempered by interest rates. These two characterizations of the savings-investment link have very different implications for the path of capital accumulation and, therefore, growth. This suggests that historians who build dynamic models of the past, in which capital formation is determined endogenously, should pay particular attention to the closure rule incorporated. Taylor and Lysy (1979) have demonstrated the power of imposing different closure rules. If the choice of closure rule is changed, the system dances to a different (but still predictable) tune, however intricate and impenetrable the model structure may appear at first glance. Not only does this suggest a potential difficulty with the macroeconomic implications of particular model specifications, but it also alerts us to one aspect of the "black box" problem commonly associated with large-scale GE models.

One implication of Taylor and Lysy's work is that some GE modelers did not themselves understand the macro implications of the models they had constructed. A similar reservation has been suggested by the work of Whalley anbd Yeung (1984) in their discussion of closure rules applied to the external sector. They conclude that the choice of closing rule "can be sufficiently important that it can considerably affect the perceived impact of policy changes, even when trade accounts for only a relatively small fraction of total activity in the economy." The major types of closing rule applied to the external sector involve setting the exchange rate as the "price" of external balance. The exchange rate modeling is, however, very weak in most models. This is no surprise since the exchange rate is a financial magnitude determined by models with no financial sector specified. The absence of a macroeconomic overlay is not the sole problem with the treatment of the overseas sector in most GE models. Whalley and Yeung severely criticize the tacking on of a partial equilibrium system of simple import and export equations to the general equilibrium model of the domestic economy. They show moreover that the import and export demand elasticities applied in such models are not what most researchers intend. The recommendation of Whalley and Yeung is that the assumptions of the small open economy be everywhere invoked or, if this is implausible for a particular economy, that the trade functions be modeled as excess demand equations applied to the rest of the world.

We have examined the black box problem as it leads to unintended consequences in the context of particular models. A more familiar difficulty is found when using GE models as a means of telling a historical story. By its very nature, the use of GE techniques makes a virtue out of complexity; often, it is extremely difficult to unravel the mechanism by which the impact of changes of an exogenous element on the vector of endogenous variables operates. The extent of mystification will usually increase along with the size and sophistication of a model. It is no surprise, therefore, that there has been occasional bewilderment on the part of economic historians (and economists) when trying to work out what is central to a model's results. As Kahn (1981) has noted, citing an enormous model as an explanantion of a historical phenomenon is unlikely to demonstrate any advanced understanding of the event in question. To paraphrase Joan Robinson, the last thing we require is a 1:1 road map of the past. In response, some economists have advocated building miniature versions of large-scale models to aid exploration and explication of model structure. A successful implementation of this procedure is that of the BOTE (back of the envelope) version of the ORANI model developed by Dixon, Parmenter, and Powell (1984). Similarly, Kahn attempts to reduce Williamson's large-scale (72-equation) model of late nineteenth-century America to a more manageable size. He found it possible to replicate two of Williamson's major findings, the unimportance of the closing of the frontier to the decline in the growth rate of GNP per worker, and the role of transport improvements in opening up the Midwest, with much simpler and more succinct versions of the underlying model. In the case of the frontier, a simple sources of growth calculation à la Denison provided almost identical results on the effect of an exogenous decline in the growth of the stock of land on output growth per capita as did the much more complex GE system. As James (1984, p. 239) and Kahn (1981, p. 36) note, however, we should not glean from this result the conclusion that the mega-model is irrelevant. Until the complicated computer model is organized and the particular counterfactual simulated, it is impossible to determine whether the interaction effects that are the core of the GE approach are important or can be dismissed. Being able to determine even this represents an advance in our stock of knowledge of the past. Indeed, the primary virtue of model miniatures is in developing a better appreciation and explanation of the results of the full-scale exercise.[22]

As an extreme version of the issue of model specification, we should make mention of David's argument concerning the appropriateness of equilibrium modeling for historical purposes. The existence of indivisibilities and resultant scale economies, the presence of learning by doing,

> strike a damaging blow at the body of theory which represents a decentralized market economy as attaining, or always tending to attain a general equilibrium configuration in the prices and quantities of a pre-specified array of inputs and outputs. . . [these factors] also remove the mathematical basis for supposing that market configurations we might still wish (albeit with shaken confidence) to treat as equilibrium solutions will be globally *stable* equilibria. Yet, upon just that supposition rest many of the economist's casual empirical applications of the methods of comparative statics and comparative dynamics. (David 1975, pp. 8–9)

The application of GE techniques to history becomes, then, partly a matter of faith, partly of optimism that the method is, if not entirely appropriate, then at least instructive.[23]

IV

The procedure for GE exercises may be summarized as: take a question, problem, or hypothesis; design a model to bring out the central issue and the core relationships to its testing; calibrate the model to the existing economy; then shock the model toward a new counterfactual equilibrium by adjusting a key behavioral or institutional parameter. Compare the new result to the old and interpret contrasts and similarities.

This section examines methods of calibration and simulation. The key issue here is data. Numerical GE analysis, whether analytical or computable, obviously requires numbers. Data are required for calibrating the model to fit the known historical facts of the base economy, and to test the validity of a particular theoretical framework of an economy. Required data include descriptive structural information and material on core behavioral parameters. The more ambitious and complete the model, the more pressing the requirements for statistical information, very often of precisely the sort that is unavailable for historical economies. Moreover, it is often the case that among the statistical facts that do exist, some are incompatible with others. In this context, there are distinct advantages of working in the GE framework: inconsistencies have to be resolved; the stylized facts for a particular period can be checked against a well specified theoretical model of economic behavior; while the modeling procedure itself will often produce new data of some interest.[24]

In general, each exercise in the GE tradition will set up its own data problems, which can only be solved on an order basis. At the most basic level, the GE researcher should be guided by the principle of Occam's Razor in establishing a model. However, it is possible to make some general statements concerning data sources and problems. To this end, we examine the Social Accounting Matrix and Jones-type models described in section III.

The major tasks of data collection and preparation for GE analysis may be divided into two parts: organization of the data to fit a benchmark equilibrium of the economy to be analyzed and the choice of key behavioral parameters that will determine the outcome of model simulations. The simplest example of a benchmark equilibrium is the input-output table, in which the double-entry accounting rules force each sector's outgoings and incomings to be equal. The input-output table provides a snapshot of the resources flows that characterize an economy in equilibrium. These matrixes move from being descriptive to being predictive only when certain behavioral criteria are attached in the form of a model structure. Similarly with the Jones-type models. In this case, the structural characteristics of the model will include the input-output coefficients, the structure of production and final demands, and the sectoral factor shares. The data that are used to construct the initial equilibrium will be derived from a variety of sources. These sources are rarely compatible, and data reconciliation is invariably required to determine a consistent benchmark equilibrium of the economy. It is worth seeing how these problems arise and how they çan resolved.

The context in which we look at these issues is the Social Accounting Matrix. Mapping the resource flows that characterize the initial equilibrium in the SAM format highlights the problems of data inconsistency and incompleteness and also provides a method for resolution. In general, the sources of information for a SAM will be a census of manufactures and an accompanying wages and earnings enquiry, incorporating material on interindustry transactions and the breakdown of value added between factor accounts; a household budget survey, which will provide details of household expenditures on the output of industry, agriculture, and services; and aggregate national income accounts, which will contain generally reliable estimates of the marginal entries in the table.

Organizing the data in the form of a SAM suggests the possibility of incompatibility in the cell entries, given that the historian will be required to draw data from a range of different sources, of varying degrees of quality, compatibility, and completeness. Considering the statistical sources for a typical SAM will make it clear how problems of inconsistency may arise: there may be some conflict, for instance, between the estimates of total earnings as derived from an earnings enquiry and a household expenditure survey. Budget surveys are notoriously unreliable with regard to the reporting of incomes and of certain expenditures: in Britain in the 1970s the reported expenditure on alcoholic beverages was only 60 percent of the known total of national consumption. The expenditure, income, and output methods of computing GNP invariably give different measures of national income. A major virtue of working within the framework of a SAM is that it emphasizes the interdependence of the data sources embedded in the general equilibrium structure. Presentation of data in this format forces the historian to consider the issues of compatability and consistency and to make explicit judgments about the relative reliability of the component blocks of data.

There are two procedures that can be followd in attempting to resolve data inconsistencies and missing entries in the SAM. The simplest is to make informal adjustments according to a subjective evaluation of the comparative virtues of the various data sources. Balancing by hand is commonly applied; in cases where the inconsistencies are of small order, this will generally be sufficient. There are, however, more formal statistical adjustment procedures which utilize the accounting requirements imposed by tabular form. The simplest of these solutions is the RAS, biproportional matrix method first used for updating input-output tables with minimal additional information (Bacharach 1971).

If a complete input-output table is available for a particular year, and an additional table is required for a year in which knowledge is restricted to the marginal totals in the matrix (the total value of output and total value of intermediate inputs by sector), the RAS method serves as a straightforward, albeit mechanical means of estimating the input-output entries for the new observations. The RAS procedure pivots on the original cell entries; firstly, it adjusts proportionally all the entries to meet the new column total. This will lead to imbalances in the row total and the cell entries; the next step is to adjust proportionally each cell entry to meet the new row total. The column total will no longer hold, and the proportional adjustment to the column marginal is again used. Each iteration brings the cell entries closer to compatibility with the row and column totals of the new observation. The final row (R) and column (S) multipliers when applied to the original input-output matrix (A) will establish the structure of intermediate relationships consistent with the new marginal observations. This route has been taken to update input-output tables to results of more recent production census, but can also be used to back-date tables as well. I have generated input-output tables for Britain in the Census of Production years of 1924 and 1930 from the Barna matrix of 1935, using a variant of the RAS approach (Thomas 1985b). It would certainly be possible to generate such tables for the United States for 1879, 1889, 1904, and 1909, using the Whitney input-output matrix for 1899, by applying the same procedure.

The disadvantage of the pure RAS approach for balancing social accounting matrixes is that it cannot easily handle missing entries and makes a very simple judgment of the differrential quality of information within a matrix: *all* decisions are made according to the authority of the column and row totals. The notion of matrix balancing as a constrained estimation problem is retained in more recent adjustment procedures that in addition take into account the researcher's knowledge about the relative accuracies of the data points. These techniques, which are most closely associated with Stone (1942, 1961a,b, 1968, 1970, 1977), are mechanical in form but have the advantage of flexibility, so that different assumptions about the relative virtues of each data set can be easily integrated and new results produced.

The constraints in this procedure are the accounting relationships that must be satisfied. Thus, incomes and receipts of any institution in a SAM must be equal in equilibrium, such that household expenditures (including savings) must exhaust incomes, and each industry's total costs equal total sales. The adjustment procedure also requires the formation of a variance matrix of the original estimates of each cell entry. This matrix shows the tolerance of estimates to the demands of the accounting constraints. If the expected variance of a cell entry is zero, then that entry is fixed and balancing has to take place around it. Construction of such a variance matrix is by no means a straightforward task and requires familiarity with the statistical sources of the SAM, their strengths and weaknesses, and an ability to turn judgments of comparative reliability into indexes of "probable range of error."

This system can be extended to incorporate cases where there are certain cell entries which are nonzero, but unknown a priori. Thus, for example, many household expenditures surveys do not include questions about total expenditure. Providing that the number of unknowns is less than the number of restrictions, we can, by substitution, rearrange the restrictions such that each constraint accounts for one unknown cell, thus determining the full solution uniquely.

The Stone procedure, though labor intensive, is quite straightforward in operation. For small and medium-sized SAM's ($n < 100$), it provides a feasible algorithm for improving the quality of raw data by pursuing the dictates of accounting consistency and incorporating the researcher's intuitions regarding the reliability of the underlying data. The stength of the procedure is that it caters to such intuitions in a systematic and formal manner, which is in most cases to be preferred to matrix balance by legerdemain, which sometimes appears to be the major statistical technique used by national income accountants. The disadvantage is that the system may appear to be more sophisticated and of greater intrinsic worth than it merits. The core concept, that of a variance matrix drawn from the statistican's insights, has limited statistical tolerance. The entries in this matrix are, at best, guesses and are not based on any statistical criteria that can determine standard errors in a probabilistic framework. We are merely quantifying the researcher's subjective evaluation of source reliability; the language of mathematical statistics is of dubious worth in evaluating the results of the adjustment procedure (Byron 1978). The establishment of the variance matrix is clearly an uncertain process, and it would behoove any researcher to test the sensitivity of the constrained solution by positing alternative indices of reliability.[25]

Once we have achieved consistency and full information about the structural conditions of the model simulation, we need also pay attention to the source of behavioral parameters. Parameters are the fixed constants that map exogenous factors into the endogenous solution. In Jones-type models, the behavioral parameters are the elasticities that govern consumption and production decisions: the price and income elasticities of domestic and foreign demand, and the sectoral elasticities of factor substitution in production. The choice of parameters will determine the results of any particular model simulation. It is therefore necessary to pay close attention to the sources of such parameters and their reliability. The usual method of setting parameter values is to take a single best-guess estimate from a search of the literature. An alternative is to employ stochastic estimation techniques to establish parameters (Mansur and Whalley 1984). It is clearly the case, however, that historians will be able to rely upon econometrically derived data only in rare cases. There is certainly no potential for the system estimation techniques favored by Jorgenson (1984, 1985). Indeed, the problem for historians is even more marked. For some economies the data on production technologies and consumption behavior is readily available. This is not the case universally, however, and somehow the missing gaps have to be filled. There are a number of options available.

The range on the values of parameters is limited by the calibration requirements of the GE model. Not only is it necessary to ensure that the structural conditions of the model be chosen to fit the base equilibrium, but it is also necessary to calibrate the model such that it reproduces base-year data as a model solution. Before the model can be calibrated, it is necessary to set the values on the parameters that determine the model solution. Clearly, however, these have to be internally consistent to ensure calibration. In certain cases, the observed equilibrium alone will be sufficient to establish uniquely the values for certain parameters. Only one set of factor share data, for example, will be consistent with the benchmark equilibrium in a Cobb-Douglas world. More generally, the form of model specification will restrict parameter values (Mansur and Whalley 1984, pp. 100–103). These factors may be termed the theoretical and empirical requirements of ensuring model consistency. To this we may add the systems approach of Frisch (1959). In the case of consumer behavior, the major source of structural information is the budget survey. This provides data on the proportion of expenditure devoted to each commodity type at each level of household income. Budget surveys, however, rarely provide information on price variations and cannot be used directly to estimate price elasticities of demand. The budgets will, however, provide estimates of budget shares by commodity and can be used to estimate income (or expenditure) elasticities. The Frisch (1959) technique allows for the calculation of all own- and cross-price elasticities for consumption from knowledge of these variables alone. In this case, the combination of the empirical evidence from the benchmark equilibrium allied to the theory of demand determines the choice of parameter values.

A second possibility is to borrow data from other economies of similar type and structure. Thus, Kelley, Williamson, and Cheetham (1972) in their model of Meiji Japan used production technology data from developing South-East Asian economies of the 1960s. This is, perhaps, an extreme version. Other historians have used stylized facts regarding consumption and production elasticities to generate missing data. Thus, Weisskoff's study of consumption functions (1971) and Houthakker's seminal article on Engel elasticities (1957) provide key data on household expenditure behavior. Mansur and Whalley (1984, p. 109) also provide a series of "central tendency estimates" of own-price elasticities of household demand functions, derived from a considered literature search. On the production side, the crucial parameter is that of the elasticity of capital-labor substitution. This is an area of much confusion in the literature, especially given the inconsistencies between cross-section and time-series econometric estimates of the variable (Berndt 1976). On average, cross-section estimates suggest Cobb-Douglas production technologies, while time-series estimation suggests elasticities of about 0.5. Caddy (1976) has provided central tendency values of the substitution elasticities at a sectoral level. Finally, many recent models of the international economy have used the central tendency estimates of trade elasticities drawn up by Stern, Francis, and Schumacher (1976). In the absence of hard econometric investigation of price and income elasticities in international trade in the nineteenth-century, there is little alternative for the historian but to use these data. Models that use the Armington (1969) assumption of differentiated products in international trade can call on Alaouze's (1977) estimates for Australia in the 1970s. Most of these data are derived from empirical treatment of contemporary economies. Is it reasonable to apply these to GE models of the past, given the effects of changing tastes and technology?

Data are not only borrowed across time, but also across national boundaries. Also, data borrowing applies not only to behavioral parameters but also to structural information such as capital-output ratios or input-output coefficients. Both of these may seem safer procedures. But, to what extent is it valid to assume that technological relationships are similar across countries? Clearly, the theoretical response is that they are not. Empirically, however, it has been noted that input-output coefficients vary across countries within a relatively narrow range (Watanabe 1961). Historians, however, need to be rather more circumspect in transferring production parameters across frontiers, given the extent of technology lags and the variation in factor and resource prices between countries. For example, Rostas' data (1948) demonstrated clearly that U.S. labor-output ratios were far higher (twice as high in blast furnaces) than were British in the interwar period, and could not simply be explained by scale economies. Comparisons of input-output coefficients for Britain in 1907 and the United States in 1899 (and again in 1935 and 1939 respectively) suggest contrast rather than similarity (Thomas 1985b). As with the other suggested sources, using such data is not necessarily appropriate, although it may be better than nothing in the setting up of a model. Obviously, it is necessary to employ extensive sensitivity analysis to ensure that the model results do not hinge crucially on the choice of a particular parameter.[26]

In linearized GE models, the calibration of a model is not to a benchmark equilibrium set in level form, but to the growth rates of the system. For historians, the aim is to calibrate the initial model as closely as possible to the actual record of the past. How do we evaluate the accuracy and acceptability of the results obtained from a simulation study of this type? In Williamson's recent volume on long trends in income inequality in Britain, he compares series of actual and predicted growth rates for his endogenous variables. How can we tell how good these are? Williamson had distinguished five reasons why particular estimates may be at variance with the historical record (1985, pp. 122–135):

1. The model is in error.
2. The estimated historical "facts" are in error.
3. The underlying structural estimates of the model are in error.
4. The estimated rates of change in the exogenous variables are in error.
5. There are errors in the structure of unknown exogenous variables.

Williamson undertakes "extensive sensitivity analysis" (1985, p. 126) to test the relative importance of these factors to the overall performance of the model. On this basis, he concludes that, in the case of his model, the major scope for error in the simulations lies in flaws in the model or in the historical facts. Such a judgment suggests a very useful gain from CGE modeling—the ability to sound out the feasibility of certain historical data estimates within a theoretically rigorous framework of analysis.

A model may be rigorous, but is it the right one? How can we determine our preference for one model formulation over another? How valid or appealing are the assumptions used to build a GE model and make it operational? To what extent do the results hinge on the validity of such assumptions?

In this response to the question, *Did British Capitalism Breed Inequality?*, Williamson recognizes three pivotal assumptions which may be questioned when applied to industrializing Britain: full employment; perfectly integrated capital markets; and the small-country assumption (Williamson 1985). None of these need be built into a GE model, and the question is whether any of them belong in a model of nineteenth-century Britain. O'Brien (1983) has challenged the first two assumptions. An additional question mark hangs over the use of the small-country assumption. It seems likely that a country that accounted for over 35 percent of world trade in manufactures between 1876 and 1895 (Hilgerdt 1945) and over 50 percent in certain key sectors (cotton textiles, iron and steel goods, shipbuilding, railway stock, coke) should be considered a large country, given that changes in British export volumes would have had an effect on world prices (Tyszynski 1951). A plausible case can also be made that Britain was a large-country importer in the midnineteenth-century, given its dominance of markets for foodstuffs and raw materials.[27] Certainly, McCloskey's (1980) calculation of the optimal tariff in 1881 was predicated on this belief, and James and Skinner (1985) have made a similar assumption for Britain in 1859.[28] Notwithstanding the problems with external sector modeling noted above, the impact of the small-country assumption requires formal testing within the structure of the model. In general terms, as Williamson notes, it is incumbent upon both modelers and their critics to undertake sensitivity analysis to test the crucial nature of assumptions as well as to identify the critical parameters in the model. Numerical experimentation with various model specifications is required before a model is used to perform counterfactual simulations.

How should we determine whether one set of results is superior to another within the range of numerical experimentation undertaken? If the major source of difficulty is to be found within the model, then we should have a mechanism whereby we can evaluate the vulnerability of the estimates of the endogenous variables to different model specification. Classical probability theory in its application to econometric work suggests a number of possible means of evaluating the quality of calibration. However, since the degree of interdependence between variables is a key characteristic of the GE system, full information maximum likelihood procedures are not appropriate. It is preferable to pursue limited information techniques of the sort that underlie two-stage least-stage estimators. In this case, we set up two different methods of evaluating the results of a model simulation. The first is to minimize a loss function of the form:

$$\min L = (a - a*)^2 + (b - b*)^2 + \cdots + (n - n*)^2 \qquad (4.25)$$

where a, b, ..., n are the actual estimates of the growth rates of the endogenous variables, and a*, $b*$, ..., $n*$ are the predicted values from the model. The disadvantage of this loss function is that it does not take into consideration the interdependence of the endogenous variables. Put crudely, if our interest is in charting the growth rate of real GNP per capita, we will not be equally impressed by the accuracy of the model's simulation of the production of dwellings and of dolls' houses. The implication here is to set up a loss function that weights the accuracy of particular predictions by their significance in the overall model. This suggests a loss function of the form

$$\min L = (a - a*)^2(dX/da) + (b - b*)^2(dX/db) + \cdots + (n - n*)^2(dX/dn) \qquad (4.26)$$

where dX/da is the derivative of the objective function with regard to changes in the endogenous variable. Of course, the very use of terminology such as "minimizing the loss function" is misleading. To begin with, as we have noted, there is the possibility that the "actual" values being used as the basis for comparison are in error. Moreover, in contrast to econometric practices, the GE model builder is not operating within formal statistical procedures that minimize least squares as the estimation procedure. The researcher is not sampling the population of possible results—each run of the model is designed to test its sensitivity to changes in its structure or data framework in the context of previous results. In contrast to econometric methods, contingent search procedures are both acceptable and necessary in GE calibration. The amount of search using sensitivity analysis that can be undertaken is limitless in principle, and needs to be bounded by pragmatic considerations. The best procedure is to examine the likely sources of bias and error, and to use the loss function as a means of distinguishing between these. Since there is no formal probabilistic foundation to this procedure, there is no table of values to say whether the predicted values are within acceptable confidence limits of the "known" actual values. The best we can do is to experiment and choose the most effective model simulation.

The role that sensitivity analysis plays is not limited to exploration of the effects of model specification on the accuracy of calibration. Another area of potential importance is that of parameter uncertainty and its effects on the accuracy of counterfactual simulations. Given that many of the parameters in a typical GE model are borrowed data or are "guesstimates," understanding the effects of parameter instability is clearly of some importance to understanding the message of the model. Until recently, this issue has not been formally treated in the GE modeling literature. The standard approach has been to undertake extensive analysis of the sensitivity of model results to parameter changes. Pagan and Shannon (1985) suggest more rigorous sensitivity testing procedures for log-linear GE models. They argue that recalibration of a model in the face of different parameter estimates is an inefficient method of proceeding. "Users can never be sure that the parameters selected for variation are the important ones nor that the combination of values considered are not biased towards a particular outcome" (Pagan and Shannon 1985, p. 104). Furthermore, a recalibration exercise for one variant of a particular model may suggest one set of key parameters, but these may not be critical for all sensitivity tests on the same model. The key problem is that of interdependence in the GE system. Pagan and Shannon suggest two measures for measuring overall sensitivity of the model to parameter variation; these rely upon mean-variance and extreme bounds measures respectively. The advantage of the latter is that it can be decomposed fairly simply to measure the contribution of individual parameters to overall model instability. The disadvantage of the approach is that it is based on an estimate of the confidence intervals that surround the parameter point estimate as used in the base model run. The *t* statistics used to calculate the bounds will clearly be subjective in the majority of cases. This makes the approach similar to the Stone system of matrix adjustment. The conclusion of numerical experiments with the two measures is that, because *t* statistics are usually quite low, quite large changes in parameter values (perhaps up to 50 percent) are necessary to develop a real sense of the sensitivity of results to the probable range of parameter values. The extreme bounds measure is helpful in analysis of linearized GE models, given its reliance on the derivatives of the matrix of endogenous variables, which can be quite easily calculated for such models. The Pagan-Shannon approach has been used by Kimbell and Harrison (1984) to useful effect.

Once the model has been specified, the numbers chosen to reproduce resource flows in the benchmark equilibrium, and the system calibrated successfully to the historical record, the historian can undertake counterfactual analysis to test hypotheses and to determine critical institutional and behavioral elements in the record of the past. What are some of the issues for which GE analysis as developed in this chapter may be useful?

V

A contribution to a volume entitled *The Future of Economic History* should certainly make some suggestions for future research. The following topics form one possible agenda:

Trade

There are any number of questions in understanding the relationships between trade and domestic development and welfare that would repay investigation in a GE framework. Many of these already have been examined from this perspective. The most obvious of these is the question of tariff protection. What was the effect of tariffs on the distribution of factoral income? Did the tariff reduce economic welfare and growth? What was the optimal tariff? What was the incidence of the tariff on particular production sectors of the economy? Was the political economy of tariff making linked to the resource reallocating effects?

One possible extension of the literature on tariffs would be to undertake comparative dynamics of the tariff. The question of the contribution of the postbellum United States tariff to industrialization, for example, cannot easily be assessed using static models. A full evaluation requires modeling of the effects to tariffs on savings and investment. Similarly with measures of the optimal tariff. James (1981) has calculated the tariff that maximizes income. This is, however, a calculation holding the capital stock constant. An alternative would be to calculate the tariff that maximizes growth, using a model that endogenizes the capital stock. If we were truly serious about measuring the contribution of the tariff to U.S. development, we would need to model the economy with and without tariffs for the entire nineteenth-century. This would be no mean feat. The results of such a model would also help us to understand better the sources of comparative advantage in the U.S. economy, and would offer another perspective on the labor scarcity debate: was the United States capital abundant and was labor scarce relative to Great Britain, and to what extent was this a function of the tariff?

In the case of the United Kingdom, there has been debate over the contribution of the General Tariff of 1932 to recovery from the Great Depression. Capie (1978) has used effective protection rates to measure the resource reallocating effects of import duties. It has become generally recognized, however, that the effects of factor substitution in production and of commodity substitution in consumption, particularly in a world with nontraded goods, are likely to make effective protection rates a bad predictor of the sectoral effects of a tariff (Taylor and Black, 1974). A GE treatment would be much more profitable. Setting up such a model is, however, complicated by the flotation of sterling after 1931. It is therefore necessary to incorporate a model subsystem of the exchange rate. As we have noted in our discussion of external closing rules, however, the exchange rate regime is not among the most developed parts of GE analysis. Krueger and Porter (1984) suggest the integration of the asset pricing model of exchange rate determination. In this model, tariffs under floating exchange rates may increase GNP, at least in the short run (Eichengreen 1981). If we could replicate this in a GE model of the interwar economy, this would be a significant result. Possible improvements in the specification of the financial sector in GE models which would make this a feasible exercise have been suggested by Feltenstein (1984).

The problem of exchange rate determination is less pressing in a fixed rate world. An issue that would repay investigation in a GE framework is the calculation of the effects of the overvaluation of sterling in the stagnating British economy of the 1920s. This would be particularly rewarding in helping to understand the issue of the rise of the new industries in this period. To what extent was the rise of such sectors as pharmaceuticals, light engineering, vehicles, and electrical goods the result of the pound sterling being overvalued by some 10 percent of its equilibrium exchange rate? By reducing the price of imports and creating difficulties for traditional export industries, did overvaluation redistribute resources toward a phalanx of consumer goods industries (Jones 1985; Thomas 1985b)?

Still thinking about tariffs, much of the contemporary use of multisectoral GE models in international trade has been directed to the question of the gains from trade liberalization. The links between free trade, reciprocity, and growth are clearly ripe for historical investigation as well—the size and distribution of gains from trade from the establishment of the Zollverein in 1834 being one such example. Yet integration and the gains from trade are not just the province of trade liberalization policies and the establishment of custom unions: there is also the question of political integration. The impact of the unification of Italy in 1861 on the overall economy and on the fortunes of the individual nation-states that came together in union could be examined in the context of the multiregional GE model. Similarly, the issue of whether there were any further gains in welfare from political consolidation of the German confederation, some forty years after the establishment of the Zollverein, is amenable to GE techniques. Similar studies of the Augsleich of 1867 on the economic progress of Austria and Hungary; of the political unification of Castile and Aragon in the sixteenth-century; of Australian federation in 1901, could be conceived. The converse is also true: the collapse of the Austro-Hungarian empire in 1918 and its effect on the successor states; the separation of Ireland from the rule of Westminster (with a new tariff code and system of subsidies to foreign capital inflows to replace cross-subsidization within the British system of public finance); the partition of Pakistan and India in the break up of the Jewel of the Crown, all are possible candidates for GE treatment.

Taxes

Public finance issues have dominated applied GE analysis in the United States. The first applications of fixed-point theorems to numerical economic modeling measured the incidence of corporate taxation in the United States (Harberger 1962, 1966; Shoven and Whalley 1972; Fullerton, Shoven, and Whalley 1978). Many of the most sophisticated developments in the field have arisen in treatment of tax issues. The use of GE models to tackle public finance questions in historical perspective has been distinctly limited. Outside of tariffs (analyzed under "Trade" above), the sole application to a historical question that I am aware of is my own work on the impact of the welfare reforms undertaken by the Liberal administration in England in 1906–1910 on the pattern of income distribution (Thomas 1983a). It would be possible to undertake analyses of the effects of the 16th amendment and the introduction of income taxation on United States income distribution, or a reprise of the classic Barna study of the *Redistribution of Incomes* (1945) on the effects of the British system of taxation. Both are primarily distributional questions and the general points raised under "Income Distribution" below extend to these exercises.

Industrial Organization

In the standard economic history texts of interwar Britain, it is claimed that the extent of rationalization of production in response to excess capacity in such staple industries as cotton, shipbuilding, and iron and steel was suboptimal. By rationalization, it is meant that there was an excess supply of the products of these industries at the ruling price, the result, it is argued, of the anarchical nature of atomistic competition in an uncertain world. Implicit in this criticism of the industrial organization of the period is a counterfactual whereby a single multiplant monopolist organizes production. A possible GE application would be to test the validity of this argument.

In the work of Chandler (1977) and others on the rise of the corporate economy in the late nineteenth-century United States economy, little attention has been given to the impact of the structure of tariffs on the size distribution and profitability of firms. Chandler has argued that the developments of large-scale corporations were entirely independent of the shape and level of the tariff. Tariffs would, ceteris paribus, be expected to reduce the concentration of industry by shoring up small, inefficient firms. The recent work of Harris (1984) on integrating the stylized facts of the industrial organization literature with the traditionally atomistically competitive environment of the GE model would be particularly interesting in an analysis of this question.

Income Distribution

Two areas of work on income distribution have claimed the attention of GE modelers: the short-run incidence of taxation and its effects on welfare, and the long-run pattern of changes in distribution and its explanation. Such little work as has been undertaken on the former is summarized under "Trade" and "Taxes" above. The latter has been the focus of two large-scale GE exercises undertaken by Williamson (1980, 1985).

GE models analyze income distribution from the production function approach rather than the human capital approach favored by most analysts of income distribution. The production function approach posits that changes in inequality, over time or in response to particular policy program, can be simulated by changes in the relative price of factors. GE models concentrate on factorial income distribution, and move to analysis the inequality of personal (or household) incomes by applying the factor prices to the known (and fixed) assets of individuals and families in order to generate an estimate of their income. Since households own a portfolio of assets (labor skills, capital, land, etc.), a shift in relative factor prices will change the level and distribution of incomes. This seems a reasonable (if mechanical) way to characterize short-run changes in inequality, but it is hazardous in the longer term, when factor price changes are likely to alter the supply of factors.

In Williamson's work, the wage ratio of unskilled and skilled labor serves as the index of inequality. This is simulated and analyzed for nineteenth-century Britain and the United States. How well a simple wage ratio works as a surrogate for changes in the entire distribution of incomes may be open to question. More significant, however, is the lack of any supply-side explanation in Williamson's work, which asumes that the growth in all factors of production, including skills, can be taken as exogenous and in no way a response to changes in relative prices. Human capital theory alerts us to the responsiveness of investment in skills to the reward structure implicit in the factor price ratios. We need supply as well as demand to understand trends in inequality. Once again, long-run simulations are dynamic exercises that require endogenous treatment of savings and investment.

Relative Prices

One of the major unsolved issues in the economic history of interwar Britain is the origins of unemployment. Recently, there has been a renaissance of the argument that the real wage was too high. The claim, to be more precise, is that the real wage in certain sectors was too high. Beenstock, Capie and Griffiths (1984) posit that the real wage in manufacturing was above equilibrium, leading to an excess supply of labor and a reduction in employment demand. An interesting general equilibrium exercise would be to ask, how low would the real wage have needed to be to clear the labor market using the demand and supply elasticities implicit or explicit in the neoclassical explanation of unemployment? What was the structure of market clearing wages across sectors? This issue could be generalized to other economies. The recent additions to the literature on the effects of rigid wages would be very helpful in this area (Nguyen, 1985).[29] The major difficulty, however, is with the poor integration of macroeconomic mechanisms with the microoriented world of Walrasian CGE modelling. The macro theorist looking at the interwar period is likely to consider such factors as the real balance effect, the role of expectations (inflationary and business), and uncertainty. It is hard to see how, with current GE models, these factors could be embedded in a micro-based framework of interwar Britain. Experimentation continues with developing macro overlays that are consistent with the Walrasian underpinnings of GE analysis (Feltenstein 1984; Slemrod 1983; Robinson and Tyson 1984), and progress can be expected along these lines.

VI

A puzzling issue is why such little work has been done with GE models by economic historians? It is scarcely the case that there is a restricted number of issues that would repay investigation in this form: in one sense, all historical questions are GE in scope. The list of possible applications above makes no claims to be a complete agenda of historical questions that would repay investigation using GE techniques. In conjunction with the suggestions made by James (1984), these do, however, suggest a wealth of directions to which the GE modeler could turn in his quest for a better understanding of the past. It must be said that establishing an agenda for future research is easier than undertaking any of the suggested exercises. But the scope and the potential is there.

Given the wealth of issues ripe for GE analysis, why has there been such a restricted market for GE techniques in historical research? We can distinguish four major constraints on the development of GE modeling in economic history: theoretical, empirical, computational, and methodological. GE modeling is not a simple or straightforward task; it requires a good deal of data grubbing, collection, and reconciliation; it requires a sound understanding of the theoretical underpinnings of equilibrium analysis; and an aptitude and desire to cut away at the "extraneous" elements of the historical reality to arrive at a workable and parsimonious version of the model to put into operation. Finally, there is a minimum level of computational competence required to put the grand schemes of GE analysis into operation.

The requirements of computational competence are rapidly declining as new and simpler algorithms are developed, and as the suitability of linearized versions of equilibrium algebra increases. Problems of data availability will doubtless be solved given the ingenuity of new economic historians in this direction, while the theoretical difficulties of designing GE models will decline with learning by doing. A more important reason for the restricted market for GE models may lie in the perceived quality of their performance up to date, and the questioning of the historical appropriateness of the methodology as a whole and of many of the assumptions made in setting up these models. Economic history is a fragile balance of economics and history and modeling the past using the methods and perspectives of the present is not always an appealing construct for the historian.

Nevertheless, the increased sophistication of GE models and techniques applied to contemporary economies will benefit economic history in the longer term. Economic historians learn by the mistakes (and successes) made in the parent disciplines. It should be obvious from this chapter that great strides have been made in making GE models more pertinent to the real world and more intelligible to consumers of the product. With these developments, and given the evident importance of general equilibrium factors in explaining growth and development in the past, GE models are likely to increase in quality, sophistication and influence in the future.

Notes

1. The exceptions to this general statement include Williamson's (1985) study of inequality in nineteenth-century Britain; Siriwardana (1985) on the Australian colony of Victoria in the 1880s; Karlström (1985) on Swedish industrialization; and James' and Skinner's (1985) analysis of the labor scarcity debate using a GE approach.

2. The taxonomy is from Challen and Hagger (1983). Keynes refers to the theoretical impetus to the model, Klein to the econometrician who first developed empirical analysis of this type. Historical examples of this form of modeling include Thomas (1976, 1981) for the United Kingdom; Klein (1950) and Norman (1969) for the United States; and Valentine (1985) for Australia.

3. With respect to expenditures, for example, distinctions are typically made between private and public agents, and—among private expenditures—between consumption and investment.

4. This statement ignores the prior claims of Quesnay's Tableau Economique. Quesnay's approach was neglected until Leontief rediscovered the approach (1941, p. 9). One other precursor of input-output methods was Colquhoun (1815, pp. 66, 89–96), whose social tables included a valuation of inputs from agriculture to industry and domestic consumption. For an interpretation of Quesnay in the framework of Leontief and Social Accounting Matrices respectively, see Phillips 1955 and Barna 1975.

5. McCloskey has employed the same perspective in his analysis of Kennedy's recent work on structural change in the British economy at the close of the nineteenth-century. The McCloskey critique, however, suggests refinement rather than abandonment of the input-output method. The original application of input-output methods to development planning was to calculate the consistency of particular final demand projections with known resource endowments. This is precisely what McCloskey asks of Meyer and Kennedy (see Kennedy 1982 and McCloskey's comments thereon).

6. It is not correct to say that prices are not a part of the model. However, prices fit into the Leontief structure as an output not as an input: prices are set by cost-plus rules rather than by response to excess demands in input, factor, and output markets. Once factor prices are known it is possible to generate goods prices using matrix inversion techniques. This cost-plus method has produced satisfactory medium-term forecasts of prices (see Watanabe and Shishido 1970; Mathur 1977; and Haig and Wood 1976).

7. Equation 4.3' suggests that incremental input-output coefficients may be an alternative to the imposition of constant average a_{ij}. Their use would perhaps make the results of input-output calculations more acceptable, although it is not clear where most historians would find the data to estimate them.

8. This point is distinct from the critique that input-output methods are essentially static, in the sense that they do not embody investment behavior, treating the vector of demands for capital goods as being as exogenous as all other final demands. I do not propose to deal with dynamic input-output methods. For a brief review, the reader is referred to Taylor (1975, pp. 50–59).

9. Available methods for finessing the burden of data are discussed in section IV. The versatility of the SAM is addressed in Thomas (1985a).

10. Williamson (1979, 1985), although concerned with long-run issues of growth and development, maintains the specific factor assumption in his modeling exercises.

11. In our case, the net effect is to lower service output.

12. I do not discuss optimizing models in this chapter since their usefulness to historians is distinctly limited. A very helpful discussion of linear programming in static and dynamic forms is given by Taylor (1975, pp. 59–95).

13. The FPRR is only viable in models with full factor mobility. Another possible means of making the search for Walrasian equilibrium more efficient is to exploit information about the derivatives of the excess demand functions. This use of a "Jacobian algorithm" is suggested and discussed by Ginsburgh and Waelbroeck (1981, pp. 107–143).

14. These methods require an understanding of the mechanics of each application. Dervis et al. suggest that the *tâtonnement* algorithm is likely to become "finicky and/or inefficient" in cases where there are significant interactions between markets (1982, p. 492). In the spirit of some comments in section IV below, this could be considered a good thing if it makes the researcher more thoughtful about the properties of the model in use.

15. Log-linear methods are also used in identity planning models. These too are based on the circular flow but from the macro perspective of the national income identity. They are essentially macro models expressed in continuous time. (See Taylor, et al. 1980.)

16. The following is based largely on Jones 1965.

17. Neary (1978) has generalized the argument for sector-specific capital to long-run as well as short-run problems.

18. Although much of the exploratory work of GE models in historical setting took place in an American context it is not the case that examples are limited to United States case studies. The work of Hueckel (1973), and later Williamson (1984), on the effects of the Revolutionary and Napoleonic Wars on British economic growth; Williamson (1985) on the source of inequality in Britain, following his work with Lindert (1980) on the United States case; the structure of the Atlantic slave trade (Darity, 1982); Kelley and Williamson's (1974) model of Japanese development in the Meiji period; O'Grada and Neary's (1985) work in progress on Eire in the 1930s: these are all testimony to the geographical range of GE applications in economic history. The list also serves to underline the almost complete monoploy of GE modeling by Anglo-Saxon scholars, and by Jeffrey Williamson in particular.

19. The judgment of Taylor and Cardoso is that, "three-year forecasts of variables were. . . quite close to level solutions of the full model. Accuracy seemed to deteriorate fairly rapidly for periods longer than three years" (Taylor, Bacha, Cardoso, and Lysy 1980, p. 53, *n.* p. 4).

20. For a recent empirical treatment of the Johnson-Gorman analysis of optimal tariffs and retaliation see Whalley 1985, pp. 221–249.

21. The term "closure" has several meanings in GE analysis. The most basic meaning is that of a model fulfilling Walras' Law, such that there is sufficient information to provide a solution. Closure may also refer to the process of soultion itself.

22. They also assist in removing computer errors from larger models.

23. At a more practical level, we should note the significant contributions of Harris (e.g., 1984) in integrating scale economies in a CGE framework.

24. The GE simulation of Anglo-American comparisons in the 1850s by James and Skinner (1985), for example, generated capital-labor ratio estimates for British unskilled and skilled manufacturing. These data were previously unknown.

25. Van der Ploeg (1982) has extended the adjustment algorithm to incorporate adjustment of a sequence of observations with autocorrelated, systematic, trend and cyclic components in the residual errors. This would be of particular value in generating consistent

long-series estimates of national income. This, of course, is the context within which techniques for balancing accounts was first developed. The pioneering work of Stone, Meade, and Champernowne (1942) was organized to clear up the usual difficulty of inconsistency between national income measures calculated from the income, expenditure, and product sides. Such discrepancies have long since plagued those developing long-series estimates of GDP. See, for example, Feinstein (1972).

26. Model simulations are, for example, not particularly sensitive to changes in input-output coefficients. The choice of the elasticity of substitution is likely to be much more pivotal in establishing a model's results.

27. Between 25 and 30 percent of total world trade in primary products was directed toward British ports between 1876 and 1900 (Hilgerdt 1945).

28. James and Skinner also assume that transport costs and tariffs meant that the United States was facing a downward-sloping world supply curve. See also James' (1981) calculation of the optimal tariff for the United States in 1859.

29. As with an analysis of the general equilibrium effects of trade union activity. (See Johnson and Mieszkowski 1970).

References

Adelman, I., and S. Robinson. 1978. *Income Distribution Policies in Developing Countries*. Standford: Standford University Press.

Alauze, Chris M. 1977. Estimates of the elasticity of substitution between imported and domestically produced goods classified at the input-output level of aggregation. IMPACT Project Working Paper 0–13. Canberra: Industries Assistance Commission.

Armington, Paul S. 1969. A theory of demand for products distinguished by place of production. *Intenational Monetary Fund Staff Papers* 16:159–76.

Arrow, Kenneth J., and Gerard Debreu. 1954. Existence of an equilibrium for a competitive economy. *Econometrica* 22:265–290.

Arrow, Kenneth J., and Frank Hahn. 1971. *General Competitive Analysis*. San Francisco: Holden-Day.

Auerbach, Alan J., and Laurence J. Kotlikoff. 1983. National savings, economic welfare and the structure of taxation. In Martin Feldstein (ed.), *Behavioral Simulation Methods in Tax Policy Analysis*. Chicago: University of Chicago Press.

Bacharach, Michael. 1971. *Bi-proportional Matrices and Input-Output Change*. Cambridge: Cambridge University Press.

Barna, T. 1945. *Redistribution of Income through Public Finance in 1937*. Oxford: Oxford University Press.

Barna, T. 1952. The interdependence of the British economy. *Journal of the Royal Statistical Society* ser. A 115:29–77.

Barna, T. 1975. Quesnay's *Tableau* in modern guise. *Economic Journal* 85: 485–496

Barten, Anton P. 1977. The systems of consumer demand functions approach: A review. *Econometrica* 45:23–51.

Bator, F.M. 1957. The simple anlaytics of welfare maximization. *American Economic Review* 47:22–59.

Beenstock, M., F. Capie, and B. Griffiths. 1984. Economic recovery in the United Kingdom in the 1930s. In *The United Kingdom Economic Recovery in the 1930s*. Panel Paper 23, Bank of England Panel of Academic Consultants.

Berndt, Ernst R. 1976. Reconciling alternative estimates of the elasticity of substitution. *Review of Economics and Statistics* 58:59–68.

Bertram, G.W. 1963. Economic growth in Canadian industry. *Canadian Journal of Economics and Political Science* 29:159–184.

Bertram, G.W. 1973. The relevance of the wheat boom in Canadian economic growth. *Canadian Journal of Economics* 6:545–566.

Boadway, Robin, and John M. Treddenick. 1978. A general equilibrium computation of the effects of the Canadian tariff structure. *Canadian Journal of Economics* 11:424–446.

Borges, Antonio, and Lawrence H. Goulder. 1984. Decomposing the impact of higher energy prices on long-term growth. In H.E. Scarf and J.B. Shoven (eds.), *Applied General Equilibrium Analysis*. New York: Cambridge University Press.

Bovenberg, Lars, and Wouter J. Keller. 1983. Non-linearities in applied general equilibrium models. Unpublished manuscript, Netherlands Central Bureau of Statistics.

Brown, Alan, and Angus Deaton. 1962. Models of consumer behaviour: A survey. *Economic Journal* 79:1145–1236.

Brown, F., and J. Whalley. 1980. General equilibrium evaluations of tariff-cutting proposals in the Tokyo Round and comparisons with more extensive liberalization of world trade. *Economic Journal* 90:836–866.

Byron, R.P. 1978. The estimation of large social accounting matrices. *Journal of the Royal Statistical Society* ser. *A* 141:359–397.

Caddy, Vern. 1976. Empirical estimation of the elasticity of substitution: A review. IMPACT Project Preliminary Working Paper OP-09. Melbourne: Industries Assistance Commission.

Cairncross, A., and Barry J. Eichengreen. 1983. *Sterling in Decline: The Devaluations of 1931, 1949 and 1967*. Oxford: Oxford University Press.

Cambridge, Department of Applied Economics. 1962–1974. *A Programme for Growth*. Cambridge: Chapman and Hall.

Capie, Forest. 1978. The British tariff and industrial protection in the 1930s. *Economic History Review* 31:399–409.

Carrin, G., Jan W. Gunning, and Jean Waelbroeck. 1983. A general equilibrium model for the world economy: Some preliminary results. In B.G. Hickman (ed.), *Global International Economic Models*. Amsterdam: North-Holland.

Carter, Anne P. 1970. *Structural Change in the American Economy*. Cambridge, MA: Harvard University Press.

Caves, R.E. 1965. Vent for Surplus: Models of Trade and Growth. In

R.E. Baldwin (ed.), Trade, *Growth and Balance of Payments*. Amsterdam: North-Holland.
Challen, D.W., and A.J. Hagger, 1983, *Macroeconometric Systems: Construction, Validation and Applications*. London: Macmillan.
Chambers, J.E. and D.F. Gordon. 1966. Primary products and economic growth: An empirical measurement. *Journal of Political Economy* 74:315–332.
Chandler, Jr., A.D. 1977. *The Visible Hand: The Managerial Revolution in American Business*. Cambridge, MA: Belknap Press.
Chenery, Hollis B., et al. 1974. *Redistribution with Growth*. London: Oxford University Press.
Chenery, Hollis B., Shuntaro Shishido, and Tsunehiko Watanabe. 1962. The pattern of Japanese growth, 1914–1954. *Econometrica* 30:98–139.
Clements, Kenneth W. 1980. A general equilibrium econometric model of an open economy. *International Economic Review* 21:469–488.
Colquhoun, Patrick. 1815. *Treatise on the Wealth, Power, and Resources of the British Empire*. London: Joseph Mawman.
Conrad, A.H., and J.R. Meyer 1965. *Studies in Econometric History*. London: Chapman and Hall.
Cook, L.H., and E. Sieper. 1984. Minerals sector growth and structural change. In L.H. Cook and M. G. Porter (eds.), *The Minerals Sector and the Australian Economy*. Sydney: Allen & Unwin.
Cooper, Russell, Keith McLaren, and Alan Powell. 1983. Short-run macroeconomic closure in applied general equilibrium modellings: Experience from ORANI and agenda for further research. In John Piggott and John Whalley (eds.), *New Developments in Applied General Equilibrium Analysis*. New York: Cambridge University Press, 1985.
Corden, W.M. 1984. Booming sector and Dutch disease economics: Survey and consolidation. *Oxford Economic Papers* 36:359–380.
Corden, W.M., and J. Peter Neary. 1982. Booming sector and deindustralization in a small open economy. *Economy Journal* 92:825–848.
Darity, Jr., William A. 1982. A general equilibrium model of the eighteenth-century Atlantic slave trade: A least-likely test for the Caribbean school. In Paul Uselding (ed.), *Research in Economic History* 7:287–326.
David, Paul A. 1975. *Technical Choice, Innovation, and Economic Growth*. Cambridge: Cambridge University Press.
Deardorff, A.V., and R.M. Stern. 1981. A disaggregated model of world production and trade: An estimate of the impact of the Tokyo Round. *Journal of Policy Modeling* 3:127–152.
Debreu, Gerard. 1959. *Theory of Value*. New York: John Wiley.
Dervis, Kemal, Jaime de Melo, and Sherman Robinson. 1981. A general equilibrium analysis of foreign exchange shortages in a developing economy. *Economic Journal* 91:891–906.
Dervis, Kemal, Jaime de Melo, and Sherman Robinson. 1982. *General Equilibrium Models for Development Policy*. New York: Cambridge University Press.

Dixon, Peter B., Brian R. Parmenter, and Alan. A. Powell. 1984. The role of miniatures in computable general equilibrium modelling. *Economic Modelling* 1:421–428.

Dixon, Peter B., Brian R. Parmenter, and Russell J. Rimmer. 1984. Extending the ORANI model of the Australian economy: Adding foreign investment to a miniature version. In Herbert E. Scarf and John B. Shoven (eds.), *Applied General Equilibrium Analysis*. New York: Cambridge University Press.

Dixon, Peter, B.R. Parmenter, John Sutton, and D.P. Vincent. 1982. *ORANI: A multisectoral model of the Australian economy*. Amsterdam: North-Holland.

Dorfman, Robert, Paul A. Samuelson, and Robert Solow. 1958. *Linear Programming and Economic Analysis*. New York: McGraw-Hill.

Edelstein, Michael. 1982. *Overseas Investment in the Age of High Imperialism*. New York: Columbia University Press.

Eichengreen, Barry J. 1981. A dynamic model of tariffs, output and employment under flexible exchange rates. *Journal of International Economics* 11:341–360.

Feinstein, C.H. 1972. *National Income, Expenditure and Output of the United Kingdom, 1855–1965*. Cambridge: Cambridge University Press.

Feldstein, Martin, and Daniel R. Feenberg. 1983 Alternative tax rules and personal saving incentives: Microeconomic data and behavioral simulations. In Martin Feldstein, (ed.), *Behavioral Simulation Methods in Tax Policy Analysis*. Chicago: University of Chicago Press.

Feltenstein, Andrew. 1980. A general equilibrium approach to the analysis of trade restrictions, with an application to Argentina. *International Monetary Fund staff Papers* 27:749–784.

Feltenstein, Andrew. 1984. Money and bonds in a disaggregated open economy. In Herbert E. Scarf and John B. Shoven (eds.), *Applied General Equilibrium Analysis*. New York: Cambridge University Press.

Fishers, Franklin M. 1976. The stability of general equilibrium: Results and problems. In Michael Artis and A.R. Nobay (eds.), *Essays in Economic Analysis*. New York: Cambridge University Press.

Fisher, Franklin M., and Peter Temin. 1970. Regional specialization and the supply of wheat in the United States, 1867–1914. *Review of Economics and Statistics* 52:134–149.

Fogel, Robert W. 1964. *Railroads and American Economic Growth*. Baltimore: Johns Hopkins University Press.

Forsyth, Peter J., and Stephen J. Nicholas. 1983. The decline of Spanish industry and the Price Revolution: A neoclassical analysis. *Journal of European Economic History* 12:601–611.

Frankel, Jeffrey. 1982. The 1807–1809 embargo against Great Britain. *Journal of Economic History* 42:291–308.

Frisch, Ragnar. 1959. A complete scheme for computing all direct and cross price elasticities in a model with many sectors. *Econometrica* 27:117–196.

Fullerton, Don. 1983. Transition losses of partially mobile industry-specific capital. *Quarterly Journal of Economics* 98:107–125.

Fullerton, Don, and Roger H. Gordon. 1983. A reexamination of tax distortions in general equilibrium models. In Martin Feldstein (ed.), *Behavioral Simulation Methods in Tax Policy Analysis*, Chicago: University of Chicago Press.

Fullerton, Don, Yolanda K. Henderson, John B. Shoven. 1984. A comparison of methodologies in general equilibrium models of taxation. In Herbert E. Scarf and John B. Shoven (eds.), *Applied General Equilibrium Analysis*. New York: Cambridge University Press.

Fullerton, Don, A. Thomas King, John B. Shoven, and John Whalley. 1981. Corporate tax integration in the United States: A general equilibrium approach. *American Economic Review* 71:677–691.

Fullerton, Don, John B. Shoven, and John Whalley. 1978. General equilibrium analysis of U.S. taxation policy. In *1978 Compendium of Tax Research*, Office of Tax Analysis, U.S. Treasury Department, Washington, DC: U.S. Government Printing Office. Pp. 23–55.

Ginsburgh, Victor, and Sherman Robinson. 1984. Equilibrium and prices in multisector models. In Moshe Syrquin, Lance Taylor, and Larry E. Westphal. (eds.), *Economic Structure and Performance: Essays in Honor of Hollis B. Chenery*, Orlando, FL: Academic Press.

Ginsburgh, Victor, and Jean Waelbroeck. 1981. *Activity Analysis and General Equilibrium Modelling*. Amsterdam: North-Holland.

Ginsburgh, Victor, and Jean Waelbroeck. 1984. Planning models and general equilibrium activity analysis. In Herbert E. Scarf and John B. Shoven (eds.), *Applied General Equilibrium Analysis*. New York: Cambridge University Press.

Gorman, W.M. 1957. Tariffs, retaliation, and elasticity of demand for imports. *Review of Economic Studies* 25:137–162.

Griliches, Zvi. 1969. Capital-skill complementarity. *Review of Economics and Statistics* 51:465–468.

Griliches, Zvi, and V. Ringstad. 1971. *Economies of Scale and the Form of the Production Function*. Amsterdam: North-Holland.

Habakkuk, H.J. 1962. *American and British Technology in the Nineteenth-Century*. Cambridge: Cambridge University Press.

Haig, B.D., and M.P. Wood. 1976. A dynamic model for analysing price changes. In Karen R. Polenske and Jiri V. Skolka (eds.), *Advances in Input-Output Analysis*. Cambridge, MA: Ballinger.

Haines, Michael. 1979. Industrial work and the family life cycle, 1889–1890. In Paul Uselding (ed.), *Research in Economic History* 4:289–356.

Harberger, Arnold C. 1962. The incidence of the corporation income tax. *Journal of Political Economy* 70:215–240.

Harberger, Arnold C. 1966. Efficiency effects of taxes on income from capital. In M. Krzyzaniak (ed.), *Effects of Corporation Income Tax*. Detroit: Wayne State University Press.

Harley, C.K. 1974. Skilled labor and the choice of techniques in Edwardian industry. *Explorations in Economic History* 11:392–414.

Harris, Richard. 1984. Applied general equilibrium analysis of small open economies with scale economies and imperfect competition. *American Economic Review* 74:1016–1032.

Harrison, Glenn W., and Larry J. Kimbell. 1983. How robust is numerical general equilibrium analysis? London, Ont.: University of Western Ontario.

Hawke, G.R. 1975. The United States tariff and industrial protection in the late nineteenth-century. *Economic History Review* 28:84–99.

Hilgerdt, Folke. 1945. *Industrialization and Foreign Trade*. Geneva: League of Nations.

Houthakker, Hendrick S. 1957. An international comparison of household expenditure patterns, commemorating the centenary of Engel's Law. *Econometrica* 25:532–551.

Hueckel, Glenn. 1973. War and the British economy, 1793–1815: A general equilibrium analysis. *Explorations in Economic History* 10:365–396.

James, John A. 1978b. The welfare effects of the antebellum tariff: A general equilibrium analysis. *Explorations in Economic History* 15:231–256.

James, John A. 1981. The optimal tariff in the antebellum United States. *American Economic Review* 71:726–734.

James, John A. 1984. The use of general equilibrium analysis in economic history. *Explorations in Economic History* 21:231–253.

James, John A., and Jonathan S. Skinner. 1985. The resolution of the labor scarcity paradox. *Journal of Economic History* 45:513–540.

Johansen, Leif. 1960. *A Multi-Sectoral Study of Economic Growth*. Amsterdam: North-Holland. (2nd edition, 1975.)

Johansen, Leif. 1968. Explorations in long-term projections for the Norwegian economy. *Economics of Planning* 8:70–117.

Johnson, Harry G. 1953. Optimal tariffs and retaliation. *Review of Economic Studies* 21:142–153.

Johnson, Harry G. 1958. *International Trade and Economic Growth: Studies in Pure Theory*. Cambridge: Harvard University Press.

Johnson Harry G., and Peter M. Mieszkowski. 1970. The effects of unionization on the distribution of income: A general equilibrium approach. *Quarterly Journal of Economics* 84:539–561.

Jones, M.E.F. 1985. The regional impact of an overvalued pound in the 1920s. *Economic History Review* 38:393–401.

Jones, Ronald W. 1965. The structure of simple general equilibrium models. *Journal of Political Economy* 73:557–572.

Jones, Ronald W. 1971. A three-factor model in theory, trade, and history. In Jagdish Bhagwati et al. (eds.), *Trade, Balance of Payments, and Growth*. Amsterdam: North-Holland.

Jorgenson, Dale W. 1984. Econometric methods for applied general equilibrium modelling. In Herbert G. Scarf and John B. Shoven (eds.), *Applied General Equilibrium Analysis*. New York: Cambridge University Press.

Jorgenson, Dale W., and Barbara M. Fraumeni. 1981. Relative prices and technical change. In E. Berndt and B. Field (eds.), *Modeling and Measuring Natural Resource Substitution*. Cambridge: M.I.T Press.

Jorgenson, Dale W., and Daniel Slesnick. 1985. General equilibrium analysis of economic policy. In John Piggott and John Whalley, (eds.), *New Developments*

in Applied General Equilibrium Analysis. New York: Cambridge University Press, pp. 293–370.
Kahn, Charles 1981. The use of complicated models as explanations: A reexamination of Williamson's late 19th century America. Unpublished manuscript.
Kärlstrom, Urban. 1985. *Economic Growth and Migration during the Industrialization of Sweden: A General Equilibrium Approach*. Stockholm: Economic Research Institute.
Kehoe, Timothy. 1980. An index theorem for general equilibrium models with production. *Econometrica* 48:1211–1232.
Kehoe, Timothy, and J. Serra–Puche. 1983. A computational general equilibrium model with endogenous unemployment. *Journal of Public Economics* 22:1–26.
Keller, Wouter J. 1980. *Tax Incidence: A General Equilibrium Approach*, North-Holland.
Kelley, Allen C., and Jeffrey G. Williamson. 1974. *Lessons from Japanese Development: An Analytical Economic History*. Chicago: University of Chicago Press.
Kelley, Allen C., and Jeffrey G. Williamson. 1983. A computable general equilibrium model of Third World urbanization and city growth: Preliminary comparative statics. In A. Kelley, W. Sanderson, and J. Williamson (eds.), *Modeling Growing Economies in Equilibrium and Disequilibrium*. Durham, NC: Duke University Press.
Kelley, Allan C., Jeffrey Williamson, and R.J. Cheetham. 1972. *Economic Dualism in Theory and History*. Chicago: Chicago University Press.
Kennedy, William P. 1982. Economic growth and structural change in the United Kingdom, 1870–1914. *Journal of Economic History* 42:105–114.
Kimbell, Larry J., and Glenn W. Harrison. 1983. On the solution of general equilibrium models. Unpublished manuscript, University of Western Ontario.
Kimbell, Larry J., and Glenn W. Harrison. 1984. General equilibrium analysis of regional fiscal incidence. In Herbert E. Scarf and John B. Shoven (eds.), *Applied General Equilibrium Analysis*. New York: Cambridge University Press.
Kindleberger, Charles P. 1964. *Economic Growth in France and Britain 1851–1950*. Cambridge, MA: Harvard University Press.
King, A. Thomas. 1977. Computing general equilibrium prices for spatial economies. *Review of Economics and Statistics* 59:340–350.
Klein, L.R. 1950. *Economic Fluctuations in the United States 1921–1941*. New York: John Wiley.
Klein, L.R. 1953. On the interpretation of Professor Leontief's system. *Review of Economics Studies* 20:131–136.
Kotlikoff, L.J., and S. Pinera. 1977. The Old South's stake in the interregional movement of slaves, 1850–1860. *Journal of Economic History* 37:434–450.
Krueger, A.O., and M.G. Porter. 1984. The asset theory of exchange rate determination and the resources boom. In L.H. Cook and M.G. Porter (eds.), *The Minerals Sector and the Australian Economy*. Sydney: Allen & Unwin.
Leontief, W.W. 1936. Quantitative input-output relations in the economic system of the United States. *Review of Economics and Statistics* 18:105–125.

Leontief, W.W. 1941. *The structure of the American economy 1919–1939*. New York: Oxford University Press.

Lewis, Frank. 1979. Explaining the shift of labor from agriculture to industry in the U.S. *Journal of Economic History* 39:681–698.

Lipton, D., James Poterba, J. Sachs, Lawrence Summers. 1982. Multiple shooting in rational expectations models. *Econometrica* 50:1329–1333.

Maddock, Rodney, and Ian McLean. 1984. Supply side shocks: The case of Australian gold. *Journal of Economic History* 44:1047–1067.

Manne, Alan S. 1983. A three-region model of energy, international trade and economic growth. In B.G. Hickman (ed.), *Global International Economic Models*. Amsterdam: North-Holland.

Mansur, Ahsan, and John Whalley. 1982. A decomposition algorithm for general equilibrium computation. *Econometrica* 50:1547–1557.

Mansur, Ahsan, and John Whalley. 1984. Numerical specification of applied general equilibrium models: Estimation, calibration, and data. In Herbert E. Scarf and John B. Shoven (eds.), *Applied General Equilibrium Analysis*. New York: Cambridge University Press.

Mathur, P.N. 1977. A study of sectoral prices and their movements in the British economy in an input-output framework. In Wassily Leontief (ed.), *Structure, System and Economic Policy*. Cambridge: Cambridge University Press.

McCloskey, Donald N. 1970. Did Victorian Britain fail? *Economic History Review* 23:446–459.

McCloskey, Donald N. 1980. Magnanimous Albion: Free trade and British national income, 1841–1881. *Explorations in Economic History* 17:303–320.

McCloskey, Donald N. 1981. *Enterprise and Trade in Victorian Britain: Essays in Historical Economics*. London: Allen & Unwin.

McKenzie, Lionel W. 1959. On the existence of general equilibrium for a competitive market. *Econometrica* 27:54–71.

Meade, James. 1955. *The Theory of International Economic Policy*. London: Oxford University Press.

Melo, Jaime de. 1978. Estimating the costs of protection: A general equilibrium approach. *Quarterly Journal of Economics* 92:209–226.

Melo, Jaime de. 1980. Tariffs and resource allocation in partial and general equilibrium. *Weltwirtschaftliches Archiv* 116:114–130.

Metzler, L. 1949. Tariffs, the terms of trade and the distribution of national incomes. *Journal of Political Economy* 57:1–29.

Meyer, J.R. 1955. An input-output approach to evaluating the influence of exports on British industrial production in the late 19th century. *Explorations in Entrepreneurial History* 8:12–34.

Neary, J.P. 1978. Short-run capital specificity and the pure theory of international trade. *Economic Journal* 88:448–510.

Nguyen, Trien. 1985. General equilibrium with price rigidities. In John Piggott and John Whalley (eds.), *New Developments in Applied General Equilibrium Analysis*. New York: Cambridge University Press.

Norman, M.R. 1969. The Great Depression and what might have been: An econometric model simulation study. Unpublished dissertation, University of Pennsylvania.

O'Brien, Patrick K. 1983. The impact of the Revolutionary and Napoleonic Wars, 1793–1815, on the long run growth of the British economy. Unpublished manuscript.

O'Grada, Cormac, and J.P. Neary. 1985. Protection, economic war and structural change: The 1930s in Ireland. Paper presented to the First World Cliometrics Congress, Evanston, Illinois.

Pagan, Adrian, and John Shannon. 1985. Sensitivity analysis for linearized computable general equilibrium models. In John Piggott and John Whalley (eds.), *New Developments in Applied General Equilibrium Analysis*. New York: Cambridge University Press.

Passell, Peter, and Maria Schmundt. 1971. Pre-Civil War land policy and the growth of manufacturing. *Explorations in Economic History* 9:35–48.

Passell, Peter, and Gavin Wright. 1972. The effects of pre-Civil War territorial expansion on the price of slaves. *Journal of Political Economy* 80:188–202.

Phillips, Almarin. 1955. The tableau economique as a simple Leontief model. *Quarterly Journal of Economics* 69:137–144.

Piggott, John, and John Whalley. 1981. A summary of some findings from a general equilibrium tax model for the United Kingdom. In *Carnegie-Rochester Conference Series on Public Policy* 14. Amsterdam: North-Holland.

Piggott, John R., and John Whalley. 1985. *Applied General Equilibrium Analysis: An Application to U.K. Tax Policy*. New York: Cambridge University Press.

Pope, Clayne. 1972. The impact of the ante bellum tariff on income distribution. *Explorations in Economic History* 9:375–421.

Powell, A.A. 1981. The major streams in economy-wide modeling: Is rapprochement possible? In J. Kmenta and J.B. Ramsey (eds.), *Large-Scale Macro Econometric Models: Theory and Practice*. Amsterdam: North-Holland.

Pyatt G., and Alan Roe. 1977 *Social Accounting for Development Planning*. Cambridge: Cambridge University Press.

Richardson, H.W. 1962. The basis of economic recovery in the Nineteen–thirties: A review and a new interpretation. *Economic History Review* 15: 344–353.

Robinson, Sherman, and Laura D'Andrea Tyson. 1984. Modeling structural adjustment: Micro and macro elements in a general equilibrium framework. In Herbert E. Scarf and John B. Shoven (eds.), *Applied General Equilibrium Analysis*. New York: Cambridge University Press.

Rostas, L. 1948. *Comparative Productivity in British and American Industry*. Cambridge: Cambridge University Press.

Samuelson, Paul A. 1947. *Foundations of Economic Analysis*. Cambridge, MA: Harvard University Press.

Samuelson, Paul A. 1951. Abstract of a theorem concerning substitutability in open Leontief models. In Tjalling Koopmans (ed.), *Activity Analysis in Production and Allocation*. New York: John Wiley.

Samuelson, Paul A. 1971. Ohlin was right. *Swedish Journal of Economics* 73: 365–384.

Scarf, Herbert E. 1967. On the computation of equilibrium prices. In W. Fellner (ed.), *Ten Essays in Honor of Irving Fisher*. New York: John Wiley.

Scarf, Herbert E. 1969. An example of an algorithm for calculating equilibrium prices. *American Economic Review* 59:669–677.

Scarf, Herbert E. 1981. The computation of equilibrium prices: An exposition. In K.J. Arrow and M.D. Intrilligator (eds.), *The Handbook of Mathematical Economics*, vol. 2. New York: North-Holland.

Scarf, Herbert E. 1983. Fixed-point theorems and economic analysis. *American Scientist* 71:289–296.

Scarf, Herbert E. 1984. The computation of equilibrium prices. In Herbert E. Scarf and John B. Shoven (eds.), *Applied General Equilibrium Analysis*. New York: Cambridge University Press.

Scarf, Herbert E., with collaboration of Terje Hansen. 1973. *The Computation of Economic Equilibria*. New Haven, CT: Yale University Press.

Scarf, Herbert E., and John B. Shoven, eds. 1984. *Applied General Equilibrium Analysis*. New York: Cambridge University Press.

Sen, Armartya K. 1965. The money rate of interest in the pure theory of growth. In F.H. Hahn and F.P.R. Brechling (eds.), *The Theory of Interest Rates*. London: St. Martin's Press.

Shoven, John B., and John Whalley. 1972. A general equilibrium calculation of the effects of differential taxation of income from capital in the U.S. *Journal of Public Economics* 1:281–321.

Shoven, John B., and John Whalley. 1973. General equilibrium with taxes: A computation procedure and an existence proof. *Review of Economic Studies* 40:475–490.

Shoven, John B., and John Whalley. 1974. On the computation of competitive equilibrium in international markets with tariffs. *Journal of International Economics* 4:341–354.

Shoven, John B., and John Whalley. 1984. Applied general equilibrium models of taxation and international trade: Introduction and survey. *Journal of Economic Literature* 22:1007–1051.

Siriwardana, A.M. 1985. A multisectoral general equilibrium model of tariff protection in the colony of Victoria in 1880. Unpublished Ph.D. thesis, La Trobe University.

Slemrod, Joel. 1983. A general equilibrium model for taxation with endogenous financial behavior. In Martin Feldstein (ed.), *Behavioral Simulation Methods in Tax Policy Analysis*. Chicago: University of Chicago Press.

Staelin, C.P. 1976. A general equilibrium model of tariffs in a noncompetitive economy. *Journal of International Economics* 6:39–63.

Stern, Robert M., J. Francis, and B. Schumacker. 1976. *Price Elasticities in International Trade: An Annotated Bibliography*. London: Macmillan.

Stone, R. 1954. Linear expenditure systems and demand analysis: An application

to the pattern of British demand. *Economic Journal* 64:511–527.
Stone, R. 1961a. *Input-Output and National Accounts*. Paris: O.E.C.C.
Stone, R. 1961b, Social accounts at the regional level: A survey. In W. Isard and J.H Cumberland (eds.), *Regional Economic Planning, Techniques of Analysis*. Paris: O.E.E.C.
Stone, R. 1968. Input-output projections: Consistent prices and quantity structures. *L'Industria* 2:212–224.
Stone, R. 1970. *Mathematical Models of the Economy and Other Essays*. London: Chapman and Hall.
Stone, R. 1977. The development of economic data systems. In G. Pyatt et al. (eds.), *Social Accounting for Development Planning with Special Reference to Sri Lanka*. Cambridge: Cambridge University Press.
Stone, R., J.E. Meade, and D.G. Champernowne. 1942. The precision of national income estimates. *Review of Economic Studies* 9:111–125.
Taylor, Lance. 1975. Theoretical foundations and technical implications. In Charles R. Blitzer, Peter B. Clark, and Lance Taylor (eds.), *Economy-Wide Models and Development Planning*. Oxford: Oxford University Press for the World Bank.
Taylor, Lance. 1979. *Macro Models for Developing Countries*. New York: McGraw-Hill.
Taylor, Lance, and Frank J. Lysy. 1979. Vanishing income redistributions: Keynesian clues about model surpises in the short run. *Journal of Development Economics* 6:11–29.
Taylor, Lance, and Stephen L. Black. 1974. Practical general equilibrium estimation of resource pulls under trade liberalization. *Journal of International Economics* 4:37–58.
Taylor, Lance, Edmar L. Bacha, Eliana A. Cardoso, and Frank J. Lysy. 1980. *Models of Growth and Distribution for Brazil*. London: Oxford University Press.
Temin, Peter. 1966. Labor scarcity and the problem of American industrial efficiency in the 1850s. *Journal of Economic History* 26:277–298.
Temin, Peter. 1971a. General equilibrium models in economic history. *Journal of Economic History* 31:58–75.
Temin, Peter. 1971b. Labor scarcity in America. *Journal of Interdisciplinary History* 1:251–264.
Thomas, Mark. 1983a. The liberal welfare reforms and the distribution of income, 1906–1910. Paper presented to Cliometrics Conference, Iowa City.
Thomas, Mark. 1983b. Rearmament and economic recovery in the late 1930s. *Economic History Review* 36:552–579.
Thomas, Mark. 1984. An input-output approach to the British economy, 1890–1914. Unpublished Ph.D. thesis, Oxford University.
Thomas, Mark. 1985a. Applying the social accounting matrix to historical problems. *Historical Methods* 18:85–95.
Thomas, Mark. 1985b. Structure and structural change in the British economy, 1900–1950. Manuscript in progress.

Thomas, T.J. 1976. Aspects of U.K. macroeconomic policy during the interwar period: A study in econometric history. Unpublished Ph.D. thesis, Cambridge University.

Thomas, T.J. 1981. Aggregate demand in the United Kingdom 1918–45. In Roderick Floud and Donald McCloskey (eds.), *The Economic History of Britain since 1700: Vol. 2, 1860 to the 1970s*. Cambridge: Cambridge University Press.

Thorbecke, Erik. 1978. The social accounting matrix and consistency-type planning models. Paper presented to the World Bank SAM Conference, Cambridge University.

Todd, Michael J. 1984. Efficient methods of computing economic equilibria. In Herbert E. Scarf and John B. Shoven (eds.), *Applied General Equilibrium Analysis*. New York: Cambridge University Press.

Tyszynski, H. 1951. World trade in manufactured commodities, 1899–1950. *Manchester School* 19:272–304.

Valentine, T.J. 1985. The battle of the plans: A macroeconometric model of the interwar economy. Working Papers in Economic History, Australian National University, Canberra.

Van der Ploeg, F. 1982. Reliability and the adjustment of sequences of large economic accounting matrixes. (with discussion), *Journal of the Royal Statistical Society* Series A 145:169–194.

Vickery, E. 1974. Exports and North American economic growth: "structuralist" and "staple" models in historical perspective. *Canadian Journal of Economics* 7:32–58.

Von Tunzelmann, G.N. 1982. Structural change and leading sectors in British manufacturing, 1907–1968. In C.P. Kindleberger and G. di Tella (eds.), *Economics in the Long View*, vol. III. C. New York: New York University Press.

Watanabe, Tsunehiko. 1961. A test of the constancy of input-output coefficients among countries. *International Economic Review* 2:340–350.

Watanabe, Tsunehiko. 1975. Quantitative foundations and implications of planning processes. In Charles R. Blitzer, Peter B. Clark, and Lance Taylor (eds.), *Economy-Wide Models and Development Planning*. Oxford: Oxford University Press for the World Bank.

Watanabe, Tsunehiko, and Shuntaro Shishido. 1970. Planning applications of the Leontief model in Japan. In Anne Carter and A. Brody (eds.), *Applications of Input-Output Analysis*. Amsterdam: North-Holland.

Watkins, M.H. 1963. A staple theory of economic growth. *Canadian Journal of Economics and Political Science* 29:141–158.

Weisskoff, Richard. 1971. Demand elasticities for a developing economy: An international comparison of consumption patterns. In Hollis B. Chenery (ed.), *Studies in Development Planning*, Cambridge, MA: Harvard University Press.

Weizman, Martin L. 1971. Shiftable versus non-shiftable capital: A synthesis. *Econometrica* 39:511–529.

Whalley, John. 1975. How reliable is partial equilibrium analysis? *Review of Economics and Statistics* 57:299–310.

Whalley, John. 1977. The United Kingdom tax system, 1968–1970: Some fixed point indications of its economic impact. *Econometrica* 45:1837–1858.
Whalley, John. 1985. *Trade Liberalization among Major World Trading Areas: A General Equilibrium Approach*. Cambridge, MA: M.I.T Press.
Whalley, John, and Bernard Yeung. 1984. External sector closing rules in applied general equilibrium models. *Journal of International Economics* 16:123–138.
Whitney, W.G. 1968. *The Structure of the American Economy in the Late Nineteenth Century*. Unpublished Ph.D. thesis, Harvard University.
Williamson, Jeffrey G. 1967. Consumer behavior in the nineteenth century: Carroll D. Wright's Massachusetts workers in 1875. *Explorations in Entrepreneurial History* 4:98–135.
Williamson, Jeffrey G. 1974. *Late Nineteenth-Century American Development*. Cambridge: Cambridge University Press.
Williamson, Jeffrey G. 1979. "Inequality, accumulation and technological imbalance: A growth equity conflict in American history?" *Economic Development and Cultural Change* 27:231–253.
Williamson, Jeffrey G. 1980. Greasing the wheels of sputtering export engines: Midwestern Grains and American growth. *Explorations in Economic History* 17:189–217.
Williamson Jeffrey G. 1984. Why was British growth so slow during the industrial revolution? *Journal Economic History* 44:687–712.
Williamson, Jeffrey G. 1985a. *Did British Capitalism Breed Inequality*? Boston: Allen & Unwin.
Williamson, Jeffrey G., and Peter H. Lindert. 1980. *American Inequality*. New York: Academic Press.
Williamson, Oliver. 1981. The modern corporation: Origins, evolution, attributes. *Journal of Economic Literature* 19:1537–1568.

5 ECONOMIC HISTORY AND HISTORICAL DEMOGRAPHY: PAST, PRESENT, AND FUTURE

Michael R. Haines

A concern with the study of population has a long tradition in economics, beginning with the economic and demographic model proposed by T.R. Malthus in 1798 and 1803 (Peterson 1979: Blaug 1978, pp. 69–79). This was the basis, along with the wages fund doctrine, of classical labor market theory (e.g., Ricardo). More recently, development economists have devoted considerable attention to the problems of economic-demographic interrelations in the modernization process. To quote Simon Kuznets, "We begin with the growth of population, for it is people who produce economic growth and consume its yield; and the increase in population is a distinctive characteristic and condition of modern economic growth" (Kuznets 1966, p. 34). Part of the interest in the study of population arose out of a concern

---

My original intention in writing this essay was to survey the field in a thorough manner. I quickly came to the conclusion that such an ambition was an impossible task, given the very rapid proliferation of research in historical demography in recent years. The compromises that had to be made have meant that the work of a large number of scholars could not be mentioned. To those individuals I offer my apologies in advance. The omissions should never be interpreted as implying lesser worth. It was simply impossible to do everything. Many of the decisions for inclusion or exclusion were arbitrary and, as often as not, had to do with the vagaries of memory. Several individuals, among them George Alter, Kenneth Wachter, Douglas Anderton, and Jeffrey Williamson, provided me with abundant materials upon request. I wish to thank them for their cooperation and Alex Field and Carl Mosk for useful comments.

with present-day developing countries, but part also derived from an interest in understanding the historical experience of developed countries. (See, for example, Easterlin 1967, 1968; T.P. Schultz 1981; United Nations 1973, ch. XIV). Indeed, definitions of modern economic growth now include the demographic transition from high to low levels of fertility and mortality as a necessary and integral component of the modernization process.

Associated with this interest in population has been the growth of the specialized subfield of economic demography. A number of sessions at recent meetings of the Population Association of America have been devoted to this area, including a special day-long seminar prior to the 1985 meetings. The field now has a specific outlet for publication (*Research in Population Economics*); and journals such as *Population and Development Review*, *Demography*, *Population Studies*, *Population*, and *Genus*, as well as more strictly economic journals, such as the *American Economic Review* and the *Journal of Political Economy*, increasingly publish articles in this field. Some of the methods developed in this area are being applied to historical research, the results of which are appearing in economic history and other historical journals (e.g., *Journal of Economic History*, *Economic History Review*, *Explorations in Economic History*, *Journal of European Economic History*, *Social Science History*, *Journal of Social History*, *Journal of Family History*, and *Historical Methods*).

The present essay surveys some aspects of the study of population of particular interest to researchers in economic history. Primary emphasis will be (a) on methodology and sources, and (b) on the substantive study of fertility, mortality, marriage, and economic-demographic interrelations. Secondary emphasis is placed on other topics with important demographic content, such as household and family structure, internal and international migration, and labor force demography. Inevitably some authors and researchers will not be mentioned, and for this I apologize in advance. There is simply too much material. The field of historical demography is an area of rapid growth in the social sciences; and the rate of production of papers, articles, books, and monographs is considerable and apparently growing. The objective here is to provide an up-to-date although noncomprehensive survey of present research and an evaluation of future prospects.

Historical demography is a field that has been well surveyed before, most recently by Henry (1967), Hollingsworth (1969), Dupaquier (1974), and Willigan and Lynch (1982). It has abundant source materials, and indeed it is in part the volume and quality of these data that has attracted economic historians. For the modern era (since, say, 1500 A.D.), these sources would include parish registers (of baptisms, marriages, and burials), tax lists, published censuses and civil registration materials, manuscript originals of censuses and civil vital registration, special surveys, marriage contracts, genealogies, family books, population registers, wills and probate records, records of institutional populations, passenger ship manifests and lists, and military conscription and pension records. There exists a veritable treasure trove of such materials which remain only partially or wholly unexploited. The future of historical demography in economic history lies, in part, in gathering, organizing, and analyzing such data.[1] Examples of some of the uses to which these data sources can be put will be given below.

Methodology and Sources

One reason historical demography has attracted quantitative historians is because of its orientation toward measurement and estimation. A core of demographic techniques has been built up over time, perhaps best summarized in the encyclopedic work *The Methods and Materials of Demography* by Henry Shryock, Jacob Siegal, and associates (U.S. Bureau of the Census, 1971). There have been, however, significant advances since this work was published, particularly in the application of models and indirect techniques of estimation: "One area of demographic analysis for developed countries in which the [indirect] techniques have proved useful is historical demography, where the data cannot always be assumed to be accurate" (United Nations 1983, p. 1).

Methods of estimating more complete demographic information and structures from limited data are of particular importance for research in economic history. Basic demographic structures and events, reflected in birth and death rates, population size and structure, growth rates, the composition and growth of the labor force, marriage patterns and rates, household composition, the magnitude and nature of migration flows, causes of death, urbanization and spatial population distribution, etc., determine the human capital of society both as producers and consumers and also how that human capital reproduces, relocates, and depreciates (Becker 1975; T.W. Schultz 1981). Demographic events are important both as indicators of social and economic change and as integral components of modern economic growth.

Some of the measures used in demography are relatively straightforward, such as crude birth and death rates, rates of natural increase, and even age-specific birth and death rates. Some of the age-specific measures must be summarized, however, if the information is to be readily used.

One technique of summarizing age-specific mortality rates is the life table, discussed in depth below. It takes age-specific death rates (for cross-sections of a population at various ages at a point in time—which generates what is known as a period life table or a synthetic cohort life table—or for an actual cohort of people born in the same period and followed over time—which provides a cohort life table) and converts them into various other measures. These other measures include the expectation of life at any age (i.e., the average number of years of life remaining if that group experienced the age-specific mortality rates embodied in the life table), the probability of surviving between any two ages, and the probability of dying between any two ages. Life tables are quite flexible and can be extended to multiple risks, such as various causes of death, or to nonmortality risks, such as migration and marriage. (These are known as multiple-decrement or increment-decrement life tables.) Age-specific mortality rates may also be summarized by various forms of standardization, or weighting, using either standard population weights (direct standardization) or standard death rate weights (indirect standardization).[2]

Similarly, age-specific fertility rates can be conveniently summarized. One approach is direct or indirect standardization, analogous to that done for death rates. There is also the total fertility rate (the sum of age-specific birth rates), which can be interpreted as the average number of births a woman would have if she survived her whole reproductive life and if she experienced the rates of childbearing given by the age-specific data. (If this were calculated for cross-sectional or period data, then it could be interpreted as applying to a synthetic cohort.) The gross reproduction rate is the same as the total fertility rate, except that it applies to female births only. Finally, the net reproduction rate adjusts the gross reproduction rate for the mortality of mothers and their daughters and may be interpreted as the rate at which a generation of women reproduce themselves.

The importance of measurement techniques and conventions and their interpretation lies in their ability to summarize and convey to the reader and the researcher the magnitudes and dynamics of population change. For example, it has been a matter of debate whether the acceleration of population growth in Europe just prior to, and during the early stages of, the Industrial Revolution was due to rising birthrates or declining death rates or, if some combination of both, in what proportion (McKeown 1976; Habakkuk 1972). If birthrates played a role, was it changes in marital fertility or nuptiality which were influential? If death rates were crucial, which causes of death and which age groups were most affected? The monumental work *The Population History of England, 1541–1871* (1981) by E. A. Wrigley and Roger Schofield was undertaken precisely with such questions in mind. Measurement tools permit us to disentangle (at least in part) the proximate causes of important demographic changes which, in turn, point the way to the study of more fundamental socioeconomic influences, such as food supply, public health, life cycle earnings patterns, urbanization, etc. Economic growth and development are intimately related to population growth and change. Demographic measurement permits an analysis of the latter.

Model Life Tables and Stable Populations.

Among the techniques that have proven very useful in estimating the overall mortality experience of a population, given very limited data, are model life tables. (A summary of current model life table systems may be found in United Nations 1983, pp. 12–21.) First created by the United Nations in the 1950s as a method of estimating mortality for developing countries with limited and defective data (United Nations 1955), there have been several model life table systems created since then. The most well known is that of Ansley Coale and Paul Demeny (1966), which was recently revised (Coale, Demeny, and Vaughan 1983). It is an empirically based, inductively derived system. It is not based on any real theory about the structure of mortality largely because such theory is lacking or has proven inadequate. The one area of demographic theory used in the system is that of stable population analysis (see below), which *has* proven extremely fruitful. The Coale and Demeny system has enjoyed wide popularity in historical work because of ease of application and the fact that it is based partly on the historical experience of presently developed countries. Of the 192 actual life tables used in its construction, 39 came from the period prior to 1900 and 84 from the period 1900–1945. Of the total, 176 came from Europe, North America, Australia, and New Zealand, while only 16 came from other areas (Taiwan, Japan, South Africa, and Israel). One weakness is thus a lack of representation of LDC experience. Also the particular mortality patterns (North, East, South, and the residual West model) may not fit historical mortality experience well. This seems to have been the case for the United States prior to 1900 (Haines 1979a), although splicing of the systems can improve the fit (see, for instance, Wrigley and Schofield 1981, appendix 14). An advantage of the Coale and Demeny models is that once the appropriate regional family has been chosen, only one parameter (e.g., a death rate at some age) is necessary to fit a table. Thus, for example, it is possible to infer death rates at all ages given the death rate at only one age.

Other model life table systems have been constructed by Ledermann (1969), Brass (1963, 1975), and, most recently the United Nations (1982). The Ledermann system has not been as extensively used as the Coale and Demeny model, although it was based on many of the same actual life tables. It is rather flexible, but fitting requires one or two parameters that may not be readily available. The Brass logit model is quite simple in computation and use, but also requires two parameters. It is very flexible in that the shape and level of the mortality schedule may be altered if there is sufficient information to warrant the parameter choices. A further advantage is that an appropriate contemporary "standard" life table can easily be used if a suitable overall historical life table exists. Extensions of the Brass model to three or four parameters have been developed (Zaba 1979), and an extension of the logit system has been proposed to a four-parameter relational system, which can be reduced to a two-parameter model (Ewbank, Gomez de Leon, and Stoto 1983). But, again, the same lack of data that prompts the use of model life tables in the first place may preclude the fitting of more than one or two parameters.

Finally, the latest United Nations (1982) system is based on 36 pairs of life tables (one for each sex) from the recent experience of developing countries. It thus has the advantage of being closer to contemporary LDC mortality patterns. Indeed four such patterns are identified within the system: the Latin American, the Chilean, the South Asian, and the Far Eastern. These patterns may or may not be appropriate to use for particular historical populations. Actual historical information will be necessary, but these tables certainly should be considered. Further, the construction of the tables themselves used a procedure analogous to the Brass logit model, which makes computation of new tables from estimates of one to three parameters (beyond the choice of pattern) relatively simple.

Accompanying model life table systems are model stable populations, based on the original work of Alfred Lotka (Lotka and Sharpe 1911; United Nations 1967, 1983, pp. 21–22). The concept involves the notion that a closed population with constant fertility and mortality schedules will converge to a constant age distribution. This is useful for historical work if conditions are met, if only approximately. For example, if an historical age structure is known and if an appropriate life table can be inferred, then the birthrate can be estimated. In general, for a closed population with a recent history of relatively constant rates, if any two of the three pieces of necessary information (age structure, mortality rates, fertility rates) are known, the other can be estimated (United Nations 1983, ch. VII). Such methods have been applied, for instance, in reconstructing the demographic history of the American black population (Eblen 1974; Meeker

1976). Since the age structure is much more influenced by birthrates than by death rates, quasi-stable population models with constant birthrates and changing death rates have been constructed (Coale 1972, ch. 5). This has perhaps a greater degree of applicability to real historical populations. A weakness of all these procedures is the assumption of a closed population, something unlikely to be true for some historical case studies, particularly urban and other local areas. Although data can be corrected if estimates of net migration are available, this is usually impossible in practice.

A recent outgrowth of stable population analysis is the application of stable population relationships to nonstable populations—as developed by Preston and Coale (1982). One development of this is the estimation of adult mortality levels from data on population by age and sex in successive censuses (Preston and Bennett 1983; Coale 1984; Bennett and Horiuchi 1981). Two papers have appeared that apply to estimation of adult mortality for England and Wales, 1841–1901 (Lentzner 1985), and for Spain, 1769–1797 (Cachinero-Sanchez 1985). These methods show promise and further extensions may be expected (e.g., Coale, John, and Richards 1985), but again require that the population under study be closed to migration, or at least that there be a correction for migration.

Models of Fertility, Marriage, and Infant Mortality

Other models have been implemented to describe female nuptiality and fertility. The nuptiality model of Coale (Coale 1971; Coale and McNeil 1972) characterizes marriage by a cumulative density function with parameters describing the age at which first marriages begin, the ultimate proportion ever married, and a scale factor giving the number of years of nuptiality in the given population that are equal to a one-year "marriage rate" in the standard population (i.e., the "speed" of the marriage process). The standard population is Sweden, 1865–1869. Despite the fact that this model is based on an historical European standard, it has not been much used in historical analysis. This is probably because, for any historical population under study, either marital status by age and sex is known, in which case the Coale nuptiality model may not be needed, or it is not known, in which case it might not be possible to fit the nuptiality model to the population under study. Also, other measures of nuptiality are more popular, such as the singulate mean age of first marriage (Hajnal 1953; 1965), the proportion of women married at age 20–24, the proportion never-married at older ages (e.g., ages 45–54), or the index of proportion married (see below). (Examples of this approach may be seen in Knodel and Maynes 1976; Crafts 1978; M. Anderson 1976; Woods and Hinde 1985; and Teitelbaum 1984, ch. 5.) One area where the model has been applied is in conjunction with the Coale and Trussell (1974, 1978) model of marital fertility in order to give estimates of age-specific overall fertility rates and the total fertility rate (the sum of the age-specific rates). One example of such an application is Warren Sanderson's reestimation of fertility and nuptiality for the United States in the nineteenth century (Sanderson 1979).

The Coale-Trussell fertility model itself has found wider application. It is based on the notion that there is a model pattern of departure from natural fertility (Henry 1961; Leridon 1977; Leridon and Menken 1979) as fertility control is increasingly practiced. Natural fertility is defined as fertility behavior in which the behavioral (as opposed to the biological) probability of moving from one parity (i.e., achieved number of children ever born) to the next parity does not depend upon parity already achieved. The Coale-Trussell model assumes an average pattern of natural fertility (from contemporary and historical data), natural fertility for all women at ages 20–24, and model pattern of deviation from natural fertility at other ages. It generates two parameters: the overall level of natural fertility at ages 20–24 and the degree of departure from natural fertility, interpretable roughly as the degree of fertility control. (For examples of applications, see Mosk 1983, ch. 3; Weir 1983, 1984a; Haines 1979b, chs. 4 and 5, 1980; and Knodel 1979). Although this fertility model is valuable, difficulties in inferring contraceptive behavior from age-specific fertility data arise when spacing as well as stopping behavior occurs early in fertility decline, since these produce a nonstandard pattern of deviation from natural fertility. Also, when nuptiality patterns are quite different from those of the populations underlying the model, marital duration effects may intervene and produce poor parameter estimates if only women's age is used (Page 1977; Mineau and Trussell 1982).

Other models—or standard patterns—of fertility and mortality, now called "biometric," have been proposed and have potential usefulness in historical applications. (For summaries, see Menken 1975; Willigan and Lynch 1982, ch. 18.) Two fertility models have been suggested by William Brass. The first approximates overall age-specific fertility and is in the form of a simple polynomial whose parameters include only level of fertility and location on the age scale (Brass 1975, ch. IV). The second, more flexible, is a relational Gompertz model (so named for the use of a Gompertz double-exponential distribution) which relates any overall age-specific fertility to a standard schedule via two parameters: the first giving the age at which half of total childbearing has occurred,, and the second giving the degree of concentration (or "peakedness") of the schedule (United Nations 1983, pp. 25–26). The latter has potential applications in adjusting or smoothing age-specific birthrates or, as also in the case of the Coale-Trussell model, comparing different distributions. Both are often used in conjunction with the *P*/*F* ratio method, which uses cumulative fertility to adjust age-specific fertility rates (see below and United Nations 1983, ch. II).[3] Other efforts have been directed to modeling age-specific fertility using other analytical expressions (for example, Romaniuk 1973; Mitra and Romaniuk 1973).

Biometric methods have been used in the analysis of infant mortality. Bourgeois-Pichat has developed a technique for determining the relationship between neonatal mortality (i.e., mortality in the first month of life) and postneonatal mortality (i.e., mortality in the next eleven months). This method was tested against historical German data by Knodel and Kintner (1977) and was found to have been affected by variant patterns of breastfeeding. Thus what the method might have diagnosed as underreporting of infant deaths or errors in age statements were actually real differences in age patterns of mortality because of differences in extent and length of breastfeeding. (See also Kintner 1985.) Nonetheless, the method may have potential uses in evaluation of historical data.

The Proximate Determinants of Fertility.

There have been historical applications of the analysis of the "proximate determinants" of fertility behavior. (For a summary, see Bongaarts and Potter 1983.) The approach was early developed by Davis and Blake (1956), Henry (1953, 1957), and Potter (1963), and has been clarified and refined by Bongaarts. These methods are designed to break down the female reproductive period and birth intervals into measurable, distinct, and meaningful components: age at marriage or entrance into a sexual union, age at menopause, duration of gestation, duration of postpartum infecundability, time added by spontaneous intrauterine mortality, and waiting time to conception. Waiting time to conception may be subdivided into effects of contraception, induced abortion, breastfeeding, and biological subfecundity. Such variables mediate between fertility outcomes, on the one hand, and the socioeconomic variables that are hypothesized to influence fertility differentials, fluctuations, levels, and trends, on the other. The chief historical populations studied with this approach have been natural fertility groups in small communities in Europe (England, France, Belgium, Germany) and North America (colonial United States and French Canada). (See Bongaarts and Potter 1983, ch. 2—who used data from Wilson 1980; Leridon 1977; Charbonneau 1979; Knodel 1977b, 1978, 1979, 1983; and other sources.) The application to populations experiencing fertility decline have been confined largely to present-day developing nations (especially those with World Fertility Survey data), but use with historical transition populations is potentially fruitful where the data permit. These would include genealogical populations such as those constructed by Knodel for Germany and for the United States by the Mormon Historical Demography Project (see below).

The Coale Indices

A methodological innovation that is not particularly complex and which has had widespread application in historical demography is the set of Coale indexes: I_f, the index of overall fertility; I_g, the index of marital fertility; I_m and I_m^*, the indexes of proportions married; and I_h, (the index of illegitimate fertility (Coale 1967, 1969). The virtue of these indices for historical work is that they have relatively moderate data requirements: aggregate birth data by legitimacy status and census data by age, sex, and marital status. There is also an intuitively appealing interpretation. For example, I_f gives the ratio of actual births for a given population of women to the births that the same group of women would have experienced if they had had the fertility of married Hutterite women in the United States in the 1920s (the highest fertility group ever observed). I_g measures the same for married women in the given population, and I_h provides an index for unmarried women. The fertility indices (I_f, I_g, I_h) thus furnish a form of indirect standardization with a value of 1.0 being historically close to maximum human reproduction. I_m and I_m^* are different, being ratios of the weighted age distributions of married women in the given population to the weighted age distribution of total women (or the sum of the Hutterite weights in the case of I_m^*) in the given population.[4] These indices have been widely used, most particularly by the European Fertility Project at the Office of Population Research at Princeton University, for which, indeed, the measures were developed (Coale 1969). Thus far, monographs and articles have been produced for Portugal, Italy, Germany, France, Belgium, Britain, Switzerland, and Russia (Livi-Bacci 1971, 1977; Knodel 1974; 1977a; E. Van de Walle 1974, 1978; Lesthaeghe 1977; Teitelbaum 1984; F. Van de Walle 1975, 1980; Coale, Anderson, and Harm 1979). Susan Watkins (1981) has done an analysis of European marriage patterns 1870–1960, using the nuptiality indices, and a volume has been prepared which summarizes a number of the major overall findings (Coale and

Watkins 1986).[5] While the Coale indices are only a form of indirect standardization, the modest data requirements, easy intuitive interpretation, ease of calculation, and current wide utilization will insure that they will be commonly used in the future.

Genealogies, Population Registers, and Other Sources

Genealogies, and methodologically related sources such as population registers, have already been used for Germany, the United States, Belgium, Sweden, China, and Japan (Willigan and Lynch 1982, ch. 5), as well as for special groups such as the British peerage (Hollingsworth 1964) and the Genevan bourgeoisie from the sixteenth to the twentieth centuries (Henry 1956). Such detailed sources, although posing difficulties of selectivity and generality, missing observations, accuracy, and analysis, promise to be a source for considerable future research. For population registers, a pioneer study of the Belgian commune of La Hulpe has been carried out by Etienne van de Walle and his colleagues (E. van de Walle 1976; Watkins and McCarthy 1980; Gutmann and van de Walle 1978; and Watkins and Gutmann 1983). Similar work is being done by George Alter for Verviers, also in Belgium. A number of scholars have begun to exploit population registers from Tokugawa Japan (c1600–1868) (Smith 1977; Hanley 1977; Hanley and Yamamura 1977). A project to exploit the Swedish population registers is also in progress (see, for instance, Agren et al. 1973).

Genealogical sources are now being subjected to relatively extensive exploitation. A notable example is the Mormon Historical Demography Project (Bean, May, and Skolnick 1978; Skolnick, et al. 1979; Bean et al. 1980). A number of papers have been forthcoming, particularly on fertility and nuptiality (Skolnick et al. 1978; Mineau, Bean, and Skolnick 1979; Mineau 1980; Mineau and Trussell 1982; Willigan et al. 1982; Bean, Mineau, and Anderton 1983; Anderton and Bean 1985; see also Kunze 1979). Linkages from the genealogical data to census wealth and probate data may furnish means to study further the demographic and life cycle correlates of wealth holding (Kearl and Pope 1983; Soltow 1975; Jones 1980). Robert Fogel's NBER project on "The Economics of Mortality in North America, 1650–1910" has also generated some use of genealogies for fertility and mortality analysis (Bourne 1986; Fogel 1984). Another extensive use of genealogical-type sources has been the work of John Knodel with German village *Ortsippenbucher* (Knodel 1968, 1977b, 1978, 1979; Knodel and Shorter 1976; Knodel and Kintner 1977). These sources have proven extraordinarily valuable in the investigation of natural fertility. Some particular groups, like the American Quakers (Wells 1971) or the bourgeoisie of Geneva (Henry 1956), have provided genealogical evidence on early fertility decline. An imaginative use of genealogies has been their application to the study of migrant behavior in the United States (Adams and Kasakoff 1980, 1984), although the generality of those may be difficult to establish.

There are, of course, parish registers and other nominal lists of births or baptisms, marriages, and deaths or burials, which have provided a wealth of material to date and promise to furnish much more. Among the most well-known users of parish registers have been the researchers following Louis Henry of INED (Institute Nationale d'Études Démographiques), who have been exploiting French parish registers from the seventeenth to the nineteenth-centuries to study fertility, nuptiality, and mortality. (For convenient summaries, see Dupaquier 1979; D.S. Smith 1977; Leridon 1977; Willigan and Lynch 1982, chs. 3 and 18; Weir 1983; Henry 1972a, 1972b, 1978a, 1978b; and Henry and Houdaille 1973, 1978, 1979.) Similar data have been collected and analyzed for colonial America, much of it for New England but some for the middle colonies and a bit for the southern colonies. A number of the important papers in colonial demography have been reprinted and discussed in Vinovskis 1979.) The French Canadian population of Quebec has also been analyzed using local parish records (Charbonneau 1979; Desjardins, Beauchamp, and Légaré 1977). The Historical Demography Research Project at the University of Montreal is an ambitious attempt to reconstitute that population from local records and extensive computer linkage. The consequence is that we have better information for some areas of seventeenth- and eighteenth-century North America than we do for much of the nineteenth century.

It is important that we attempt to link more purely demographic data with other economic and social information. Additional sources that provide demographic linkages to economic phenomena are special purpose surveys, particularly family budget data. (For an account of these, see Williamson 1967.) Carroll Wright's surveys of Massachusetts workers in 1874 and of American and European workers in 1889–1890 have been used to study fertility and some of the demographic correlates of income, savings, poverty, consumption, and the family life cycle (Modell 1978; Kelley 1972; Haines 1979b, ch. 6, 1979c, 1981, 1985; Lees 1980). There remain some manuscript or published micro sources to be exploited (e.g., the 1917–1918 and the 1934–1936 budget surveys, as well as a number of state surveys in the United States), and published data for other countries (Fishlow 1973; Alter 1984).

Historical mortality research, like other areas of historical demography, often suffers from a lack of age-specific data. One recent development is to exploit insurance and annuity data to construct mortality estimates (Alter 1983a, 1983b; Alter and Riley forthcoming). Since there appears to be a fair amount of such information available, this seems a promising direction, with further implications for appraisal of wealth and behavior towards risk.

One additional data base, which is familiar to me and contains potential for further demographic research, is the archive of the Philadelphia Social History Project. A description of the basic sources, including micro level data from the U.S. censuses of population and manufacturing from 1850–1880, as well as aggregated data from small geographic units (the "grid squares") within Philadelphia County, may be found in Hershberg (1976). Work has been done (and is currently still in progress) on labor force structure and activity, manufacturing and industrial structure, migration, family structure and family economy, poverty, discrimination, mortality, and fertility. (A number of papers appear, or are reprinted in, Hershberg 1981. See also Haines 1980a; Condran and Cheney 1982; Cheney 1984; Condran, 1984.) The data base is currently being archived at the University of Pennsylvania.

"The Population History of England" and Family Reconstitution

A major project has been underway for many years in England at the Cambridge Group for the History of Population and Social Structure, supervised by E. A. Wrigley, Roger Schofield, Peter Laslett, and Richard Wall. Parish registers were instituted in England as early as 1538 (although the quality of many early registers was severely deficient), and the Cambridge Group has aimed at two strategies to utilize these lists of baptisms, burials, and marriages. The first strategy, summarized in the monumental and important volume by Wrigley and Schofield, *The Population History of England, 1541–1871* (1981), attempts to utilize the aggregate numbers of baptisms, marriages, and burials by year to obtain estimates of standard demographic measures.[6] The estimates of aggregate baptisms, marriages and burials were based on a nonrandom sample of 404 parishes (about 4 percent of all parishes). This sample overrepresented larger parishes, and so the 52 smaller parishes had to be given larger weights, decreasing the reliability of the estimates. The data were evaluated in a number of ways for completeness and accuracy. Gaps and assumed defective registration were filled in. The baptisms and burials had then to be converted to births and deaths, confronting, among other things, the problems of nonconformist religious practice and of delayed baptisms increasing the proportion of infant deaths neither registered as a baptism nor a burial. The whole issue of residual underregistration is troublesome and not fully resolved; but the care and thoughtfulness of the research on this is evident.

Once these time series have been constructed, they can be evaluated in themselves for fluctuations and cycles and by measures used only with series of vital events (such as aggregate natural increase, ratio of births to deaths, ratio of births to marriages). The techniques for the evaluation of cycles in economic and demographic data have become quite sophisticated and owe much to the pioneering work of Ronald Lee, who has applied spectral analysis, distributed lag models, and other time series methods to historical data on births, deaths, marriages, prices, and harvests (Lee 1973, 1975, 1977, 1978; Wrigley and Schofield 1981, ch. 9 and appendix 16; Willigan and Lynch 1982, ch. 13). One of the major problems with such series is precisely that they lack population estimates necessary for the denominators for rates. This problem was solved by an ingenious technique known as "aggregative back projection," which grew out of some original work by Ronald Lee (Lee 1974; Wrigley and Schofield 1981, ch. 7 and appendix 15). It involves beginning at a benchmark point (the census of 1871) and backward projecting the population by age and sex, making allowance for estimated net migration, using estimated model life tables, and making certain that the annual deaths are the same as those in the actual population and that each age cohort is accurately projected back to the correct number of births. Aggregative back projection produces estimates not only of total population size, but also of the age structure. It is, however, a process fraught with dangers of cumulated errors, although the constraint of the annual births and deaths is an important check. The assumptions of using the third English life table of 1838–1854, extended above age 50 by Coale and Demeny Model North, and of using nineteenth-century Swedish data for the age schedule of net migration might introduce biases, although the authors go to some lengths to check the sensitivity of the estimates to these and other assumptions. More recently, Ronald Lee (1985) has criticized the back projection technique as suffering from a type of identification problem (i.e., it only predicts one of an infinite number of possible demographic "pasts"). He proposes instead the less ambitious inverse projection technique, which explicitly requires outside information on population size at various dates. Replicating the analysis with inverse instead of back projection, Lee finds that the Wrigley-Schofield results are not materially altered. But he also notes that the Wrigley and Schofield reconstruction cannot provide independent evidence for general levels of population before the mid-eighteenth century. It only can allow us to interpolate between various benchmarks given by external evidence and then help fill in the demographic past with much richer detail. Interestingly, the Wrigley-Schofield figures are indeed similar to some earlier estimates of population size (e.g., Gregory King's 1695 estimate and Rickman's average estimates for 1600–1670 published in the 1841 census), but not with others (e.g., the Compton census of 1676). The back projected age structure differs from the much cited Gregory King numbers for 1695. Overall, however, these results are the best to date, although they are certainly not going to be the last word. Further refinements, some of them based on additional research and modeling by the Cambridge Group itself, are most probable.

The second strategy is presented in a separate paper (Wrigley and Schofield 1983) and involves the use of the family reconstitution technique. Indeed, much of the detailed information in the book on age-specific birth rates, age at marriage, proportions married by age, and age patterns of mortality had to come from this source. Family reconstitution was developed by Louis Henry and his colleagues to use parish register documents (Fleury and Henry 1976; Willigan and Lynch 1982, chs. 3 and 8). Since lists of vital events cannot provide rates without a base population at risk, one method of obtaining the base population is to "reconstitute" families by linking vital events for the same person and linking family members together. In effect, an artificial genealogy is constructed. Using hand and computer linkage and various rules for probable matches, a certain proportion of all families in a community can be recreated over time; and, for them, vital rates may be calculated. A major drawback is that only a part of a community may be reconstituted. Only partial information may be available for some individuals. Marriage records often lack age data, so linkage to baptism or burial records is necessary. Migration causes individuals to be "lost." Many families deemed to be reconstituted still lack some dates or have imputed information. Usually less mobile and more prominent families are likely to be completed, with potential biases in the results. Also, smaller, more rural communities are often chosen because of (supposedly) less geographic mobility. An example of an early finding that was probably unwarranted both for reasons of interpretation and representativeness was Wrigley's supposition (on the basis of the results for the parish of Colyton) that control of fertility within marriage was important in preindustrial England (Wrigley 1966). Nonetheless, it is a powerful way to make use of available data. Wrigley and Schofield (1983) reported results of thirteen such reconstitutions and found that they tended to support the aggregative findings (although there may be some element of circularity here to the extent that the reconstitution findings were used as a basis for the aggregative results). A large number of French communes (forty) have thus been analyzed (see Weir 1983, table 46 and appendix A), as well as several in colonial America (Vinovskis 1979) and much of French Canada (Desjardins, Beauchamp, and Legare 1977).

Family reconstitutions can be very valuable to the study of social and economic history in that the linkages can be made not only to demographic events but also to a number of other sources (e.g., assessment and tax lists; wills and probates; parish account books; court records; military service and pension records), which can be used for more than strictly demographic analysis. An example of this may be found in the work of David Levine and Keith Wrightson (Levine 1977; Wrightson and Levine 1979). Further work in this area may be expected, if only because small local studies are tractable and intellectually satisfying. Synthetic studies are being done, and the possibilities are considerable for the linkage of economic and demographic data. For example, Wrigley, Schofield, and Lee discuss interactions and lags between economic events (price changes, harvest failures) and demographic occurrences (changes in birth, marriage, and death rates). Crisis mortality has received particular attention (Wrigley and Schofield 1981, chs. 8–11; see also, Weir 1984a; Olney 1983; Lindert 1983; *Journal of Interdisciplinary History* 1983). Natural fertility and family limitation have been investigated using such studies (Bongaarts and Potter 1983, ch. 2), as well as the importance of marriage as a means of aggregate population growth regulation (D.S. Smith 1977; Wrigley and Schofield, 1981; Weir, 1984a, 1984b). The stories told at a macro level will certainly need support from micro level-data if at all possible.

Own-Children Methods and Historical Census Data

A methodology that has become popular with the availability of manuscript censuses and similar documents is own-children analysis. Actually, this method covers a whole range of techniques which employ data on children linked to one or both parents, including analysis of census and survey questions on children ever born and children surviving. Most commonly, it applies to fertility analysis which links women to their surviving own-children present in the household and then backward projects the women and children to obtain birthrates in some range of years (usually no more than fifteen) prior to the census or survey (United

Nations 1983, pp. 182–195). It was first developed by Grabill and Cho (Grabill and Cho 1965; Cho, Grabill, and Bogue 1970; Cho 1973). It is superior to simple methods of reverse projection (from aggregate census data) since it provides age-specific birthrate estimates.[7] Hareven and Vinovskis (1975, 1978) applied the method to samples of the 1880 U.S. census for parts of Boston and for five other Massachusetts towns. They used age-standardized martial child-woman ratios, which require no adjustments for child and adult female mortality, for underenumeration, or for children missing from their mothers for reasons other than mortality. These age-adjusted ratios are a measure of net or effective fertility (i.e., surviving children), and they may be calculated for either married women or all women. They are not, however, comparable to many standard fertility measures (age-specific overall or marital fertility rates, total fertility rates, total marital fertility rates, gross and net reproduction rates).

Age-standardized marital child-woman ratios have become relatively popular, given the relative ease of computation, and have been applied to manuscript census data for various areas in the United States (Hareven and Vinovskis 1975, 1978; Haines 1979b, chs. 4 and 6; Zunz 1982; Mason, Weinstein, and Laslett 1985), Canada (Katz, Doucet, and Stern 1982, pp. 335–344), England (Haines 1979b, ch. 5), and France (Tilly 1977). The potential of the method is only realized, however, with calculation of standard demographic measures (age-specific overall and marital fertility rates and measures derived from them). This has been done for the whole United States from the 1900 public use sample (Tolnay, Graham, and Guest 1982), for other areas of the United States (Haines, 1979b, chs. 4 and 6, 1980a), and for England and Wales (Haines 1979b, ch. 5; Woods and Smith 1983). The more refined application requires appropriate adjustments for mortality, underenumeration, and children absent for reasons other than mortality; and these may not always be easy to obtain (see Haines, 1979b, pp. 114–148).[8]

The own-children method holds a great deal of promise, but it has been limited by the difficult chore of obtaining population listings (censuses, surveys, etc.) of adequate quality, making the own-child linkages, and performing the tasks of estimation. As an illustration, the United States census manuscripts prior to 1850 are virtually unusable for this because only heads of household were listed with summary information on household composition. Linkage of women and their children is too uncertain. From 1850 to 1870, the censuses listed each individual separately by name, and it is possible to infer relationships from name, age, sex, and order of enumeration. Only in 1880 did the United States census begin to provide information on marital status and relation to head of household, very useful in making the linkages. Finally, in 1900 and 1910, the United States censuses provided data on children ever born, children surviving, and duration of current marriage (U.S. Bureau of the Census 1979). In contrast, the English censuses gave nominal listings, relationship to head of household, and marital status from 1851 (Wrigley, 1972; Lawton, 1978). The New York State censuses had the same information from 1855. Sampling, linkage, and editing have been made easier and less costly by the availability of microcomputers, but the tasks are still large.[9] Currently, public use samples of American censuses are available for 1900 and 1960–1980. Samples will soon be ready for 1910, 1940, and 1950. It would seem likely that, in the future, demographic public use samples will be done for the censuses of 1850–1880. (The 1890 census was largely destroyed in a fire.) Two samples exist of linked population and agriculture schedules for the rural North and for the rural South in the United States in 1860 (the Bateman-Foust and the Parker-Gallman samples) (Bateman and Foust 1974; Foust 1976). While these samples are very valuable for the study of agricultural productivity and structure (see, for example, Fogel and Engerman 1974, ch. 6, 1977; Wright 1978), they were not initially constructed for demographic analysis. The difficulties in using these samples for demographic research are illustrated by the elaborate procedures for matching used by Easterlin, Alter, and Condran in their efforts to test the land availability—bequest hypothesis for the antebellum United States with the Bateman-Foust data (Easterlin, Alter, and Condran 1978, esp. appendix A; Easterlin 1976). A public use sample has also been done for England and Wales for the census of 1851, and efforts are underway for several of the later censuses at the Cambridge Group for the History of Population and Social Structure.

Future research would be facilitated by more comprehensive census public use samples: for example, for the United States censuses of 1850–1880, 1920, and 1930; for England and Wales, 1861–1911; for Scotland and Ireland, 1851–1911; for Sweden and for other European countries for which manuscripts exist and are available; and for states of the United States (such as New York).[10] Many of these materials have been microfilmed by the Genealogical Society in Salt Lake City, Utah, and are available subject to certain restrictions. (For example, the Registrar General of England and Wales has a 100-year rule for public release of data, as does the government of Belgium, while the U.S. Bureau of the Census has a 72-year rule. Ireland will apparently allow public access with some permission within the 100-year period. Many state and local governments, both in the United States and elsewhere, have varied rules but often require special permission.) There are limits to the general conclusions that can be drawn from local samples, although, given the logistical problems of large-scale sampling, it is easy to see why regional studies are done.

Some censuses contain additional information useful for demographic estimation—information on parity (children ever born), child survival (number of livebirths surviving), and duration of marriage. The 1900 and 1910 censuses of the United States, the 1911 censuses of England and Wales, Scotland, and Ireland, and the 1910 Swedish census contain such information, which is valuable even in published form if it is tabulated appropriately. The 1865 New York State census has data on children ever born, as does the Massachusetts census of 1885. Some of this information is available in the form of microsamples (e.g., the 1900 and—soon—1910 United States censuses), and some potentially could be thus organized (e.g., the 1911 United Kingdom censuses, portions of the 1865 New York census).[11] The quality of such information is sometimes problematic: misstatement of women's ages or marital durations, use of current rather than first marriage duration, omission of children in responses, non-response recorded as zero, etc. (United Nations 1983, pp. 27–29). There are, however, techniques to appraise, analyze, and adjust such data (United Nations 1983, pp. 27–29, appendix II; Ewbank 1982); and, with care, they can prove extremely valuable.

Information on children ever born and children surviving can be used to estimate both fertility and mortality. Perhaps the most common application is in the estimation of childhood mortality via systems of model life tables (Sullivan 1972; Trussell 1975; United Nations 1983, ch. III). These methods use the proportion of children who are dead to groups of women of particular ages or marital durations, whose experience is adjusted for fertility patterns, to find a standard demographic parameter in a model life table system. The parameter is $q(a)$, the proportion of children dying before age a. (Age a varies according to the age or marital duration group of mothers chosen). A variant of these methods is the backward projection of the age structure of surviving own children for some group of women (usually aged 20–34 years or married 0–14 years) to find the correct model life table that just equates total children ever born with the backward projected population (Preston and Palloni 1978). These procedures have been applied to the 1900 United States census, using Coale and Demeny's Model West, as well as to the 1865 New York State census and the 1911 Census of Marriage and Fertility of England and Wales (Preston and Haines 1984; Haines 1977; Preston, Haines, and Pamuk 1981). One variant of the method has been applied to a sample of women aged 55 and over from the 1900 United States census by Smith (D.S. Smith 1983). Another variant uses a ratio of actual to expected child deaths to create a child mortality index (Preston, Haines, and Pamuk 1981; Haines and Preston 1984). It is useful both for tabulation and for multivariate analysis, since it can be calculated at the group and at the individual level. Finally, in addition to establishing mortality levels and differentials, it is possible, using these methods, to estimate time trends for a period of 15–20 years prior to the census (Haines and Preston 1984).

Data on parity may be used to estimate fertility. If it is believed that parity data for younger women are more accurate than registered or survey birth data, then parity data can be used to correct the registration or survey data for level, while assuming that the correct "shape" of the age-specific birth schedule is given by the registration or survey data. If parity is available in two successive censuses or surveys, age-specific fertility estimates also can be made (United Nations 1983, ch. II).

One very imaginative application of historical parity data, the cohort-parity method, has been developed by Paul David and Warren Sanderson and applied to the 1900, 1910, and 1940 United States censuses (David and Sanderson 1986).[12] It was necessary to correct the calculated mean parity for older women for selectivity due to mortality and marital dissolution. This was done by using a group of statistical models for correcting censored distributions, where the censoring is not independent of the attributes to be estimated. This is, in itself, an interesting example of the usefulness of some seemingly arcane methods drawn from other disciplines. Then the cohort-parity analysis was applied to these corrected data to estimate the proportion of the female population which had, or had not, controlled their fertility. It is possible to separate fertility controllers into "active" (i.e., those who actually did restrict family size) and "passive" (i.e., those who would control if it were necessary). One of the unique features of this model is the incorporation of Page's (1977) observation that model marital fertility schedules that incorporate only age, and not marital duration, can produce misleading results. In particular, women marrying late seem to maintain higher age-specific marital fertility rates longer in their reproductive lives, possibly in order to compensate for a late start in childbearing (Mineau and Trussell 1982). To correct for this, David and Sanderson have developed a model distribution of natural fertility by both age and marital duration using the 1911 census of Ireland. Using this method and the censuses of 1900, 1910, and 1940, they are able to estimate the full distribution of completed marital parity, the proportion of American marriage cohorts 1855–1859 to 1915–1919 ever controlling actively during completed reproductive lifetimes, aggregate effectiveness of control (the ratio of active controllers to couples desiring control), and the mean completed parity of controlling and noncontrolling women. This is a very imaginative methodology which makes use of existing data. Interestingly enough, one of the conclusions from analysis extended from this work is that spacing as well as stopping behavior were important in the nineteenth century American fertility transition (David and Sanderson 1984). Although other researchers using similar data have concluded that only stopping was important (Tolnay and Guest 1984), it is significant that recent work with the genealogical data of the Mormon Historical Demography Project has concluded that spacing was an important component of the fertility decline in the United States (Anderton and Bean 1985). This seems to place the American experience once again at variance from that of Europe (Knodel and van de Walle 1982).

Demographic Simulation

In order to answer a number of "what if" questions in historical demography, some researchers have turned to demographic simulation. One of the original questions to have spurred this interest was: If one observes in a particular nominal listing (e.g., a census manuscript) a certain distribution of household structures (nuclear, stem, extended, expanded, solitary, etc.), is this the product of particular residence rules or of demographic forces (age-specific birth, death, migration, and marriage rates)? (Wrigley 1969, pp. 131–134). This sort of query prompted Eugene Hammel, Kenneth Wachter, and their colleagues to develop the SOCSIM microsimulation model to do what they call "experimental history" (Hammel and Wachter 1977; Wachter, Hammel, and Laslett 1978). There are two sorts of simulation: microsimulation, which runs a series of hypothetical households and individuals through the model, subjecting them to various demographic processes and residence rules and then checking the outcomes after the passage of a certain amount of simulation "time"; and macrosimulation, which follows a population at the level of aggregative rates and levels. The SOCSIM model is an example of the former. Macrosimulation has been used to study birth intervals and natural fertility. It is reasonably straightforward and, with a language such as DYNAMO, could be used on microcomputers (Willigan and Lynch 1982, ch. 15—examples using the REPMOD simulation can be found in Willigan et.al. 1982; and Bongaarts and Potter 1983, ch. 6). Since these approaches offer answers to some of those nagging "what if" questions in economic and social history and historical demography, more can be expected in the future. The availability of packages for microcomputers will certainly have an impact. Simulations can *help* provide answers for questions such as: How large or small a value for some outcome variable is really large or small in a statistical sense? How sensitive are certain results to choices in parameters, rules, constants, and particular assumptions?

Statistical and Econometric Methods

Historical demography, like economic history, should benefit from advances made in statistics and econometrics. Many of the data sets produced in historical demography are time series. Developments in distributed lag models, covariance analysis, pooled time series–cross-section regression, vector autoregression, spectral analysis, ARMA (autoregressive, moving average) models (also known as Box-Jenkins models), and other time series statistical techniques offer considerable promise (Maddala 1977; Willigan and Lynch 1982, ch. 13).[13] Ronald Lee (1973, 1975, 1977, 1978; Wrigley and Schofield 1981, ch. 9) has worked extensively with spectral analysis. It has been applied by Jorde and Harpending (1976) to study the historical relationship between birthrates and rainfall, and by Neal (1976) to cycles in the trans-Atlantic migrations of the nineteenth century. Distributed lag regression models have also been used with success on English data by Lee (Wrigley and Schofield 1981, ch. 9, which was written by Ronald Lee) and by Olney (1983), to French data by Richards (1983), and comparatively to both English and French data by Weir (1984a). It is possible that such distributed lag models may also be made simultaneous structural models (e.g., Richards 1983). McDonald (1979) has used ARMA models to analyze Australian fertility data 1921–1975. Toni Richards (1977) provides an example of the application of pooled time series–cross-section regression to study the German fertility decline. Many possibilities exist, and their exploration should be assisted by microcomputer packages such as RATS (regression analysis of time series) and GAUSS, which contain many time-series related statistical procedures (including nonlinear and maximum-likelihood methods, ARMA models, simultaneous-equations models, and spectral analysis). A recent work by Mary Breckenridge (1983) has applied time series techniques developed by Tukey to historical Swedish demographic data.

Other multivariate techniques, not specifically related to time series, offer possibilities, Log-linear models have been proposed to deal with analysis of unordered categorical variables (Bishop, Fienberg, and Holland 1975; Fienberg 1977; Willigan and Lynch 1982, ch. 14), but have not found wide acceptance. One recent example has applied a log-linear model to the analysis of social mobility in the nineteenth century (Kousser, Galenson, and Cox 1982). There remain, however, problems of application and interpretation which render log-linear analysis less attractive than conventional regression analysis.

The prognosis is that regression will remain a preferred technique among economic historians educated in the current econometric curricula. A number of variants of regression analysis have proven illuminating and fruitful. Multiple classification analysis (a variant of OLS regression) is valuable because it provides easily interpretable results (e.g., Haines 1979b, ch. IV), while logit and probit regression have the advantage of ease of interpretation and better statistical properties for limited dependent variables (e.g., Goldin 1979, 1981). Another variant of conventional regression that holds promise is hazards or proportional hazards modeling (Trussell and Hammerslough 1983; Menken et al. 1981). It copes with the problems posed by individual-level data with stochastic, discrete events, such as mortality and nuptiality. A difficulty with this method is that it first requires a tedious tabulation stage before the data are entered into the statistical model. Improvements in computer software should alleviate this, however. In another and simpler approach, Haines and Preston (1984) have proposed a specially constructed dependent variable to study child mortality.

Among other methodologies with promise for future use would be mobility table analysis (Hout 1983), which has potential applications in migration and nuptiality studies; and the use of LISREL, a combination of confirmatory factor analysis and covariance structure models (Long 1983a, 1983b). Multiple-decrement or increment-decrement life tables have already been used for analysis of cause of death and nuptiality (e.g., Preston, Keyfitz, and Schoen 1972) and should find further use in historical work. Overall, then, new data and methods hold much promise for the future of historical demography and its connection to economic history.

The Historical Study of Fertility and Nuptiality

The historical study of fertility and marriage has often emphasized the "theory of the demographic transition" from high to low levels of fertility and mortality. The more conventional "ideal type" of this model (since it really is not a theory in the scientific sense) has identified a pretransition stage with high and reasonably stable natural fertility and high and fluctuating mortality. This is supposed to be followed by a reduction in mortality variation and then a decline in mortality, followed, in turn, by a stage of fertility decline, and finally succeeded by an era of low mortality and low, but fluctuating, fertility. Economic forces have been deemed to play a central role in this process. Frank Notestein (1953) made what is regarded as a classic statement of the theory of the demographic transition. His comments on fertility decline are illuminating:

> The new ideal of the small family arose typically in the urban industrial society. It is impossible to be precise about the various causal factors, but apparently many were important. Urban life stripped the family of many functions in production, consumption, recreation, and education. In factory employment the individual stood on his own accomplishments. The new mobility of young people and the anonymity of city life reduced the pressures toward traditional behavior exerted by the family and community. In a period of rapidly developing technology, new skills were needed, and new opportunities for individual advancement arose. Education and a rational point of view became increasingly important. As a consequence the cost of child-rearing grew and the possibilities for economic contributions by children declined. Falling death-rates at once increased the size of the family to be supported and lowered the inducements to have many births. Women, moreover, found new independence from household obligations and new economic roles less compatible with childbearing. (Notestein, 1953, quoted in Coale 1974, p. 54)

A number of researchers have attempted to identify not only the magnitude and timing of the fertility transition, but also its socioeconomic correlates. The European Fertility Project is an outstanding example, with monographs on Portugal, Italy, Britain, Russia, Belgium, Germany, and France; further monographs expected on Switzerland, France, and Denmark; a number of papers; and a summary volume (Livi-Bacci 1971, 1977; Teitelbaum 1984; Coale, Anderson, and Harm 1979; Knodel 1974, 1977b; Lesthaeghe 1977, 1980, 1983; E. van de Walle 1974, 1978; F. van de Walle 1975, 1980; Coale and Watkins 1986). Analyzing subnational geographic units (usually provinces) and utilizing the Coale indexes (I_f, I_g, I_m, I_m^*, I_h), a number of essential descriptive findings have emerged (Watkins 1986, pp. 429–435). With the exception of France, an early decliner (E. van de Walle 1978) and some isolated small geographic areas and particular groups, the decline in European fertility took place after about 1870 and was largely complete by 1960. Declines in marital fertility exceeded declines in overall fertility, and indeed changes in marital fertility were the driving force. Nuptiality, after about 1930, actually moved to counter declines in marital fertility. That is, age at marriage fell, proportions of women married at various ages rose, and the proportion of the female population remaining permanently celibate fell (Watkins 1985). Once the decline by province began, it almost never stopped or reversed until a low level of marital fertility had been reached. The decline and geographic spread were relatively swift, once initiated. Further, the decline spread across Europe much like an epidemic, generally from west to east, but the geographic pattern was varied. Geographically adjacent areas often experienced quite different patterns, the difference often being linguistic and cultural rather than strictly economic. (For example, such was the case in Belgium, where French-speaking Walloon areas showed early declines while adjoining Flemish-speaking areas had later declines and initially higher levels.)

Beyond the European Fertility Project, analysis of population aggregates and small local area studies for Germany, France, and England (Knodel 1978, 1979, 1983; Dupaquier 1979; Weir 1983; Wrigley and Schofield 1981, 1983), have revealed natural fertility to have been the rule in western Europe prior to the mid-nineteenth century. But there were also significant variations from place to place and over time. Many of these differences were unrelated to economic factors and were more closely associated with such things as differences in breatfeeding practices. It also appears that variations in nuptiality were quite important, causing, for example, the gross reproduction rate in England to vary between 1.81 and 3.06 during the period 1541 and 1871 (Wrigley and Schofield 1981). There is further evidence that nuptiality and natural fertility may have interacted in a homeostatic fashion to keep pretransition population growth rates at relatively low levels. The importance of economic factors in differential secular change in nuptiality across regions and groups is a vital topic which is emerging, following the lead of Wrigley and Schofield (1981) and other scholars using the Wrigley-Schofield data as well as a variety of other sources. For example, recently Weir (1984a) has disputed the claim that pretransition France was a Malthusian "high pressure" demographic regime (i.e., with high fertility and periodic endogenous mortality crises) while England was a "low pressure" regime (i.e., with oveall fertility modulated by significant nuptiality adjustments). Further time series analysis, such as that done by Richards (1983), Breckenridge (1983), and Lee (1978, 1981) will be of considerable value here.

The search for explanatory and causal factors in the European fertility decline has been less successful. Knodel and van de Walle (1979, 1982) have worked for some time on identifying threshold levels of various indicators of modernization and socioeconomic development relevant to the date of an irreversible 10-percent decline in marital fertility. The conclusion is that the marital fertility decline took place under a very wide variety of social, economic, and demographic conditions. For example, at the date of 10-percent decline, the percentage of the male labor force in agriculture ranged from 13 percent in Scotland and 15 percent in England and Wales (1892) to 70 percent in Bulgaria (1912), and 73 percent in Hungary (ca. 1890). Percentage of the rural population ranged from 85 percent in Finland (1910) and 84 percent in Hungary (ca. 1890) to 26 percent in the Netherlands (1897) and 28 percent in England and Wales (1892). The percentage of the population in cities of over 20,000 inhabitants ranged from 7 percent in Bulgaria (1912) and France (ca. 1800) to 57 percent in England and Wales (1892) and 49 percent in Scotland (1894).

The relationship between education and fertility has also not proven consistent historically. Percentages of the population aged 10 or 15 and over who were illiterate ranged from quite low in such countries as Germany (1890), Switzerland (1892), Denmark (1900), and Norway (1904) to 60 percent in Bulgaria (1912), 46 percent in Spain (1918), and 49 percent in Hungary (ca. 1890) at the date of 10-percent decline in marital fertility. While there is considerable evidence in the mid-twentieth century of an inverse correlation between parents' education and fertility (Cochrane 1979), the relationship is less clear historically, especially when literacy is used instead of the number of years of schooling attained (Graff 1979). A number of historical studies, including some in the European Fertility Project, have come up with no relation, or even a positive one, instead of the expected negative relation between parental literacy and fertility. On the other hand, some authors, such as Vinovskis (1976) in his study of interstate fertility differentials in the United States in 1850 and 1860, believe that the role of literacy is seriously underestimated. For example, Crafts (1984a, 1984b) estimates that as much as 50 percent of the pre-1895 decline in marital fertility in England and Wales can be accounted for by declines in illiteracy, which is interpreted as a proxy for information costs in family limitation. Thus the relation of literacy and education to fertility historically is neither simple nor necessarily unidirectional. More inquiry on this potentially rich area is indicated.

More recently attention has been switching from parental to child educaton. Caldwell (1982, ch. 10) has proposed that the rise of modern mass education has had an important influence on fertility decline, particularly by increasing the diffusion of middle-class values and knowledge of family limitation practices, but also by increasing child costs. As parents invest more in the human capital of their children, the net flow of resources switches from children to parents over to parents to children. Net child costs rise and fertility declines (Caldwell 1982, chs. 4–5). Related to this is the view of Becker (1981, ch. 6) that parents choose fewer children and more "quality" per child over time because of the decline of the implicit price of child "quality." This latter has been, in turn, caused by increased returns to human capital in the course of economic growth and development (T. W. Schultz 1981). Recently, Tan and Haines (1984) have shown that fertility declines seem to occur at a time of relatively high level of primary school enrollment and the beginnings of rapid increases in secondary school enrollments. But much more work will have to be done on these issues historically to provide consistent stories in which the simultaneous effects of other variables are appropriately disentangled. Similarly, Caldwell's notions of intergenerational resource and wealth transfers are very challenging, but empirical testing will be difficult. Some data sets, including the Mormon genealogical data base (Bean, May, and Skolnick 1978), may have the necessary historical information, and some work is already proceeding in that direction (e.g., Bourne 1986).

Another major characteristic of the fertility decline in Europe was that it appears that knowledge of effective family limitation practices was largely absent from many areas prior to the decline. That is not to say that it was not possible to limit family size. Knowledge of contraception was present even in the ancient world (Himes 1936). It was simply quite difficult to achieve effective family limitation with the technology and knowledge available. Sustained fertility declines did take place earlier among particular groups, such as the Jews of Italy and the bourgeosie of Geneva, and in both the United States and France from at least 1800 (Livi-Bacci 1977, pp. 41–44; Henry 1956; Yasuba 1962; E. van de Walle 1978, 1980). But, as David and Sanderson have shown for a period as late as the 1890s and 1900s, it was a problem to achieve a small family size in a regime of inefficient contraceptive technology (David and Sanderson, 1986). Both spacing and stopping behavior were required. Anderton and Bean (1985), studying nineteenth-century American genealogical data, have reached a similar conclusion. The consequence was a substantial amount of unwanted fertility, as evidenced by extremely lax child care practices and relative indifference to infant and child loss (Knodel and van de Walle 1982, p. 271). Work with microdata sets for Germany and England reveals relatively little evidence of stopping or deliberate spacing among most of the population until the later nineteenth century. Although some of this evidence comes from the use of Coale and Trussell m values, which may be limited, there is other supporting information such as mean birth intervals, mean age of mother at last birth (adjusted for mothers' mortality), and proportion of childbearing by women beyond age 30 (Knodel 1979; Wrigley and Schofield 1983; Haines 1979b, ch. V). One additional piece of evidence on this is that both marital and nonmarital fertility rates declined together. Since, presumably, motivation for fertility control was greater among unmarried women, this is interpreted as evidence of technological limitations. Additional work with, and interpretation of, microdata sets (e.g., census manuscripts, genealogies, family books, populations registers) will furnish greater insight here, as will the study of literary sources, diaries, medical literature, etc. to determine perceptions and the extent of diffusion of existing knowledge.

Infant mortality, or rather infant and child mortality (e.g., survival to age 15 or 20) (Matthiessen and McCann 1978), played an ambiguous role in historical fertility decline. It has been hypothesized that declines in infant and child mortality lead to decreases in fertility first, because of a biological mechanism lengthening birth intervals (partly through prolonged lactation) and, second, because of a behavioral mechanism in which parents perceive that fewer births are necessary to obtain a target surviving family size (Preston 1978, ch. 1). The historical evidence is mixed. Marital fertility declined in Ireland well after the onset of a decline in infant mortality. This was not true in Germany and Belgium, where levels of infant mortality remained very high while fertility was declining. The prolonged fertility decline in the United States prior to the Civil War may have taken place despite *rising* mortality rates (Fogel 1984). If child survival had an effect on fertility decline, one certainly would have expected substantial changes in infant and child mortality prior to, or at least accompanying, fertility decline. Such was not universally the case. Cross-sectional results for small geographic areas in England and Wales and in Prussia in the mid and late nineteenth century showed ambiguous and often statistically insignificant relationships between infant mortality and either overall or marital fertility (Haines 1979b, ch. III).

Thus the influence of the socioeconomic context on fertility, so forcefully spelled out by the theory of the demographic transition, has not proven to be predictable or strong. This has been shown especially true for aggregate data for smaller geographic areas for which, as a statistical matter, such relationships should be quite marked. In particular cases and in the cross-section, the relationships may be strong, highly correlated, and in the predicted direction. But the results are not consistent across countries. In some instances, such as Germany (Richards 1977) and Belgium (Lesthaeghe 1977), the effect of region alone was an extremely powerful predictor of decline. In Russia it was often not the Western nationalities themselves that were responsible for lower fertility and earlier decline, but the characteristics of areas and regions in which Western nationalities were present.

An important modification has been proposed by Ron Lesthaeghe (1980, 1983). One of the best predictors of fertility differentials and change in Belgium since 1880 was an index of industrialization and urbanization (derived from several economic and demographic measures combined using principal components methods) and of secularization (measured as the percent voting socialist or liberal in 1919) (Lesthaeghe 1977, ch. 5). The concept of secularization has been carried forward to cover fundamental changes in the ideational structure of societies in which, as Ansley Coale has pointed out (Coale 1974, pp. 65–67), fertility control becomes a choice variable only when the cultural context permits it. Once this is true, if the technology of family limitation permits and if it becomes socially and economically advantageous to control fertility, declines proceed rapidly. The hypothesis that a change in ideology, from one emphasizing community and family authority and exchange patterns to one exemplifying individual choice and rationality, is consistent with the phenomenon of a rapid and irreversible fertility decline, occurring across a wide variety of countries with greatly differing socioeconomic levels, within a relatively short span of time (roughly 30 years). Advances in the technology of family limitation only assist this process, since both France and the United States were already experiencing declines with existing, inefficient technology prior to most of Europe. Advances in urbanization and industrialization also made family limitation in *some* cases more advantageous, but the cultural context appears to have been crucial.

Where does this leave economic historians? The discipline of economic history is not used to dealing with the concept of culture, meaning, in general, a system of expectations expressing itself in behavior and in physical artifacts. Nonetheless, despite the lack of familiarity, economists and economic historians can combine the concept of culture with economic models and, more widely, with all sorts of optimizing models of human behavior. Recently, in two articles on England and Wales, Crafts (1984a, 1984b) has argued that differential child costs were important in explaining cross-sectional differentials in legitimate fertility in 1911 and that changes in child costs were important in explaining the fertility decline 1877–1938. Economic structure (e.g., female labor force activity, proportions of labor force in mining and textiles) was also significant. And yet the concept of child costs must embody subjective elements—perceptions of future benefits, as well as present and future costs, which influence investment in the human capital of children. Economists often relegate such considerations to the category of tastes and preferences, which are usually not investigated.[14] There is no reason, other than the obvious complications to modeling, not to investigate them and thus try to explain perceived costs and benefits of children. Child costs can be, and have been, treated in historical context. (See, for example, Lindert 1978, 1980; and comments by Mueller 1980.) This area would benefit from further theoretical work and collection of empirical information.

As has already been mentioned, two of the more interesting (and troublesome) cases of fertility decline are those of France and the United States. (To this group may also be added Canada.) In these countries, fertility decline preceded substantial industrialization and urbanization. Present evidence points to a decline in both from the late eighteenth century. The cases are interesting because they were largely agrarian societies which nevertheless experienced this prolonged and dramatic sociodemographic change—a possible lesson for developing nations today. The cases are, however, quite different—the United States and Canada were land abundant, relatively literate, and newly settled; France was long settled and much less literate. Recent work on France (E. van de Walle 1978, 1980) shows a strong inverse relation between marital fertility and nuptiality across *départements*, pointing to a continuation of the kind of homeostatis observed by Smith (1977) for earlier periods. Once this is taken into account, France also showed higher marital fertility in *départements* with higher mortality and lower revenue per land unit (E. van de Walle 1978). Thus, high mortality and lower income were related to high fertility; but the decline itself is not explained, since the timing and course of mortality and rural income are unclear. Van de Walle makes a plea for more microstudies, cohort analysis, and comparative work—pleas that should be answered in future research, some of which is underway.

In contrast to France, the United States and Canada were land rich and newly settled. The leading theory of American fertility decline is the land availability hypothesis, essentially a child cost view. That is, fertility was highest when there was an abundance of cheap improved land, presumably making it easier to endow children with adequate farm sites nearby.[15] This was first proposed by Yasuba (1962), having discovered that, prior to 1860, more densely populated states had lower child-woman ratios. Density was interpreted as a proxy for land availability. More refined measures and statistical techniques were used by Forster and Tucker (1972), but the Yasuba results were confirmed and reinforced. Work on colonial populations in New England indicates that this was happening even prior to 1800 (Lockridge 1968). Tests with county-level data (Leet 1976) and with microdata from the 1860 census (Easterlin 1976; Easterlin, Alter, and Condran 1978) have also supported Yasuba's results. Canada, an analogous case, has been studied by McInnis (1977), with similar results. The competitor view, exemplified by R. G. Potter (1965) and Vinovskis (1976), emphasizes more conventional socioeconomic variables, including urbanization and education. And it must be noted that the Yasuba results show a much stronger effect of urbanization and industrialization by 1850 and 1860. Also, as Vinovskis (1978) has indicated, urban child-woman ratios fell right along with the rural ones. Imbalanced sex ratios apparently led to higher marriage probabilities for females on the frontier (T'ien 1959). Finally, after 1860, a more conventional set of socioeconomic changes dominated the continuing fertility decline in the United States (and in France as well) as industrial and urban growth proceeded. Further work with microdata sets (e.g., Bourne 1986, and the Morman Historical Demography Project: Bean, May, and Skolnik, 1978) will shed some additional light on the issues, but it is not clear that the relative importance of the different factors will ever be fully assessed.

Some most useful work has recently been advanced by the Stanford Project on the History of Fertility Control. In addition to the work of Paul David and Warren Sanderson (1986) already mentioned, there has been an effort to reexamine the land availability–bequest model (e.g., Easterlin 1976) in explaining the rural fertility decline in the antebellum United States (David and Sundstrom 1984; Sundstrom and David 1985). Using a model of life cycle fertility, savings, demand for old-age support, and bargaining within the family, David and Sundstrom believe that development of nonagricultural labor market opportunities for farm children had more to do with rural American fertility decline than did the gradual erosion of the frontier and the disappearance of inexpensive bequests. It is a direction worth pursuing. In another connection, the Stanford Project has also been working with state-of-the-art statistical techniques applied to a microeconomic model of rational child spacing for purposes of family limitation (David, Mroz, and Wachter 1985; David and Mroz 1985). Applying the model (which allows for individual-level covariates, ecological covariates, and unobserved heterogeneities, and also interactions between fertility, infant mortality, and family limitation) to INED data for rural communes in northern France in the eighteenth-century, evidence is found for family limitation on the part of some families, especially those with many daughters. The results may shed some light on the early fertility decline in France and constitute some critique of the natural fertility view of preindustrial Europe.

The field of differential fertility still appears open and rich with possibilities, despite the considerable work already done. Often differential fertility has been studied to obtain clues as to the roles of various factors in the demographic transition. Analysis of a time series of cross-sections concerns itself immediately with differentials and only by extension with the issue of fertility decline. Unfortunately it has more often been used to study the latter rather than differentials. Research on historical fertility differentials for the presently developed countries has revealed, in general, higher fertility in rural than in urban areas; higher fertility among manual than among white collar and professional occupations; higher fertility among lower income and wealth groups; higher fertility among the illiterate and less-educated groups; lower fertility among wage-earning women (though not necessarily among self-employed workers in the home); and higher fertility among certain religious, racial, and ethnic groups, such as blacks in the United States, Catholics in Germany and the United States, and the French Canadians (United Nations 1973, pp. 96–105).

The actual historical record is not as clear, however. For example, Graff (1979) has found that differential fertility by literacy status in historical studies has led to ambiguous results, with differing directions of the relationship and often statistically insignificant results. Information on number of years of schooling, which has produced much more consistent inverse correlations with fertility among contemporary populations (Cochrane 1979), is frequently unavailable in historical data. Although ecological correlations sometimes are strong (e.g., Vinovskis 1976), it is not clear that what we observe at present was also true in the past. For example, occupation and class differentials in fertility in England and Wales appear to have become more pronounced during the fertility decline before closing up again (Innes 1938). In the Pennsylvania anthracite region (Haines 1979b, ch. IV) fertility among farmers was initially higher than that among all other occupational groups in 1850, but dropped to a middle rank by 1900. While fertility in urban areas was often lower than in rural places, it often depended upon the type of urban place. For instance, cities based on mining and heavy industry have often had fertility higher than surrounding rural environments, in contrast to cities based on commerce and administration (Wrigley 1961; Haines 1979b). While the foreign-born in the United States often had fertility higher than that of the native population, it was not always true. For instance, the differentials apparently shifted in Philadelphia between the 1840s and the 1850s (Haines 1980a).

Most of the theory related to differential fertility has either to do with differences in the relative costs and benefits of children (Easterlin 1978; Lindert 1978), or with issues of norms or tastes (Ryder 1973). The issue of norms or tastes can often be posed as one of constraints or of costs, such as the additional psychological cost of fertility regulation among Roman Catholics (Easterlin 1978). The concepts of costs, benefits, and constraints hold some promise for additional progress in historical research on these issues. While it is true that additional work will be needed simply to uncover and measure fertility differentials at various places and times, the task of explanation is pressing. For example, why do fertility differentials exist between racial and ethnic groups? One viewpoint, the socioeconomic characteristics hypothesis, states that once all relevant socioeconomic differences are taken into account, fertility differences by race and ethnicity should disappear (Bean and Marcum 1978). Since income, wealth, education, occupation, residence, and other factors are frequently highly correlated with race or ethnic background, this is a plausible view. A competing view is the minority group status hypothesis which states that minority groups may protect themselves by either having many children or having relatively few "high-quality" children (Bean and Marcum 1978, pp. 193–199). The problem here is that the effect of minority status on fertility can be in either direction. All we know a priori is that the fertility of minority groups should be different from that of the dominant majority. An improved understanding of which factors influence the relative costs and benefits of children— and in which direction—would help here. Researchers studying the United States in the nineteenth and twentieth centuries have been particularly interested in these issues, due to the country's considerable ethnic and racial diversity. The peculiar fertility pattern of American blacks has attracted much attention, with relatively high rural fertility and surprisingly low urban fertility (Engerman 1978; Haines 1980b; Tolnay 1980). There has been dispute over the relative roles of disease and morbidity (creating infertility) versus socioeconomic and demographic factors in altering the costs and benefits of marriage and childbearing. (See, for example, McFalls 1973, 1981). Fertility differentials among the native and foreign-born populations of the United States have historically attracted similar interest (Haines 1979b; Guest 1982; Easterlin 1977), and the same issues prevail. Greater use of micro-level data may help shed some light on this through variations in the age structure of marital fertility.

The variant occupational and rural-urban differentials in fertility are also problematic. The effect of economic structures can be crucial. I have argued at length elsewhere (Haines, 1979b) that mining and heavy industry create economic structures (which can be interpreted as microeconomic constraints) which provide incentives for particular areas, occupations, and groups to have higher fertility. It is generally argued that urban areas encourage smaller families because of greater density, scarcer and more expensive housing, fewer child labor opportunities (in contrast to agriculture), more wage labor opportunities for women, and better enforcement of child labor laws and compulsory education statutes. Child costs are thus thought to be higher in urban areas, as also might be the rewards to greater investment in human capital (quality per child). But much depends on the actual circumstances. For instance, mining and heavy industrial areas had few female labor forces possibilities while providing good opportunities for children. Male wages peaked early in the life cycle and were relatively high, encouraging early marriage and shorter mean length of generation. Differential net in-migration of young adult males (in response to the same labor demand factors) biased sex ratios in favor of earlier and more extensive marriage of women. Higher child mortality tended to shorten birth intervals. All this combined to favor both higher (female) nuptiality and greater marital fertility in those areas and among occupational groups most affected.

Hence, in late nineteenth-century Europe some industrial cities had fertility higher than that in surrounding rural areas (Wrigley 1961). In contrast, textile centers, which made extensive use of female labor, and urban areas, with a greater demand for female domestic workers, would tend to have late and less extensive marriage among females and possibly lower marital fertility because of higher child costs due to greater opportunity cost of women's time. Some authors argue that once such influences are taken into account, the independent effect of occupation or residence should become insignificant (e.g., Bogue 1969, p. 705). But that misses the point, or perhaps is exactly the point. The structure or set of characteristics associated with a particular area, or surrounding a particular occupation, influence and are influenced by the demographic behavior of that area or group. It is the task of the economic, demographic, and social historian to disentangle and clarify such influences. One example is the work of Guest and Tolnay on the interaction of sociodemographic and economic structures on interstate fertility differentials in the United States at the turn of the century (Guest and Tolnay 1983a, 1983b). Another example is David Levine's (1977) work on four different English villages from the mid-sixteenth to the mid-nineteenth-centuries. Each village was deliberately chosen for its different socioeconomic structure. Differences in demographic behavior were indeed observed. Levine closes with a plea for greater study of fertility differentials, especially by occupation, in order better to understand the precise impact of economic change. His subsequent intensive work on the village of Terling with Keith Wrightson (Wrightson and Levine 1979) attempts to make use of a wide variety of sources to accomplish that task.

An area that has generated some attention in fertility analysis has been the study of cycles in fertility (and marriage) behavior. Perhaps the most notable is Easterlin's explanation of the post-World War II baby boom in the United States and elsewhere as a product of long swings in economic activity, migration, and cohort size phenonema (Easterlin 1968, 1973, 1980). Ronald Lee has carried that field much further with the application of techniques such as spectral analysis, and he has looked at both short-term fluctuations and longer cycles (Lee 1975, 1978, 1981). While there is not widespread interest in this, the study of cycles is almost inherently an historical issue. It seems likely that research will continue, although probably on a relatively modest scale. Still, with the long time series of data now available for England, France and several Scandinavian countries, the opportunities to study long swings in fertility and nuptiality will be attractive. (See, for example, Breckenridge 1983.)

Although a great deal concerning fertility has not been covered here, including the substantive findings of the European Fertility Project, the Cambridge Group, and INED, the area continues to attract researchers to exploit the rich data sources available. As already mentioned, linkage of fertility data to other social and economic information should provide ample opportunities to explore economic/demographic interactions and to extend and test such models as those of Easterlin, Becker, and Caldwell, among others. On-going projects (such as the Mormon Demographic History Project, the Berkeley group on demographic simulation, the NBER projects on health and mortality, to name several), as well as work by numerous individuals and small groups, can be expected to continue to extend our knowledge of historical fertility and nuptiality.

The Historical Study of Mortality

The study of mortality (and now morbidity and health) has received, in recent years, increased attention. In the post-World War II period, rapid declines in mortality in developing countries, combined with continued improvements in life expectations and in infant and child mortality in developed countries, led to reduced concern. More recently, however, mortality declines have slowed and renewed interest has been expressed both in trends and in differentials in mortality.

Historically, mortality has often been better documented than fertility, partly because of public health concerns and partly because of the applications of mortality analysis in the insurance and annuity fields (Willigan and Lynch 1982, ch. 1). The decline in mortality in the nineteenth and twentieth centuries has been well documented in two important papers by Stolnitz (1955, 1956), and also by the United Nations (1973, ch. V). Prior to the nineteenth-century, we have less adequate inforamtion, but the scholars at the Cambridge Group and INED as well as researchers on colonial French canada, the colonial United States, and Japan have been working to provide mortality as well as fertility estimates for periods before the modern statistical era (Wrigley and Schofield 1981;

Vinovskis 1978; Hanley and Yamamura 1977; T.C. Smith 1977; Desjardins, Beauchamp, and Legare 1977). John Knodel's work on infant mortality in a number of German villages is a model of the use of reconstitution techniques for mortality analysis (Knodel and van de Walle 1967; Knodel and Kintner 1977). The impact of differential breast-feeding on infant mortality historically has been much clarified by his work.

A great deal has been learned historically about the course of mortality, but more is on the way. For example, the trend of mortality in the United States in the nineteenth-century has been an area of uncertainty. Our knowledge about Massachusetts, where vital registration began in 1842, is considerable (Gutman 1956). But even there, uncertainty rules prior to the Civil War (Vinovskis 1972). Kuznets (1965, pp. 355–366) and Higgs (1973) have supposed that mortality declined in the United States after about 1870. Easterlin (1977), using the results of Preston (1976, ch. 4), noted that some part of mortality decline internationally in the twentieth-century was due to an increase in income per capita (presumably operating through better diet, clothing, shelter, and public health), and that cities had generally higher mortality in the nineteenth and early twentieth centuries (Weber 1899, pp. 343–367). He then hypothesized that mortality probably declined in the nineteenth-century United States because incomes per capita were increasing to offset the ill effects of increased urbanization. In contrast, some work using a two-parameter logit model life table system and census mortality data found that mortality improved little prior to about 1880 (Haines 1979a). More recent research by Fogel (1984), using genealogical data, actually found evidence of *rising* mortality in the antebellum United States. This is a puzzle, since income per capita was rising and areas in the supposedly healthy rural, agrarian Midwest were being settled. Data on human stature, used as an indicator of health and cumulative well-being have indicated declining terminal heights from the birth cohorts of about 1830 to those of the 1880s (See also *Social Science History* 1982, and the papers included there; and Tanner 1981.) This supports the idea of deteriorating health, morbidity, and mortality conditions in the early and mid-nineteenth-century United States, but explanation is now needed.

The recent abundance of studies of human stature (e.g., *Social Science History* 1982; Fogel et al. 1983; Steckel 1983) is an important step in assessing historical health and its relation to mortality. Work is underway on such historical data for the United States, Britain, Sweden, the Hapsburg Monarchy, and the Caribbean (see Fogel 1984). Stature and human growth are most useful indexes of cumulative nutritional status (which encompasses both dietary intake and disease conditions), and such data *are* available historically (especially for military and institutional populations). Combined with such things as friendly society health insurance and hospital records, it is possible to gain a much better understanding of historical trends and differentials in health, productivity, morbidity, and death.

One long-term on-going debate has concerned the causes of the historical mortality decline. Such things as the virtual disappearance of bubonic plague in early eighteenth-century (Biraben 1968; Appleby 1980) still remain mysterious. While it is true that, in the eighteenth-century, crisis (as opposed to endemic) mortality began to be less frequent and less severe, it remains to explain this. Helleiner (1965, 1967) believed that improved transport and more effective public and private organization played a role by reducing the incidence of local famine. Ecobiological alterations possibily reduced the virulence and incidence of some diseases (e.g., plague and scarlet fever). But there were also reductions in mortality from many other acute and chronic infectious and parasitic diseases. The beneficial role of medical science, so apparent as the twentieth-century progressed, had been offered as an explanation, but early work by McKeown and Brown (1955) and McKeown and Record (1962) showed that specific medical improvements in the eighteenth and nineteenth-centuries were not sufficient to explain the mortality declines in England and Wales. Analysis of cause of death data from the late nineteenth and early twentieth-centuries revealed, for instance, substantial declines in tuberculosis mortality without evidence of any relevant new therapies. McKeown was motivated to propose that improvements in diet, clothing, and shelter (i.e., standard of living) were central. He has proceeded (McKeown 1976; McKeown, Brown, and Record 1972) to generalize this to other countries, proposing that indeed the transport and agricultural revolutions were critical events, making foodstuffs cheaper and more readily available, improving general health, and reducing crisis mortality.

Recent work by Fogel and his colleagues (Fogel 1984) and by others (*Journal of Interdisciplinary History* 1983) on nutrition and mortality has attempted to find more precise connections via the medical literature and microdata. Even the traditional relationship between harvest failures (often measured by grain price fluctuations) and mortality crises has spurred new debate. Fogel (1984) has suggested that peaks in grain prices may have created much smaller fluctuations in consumption historically because of low price and income elasticities of demand for food. And yet crisis mortality was most likely to occur among marginal consumers who could least afford even small reductions in dietary intake. Schofield (1983; Wrigley and Schofield 1981, chs. 8–9) found that early modern England did not show considerable mortality responsiveness to variations in grain prices and therefore was a "low pressure" demographic regime. In contrast France has a much greater responsiveness of mortality to grain price variation and, along with its high natural fertility and relatively early marriage pattern, was thus the sort of "high pressure" demographic regime envisioned by Malthus. This has been challenged by Weir (1984a) who found a higher mortality responsiveness in France prior to 1740 while thereafter both France and England showed a modest short-term relationship between grain price changes and mortality fluctuations. The work of Michelle McAlpin on India (e.g., McAlpin, 1983a, 1983b) has emphasized the complexities of these connections, and clearly more extensive inquiry into the precise mechanisms is required.

The disentangling of the causes of mortality declines, fluctuations, and differentials hinges very much on the analysis of causes of death—finding more detail on proximate causes of death before formulating more hypotheses on underlying factors (e.g., McKeown 1976, 1978). A powerful start in this direction was undertaken by Preston, Keyfitz, and Schoen (1972) who compiled a large set of multiple-decrement life tables by age, sex, and cause with the available and reasonably reliable data. A number of the tables go back into the nineteenth-century. Most are for the presently developed countries in the twentieth-century, as one might expect, however. Moving the analysis still further, Preston (1976) has attempted to define model mortality patterns based on causes on death—much as Coale and Demeny (1966) created model patterns from age- and sex-specific death rates. The value here for historical analysis would be to make use of incompletely registered or enumerated cause-specific mortality data. Unfortunately, historical cause-specific mortality data also suffer from changing (and often improving) diagnosis of cause and also changes in classification of causes (nosology).

Nonetheless, some very useful analysis of historical cause of death information has been done. For instance, Condran and Crimmins (1978, 1979, 1980; Crimmins and Condran 1983) have used registration data reported in the United States censuses of 1890 and 1900 to examine mortality differentials and change by cause of death. Higher urban mortality was caused by certain communicable diseases, and public health measures were partially responsible for reducing mortality and for explaining differentials across cities. A detailed analysis of Philadelphia for the period 1870–1930 by Condran and Cheney (1982) found that analysis of cause of death contributed to a more favorable interpretation of the role of medical intervention when the definition of medical intervention was expanded to include public health activities. The complexity of the mortality reduction process is emphasized by their work. Similarly, a study of urban mortality in nineteenth-century France by Preston and van de Walle (1978) revealed an important role for public health. Cause of death data were important in that inquiry. A recent example of imaginative work with historical cause of death data is the monograph by Elizabeth Hoffman on the Italian mortality decline (Hoffman 1981). There exist numerous data with cause of death by age and sex for various subnational units and even for subgroups (e.g., race and ethnicity for the United States). Germany is a good example, where the data remain largely unexploited. (But see Kintner 1982; Haines 1976.) The British data have been more widely used (e.g., McKeown and Record 1962; McKeown 1976), but much more could be done for the nineteenth and early twentieth-centuries, despite the problems of diagnosis, underregistration, and changing classification. What is needed is something analogous to the European Fertility Project for mortality to continue the basic work of Preston, Keyfitz, and Schoen (1972) and extend it to subnational units and to population subgroups. Unfortunately, work on mortality is exceedingly data intensive, requiring extreme care in evaluation, and does not promise a quick payoff. Nonetheless, the finding of Kingsley Davis (1973) that declines in urban mortality from the nineteenth-century in the presently developed countries were more rapid than mortality declines in developing countries since 1945 is remarkable and beckons for further explanation and analysis. The fact is that cities were once very hazardous to health and longevity (Weber 1899, pp. 343–367) and became, if anything, better off than rural areas. This was a notable historical event. Research into the role of urban sanitation, public health, and medical advances will need to be pushed forward if we are to understand the complexities of this phenomenon. (The work of Cain 1977, and Condran and Cheney 1982 are instructive in this regard.)

Mortality is a powerful index of social and economic well-being. It has been used by the World Bank as one of its "basic needs" indicators (Morawetz 1977).[16] It has been proposed as an important input, for example, into the standard of living debate for Britain for the late eighteenth and early nineteenth-centuries (Hobsbawm 1957). The results of Wrigley and Schofield (1981) have been used by Lindert (1983) to revise our views on the debate. Williamson (1981, 1982, 1985a) has employed infant and adult mortality statistics to gauge the extent of urban "disamenities" in nineteenth-century England and to measure the compensating wage differentials necessary to induce people to live in urban areas. He has also attempted to measure the economic gains to Britain from the increase in expectation of life betwen the eighteenth and the twentieth-centuries (Williamson 1984a). Child mortality indexes have been used to measure the relative inequality between the United States and England at the turn of the century (Haines 1985b).

Overall, then, the study of mortality holds promise. There exist considerable published data which are, as yet, inadequately evaluated and exploited. Microdata sources, such as census records, manuscript vital statistics registers, genealogical records, insurance company and friendly society archives, etc. all can provide much potenital insight into a demographic process that not only is an important social indicator but also has a central influence on fertility and on the whole strategy of investment in human capital. After all, mortality risk was one of the chief constraints historically on the decision to improve human productivity through education, training, and health inputs.

Migration and Family Structure; Comparative Research

Discussion of remaining topics is relatively brief due to space limitations. One area that has long attracted the attention of economic historians has been that of international and internal migration, the latter related to the phenomenon of urbanization (Kuznets 1966; United Nations 1973, chs. VI and VII). The redistribution of factors of production is a substitute for trade, and migration increased dramatically in volume as technological change in transportation in the nineteenth and twentieth-centuries decreased costs and time in transit. The leading theoretical model of migration is that of labor markets; and, within that model, the human capital approach, emphasizing the costs and returns of relocation to migrants, has proven fruitful (Sjaastad 1962; Becker 1975). It is, for example, the organizing framework for David Galenson's important study of the transatlantic migration of indentured servants from Europe to the New World in the seventeenth and eighteenth-centuries (Galenson 1981). Some migrations, such as the importations of blacks as slaves to the New World (Curtin 1969) were not voluntary, but even there a human capital approach from the perspective of the demand for labor can be used. The literature on the slave trade is quite large and can be expected to grow as microrecords (e.g., ship's manifests, records of slave auctions, records of coastal trade, records of the Royal Navy from the seizure of slave ships, plantation accounts) are more fully exploited.

The more conventional approach was to use census data on population by birth and residence to measure lifetime migration. A notable example for the United States is the classic study of Population Redistribution and Economic Growth in the United States undertaken in the 1950s by Simon

Kuznets, Dorothy Thomas, Everett Lee, Hope Eldridge, Richard Easterlin, Ann Miller, and their colleagues at the University of Pennsylvania (Lee et al. 1957; Kuznets, Miller, and Easterlin 1960; Eldridge and Thomas 1964). Other estimates of net migration, using the balancing equation and other techniques have been widely prepared and analyzed for developed countries. (See, for instance, Willcox 1931.) One classic study for Britain is Arthur Redford's (1964) work on historical labor migration. More recently, Jeffrey Williamson has been examining the role of migration in Britain's urban transition and the growth of the British economy in the early stages of the industrial revolution (Williamson 1984b, 1985b). Barbara Anderson has examined the effects of modernization on internal migration in Russia in the late nineteenth-century Russia (Anderson 1977, 1980). A study of urbanization, industrialization, and internal migration in Germany in the nineteenth and twentieth-centuries by Steve Hochstadt (1981) has called into question some of the more conventional views of migration as related to urbanization. Using largely published (and some archival) aggregative data, he finds that rural places experienced gross migration flows as large as those in cities and that the flows were as likely to be related to agricultural labor demand as the demand for labor in cottage or modern industry. Finally, gross migration flows may well have diminished in Germany and elsewhere in Europe as modern economic growth created more structured and stable labor demand.

Brinley Thomas (e.g., Thomas 1954) has devoted much of his productive career to the study of internal migration as a labor market clearing phenomenon. Work by Vedder and Gallaway (1971, 1980) and by Lebergott (1964, 1970) have sought for the United States to document the neoclassical market clearing mechanisms in the face of continued forces, such as war and technical change and the opening of new resource supplies, which made for disequilibria. These efforts have been persuasive and have used largely published aggregate statistics. Examples exist for other developed countries as well (e.g., see United Nations 1973, chs. VI and VII).

The future direction lies with the use of new microdata sets. One example, already mentioned, is David Galenson's (1981) work on indentured servants in the New World. Another is Leslie Moch's work on tracing migrants from manuscript census records in France in 1906 in order to obtain career migration and occupational movements (Moch 1981a, 1981b, 1983; Moch and Tilly 1985). Still another source of great potential are the genealogical data bases being used by the Mormon Demographic History Project and the NBER project conducted by Robert Fogel at the University of Chicago. Adams and Kasakoff (1980, 1984) have been using small genealogical samples to trace migrants from the eastern seaboard of the United States in their repeated moves westward. These sources, and the painstaking and extremely time-consuming analyses that accompany them, will give us actual life histories and migration paths, particularly for repeat movers. In the past, we learned a great deal about lifetime movers (i.e., those for whom birthplace and current residence were not the same). Some microodata sets have been used to examine differences between lifetime migrants and nonmigrants, particularly with respect to labor force activity. (See, for instance, Laurie, Hershberg, and Alter 1981; Moch and Tilly 1985.) More of such work can be expected until we accumulate enough information to render strong comparative generalizations. There are also some sources, such as the 1855 New York State census or the 1900 United States census manuscripts, which allow us to analyze recent migrations because they contain questions on recent moves or the duration of residence in the United States. (See, for example, Katz, Doucet, and Stern 1978; Parkerson 1982; Davenport 1984, 1985.) Further work with such sources will be necessary. Particularly useful will be documents such as population registers such as those for Belgium (Gutmann and van be Walle 1978) and Italy (Hogan and Kertzer, 1985) which provide very detailed data. When linked to economic records, such as payrolls, probates, tax records, etc., these registers can help a great deal in creating operational tests of human capital models. But the effort required for data collection, data entry, coding, processing, and other tasks is enormous, so that results and studies will not be available soon. One interesting speculation is whether the Todaro (1976) model of rural-urban migration which has enjoyed such popularity for the study of developing countries can be tested for historical case studies.

One notable area of historical research into migration has been the study of geographic mobility within nineteenth- and twentieth-century American cities. Beginning with the work of Thernstrom (1964, 1969; Thernstrom and Knights, 1971) and Knights (1971), a number of studies have found, through attempts at census linkage, a relatively high degree of mobility. (See Parkerson 1982 for a summary of some of these studies). More recently, it has been asserted that these earlier findings may well have been an artifact of the inability to make better linkages and defects in the sources themselves, particularly for large and rapidly growing metropolitan areas (Parkerson 1982; Davenport 1985). Further efforts with microdata sources, particularly genealogical data, can be expected to shed some light on the problem; but, ultimately, the problem may not be amenable to quantitative resolution.

The study of family structure has attracted a great deal of interest among social historians and historical sociologists and anthropologists in recent years.[17] The work of the Cambridge Group—particularly Peter Laslett (Laslett and Wall 1972)—and the Berkeley group on demographic simulation (Wachter, Hammel, and Laslett 1978); Michael Anderson's pioneering work on nineteenth-century Lancashire (Anderson 1971); and Lutz Berkner's work on the stem family (Berkner 1972), have all attracted attention to the issues of the roles of rules versus choice versus demographic constraints on observed patterns of family types in nominal listings. Economic historians have not been so active in this field, but that may change. Given the increased interest in the family economy (e.g., Becker 1976, 1981; Goldin 1979, 1981; Haines 1979c; Alter 1984; Hareven 1982) and the continuing research in family labor supply models (Killingsworth 1983, ch. 2), there is a role for family structure in models of family labor supply, domestic industry, savings, and consumption (e.g., Williamson 1967; Modell 1978; Lees 1980; Haines 1979c, 1985a). The simulation exercises have found that observed family structure is relatively sensitive to the ambient mortality regime, as well as to fertility rates and rules concerning marriage ages and patterns of coresidence (Wachter, Hammel, and Laslett 1978). It has been argued, for instance, that the historically high incidence of female-headed families among the black population of the United States was as much a result of high mortality as of marriage and coresidence decisions (Hershberg 1981). Within these constraints, it certainly appears that families adopted strategies to maximize family income and consumption, and some of the factors affecting family structure, such as fertility levels, marriage patterns, and coresidence rules, may have been, at least in part, endogenous and hence a part of the strategy. This area needs exploration, again probably with microdata. For example, families that experienced relative poverty in the middle stages of the family life cycle often had large numbers of nonworking family members (especially young children). Did these families essentially choose this situation in order to have larger numbers of working family members later in the life cycle? Was this a rational form of saving in a world of imperfect capital markets and high risks (e.g., high mortality)?

The *Annales* school of social, economic, and demographic history (Willigan and Lynch 1982, ch. 21; Stoianovich 1976; R. Forster 1978; Braudel 1980) is a multidisciplinary approach designed to integrate demographic and economic history into a larger causal picture.[18] Such an approach has been labeled *total history*. As Willigan and Lynch note:

> One of the advantages of a "total history" approach to the study of historical demographic development is that it identifies different levels of human historical

> existence—biological, ecological, economic, demographic, or political—and attempts to assess varying causal relationships among these humanly conditioned dimensions of existence in order to understand both constancy and change in the past (Willigan and Lynch 1982, p. 434). Among notable examples would be the work of Fernand Braudel (1972, 1973), Marc Bloch (1966), Emmanuel Le Roy Ladurie (1967, 1974, 1978), and Pierre Goubert (1960). A considerable amount of the demographic work of I.N.E.D. on fertility and nuptiality has appeared in *Annales*.[19] Much of the work done by scholars in this school is not of the technical variety that is admired among cliometricians, but consists of the careful and imaginative use of a broad variety of sources and the integration of various disciplines. Large synthetic work should be the ultimate goal of economic historians, even though there may have to be a large amount of detailed preparatory work and numerous case studies before such synthesis is possible. That is perhaps the lesson to be learned from the *Annales* approach. In addition, economic, demographic, and social history can indeed be readable and even, at times, entertaining.

There has been a resurgence of interest in that most fascinating of demographic case studies: Ireland. The catastrophic mortality of the great famine of the 1840s, the dramatic emigration (which, significantly, predated the famine) leading to a decline in population from over 8.5 million in 1841 to about 4.5 million in 1961, the very late age at marriage, the high proportion of the population remaining permanently celibate—all these have made Ireland an historical demographic laboratory. It was a major ingredient of Kingsley Davis' "theory of multiphasic response" (1963). For the prefamine period the classic is Connell (1950). Recently, however, Joel Mokyr and Cormac O Grada have launched a major effort to reinterpret Irish population history and its interconnections to the famine and poverty (Mokyr 1983; Mokyr and O Grada 1984). With the abundance of potential microrecords, some exciting additional work is yet in prospect. I would expect, however, that increasing attention will be paid to the postfamine period (Kennedy 1973), with use being made of the original census and vital statistics records. For example, the 1911 census of marriage and fertility of Ireland is apparently available on a limited basis. Important questions need to be answered as to the dynamics of the extreme adjustment patterns of nuptiality in a regime of continued natural fertility in a poor, largely rural setting.

A final mention should be made of studies that transcend the geographic boundaries of Europe and North America. There is a flourishing literature on the economic history of the now developed former colonial areas of Australia and New Zealand. Japan, a non-Western nation that has entered the category of developed countries, has been the subject of increasing attention from demographic and economic historians partly because of its unusual sources and partly because of the interest in this non-Western success story. A starting point for the study of the demographic history of Japan is the now classic study of Irene Taeuber (1958). The Tokugawa period has inspired a good deal of work as the period of Japan's "apprenticeship." Here might be cited the work of Hanley and Yamamura (1977; Hanley 1977), as well as that of T.C. Smith (1977). A recent contribution to the area is a comparative study of Japan and Sweden by Mosk (1983), which covers the pre-modern and the modern periods in both countries and offers an explanation for (1) behavior under the natural fertility regimes prior to the demographic transition and (2) behavior during the demographic transition itself through a model of rational maximizing household behavior. This study is an encouraging application of the basic ideas of neoclassical microeconomic theory, and also offers some hope that more can be gleaned from analysis of economic variables in connection with the European Fertility Project. It is refreshing that the difficult area of comparative economic and demographic history can be so illuminating. Other areas of the developing world have come under scrutiny, but there is often a lack of suitable demographic and economic data to pursue quantitative analysis. Some former colonial areas did benefit from the statistical orientations of the colonial administrations, and the work of Michelle McAlpin on famine and demographic and economic change in India has exploited such data (McAlpin 1983a, 1983b). Latin America may prove a fertile area for such inquiries, since historical data exist and is of reasonable quality in some cases (see for instance, Arretx, Mellafe, and Somoza 1976, 1977b; Somoza 1968; Cancian, Goodman, and Smith 1978).

Conclusion

It is a difficult exercise to summarize the literature and tendencies in a field as rapidly growing as historical demography. Part of that growth may be attributed simply to the abundance and quality of historical sources in this area. But more fundamentally, there is an increasing recognition that demographic processes are integral to the explanation of much in social and economic history. There has been an increasing effort to make fertility mortality, marriage, migration, and labor force activity endogenous to the historical development process. The invention and application of new methodologies and the utilization of large, computerized data sets, many of them at the individual and household level, have made possible inquiries that could never have been attempted previously. There is every expectation that the field of historical demography will increasingly occupy the attention and efforts of economic historians. The hope is that the focus will broaden to encompass other areas of traditional concern, such as investment and consumption behavior, technical change and innovation, international trade, etc. Finally, to the numerous authors and researchers whose work was not mentioned in this chapter, I again make my apologies. Several monographs could be written at present surveying the various fields within historical demography. The interrelation with economic history has become so close that only a comprehensive review would do full justice to the subject posed in the chapter title.

Notes

1. A recent survey of sources with examples of their use may be found in Willigan and Lynch (1982 p. II).

2. Direct standardization simply consists of taking a series, such as age-specific birth or death rates, and applying a "standard" population age structure to them to generate births or deaths. These would be, in turn, divided by the total of the "standard" population to obtain a single age-standardized birth or death rate. These standardized rates could be compared to an ordinary crude birth or death rate to gauge the impact of differing age-specific rates with a constant age structure. Indirect standardization involves the application of "standard" age-specific birth, death, marriage, or migration rates to a known age structure to generate total births, deaths, etc. These can then be divided by the total of the actual population to produce another form of standardized rates for comparison with ordinary crude rates. This is usually done when there are no actual age-specific rates available or when the effect of differing age structures is of interest. An instructive example of a form of indirect standardization is the set of Coale indices (Coale 1967), discussed below.

3. The *P*/*F*—ratio method compares achieved parity (*P*), or number of children ever born, to women of some age or marital duration, to cumulated age- or marital-duration-specific birthrates (*F*). The assumption is that parity accurately gives level of fertility while the age- or duration-specific rates accurately provide the age or duration fertility pattern. Thus the *P*/*F* ratio provides a correction to the age- or duration-specific rates.

4. A description may be found in Coale (1969).

5. The Office of Population Research at Princeton University has made available tapes of the basic data generated by the European Fertility Project.

6. A useful review and critique of the methodology is provided in a review of Wrigley and Schofield's book by T.H. Hollingsworth in *Population Studies* 36(3):(1982) 495–499. A convenient short treatment of findings for the eighteenth-century is given in Lee and Schofield (1981).

7. Some reverse projection fertility estimation methods are quite sophisticated and involve more than one census. For example, Coale and Zelnik (1963) reverse projected the native white population of the United States from the decennial censuses of 1880 through 1960 to obtain estimates of age- and sex-specific errors of enumeration in these censuses and

also of white birthrates (1855–1960). A similar exercise was performed for the American black population by Coale and Rives (1973).

8. For instance, Woods and Smith (1983) make estimates of age specific marital fertility rates by social class of father for several areas in England for 1851, 1861, and 1871 by using cemetery records and model life tables to obtain class-specific child and adult female mortality differences The procedure used has its difficulties and is illustrative of the estimation problems posed by this method.

9. The 1910 United States census public use sample is being entered by mircocomputer.

10. A listing of historical published state census materials for the United States may be found in Dubest .r (1948).

11. The manuscripts of the 1885 Massachusetts census are no longer extant. The 1911 Census of England and Wales will not be available until the year 2011, although the 1911 Census of Ireland is currently accessible. Special tabulations of the 1911 Scottish census exist with the Registrar General of Scotland.

12. The 1940 United States census published extensive tabulations of parity by age of women cross-tabulated along a number of other dimensions. In addition, a special sample of the 1910 census manuscripts was made in conjunction with the 1940 census work and tabulations of parity data were also thus made for 1910 (U.S. Bureau of the Census 1943, 1945).

13. A number of valuable titles have appeared in the series *Quantitative Applications in the Social Sciences* by Sage Publications, covering a wide range of methodologies and issues.

14. There has been, however, some recent research with economic models of fertility that do include endogenous tastes (Easterlin, Pollak, and Wachter 1980).

15. A summary of the debate concerning the relationship between land availability and facility may be found in Vinovskis (1978) and Easterlin (1977).

16. The infant mortality rate and the expectation of life at birth are the summary measures so used.

17. A glance at recent issues of the *Journal of Family History* should suffice here.

18. The approach derives its name from the journal *Annales E.S.C.* which was founded by Marc Bloch and Lucien Fevre in 1929 as a reaction to the prevalent types of French historical work (narrative, biographical, political, and diplomatic). This journal has been a forum for the presentation of a large amount of historical economic, social, and demographic research.

19. A summary of these studies can be found in Weir (1983).

References

Adams, John W., and Alice B. Kasakoff 1980. Migration at marriage in colonial New England: A comparison of rates derived from genealogies with rates from vital records. In Bennett Dyke and Warren T. Morrill (eds.), *Genealogical Demography*. New York: Academic Press. Pp. 115–138.

Adams, John W., and Alice B. Kasakoff. 1984. Migration and the family in colonial New England: The view from genealogies. *Journal of Family History* 9(1):24–43.

Agren, Kurt, David Graunt, Ingrid Eriksson, John Rogers, Anders Norberg, and Sune Akerman. 1973. *Aristocrats, Farmers, and Proletarians: Essays in Swedish Demographic History*. Studia Historica Upsaliensia 42. Uppsala: Almquist and Wiksell.

Alter, George. 1983a. Estimating mortality from annuities, insurance, and other life contingent contracts. *Historical Methods* 16(1):45–58.

Alter, George, 1983b. Plague and the Amsterdam annuitant: A new look at life annuities as a source for historical demography. *Population Studies* 37(1): 23–41.

Alter, George. 1984. Work and income in the family economy: Belgium, 1853, and 1891. *Journal of Interdisciplinary History* 15(2):255–276.

Alter, George, and James Riley. Forthcoming. How to bet on lives: A guide to life contingent contracts in early modern Europe. *Research in Economic History*.

Anderson, Barbara A. 1977. Who chose the cities? Migrants to Moscow and St. Petersburg cities in the late nineteenth-century. In Ronald D. Lee (ed.), *Population Patterns in the Past*. New York: Academic Press. Pp. 277–295.

Anderson, Barbara A. 1980. *Internal Migration during Modernization in Late Nineteenth-Century Russia*. Princeton, New Jersey: Princeton University Press.

Anderson, Michael. 1971. *Family Structure in Nineteenth-Century Lancashire*. Cambridge: Cambridge University Press.

Anderson, Michael. 1976. Marriage patterns in Victorian Britain: An analysis based on registration district data for England and Wales, 1861. *Journal of Family History*1(2):55–78.

Anderton, Douglas L., and Lee L. Bean. 1985. Birth spacing and fertility limitation: A behavioral analysis of a nineteenth-century population.*Demography* 22(2):169–183.

Appleby, Andrew B. 1980. The disappearance of plague: A continuing puzzle. *Economic History Review*, 2nd ser. 33(2):161–173.

Arretx, Carmen, Rolando Mellafe, and Jorge L. Somoza. 1976. Mortality estimates in a parish of Santiago from orphanhood information. Nunoa, 1866–1871 *CELADE* ser. A, no. 145 (October).

Arretx, Carmen, Rolando Mellafe, and Jorge L. Somoza. 1977a. Adult mortality estimate based on information on age structure of deaths. An application to data for San Felipe around 1787. *CELADE* ser. A, no. 153 (February).

Arretx, Carmen, Rolando Mellafe, and Jorge L. Somaza. 1977b. Fertility estimate through the own children method. An application to data from Argentina, 1895. *CELADE* ser. A, no. 154 (February).

Bateman, Fred, and James D. Fourst. 1974. A sample of rural households selected from the 1860 manuscript censuses. *Agricultural History* 48(1):75–93.

Bean, Frank D., and John P. Marcum. 1978. Differential fertility and the minority group status hypothesis: An assessment and review. In Frank D. Bean and W. Parker Frisbee (eds.), *The Demography of Racial and Ethnic Groups*. New York: Academic Press. Pp. 189–211.

Bean, Lee L., Dean L. May, and Mark Skolnick. 1978. The Morman Historical Demography Project. *Historical Methods* 11(1):45–53.

Bean, Lee L., Geraldine P. Mineau, and Douglas Anderton. 1983. Residence and religious effects on declining family size: An historical analysis of the Utah population. *Review of Religious Research* 25:91–101.

Bean, Lee L., Geraldine P. Mineau, Katherine A. Lynch, and J. Dennis Willigan. 1980. The Genealogical Society of Utah as a data resource for historical demorgraphy. *Population Index* 46(1):6–19.

Becker, Gary S. 1975. *Human Capital*. 2nd ed. New York: Columbia University Press.

Becker, Gary S. 1976. *The Economic Approach to Human Behavior*. Chicago: University of Chicago Press.

Becker, Gary S. 1981. *A Treatise on the Family*. Cambridge, MA: Harvard University Press.

Bennett, Neil G., and Shiro Horiuchi. 1981. Estimating the completeness of death registration in a closed population. *Population Index* 47(2):207–221.

Berkner, Lutz 1972. The stem family and the developmental cycle of the peasant household: An eighteenth-century Austrian example. *American Historical Review* 77: 398–418.

Biraben, Jean-Noel. 1968. Certain demographic characteristics of the plague epidemic in France, 1720–22. *Daedalus* 97(2):536–545.

Bishop, Y.M.M., SE. Fienberg, and P.W. Holland. 1975. *Discrete Multivariate Analysis: Theory and Practice*. Cambridge, MA: MIT Press.

Blaug, Mark. 1978. *Economic Theory in Retrospect*. 3rd ed. Cambridge: Cambridge University Press.

Bloch, Marc. 1966. *French Rural History*. Translated by Janet Sondheimer. Berkeley, CA: University of California Press.

Bogue, Donald. 1969. *Principles of Demography*. New York: Wiley.

Bongaarts, John, and Robert G. Potter. 1983. *Fertility, Biology and Behavior: An Analysis of the Proximate Determinants*. New York: Academic Press.

Bourne, Jenny. 1986. New results on the decline in household fertility in the United States from 1750 to 1900. In Stanley Engerman and Robert Gallman (eds.), *Long Term Factors in American Economic Growth*. Chicago: University of Chicago Press.

Brass, William. 1963. The construction of life tables from child survivorship ratios. International Union for the Scientific Study of Population. *International Population Conference: New York, 1961*, vol. 1. London: IUSSP. Pp. 294–301.

Brass, William. 1975. *Methods for Estimating Fertility and Mortality from Limited and Defective Data*. Chapel Hill, NC: Carolina Population Center.

Braudel, Fernand. 1972. *The Mediterranean and the Mediterranean World in the Age of Philip II*, vols. 1 and 2. Translated by Sian Reynolds. New York: Harper & Row.

Braudel, Fernand. 1973. *Capitalism and Material Life*. Translated by Miriam Kochan. New York: Harper & Row.

Braudel, Fernand. 1980. *On History*. Translated by Sarah Matthews. Chicago: University of Chicago Press.

Breckenridge, Mary, B. 1983. *Age, Time, Fertility: Applications of Exploratory Data Analysis*. New York: Academic Press.

Cachinero-Sanchez, Benito. 1985. Estimating levels of adult mortality in eighteenth-century Spain. *Historical Methods* 18(2):63–70.

Cain, Louis P. 1977. An economic history of urban location and sanitation. *Research in Economic History* 2:337–389.

Caldwell, John C. 1982. *Theory of Fertility Decline*. New York: Academic Press.

Cancian, Francesca M., Louis Walt Goodman, and Peter H. Smith. 1978. The Family in Latin America. *Journal of Family History* 3(4):special issue.

Charbonneau, Hubert. 1979. Les regimes de fecondité naturelle en Amerique du Nord: Bilan et analyse des observations. In Henri Leridon and Jane Menken (eds.), *Natural Fertility*. Liege: Ordina Editions. Pp. 441–491.

Cheney, Rose A. 1984. Seasonal aspects of infant and childhood mortality: Philadelphia, 1865–1920. *Journal of Interdisciplinary History* 14(3):561–585.

Cho, Lee J. 1973. The own-children approach to fertility estimation: An elabaoration. International Union for the Scientific Study of Population. *International Population Conference: Liege, 1973*, vol. 2. Liege: IUSSP. Pp. 263–279.

Cho, Lee-Jay, Wilson H. Grabill, and Donald J. Bogue. 1970. *Differential Current Fertility in the United States*. Chicago, II: Community and Family Study Center, University of Chicago.

Coale, Ansley J. 1967. Factors associated with the development of low fertility: An historic summary. In *World Population Conference: 1965*, vol. 2. New York: United Nations. Pp. 205–209.

Coale, Ansley J. 1969. The decline of fertility in Europe from the French Revolution to World War II. In S.J. Behrman, Leslie Corsa, Jr., and Ronald Freedman (eds.), *Fertility and Family Planning*. Ann Arbor, MI: University of Michigan Press. Pp. 3–24.

Coale, Ansley J. 1971. Age patterns of marriage. *Population Studies*. 25(2): 193–214.

Coale, Ansley J. 1972. *The Growth and Structure of Human Populations: A Mathematical Investigation*. Princeton, NJ: Princeton University Press.

Coale, Ansley J. 1974. The demographic transition. IUSSP. *International Population Conference: Liege, 1973*, vol. 1. Liege: International Union for the Scientific Study of Population. Pp. 53–72.

Coale, Ansley J. 1984. Life table construction on the basis of two enumerations of a closed population. *Population Index* 50(2):193–213.

Coale, Ansley J., and Paul Demeny. 1966. *Regional Model Life Tables and Stable Populations*. Princeton, NJ: Princeton University Press.

Coale, Ansley, and Paul Demeny with Barbara Vaughan. 1983. *Regional Model Life Tables and Stable Populations*, 2nd ed. New York: Academic Press.

Coale, Ansley J., and Donald R. McNeil. 1972. The distribution by age of the frequency of first marriage in a female cohort. *Journal of the American Statistical Association* 67(340):743–749.

Coale, Ansley J., and Norfleet W. Rives, Jr. 1973. A statistical reconstruction of the black population of the United States 1880–1970: Estmiates of true numbers by age and sex, birth rates, and total fertility. *Population Index* 39(1):3–36.

Coale, Ansley J., and T. James Trussell. 1974. Model fertility schedules: Variations in the age structure of childbearing in human populations. *Population Index* 40(2):185–258.

Coale, Ansley J., and T. James Trussell. 1978. Technical note: Finding the two parameters that specify a model schedule of marital fertility. *Population Index* 44(2):203–213.

Coale, Ansley J., and Susan Cotts Watkins, eds. 1986. *The Decline of Fertility in Europe*. Princeton, NJ: Princeton University Press.

Coale, Ansley J., and Melvin Zelnik. 1963. *New Estimates of Fertility and Population in the United States: A Study of Annual White Births from 1855 to 1960 and of Completeness of Enumeration in the Censuses from 1880 to 1960.* Princeton, NJ: Princeton University Press.

Coale, Ansley J., Barbara Anderson, and Erna Harm. 1979. *Human Fertility in Russia Since the Nineteenth-Century: The Demographic Transition in a Different Historical Context.* Princeton, NJ: Princeton University Press.

Coale, Ansley J., Meredith John, and Toni Richards. 1985. Calculation of age-specific fertility schedules from tabulations of parity in two censuses. *Demography* 22(4):611–623.

Cochrane, Susan Hill. 1979. *Fertility and Education: What Do We Really Know?* World Bank Staff Occasional Papers, No. 26. Baltimore: Johns Hopkins University Press.

Condran, Gretchen A. 1984. An evaluation of estimates of underenumeration in the census and the age pattern of mortality, Philadelphia, 1880. *Demography* 21(1):53–69.

Condran, Gretchen A., and Rose A. Cheney. 1982. Mortality trends in Philadelphia: Age and cause-specific death rates, 1870–1930. *Demography* 19(1):97–123.

Condran, Gretchen, and Eileen Crimmins-Gardner. 1978. Public health measures and mortality in U.S. cities in the late nineteenth-century. *Human Ecology* 6(2):27–54.

Condran, Gretchen, and Eileen Crimmins. 1979. A description and evaluation of mortality data in the federal census: 1850–1900. *Historical Methods*. 12(1): 1–23.

Condran, Gretchen, and Eileen Crimmins-Gardner. 1980. Mortality differentials between rural and urban areas in the northeastern United States, 1890–1900. *Journal of Historical Geography* 6(2):179–202.

Connell, K.H. 1850. *The Population of Ireland, 1750–1845*. Oxford: Clarendon Press.

Crafts, N.F.R. 1978. Average age at first marriage for women in mid-nineteenth century England and Wales: A cross-section study. *Population Studies* 32(1):21–25.

Crafts, N.F.R. 1984a. A cross-sectional study of legitimate fertility in England and Wales in 1911. *Research in Economic History* 9:89–107.

Crafts, N.F.R. 1984b. A time series study of fertility in England and Wales, 1877–1938. *Journal of European Economic History* 13(3):571–590.

Crimmins, Eileen, and Gretchen A. Condran. 1983. Mortality variation in U.S. cities in 1900: A two-level explanation by cause of death and underlying factors. *Social Science History* 7(1):31–59.

Curtin, Philip D. 1969. *The Atlantic Slave Trade: A Census*. Madison, WI: University of Wisconsin Press.

Davenport, David Paul. 1984. Tracing rural New York's out-migrants, 1855–1860. *Historical Methods* 17(3):59–67.

Davenport, David Paul. 1985. Duration of residence in the 1855 census of New York state. *Historical Methods* 18(1):5–12.

David, Paul A., and Thomas Mroz. 1985. A seqential econometric model of birth spacing behavior among rural French villagers, 1749–1789. Stanford Project on the History of Fertility Control. Working Paper No. 19 (December).

David, Paul A., and Warren Sanderson. 1984. Spacing versus stopping in the past: Marital duration specific patterns of fertility control among U.S. native white women, 1880–1910. Stanford Project on the History of Fertility Control. Working Paper No. 13 (April).

David, Paul, and Warren Sanderson. 1986. Rudimentary contraceptive methods and the American fertility transition to marital fertility control, 1855–1915. In Stanley Engerman and Robert Gallman (eds.), *Long Term Factors in American Economic Growth*. Chicago: University of Chicago Press.

David, Paul A., and William A. Sundstrom. 1984. Bargains, bequests, and births: An essay on intergenerational conflict, reciprocity, and the demand for children in agrarian societies. Stanford Project on the History of Fertility Control. Working Paper No. 12 (June).

David, Paul A., Thomas Mroz, and Kenneth Wachter 1985. Rational strategies of birth spacing and fertility regulation in rural France during the ancien regime. Stanford Project on the History of Fertility Control Working Paper No. 14 (March).

Davis, Kingsley. 1963. The theory of change and response in modern demographic history. *Population Index* 29(4):345–366.

Davis, Kingsley. 1973. Cities and mortality. International Union for the Scientific Study of Population. *International Population Conference: Liege, 1973*. (Liege: IUSSP.) 3:259–282.

Davis, Kingsley, and Judith Blake. 1956. Social structure and fertility. *Economic Development and Cultural Change* 4(3):211–235.

Desjardins, Bertrand, Pierre Beauchamp, and Jacques Legare. 1977. Automatic family reconstitution: The French-Canadian seventeeth-century experience. *Journal of Family History* 2(1):56–76.

Dubester, Henry J. 1948. *State Censuses: An Annotated Bibliography of Censuses of Population Taken After the Year 1790 by States and Territories of the United States*. Washington, D.C.: GPO.

Dupaquier, Jacques. 1974. *Introduction a la demographie historique*. Paris: Gamma.

Dupaquier, Jacques, 1979. Etude comparative des donnees sur la fecondite dans 25 monographies concernant le bassin Parisien a la fin du XVIIe siecle et au debut du XVIIIe. In Henri Leridon and Jane Menken (eds.), *Natural Fertility*. Liege: Ordina Editions. Pp. 409–439.

Easterlin, Richard A. 1967. The effects of population growth on the economic development of developing countries. *Annals of the American Academy of Political and Social Science* 364(January):98–108.

Easterlin, Richard A. 1968. Economic growth: An overview. *International Encyclopedia of the Social Sciences*, vol. 4. New York: MacMillan. Pp. 395–408.

Easterlin, Richard A. 1973. Relative economic status and the American fertility swing. In Eleanor B. Sheldon (ed.), *Family Economic Behavior: Problems and Prospects*. Philadelphia: Lippincott. Pp. 170–223.

Easterlin, Richard A. 1976. Population change and farm settlement in the northern United States. *Journal of Economic History* 36(1):45–75.

Easterlin, Richard A. 1977. Population issues in American economic history: A survey and critiques. In Robert Gallman (ed.), *Recent Developments in the Study of Business and Economic History: Essays in Honor of Herman E. Krooss*. Greenwich, CT: JAI Press. Pp. 131–158.

Easterlin, Richard A. 1978. The economics and sociology of fertility: A synthesis. In Charles Tilly (ed.), *Historical Studies of Changing Fertility*. Princeton, NJ: Princeton University Press. Pp. 57–133.

Easterlin, Richard A. 1980. *Birth and Fortune: The Impact of Numbers on Personal Welfare*. New York: Basic Books.

Easterlin, Richard A., George Alter, and Gretchen Condran. 1978. Farms and farm families in old and new areas: The northern states in 1860. In Tamara K. Hareven and Maris Vinovskis (eds.), *Family and Population in Nineteenth-Century America*. Princeton, NJ: Princeton University Press. Pp. 22–84.

Easterlin, Richard A., Robert A. Pollak, and Michael L. Wachter. 1980. Toward a more general economic model of fertility determination: Endogenous preferences and natural fertility. In Richard A. Easterlin (ed.), *Population and Economic Change in Developed Countries*. Chicago: University of Chicago Press. Pp. 81–149.

Eblen, Jack E. 1974. New estimates of the vital rates of the United States black population during the nineteenth-century. *Demography* 11(2):301–319.

Eldridge, Hope T., and Dorothy Swaine Thomas. 1964. *Population Redistribution and Economic Growth: United States, 1870–1950*, vol. 3, Demographic analyses and interrelations. Philadelphia: American Philosophical Society.

Engerman, Stanley L. 1978. Changes in black fertility, 1880–1940. In Tamara K. Hareven and Maris A. Vinovskis (eds.), *Family and Population in Nineteenth-Century America*. Princeton, NJ: Princeton University Press. Pp. 126–153.

Ewbank, D.C. 1982. The sources of error in Brass's method for estimating child survival: The case of Bangladesh. *Population Studies* 36(3):459–474.

Ewbank, D.C., J.C. Gomez de Leon, and M.A. Stoto. 1983. A reducible four-parameter system of model life tables. *Population Studies* 37(1):105–127.

Fienberg, Stephen E. 1977. *The Analysis of Cross-Classified Categorized Data*. Cambridge, MA: M.I.T. Press.

Fishlow, Albert. 1973. Comparative consumption patterns, the extent of the market, and alternative development strategies. In Eliezar B. Ayal (ed.), *Micro Aspects of Development*. New York: Preager. Pp. 41–80.

Fleury, Michael, and Louis Henry. 1976. *Nouveau manuel de depouillement et d'exploitation de l'etat civil ancien*. 2nd ed. Paris: Editions de L'I.N.E.D.

Fogel. Robert W. 1984. Nutrition and the decline in mortality since 1700: Some preliminary findings. National Bureau of Eoconomic Research. Working Paper No. 1402 (July).

Fogel, Robert W., and Stanley L. Engerman. 1974. *Time on the Cross: The Economics of American Negro Slavery*, vol. 2. Boston: Little-Brown.

Fogel, R.W., and Stanley L. Engerman. 1977. Explaining the relative efficiency of slave agriculture in the antebellum South. *American Economic Review* 67(3):275–308.

Fogel, R.W., et al. 1983. Secular changes in American and British stature and nutrition. *The Journal of Interdisciplinary History* 14(2):445–481.

Forster, Colin, and G.S.L. Tucker. 1972. *Economic Opportunity and White American Fertility Ratios, 1800–1860*. New Haven, CT: Yale University Press.

Forster, Robert. 1978. Achievements of the Annales School. *Journal of Economic History* 38(1):58–76.

Foust, James D. 1976. *The Yeoman Farmer and the Westward Expansion of U.S. Cotton Production*. New York: Arno Press.

Galenson, David. 1981. *White Servitude in Colonial America: An Economic Analysis*. Cambridge: Cambridge University Press.

Goldin, Claudia. 1979. Household and market production of families in a late nineteenth-century city. *Explorations in Economic History* 16:111–131.

Goldin, Claudia. 1981. Family strategies and the family economy in the late nineteenth-century: The role of secondary workers. In Theodore Hershberg (ed.), *Phildelphia: Work, Space, Family, and Group Experience in the Nineteenth-Century*. New York: Oxford University Press. Pp. 277–310.

Goubert, Pierre. 1960. *Beauvais et le beauvasis de 1600 à 1730*. Paris: SEVPEN.

Grabill, Wilson H., and Lee Jay Cho. 1965. Methodology for the measurement of current fertility from population data on young children. *Demography* 2:50–73.

Graff, Harvey J. 1979. Literacy, education, and fertility, past and present: A critical review. *Population and Development Review* 5(1):105–135.

Guest, Avery M. 1982. Fertility variation among the U.S. foreign stock population in 1900. *International Migration Review* 16, p. 3, no. 59:577–594.

Guest, Avery M., and Stewart Tolnay. 1983a. Urban industrial structure and fertility: the case of large American cities. *Journal of Interdisciplinary History* 13(3):387–409.

Guest, Avery M., and Stewart Tolnay. 1983b. Children's roles and fertility: Late nineteenth-century United States. *Social Science History* 7(4):355–380.

Gutman, Robert. 1956. The accuracy of vital statistics in Massachusetts, 1842–1901. Unpublished Ph.D. dissertation. New York: Columbia University.

Gutmann, Myron P., and Etienne van de Walle. 1978. New sources for social and demographic history: The Belgian population registers. *Social Science History* 2(2):121–143.

Hubakkuk, H. J. 1972. *Population Growth and Economic Development since 1750*. Leicester, England: Leicester University Press.

Haines, Michael R. 1976. Population and economic change in nineteenth-century Eastern Europe: Prussian Upper Silesia, 1840–1913. *Journal of Economic History* 36(2):334–358.

Haines, Michael R. 1977. Mortality in nineteenth-century America: Estimates from New York and Pennsylvania census data, 1865 and 1900. *Demography* 14(3):311–331.

Haines, Michael R. 1979a. The use of model life tables to a estimate mortality for the United States in the late nineteenth-century. *Demography* 16(2):289–312.

Haines, Michael R. 1979b. *Fertility and Occupation: Population Patterns in Industrialization*. New York: Academic Press.

Haines, Michael R. 1979c. Industrial work and the family life cycle, 1889–1890. *Research in Economic History* 4:289–356.

Haines, Michael R. 1980a. Fertility and marriage in a nineteenth-century industrial city: Philadelphia, 1850–1880. *Journal of Economic History* 40(1):151–158.

Haines, Michael R. 1980b. Why were nineteenth-century U.S. urban black fertility rates so low? Evidence from Philadelphia, 1850–1880. Unpublished paper. Wayne State University, Department of Economics.

Haines, Michael R. 1981. Poverty, economic stress, and the family in a late nineteenth-century American city: Whites in Philadelphia, 1880. In Theodore Hershberg (ed.), *Philadelphia: Work, Space, Family, and Group Experience in the Nineteenth-Century*. New York: Oxford University Press. Pp.240–276.

Haines, Michael R. 1984. Ethnic differentials in marital fertility during fertility decline: Philadelphia, 1850–1880. Paper presented at the annual meetings of the Population Association of America, Minneapolis, Minnesota, May 2–5, 1984.

Haines, Michael R. 1985a. The life cycle, savings, and demographic adaptation: Some historical evidence for the United States and Europe. In Alice S. Rossi (ed.), *Gender and the Life Course*. New York: Aldine. Pp.43–63.

Haines, Michael R. 1985b. Inequality and childhood mortality: A comparison of England and Wales, 1911, and the United States, 1900. *The Journal of Economic History* 45(4): 885–912.

Haines Michael R., and Samuel H. Preston. 1984. Cities, ethnicity, and child mortality in the United States in 1900. Paper presented at the annual meetings of the Social Science History Association, Toronto, Ontario, 26–28 October 1984.

Hajnal, John. 1953. Age at marriage and proportions marrying. *Population Studies* 7(3):111–136.

Hajnal, John. 1965. European marriage patterns in perspective. In D. V. Glass and D. E. C. Eversly (eds.), *Population in History*. London: Arnold. Pp. 101–143.

Hammel, E. A., and Kenneth W. Wachter. 1977. Primonuptiality and ultimonuptiality: Their effects on stem-family-household frequencies. In Ronald D.Lee (ed.), *Population Patterns in the Past*. New York: Academic Press. Pp. 113–134.

Hanley, Susan B. 1977. The influence of economic and social variables on marriage and fertility in eighteenth and nineteenth century Japanese villages. In Ronald D. Lee (ed.), *Population Patterns in the Past*. New York: Academic Press. Pp. 165–200.

Hanley, Susan B., and Kozo Yamamura. 1977. *Economic and Demographic Change in Preindustrial Japan, 1600–1868*. Princeton, NJ: Princeton University Press.

Hareven, Tamara K. 1982. *Family Time and Industrial Time: The Relationship between the Family and Work in a New England Industrial Community*. Cambridge: Cambridge University Press.

Hareven, Tamara K., and Maris A. Vinovskis. 1975. Marital fertility, ethnicity, and occupation in urban families: An analysis of South Boston and the South End in 1880. *Journal of Social History* 8::69–93.

Hareven, Tamara K., and Maris A. Vinovskis. 1978. Patterns of childbearing in late nineteenth-century America: The determinants of marital fertility in five Massachusetts towns in 1880. In Tamara K. Hareven and Maris A. Vinovskis (eds.), *Family and Population in Nineteenth-Century America*. Princeton, NJ: Princeton University Press. Pp. 85–125.

Helleiner, Karl F. 1965. The Vital Revolution reconsidered. In D.V. Glass and D.E.C. Eversley (eds.), *Population in History*. Chicago: Aldine. Pp. 79–86.

Helleiner, Karl F. 1967. The population of Europe from the Black Death to the eve of the Vital Revolution. In E.E. Rich and C.H. Wilson (eds.), *The Cambridge Economic History of Europe* IV, The economy of expanding Europe in the sixteenth and seventeenth centuries. Cambridge: Cambridge University Press. Pp. 1–95.

Henry, Louis. 1953. "Fondements theoretiques des measures de la fecondite naturelle." *Revue de L'Institute Internationale de Statistique* 21(3):135–252.

Henry, Louis. 1956. *Anciennes familles genevoises: Etude demographique, XVIe–XXe siecle*. Paris: Presses Universitaires de France.

Henry, Louis. 1957. Fecondite et famille, models mathematiques. *Population* 12(3):413–444.

Henry, Louis. 1961. Some data on natural fertility. *Eugenics Quarterly* 8(2):81–91.

Henry, Louis. 1967. *Manuel de demographie historique*. Paris: Droz.

Henry, Louis. 1972a. Fecondité des marriages dans le quart sud-ouest de la France de 1720 à 1829, pt. 1. *Annales, E.S.C* 27(3):612–640.

Henry, Louis. 1972b. Fecondité des marriages dans le quart sud-ouest de la France de 1720 à 1829, pt. 2. *Annales, E.S.C.* 27(4–5):977–1023.

Henry, Louis. 1978a. Demographie historique: L'enquete de l'I.N.E.D. sur la population de la France avant 1800. *Journal de la Societé de Statistique de Paris* 119(3):229-233.

Henry, Louis. 1978b. Fecondite des marriages dans le quart sud-est de la France de 1670 à 1829. *Population* 33(4–5):856–883.

Henry, Louis, and Jacques Houdaille. 1973. Fecondité des marriages dans le quart nord-ouest de la France de 1670 à 1829. *Population* 28(4–5):873–924.

Henry, Louis, and Jacques Houdaille. 1978. Celibat et age au marriage aux XVIIIe et XIXe siecles en France. I. Celibat definitif. *Population* 33(1):43–83.

Henry, Louis, and Jacques Houdaille. 1979. Celibat et age au marriage aux XVIIIe et XIXe siecles en France. II. Age au premier marriage. *Population* 34(2):433–442.

Hershberg, Theodore, ed. 1976. The Philadelphia Social History Project. *Historical Methods Newsletter* 9(2–3):.

Hershberg, Theodore, ed. 1981. *Philadelphia: Work, Space, Family, and Group Experience in the Nineteenth-Century*. New York: Oxford University Press.

Higgs, Robert. 1973. Mortality in rural America, 1870–1920: Estimates and conjectures. *Explorations in Economic History* 10(2):177–195.

Himes, Norman E. 1936. *Medical History of Contraception*. Baltimore: Williams and Wilkins.

Hobsbawn, E.J. 1957. The British standard of living, 1790–1850. *Economic History Review* 2nd ser. 10(1):46–68.

Hochstadt, Steve. 1981. Migration and industrialization in Germany, 1815–1977. *Social Science History* 5(4):445–468.

Hoffman, Elizabeth. 1981. *The Sources of Mortality Changes in Italy since Unification*. New York: Arno Press.

Hogan, Dennis P., and David I. Kertzer. 1985. Migration patterns during Italian urbanization. *Demography* 22(3):309–325.

Hollingsworth, T.H. 1964. The demography of the British peerage. *Supplement to Population Studies* 18(2).

Hollingsworth, T.H. 1969. *Historical Demography*. Ithaca, New York: Cornell University Press.

Houdaille, J., and L. Henry. 1976. La fecondité des marriages dans le quart nord-est de la France de 1670 à 1829. *Annales de Demographie Historique* 341–392.

Hout, Michael. 1983. *Mobility Tables*. Sage University Paper Series on Quantitative Applications in the Social Sciences, ser. no. 07–031. Beverly Hills, CA: Sage Publications.

Innes, J.W. 1938. *Class Fertility Differentials in England and Wales, 1876–1934*. Princeton, NJ: Princeton University Press.

Jones, Alice Hanson. 1980. *Wealth of a Nation to Be: The American Colonies on the Eve of the Revolution*. New York: Columbia University Press.

Jorde, L.B., and H.C. Harpending. 1976. Cross-spectral analysis of rainfall and human birth rate: An empirical test of a linear model. In R.H. Ward and K.M. Weiss (eds.), *The Demographic Evolution of Human Populations*. New York: Academic Press. Pp. 129–138.

Journal of Interdisciplinary History. 1983.Hunger and history: The impact of changing food production and consumption patterns on society 14(2):

Katz, Michael B., Michael J. Doucet, and Mark J. Stern 1978. Migration and the social order in Erie County, New York, 1855. *Journal of Interdisciplinary History* 8(4):669–701.

Katz, Michael B., Michael J. Doucet, and Mark J. Stern. 1982. *The Social Organization of Early Industrial Capitalism*. Cambridge, MA: Harvard University Press.

Kearl, J.R., and Clayne L. Pope. 1983. The life cycle in economic history. *Journal of Economic History* 43(1):149–158.

Kelley, Allen C. 1972. Demographic changes and American economic development, past, present and future. In Elliott R. Morss and Ritchie H. Reed (eds.),

Economic Aspects of Population Change. U.S. Commission on Population Growth and the American Future. Vol. II of Commission Research Reports. Washington, D.C.: GPO. Pp. 9–48.

Kennedy, Jr., Robert E. 1973. *The Irish: Emigration, Marriage, and Fertility*. Berkeley, CA: University of California Press.

Killingsworth, Mark R. 1983. *Labor Supply*. Cambridge: Cambridge University Press.

Kintner, Hallie J. 1982. *The Determinants of Infant Mortality in Germany from 1871 to 1933*. Ph.D. dissertation: University of Michigan.

Kintner, Hallie J. 1985. Trends and regional differences in breastfeeding in Germany from 1871 to 1937. *Journal of Family History* 10(2):163–182.

Knights, Peter, 1971. *The Plain People of Boston, 1830–1860: A Study of City Growth*. New York: Oxford University Press.

Knodel, John. 1968. Infant mortality and fertility in three Bavarian villages: An analysis of family histories in the nineteenth-century. *Population Studies* 22(3):297–318.

Knodel, John. 1974. *The Decline of Fertility in Germany, 1871–1939*. Princeton, NJ: Princeton University Press.

Knodel, John. 1977a. Town and country in nineteenth-century Germany: A review of urban-rural differentials in demographic behavior. *Social Science History* 1(3):356–382.

Knodel, John. 1977b. Family limitation and the fertility transition: Evidence from the age pattern of fertility in Europe and Asia. *Population Studies* 31(2): 219–249.

Knodel, John. 1978. Natural fertility in pre-industrial Germany. *Population Studies* 32(3):481–510.

Knodel, John. 1979. From natural fertility to family limitation: The onset of fertility transition in a sample of German villages. *Demography* 16(4):493–522.

Knodel, John. 1983. Natural fertility: Age patterns, levels, and trends. In Rodolfo A. Bulatao and Ronald D. Lee (eds.), *Determinants of Fertility in Developing Countries*, vol. 1, Supply and demand for children. New York: Academic Press. Pp. 61–102.

Knodel, John, and Hallie Kintner. 1977. The impact of breast feeding patterns on the biometric analysis of infant mortality. *Demography* 14(4):391–409.

Knodel, John, and Mary Jo Maynes. 1976. Urban and rural marriage patterns in imperial Germany. *Journal of Family History* 1(2):129–168.

Knodel, John, and Edward Shorter. 1976. The reliability of family reconstitution data in German village genealogies (*Ortssippenbucher*). *Annales de Demographie Historique*, pp.115–154.

Knodel, John, and Etienne van de Walle. 1967. Breast feeding, fertility, and infant mortality: An analysis of some early German data. *Population Studies*. 21(2):109–131.

Knodel, John, and Etienne van de Walle. 1979. Lessons from the past: Policy implications of historical fertility studies. *Population and Development Review*

5(2):217–245.
Knodel, John, and Etienne van de Walle. 1982. Fertility decline: 3. European transition. In John A. Ross (ed.), *International Encyclopedia of Population*. New York: Free Press. Pp. 268–275.
Kousser, J. Morgan, David Galenson, and Gary W. Cox. 1982. Log-linear analysis of contingency tables: An introduction for historians with an application to Thernstrom on the "Floating Proletariat." *Historical Methods* 15(4):152–169.
Kunze, Kent. 1979. The effects of age composition and changes in vital rates on nineteenth-century population estimates from new data. Ph.D. dissertation, Department of Economics, University of Utah.
Kuznets, Simon. 1965. *Economic Growth and Structure*. New York: Norton.
Kuznets, Simon. 1966. *Modern Economic Growth: Rate, Structure, and Spread*. New Haven: Yale University Press.
Kuznets, Simon, Ann R. Miller, and Richard A. Easterlin. 1960. *Population Redistribution and Economic Growth: United States, 1870–1950*, vol. 2, Analyses of economic change. Philadelphia: American Philosophical Society.
Laslett, Peter, and Richard Wall, eds. 1972. *Household and Family in Past Time*. Cambridge: Cambridge University Press.
Laurie, Bruce, Theodore Hershberg and George Alter. 1981. Immigrants and industry: The Philadelphia experience 1850–1880. In Theodore Hershberg, (ed.), *Philadelphia: Work, Space, Family, and Group Experience in the Nineteenth-Century*. New York: Oxford University Press. pp. 93–119.
Lawton, Richard, ed. 1978. *The Census and Social Structure: An Interpretive Guide to Nineteenth-Century Censuses for England and Wales*. London: Frank Cass.
Le Roy Ladurie, Emmanuel. 1967. *Histoire du climat depuis l'an mil*. Paris: Flammarion.
Le Roy Ladurie, Emmanuel. 1974. *The Peasants of Languedoc*. Translated by John Day. Urbana: University of Illinois Press.
Le Roy Ladurie, Emmanuel. 1978. *Montaillou: The Promised Land of Error*. Translated by Barbara Bray. New York: Braziller.
Lebergott, Stanley. 1964. *Manpower in Economic Growth: the American Record since 1800*. New York: McGraw-Hill.
Lebergott, Stanley. 1970. Migration within the United States, 1800–1960: Some new estimates. *Journal of Economic History* 30(4):839–847.
Ledermann, Sully. 1969. *Nouvelles tables-types de mortalite*. Cahier No. 53 de l'Institut National d'Etudes Demographiques. Paris: Presses Universitaires de France.
Lee, Everett S., A.R. Miller, C.P. Brainerd, and R.A. Easterlin. 1957. *Population Redistribution and Economic Growth: United States, 1870–1950*, vol. 1, Methodological considerations and reference tables. Philadelphia: American Philosophical Society.
Lee, Ronald D. 1973. Population in pre-industrial England: An econometric analysis. *Quarterly Journal of Economics* 87(4):581–607.
Lee, Ronald D. 1974. Estimating series of vital rates and age structures from

baptisms and burials: A new technique, with applications to pre-industrial England. *Population Studies* 28(3):495–512.

Lee, Ronald D. 1975. Natural fertility, population cycles, and spectral analysis of births and marriages. *Journal of the American Statistical Association*. 70(350): 295–304.

Lee, Ronald D. 1977. Methods and models for analyzing historical series of births, deaths and marriages. In Ronald D. Lee (ed.), *Population Patterns in the Past*. New York: Academic Press. Pp. 337–370.

Lee, Ronald D. 1978. Models of pre-industrial population dynamics, with applications to England. In Charles Tilly (ed.), *Historical Studies of Changing Fertility*. Princeton, NJ: Princeton University Press, Pp. 155–207.

Lee, Ronald D. 1981. Short-term variation: Vital rates, prices, and weather. In E. A Wrigley and R. S. Schofield. *The Population History of England, 1541–1871*. Cambridge, MA: Harvard University Press. Pp. 356–401.

Lee, Ronald D. 1985. Inverse projection and back projection: A critical appraisal, and comparative results for England, 1539 to 1871. *Population Studies*. 39(2):233–248.

Lee, Ronald D., and R. S. Schofield. 1981. British population in the eighteenth-century. In Roderick Floud and Donald McCloskey (eds.), *The Economic History of Britain since 1700*, vol. 1, *1700–1860*. Cambridge: Cambridge University Press. pp. 17–35.

Lees, Lynn H. 1980. Getting and spending: The family budgets of English industrial workers in 1890. In John M. Merriman (ed.), *Consciousness and Class Experience in Nineteenth-Century Europe*. New York: Holmes and Meier. Pp. 169–186.

Leet, Donald R. 1976. The determinants of fertility transition in ante-bellum Ohio. *Journal of Economic History* 36(2):359–378.

Lentzner, Harold R. 1985. Adult mortality estimates from successive censuses: England and Wales in the nineteenth-century. *Historical Methods* 18(2):51–62.

Leridon, Henri. 1977. *Human Fertility: The Basic Components*. Chicago: University of Chicago Press.

Leridon, Henri, and Jane Menken, eds. 1979. *Natural Fertility*. Liege: Ordina Editions.

Lesthaeghe, Ron. 1977. *The Decline of Belgian Fertility, 1800–1970*. Princeton, NJ: Princeton University Press.

Lesthaeghe, Ron. 1980. On the social control of human reproduction. *Population and Development Review*. 6(4):527–548.

Lesthaeghe, Ron. 1983. A century of demographic and cultural change in Western Europe: An exploration of underlying dimensions. *Population and Development Review* 9(3):411–435.

Levine, David. 1977. *Family Formation in an Age of Nascent Capitalism*. New York: Academic Press.

Lindert, Peter H. 1978. *Fertility and Scarcity in America*. Princeton, NJ: Princeton University Press.

Lindert, Peter H. 1980. Child costs and economic development. In Richard A.

Easterlin (ed.), *Population and Economic Change in Developing Countries*. Chicago: University of Chicago Press. Pp. 5–69.
Lindert, Peter H. 1983. English living standards, population growth, and Wrigley-Scofield. *Explorations in Economic History* 20(2):131–155.
Livi-Bacci, Massimo. 1971. *A Century of Portuguese Fertility*. Princeton, NJ: Princeton University Press.
Livi-Bacci, Massimo. 1977. *A history of Italian fertility during the last two centuries*. Princeton, NJ: Princeton University Press.
Lockridge, Kenneth A. 1968. Land, population, and the evolution of New England society, 1630–1790. *Past and Present* 39:62–80.
Long, J. Scott. 1983a. *Confirmatory Factor Analysis*. Sage University paper series on Quantitative Applications in the Social Sciences, ser. no. 07–033. Beverly Hills, CA: Sage Publications.
Long, J. Scott. 1983b. *Covariance Structure Models: An Intrυduction to LISREL*. Sage University Paper Series on Quantitative Applications in the Social Sciences, ser. no. 07–034. Beverly Hills, CA: Sage Publications.
Lotka, Alfred J., and F.R. Sharpe. 1911. A problem in age distribution. *Philosophical Magazine* 21(124):435–438.
Maddala, G.S. 1977. *Econometrics*. New York: McGraw-Hill.
Mason, Karen Oppenheim, Maxine Weinstein, and Barbara Laslett. 1985. The decline of fertility in Los Angeles, California, 1880–1900. Research Report no. 85–83. Population Studies Center. University of Michigan (July).
Matthiessen, Poul C., and James McCann. 1978. The role of mortality in the European fertility transition: Aggregate-level relations. In Samuel H. Preston (ed.), *The Effects of Infant and Child Mortality on Fertility*. New York: Academic Press. Pp. 47–68.
McAlpin, Michelle B. 1983a. Famines, epidemics, and population growth: The case of India. *Journal of Interdisciplinary History* 14(2):351–366.
McAlpin, Michelle B. 1983b. *Subject to Famine: Food Crises and Economic Change in Western India, 1860–1920*. Princeton, NJ: Princeton University Press.
McDonald, John. 1979. A time series approach to forecasting Australian total live-births. *Demography* 16(4):575–601.
McFalls, Joseph. 1973. Impact of VD on the fertility of the U.S. black population, 1880–1950. *Social Biology* 20:2–19.
McFalls, Joseph. 1981. *Disease and Fertility*. New York: Academic Press.
McInnis, R.M. 1977. Childbearing and land availability: Some evidence from individual household data. In Ronald Demos Lee (ed.), *Population Patterns in the Past*. New York: Academic Press. Pp.201–227.
McKeown, Thomas. 1976. *The Modern Rise of Population*. New York: Academic Press.
McKeown, T. 1978. Fertility, mortality, and cause of death. *Population Studies* 32(3):535–542.
McKeown, T., and R.G. Brown. 1955. Medical evidence related to English population changes in the eighteenth-century. *Population Studies* 9(2):119–141.

McKeown, T., and R. G. Record. 1962. Reasons for the decline of mortality in England and Wales during the nineteenth-century. *Population Studies*. 16, 2:94–122.

McKeown, T., R. G. Brown, and R. G. Record. 1972. An interpretation of the modern rise of population in Europe. *Population Studies* 26(3):345–382.

Meeker, Edward. 1976. Mortality trends of southern blacks, 1850–1910: Some preliminary findings. *Explorations in Economic History* 13(1):13–42.

Menken, Jane. 1975. Biometric models of fertility. *Social Forces* 54(1):52–65.

Menken, Jane, James Trussel, Debra Stempel, and Ozer Babakol. 1981. Proportional hazards life table models: An illustrative analysis of sociodemographic influences on marriage dissolution in the United States. *Demography* 18(2): 181–200.

Mineau, Geraldine P. 1980. Fertility on the frontier: An analysis of the nineteenth-century Utah population. Ph.D. dissertation, Department of Sociology, University of Utah.

Mineau, Geraldine P., and James Trussell. 1982. A specification of marital fertility by parents' age, age at marriage and marital duration. *Demography*. 19(3):335–350.

Mineau, Geraldine P., Lee L. Bean, and Mark Skolnick. 1979. Mormon demographic history II: The family life cycle and natural fertility. *Population Studies* 33(3):429–446.

Mitra, S., and A. Romaniuk. 1973. Pearsonian type I curve and its fertility projection potentials. *Demography* 10(3):351–366.

Moch, Leslie Page. 1981a. Marriage, migration and urban demographic structure: A case from France in the Belle Epoque. *Journal of Family History* 6(1):70–88.

Moch, Leslie Page. 1981b. Adolescence and migration to Nimes, France, 1906. *Social Science History* 5(1):25–51.

Moch, Leslie Page. 1983. *Paths to the City: Regional Migration in Nineteenth-Century France*. Beverly Hills, CA: Sage Publications.

Moch, Leslie Page, and Louise Tilly. 1985. Joining the urban world: Occupation, family, and migration in three French cities. *Comparative Studies in Society and History* 27(1):33–56.

Modell, John. 1978. Patterns of consumption, acculturation, and family income strategies in late nineteenth-century America. In Tamara K. Hareven and Maris A. Vinovskis (eds.), *Family and Population in Nineteenth-Century America*. Princeton, NJ: Princeton University Press. Pp.206–240.

Mokyr, Joel. 1983. *Why Ireland Starved: A Quantitative and Analytical History of the Irish Economy, 1800–1850*. London: Allen & Unwin.

Mokyr. Joel, and Cormac O Grada. 1984. New developments in Irish population history, 1700–1850. *Economic History Review* 2nd ser. 37(4):473–488.

Morawetz, David. 1977. *Twenty-Five Years of Economic Development*. Baltimore, MD: Johns Hopkins University Press.

Mosk, Carl. 1983. *Patriarchy and Fertility: Japan and Sweden, 1880–1960*. New York: Academic Press.

Mueller, Eva. 1980. Comment on "Child costs and economic development" by Peter Lindert. In Richard A. Easterlin (ed.), *Population and Economic Change in Developing Countries*. Chicago: University of Chicago Press. Pp. 69–74.

Neal, Larry. 1976. Cross-spectral analysis of long swings in Atlantic migration. *Research in Economic History*. 1:260–297.

Notestein, Frank W. 1953. The economics of population and food supplies. I. The economic problems of population change. *Proceedings of the Eighth International Conference of Agricultural Economists*. London: Oxford University Press.

Olney, Martha L. 1983. Fertility and the standard of living in early modern England: In consideration of Wrigley and Schofield. *Journal of Economic History*. 43(1):71–77.

Page, Hilary J. 1977. Patterns underlying fertility schedules: A decomposition by both age and marriage duration. *Population Studies*. 31(1):85–106.

Parkerson, Donald H. 1982. How mobile were nineteentn-century Americans? *Historial Methods* 15(3):99–109.

Peterson, William. 1979. *Malthus*. Cambridge, MA: Harvard University Press.

Potter, J. 1965. The growth of population in America, 1700–1860. In D.V. Glass and D.E.C. Eversley (eds.), *Population in History*. Chicago: Aldine. Pp. 631–688.

Potter, Robert G., Jr. 1963. Birth intervals: Structure and change. *Population Studies*. 17(2):155–166.

Preston, Samuel H. 1976. *Mortality Patterns in National Populations*. New York: Academic Press.

Preston, Samuel H., ed. 1978. *The Effects of Infant and Child Mortality on Fertility*. New York: Academic Press.

Preston, Samuel H., and Neil G. Bennett. 1983. A census-based method for estimating adult mortality. *Population Studies* 37(1):91–104.

Preston, Samuel H., and Ansley J. Coale. 1982. Age structure, growth, attrition, and accession: A new synthesis. *Population Index* 48(2):217–259.

Preston, Samuel H., and Michael R. Haines. 1984. New estimates of child mortality in the United States at the turn of the century. *Journal of the American Statistical Association* 79(386):272–281.

Preston, Samuel H., and Alberto Palloni. 1978. Fine-tuning Brass-type mortality estimates with data on ages of surviving children. United Nations. *Population Bulletin No. 10*. New York: United Nations. Pp. 72–91.

Preston, Samuel H., and Etienne van de Walle. 1978. Urban French mortality in the nineteenth-century. *Population Studies* 32(2):275–297.

Preston, Samuel H., Michael R. Haines, and Elsie Pamuk. 1981. Effects of industrialization and urbanization on mortality in developed countries. International Union for the Scientific Study of Population, *International Population Conference, Manila, 1981: Solicited Papers*, vol. 2. Liege: IUSSP. Pp. 233–254.

Preston, Samuel H., Nathan Keyfitz, and Robert Schoen. 1972. *Causes of Death: Life Tables for National Populations*. New York: Seminar Press.

Redford, Arthur. 1964. *Labor Migration in England, 1800–1850.* 2nd ed. Edited and revised by W.H. Chaloner. Manchester, England: Manchester University Press.

Richards, Toni. 1977. Fertility decline in Germany: An econometric appraisal. *Population Studies* 31(3):537–553.

Richards, Toni. 1983. Weather, nutrition, and the economy: Short-run fluctuations in births, deaths, and marriages, France, 1740–1909. *Demography* 20(2): 197–212.

Romaniuk, A. 1973. A three-parameter model for birth projections. *Population Studies* 27(3):467–470.

Ryder, Norman. 1973. Comment on "A new approach to the economic theory of fertility behavior" by Robert J. Willis. *Journal of Political Economy* 81(2), II:565–569.

Sanderson, Warren C. 1979. Quantitative aspects of marriage, fertility and family limitation in nineteenth-century America: Another application of the Coale specification. *Demography* 16(3):339–358.

Schofield, Roger. 1983. The impact of scarcity and plenty on population change in England, 1541–1871. *Journal of Interdisciplinary History* 14(2):265–291.

Schultz, T. Paul. 1981. *Economics of Population*. Reading, MA: Addison-Wesley.

Schultz, Theodore W. 1981. *Investing in People: The Economics of Population Quality*. Berkeley, CA: University of California Press.

Sjaastad, Larry. 1962. The costs and returns of human migration. *Journal of Political Economy* 70(5):80–93.

Skolnick, Mark, Lee L. Bean, S.M. Dinetelman, and Geraldine Mineau. 1979. A computerized family history data base system. *Sociology and Social Research*: 601–619.

Skolnick, Mark, Lee L. Bean, V. Arbon, Kide Nevers, and P. Cartwright. 1978. Mormon demographic history I: Nuptiality and fertility of once-married couples. *Population Studies* 32(1):5–19.

Smith, Daniel Scott. 1977. A homeostatic demographic regime: Patterns in West European family reconstitution studies. In Ronald D. Lee (ed.), *Population Patterns in the Past*. New York: Academic Press. Pp. 19–51.

Smith, Daniel Scott. 1983. Differential Mortality in the United States before 1900. *Journal of Interdisciplinary History* 13(4):735–759.

Smith, Thomas C. 1977. *Nakahara: Family Farming and Population in a Japanese Village, 1717–1830*. Stanford, CA: Stanford University Press.

Social Science History. 1982. vol. 6, no. 4 (Fall).

Soltow, Lee. 1975. *Men and Wealth in the United States, 1850–1870*. New Haven, CT: Yale University Press.

Somoza, Jorge L. 1968. Nivel *y* diferenciales de la fecundidad en la Argentina en el siglo XIX. *The Milbank Memorial Fund Quarterly* 46(3), (July) p. 2.

Steckel, Richard. 1983. Height and per capita income. *Historical Methods* 16(1):1–7.

Stoianovich, Traian. 1976. *French Historical Method: the Annales Paradigm*. Ithaca, NY: Cornell University Press.

Stolnitz, George. 1955. A century of international mortality trends: I. *Population Studies* 9:24–55.
Stolnitz, George. 1956. A century of international mortality trends: II. *Population Studies* 10(1):17–42.
Sullivan, Jeremiah M. 1972. Models for the estimation of the probability of dying between birth and exact ages in early childhood. *Population Studies* 26(1):79–97.
Sundstrom, William A., and Paul A. David. 1985. Old-age security motives, labor markets, and farm family fertility in antebellum America. Stanford Project on the History of Fertility Control. Working Paper No. 17 (December).
Taeuber, Irene B. 1958. *The Population of Japan*. Princeton, NJ: Princeton University Press.
Tan, Jee-Peng, and Michael Haines. 1984. *Schooling and Demand for Children: Historical Perspectives*. World Bank Staff Working Papers, No. 697. Washington, D.C.: The World Bank.
Tanner, J.M. 1981. *A History of the Study of Human Growth*. Cambridge: Cambridge University Press.
Teitelbaum, Michael S. 1984. *The Birtish Fertility Decline: Demographic Transition in the Crucible of the Industrial Revolution*. Princeton, NJ: Princeton University Press.
Thernstrom, Stephan. 1964. *Poverty and Progress: Social Mobility in a Nineteenth-Century City*. Cambridge, MA: Harvard University Press.
Thernstrom, Stephan. 1973. *The Other Bostonians: Poverty and Progress in the American Metropolis, 1880–1970*. Cambridge, MA: Harvard University Press.
Thernstrom, Stephan, and Peter R. Knights. 1971. Men in motion: Some data and speculations about urban population mobility in nineteenth-century America. In Tamara K. Hareven (ed.), *Anonymous Americans: Explorations in Nineteenth-Century Social History*. Englewood Cliffs, NJ: Prentice Hall. Pp. 17–47.
Thomas, Brinley. 1954. *Migration and Economic Growth: A Study of Great Britain and the Atlantic Community*. Cambridge: Cambridge University Press.
T'ien, H. Yuan. 1959. A demographic aspect of interstate variations in American fertility, 1800–1860. *The Milbank Memorial Fund Quarterly* 37:49–59.
Tilly, Louise A. 1977. Occupational Structure, Women's Work, and Demographic Change in Anzin and Roubaix, 1872–1906. Unpublished manuscript.
Todaro, Michael P. 1976. Rural-urban migration, unemployment and job probabilities: Recent theoretical and empirical research. In Ansley J. Coale (ed.), *Economic Factors in Population Growth*. New York: Wiley. Pp. 367–385.
Tolnay, Stewart E. 1980. Black fertility in decline: Urban differentials in 1900. *Social Biology* 27(4):249–260.
Tolnay, Stewart E., and Avery M. Guest. 1984. American family building strategies in 1900: Stopping or spacing. *Demography* 21(1):9–18.
Tolnay, Stewart E., Stephan N. Graham, and Avery M. Guest. 1982. Own-child estimates of U.S. white fertility, 1886–99. *Historical Methods* 15(3):127–138.
Trussell, T. James. 1975. A re-estimation of the multiplying factors for the Brass technique for determining childhood survivorship rates. *Population Studies* 29(1):97–107.

Trussell, T. James, and Chàrles Hammerslough. 1983. A hazards-model analysis of the covariates of infant and child mortality in Sri Lanka. *Demography* 20(1):1–26.

United Nations. 1955. *Age and Sex Patterns of Mortality: Model Life Tables for Under-Developed Countries*. No. 55.XIII.9. New York: United Nations.

United Nations. 1967. *Manuals on Methods of Estimating Population. Manual IV*. Methods of estimating basic demographic measures from incomplete data. Population Studies, No. 42. New York: Department of Economic and Social Affairs, United Nations.

United Nations. 1973. *The Determinants and Consequences of Population Trends: New Summary of Findings on Interaction of Demographic, Economic and Social Factors*. New York: United Nations.

United Nations. 1982. *Model Life Tables for Developing Countries*. Population Studies, No. 77. New York: Department of International Economic and Social Affairs, United Nations.

United Nations. 1983. *Indirect Techniques for Demographic Estimation*. Manual X. New York: United Nations.

U.S. Bureau of the Census. 1943. *Sixteenth Census of the United States: 1940 Population*. Differential fertility, 1940 and 1910: Fertility for states and large cities. Washington, D.C.: GPO.

U.S. Bureau of the Census. 1945. *U.S. Census of Population: 1940*. Differential fertility, 1940 and 1910: Women by number of children ever born. Washington, D.C.: GPO.

U.S. Bureau of the Census. 1971. *The Methods and Materials of Demography*, by Henry S. Shryock, Jacob S. Siegal, and associates. Washington, D.C.: GPO. Vols. 1 and 2.

U.S. Bureau of the Census. 1979. *Twenty Censuses: Population and Housing Questions, 1790–1980*. Wshington, D.C.: GPO.

Van de Walle, Etienne. 1974. *The Female Population of France in the Nineteenth-Century: A Reconstruction of 82 Departments*. Princeton, NJ: Princeton University Press.

Van de Walle, Etienne. 1976. Household dynamics in a Belgian village, 1847–1866. *Journal of Family History* 1(1):80–94.

Van de Walle, Etienne. 1978. Alone in Europe: The French fertility decline until 1850. In Charles Tilly (ed.), *Historical Studies of Changing Fertility*. Princeton, NJ: Princeton University Press. Pp. 257–288.

Van de Walle, Etienne. 1980. Motivations and technology in the decline of French fertility. In Robert Wheaton and Tamara Hareven (eds.), *Family and Sexuality in French History*. Philadelphia: University of Pennsylvania Press. Pp. 135–178.

Van de Walle, Francine. 1975. Migration and fertility in Ticino. *Population Studies* 29(3):447–462.

Van de Walle, Francine. 1980. Education and the demographic transition in Switzerland. *Population and Development Review* 6(3):463–472.

Vedder, Richard K., and Lowell E. Gallaway. 1971. Mobility of native Americans.

Journal of Economic History 31(3):613–649.
Vedder, Richard K., and Lowell E. Gallaway. 1980. Population transfers and the post-bellum adjustments to economic dislocations, 1870–1920. *Journal of Economic History* 40(1):143–149.
Vinovskis, Maris. 1972. Mortality rates and trends in Massachusetts before 1860. *Journal of Economic History* 32(1):184–213.
Vinovskis, Maris. 1976. Socioeconomic determinants of interstate fertility differentials in the United States in 1850 and 1860. *Journal of Interdisciplinary History* 6(3):375–396.
Vinovskis, Maris A. 1978. Recent trends in American historical demography: Some methodological and conceptual considerations. *Annual Reviews in Sociology* 4:603–627.
Vinovskis, Maris, ed. 1979. *Studies in American Historical Demography*. New York: Academic Press.
Wachter, Kenneth W., with Eugene A Hammel and Peter Laslett. 1978. *Statistical Studies of Historical Social Structure*. New York: Academic Press.
Watkins, Susan. 1981. Regional patterns of nuptiality in Europe, 1870–1960. *Population Studies* 35(2):199–215.
Watkins, Susan. 1986. Conclusions. In Ansley Coale and Susan Watkins (eds.), *The Decline of Fertility in Europe*. Princeton,, NJ: Princeton University Press. Pp. 420–449.
Watkins, Susan, and Myron P. Gutmann. 1983. Methodological issues in the use of population registers for fertility analysis. *Historical Methods* 16(3):109–120.
Watkins, Susan, and James McCarthy. 1980. The female life cycle in a Belgian commune: La Hulpe, 1847–1866. *Journal of Family History* 5(2):167–179.
Weber, Adna F. 1899. *The Growth of Cities in the Nineteenth-Century: A Study in Statistics*. New York: Macmillan.
Weir, David R. 1983. Fertility transition in rural France, 1740–1829. Ph.D. dissertation, Department of Economics, Standford University.
Weir, David R. 1984a. Life under pressure: France and England, 1670–1870. *Journal of Economic History* 44(1):27–47.
Weir, David N. 1984b. Rather never than late: Celibacy and age at marriage in English cohort fertility. *Journal of Family History* 9(4):340–354.
Wells, Robert. 1971. Family size and fertility control in eighteenth-century America: A Study of Quaker families. *Population Studies* 25(1):73–82.
Willcox, Walter F. 1931. *International Migrations*, vols. 1 and 2. New York: NBER.
Williamson, Jeffrey G. 1967. Consumer Behavior in the Nineteenth-Century: Carrol D. Wright's Massachusetts Workers in 1875. *Explorations in Entrepreneurial History* 2nd ser. 4(2):98–135.
Williamson, Jeffrey G. 1981. Urban disamenitities, dark satanic mills, and the British standard of living debate. *Journal of Economic History* 41(1):75–83.
Williamson, Jeffrey G. 1982. Was the Industrial Revolution worth it? Disamenities and death in nineteenth-century British towns. *Explorations in Economic*

History 19:221–245.

Williamson, Jeffrey G. 1984a. Irish immigration, elastic labor supplies and crowding-out during the British Industrial Revolution, 1821–1861. Harvard Institute of Economic Research. Discussion Paper No. 1085. Harvard University. (September)

Williamson, Jeffrey G. 1984b. British mortality and the value of life, 1781–1931. *Population Studies* 38(1):157–172.

Williamson, Jeffrey G. 1985a. *Did British Capitalism Breed Inequality*? Boston, MA:Allen & Unwin.

Williamson, Jeffrey G. 1985b. The urban transition during the first Industrial Revolution: England, 1776–1871. Harvard Institute of Economic Research Discussion Paper No. 1146. (April) Harvard University.

Willigan, J. Dennis, and Katherine A. Lynch. 1982. *Sources and Methods of Historical Demography*. New York: Academic Press.

Willigan, J. Dennis, Geraldine P. Mineau, Douglas L. Anderton, and Lee L. Bean. 1982. A macrosimulation approach to the investigation of natural fertility. *Demography* 19(2):161–176.

Wilson, Christopher. 1980. The components of marital fertility in historical Europe. Paper presented at the IUSSP Seminar on the Analysis of Maternity Histories. London, April, 1980.

Woods, R. I., and P. R. A. Hinde. 1985. Nuptiality in nineteenth-century England. *Journal of Family History* 10(2):119–144.

Woods, R., and C. W. Smith. 1983. The decline of marital fertility in the late nineteenth-century: The case of England and Wales. *Population Studies* 37(2):207–225.

Wright, Gavin. 1978. *The Political Economy of the Cotton South: Households, Markets, and Wealth in the Nineteenth-Century*. New York: Norton.

Wrightson, Keith, and David Levine. 1979. *Poverty and Piety in an English Village: Terling, 1525–1700*. New York: Academic Press.

Wrigley, E. A. 1961. *Industrial Growth and Population Change: A Regional Study of the Coalfield Areas of Northwest Europe in the Later Nineteenth-Century*. Cambridge: Cambridge University Press.

Wrigley, E. A. 1966. Family limitation in pre-industrial England. *Economic History Review* 2nd ser. 19(1):82–109.

Wrigley, E. A. 1969. *Population and History*. New York: McGraw-Hill.

Wrigley, E. A., ed. 1972. *Nineteenth-century Society: Essays in the Use of Quantitative Methods for the Study of Social Data*. Cambridge: Cambridge University Press.

Wrigley, E. A., and R. S. Schofield. 1981. *The Population History of England, 1541–1871: A Reconstruction*. Cambridge, MA: Harvard University Press.

Wrigley, E. A., and R. S. Schofield. 1983. English population history from family reconstitution: Summary results 1600–1799. *Population Studies* 37(2): 157–184.

Yasuba, Yasukichi. 1962. *Birth Rates of the White Population of the United States,*

1800–1860: An Economic Analysis. Baltimore, MD: Johns Hopkins Press.
Zaba, B. 1979. The four-parameter logit life table system. *Population Studies* 33(1):79–100.
Zunz, Olivier. 1982. *The Changing Face of Inequality: Urbanization, Industrial Development, and Immigration in Detroit, 1880–1920*. Chicago: University of Chicago Press.

6 THEORY AND HISTORY IN MARXIAN ECONOMICS

William Lazonick

Prologue

Imagine that you are an aspiring economist, in search of "good" economic theory. An academic economist tells you to look at the top-rated economic journals, where rigorous exercises in logic abound. After a short shift in the library, you concede that the work appears rigorous enough, at least as far as technique is concerned. But (forever naive) you question whether, beneath the obvious technical sophistication, the stuff that fills the journals is all that relevant to the real world.

The academic economist suppresses a bemused smile. Well-versed in the modern history of economic thought, he answers that "the economic scholar works for the only coin worth having—our own applause" (Samuelson 1962, p. 18). If an article appears in a relevant journal and cites the relevant economics literature, it must be relevant—at least to the real world of the academic economist.

The logic of the argument seems unassailable. After all, who are you to say what good economic theory, or a good economist, is? How can a mere apprentice know what constitutes the "real world"? So you bury yourself in the relevant literature in the hopes of becoming a relevant economist.

You do not quite make it at the theoretical game, but a spark of intellectual curiosity about how the real world *really* works continues to glow somewhere inside. So you pursue an applied field such as labor economics, industrial organization, or even (if you are daring) economic history. You have the vague feeling that you are leaving your theorist friends to be masters of the guild, but they seem willing to pay you the respect befitting a well-trained and well-behaved journeyperson. In the company of your "subdisciplinarian" colleagues, you glory in the relevance of your applied work for understanding real-world problems. But you do not question the rigorous theoretical framework that is forever being embellished by the master logicians who preside over the body of economists and bestow upon the discipline scientific prestige.

So you have become an academic economist, unaware that there is another, more innovative way that, in your youth, you might have employed your scarce intellectual resources. If you had rejected from the outset the notion that "good" economic theory is what "good" economists say it is, and if you had immersed yourself for perhaps a decade (maybe two) in the rigorous study of the evolution of economic institutions, you might have developed an independent judgment on what phenomena are fundamental to the real world of economic activity, and hence what might constitute relevant theory. If, in addition, you had managed to stick around the economics profession long enough to tell your tale, you might have found yourself challenging the dominant intellectual ideology that has given irrelevant theory a life of its own, making it apparently impervious to evolving reality.

You might even have begun to question the whole methodological outlook that one must adopt to enter into the guild of economists. As far as relevance is concerned, you might have insisted that theory be the servant of reality rather than vice versa. As for rigor, you might have defined it not merely in terms of logical consistency but more fundamentally in terms of the systematic evaluation of empirical material to determine the theoretical constructs that capture the essence of reality. In turn, the chosen theoretical constructs might then have provided you with a coherent framework for exploring empirical material as well as for formulating and testing new hypotheses.

But, alas, by now pushing forty, you have long since committed your intellectual resources to the mainstream approach, and possess neither the will nor the way to engage in what might turn out to be truly innovative intellectual activity. You now have, moreover, social responsibilities to bear. You have become an academic economist to whom new aspirants turn for direction. You tell them to look at the top-rated economics journals. . . .

I. Making Use of Marx

This essay is an argument for innovation in economics. By maintaining a dialectical relation between theory and reality, relevant theory can be generated by rigorous empirical study, and can then serve as a tool to analyze how the future evolves out of the past. The discovery of the conceptual framework that embodies the essence of reality and enables us to explore the dynamics of economic development can become the defining characteristic of theoretical rigor. Logical consistency will remain critical for working out solutions, but the solutions will only become meaningful when we have explored the subject matter—the real world—to discover the nature of the problems to be solved. By integrating theory and reality, rigor and relevance can go hand in hand.

In the attempt to integrate theory and reality, we do not, fortunately, have to start from scratch. There was a time—the so-called classical period in economics—when leading economists thought that an understanding of the evolution of economic and social institutions was a prerequisite to fashioning good theory. We can learn from their insights as well as from their errors. In this regard, Karl Marx stands out in the history of economics, not only because he explicitly sought to develop a method for integrating history and theory but also because, over one hundred years ago, he attacked the growing tendency for economic theory to become divorced from social reality. For those, like myself, who believe that modern neoclassical theory has long since lost touch with the real world, Marx's approach offers methodological insights and conceptual distinctions that can help us construct an alternative theory upon adequate empirical foundations.

But we must be careful. The Marxian approach is not an immediately applicable theory of capitalist development, but only a valuable point of departure. If we accept the proposition that historical analysis can motivate and validate theoretical generalizations, it makes sense to establish the relevance of Marx's theoretical framework and conclusions for his own time before we attempt to draw upon Marx to analyze the present-day capitalist economy. Only then can we usefully accept, reject, modify, or elaborate the Marxian propositions as part of a much larger project—that goes beyond even the grand scope of Marx's endeavors—to develop a more relevant theory of the capitalist economy.

Because Marx explicitly based his theory on history, we can go back to his writings in order to evaluate how well his theories capture the essence of capitalist development as it occurred through the third quarter of the nineteenth-century. If, as I believe to be the case, Marx was on the right track in his attempt to build a relevant theory of capitalist development, it may well be that we can learn as much from Marx's empirical and analytical errors as we can from his valid insights. For if he was on the right track—that is, if we can accept as historically relevant his fundamental assumptions about the nature of the capitalist economy—then we can, with the help of historical research and logical reasoning, correct Marx's mistakes and in the process build a richer, even more relevant theory.

Unfortunately, most critical evaluations of Marx are undertaken to discourage others from taking him seriously rather than to learn from his mistakes. In response to such attacks, many, if not most, modern Marxists defend their teacher by denying that he could have erred. Even modern Marxist economists who try to ensure the empirical relevance of their own theorizing have made little effort to assess how well Marx himself carried out the task in and for his own time (see, e.g., Sweezy 1968; Mandel 1968; Braverman 1974).

My own attempt to make use of Marx has convinced me that a great deal in the way of theory needs to be added to the general framework that Marx left behind. But because I have found Marx's work (or at least my interpretation of it) so useful in guiding my own historical research, I remain convinced that to ignore Marx is to eschew valuable theoretical foundations for analyzing the dynamics of economic development and forego a valuable intellectual opportunity to discover how history and theory might be brought into the service of one another.

As a graduate student in the early 1970s, I decided that to make use of Marx the first step was to investigate how well his analysis of the rise and consolidation of British industrial capitalism stood up in the light of the wealth of historical research that had been made available in the century or so since he wrote. My criteria of evaluation included not only the factual accuracy of the arguments that Marx actually made, but also the extent to which he attempted to address all the issues that, in retrospect, appear to be central to understanding capitalist development.

My initial strategy was to evaluate Marxian theory by synthesizing the historical research of others (see Lazonick 1975). Up to a point, the synthetic approach yielded considerable insight. Nevertheless, one sign of the success of my project was that the attempt to work from the available historical material raised at least as many questions as it answered, revealing the need to probe thoroughly the core of the Marxian framework.

The pivotal arguments in Marxian theory have to do with the interaction of forces and relations of production. Forces of production are nature, technology, and human capabilities. The development of these forces creates the *potential* for economic development. Relations of production are the structures of social power within an enterprise or industry that determine the influence exercised by different classes of people over how goods are produced and how the resultant income is distributed.

The interaction of the forces and relations of production determines the dynamics of capitalist development. The Marxian dialectic argues that the forces of production—broadly speaking, technology—develop on the basis of certain relations of production—that is, a structure of social power. At some point the existing relations of production inhibit the further development of the forces of production. If further economic development is to occur the prevailing structure of social power will have to be transformed.

The hallmark of orthodox Marxism, derived largely from the way in which Marx analyzed nineteenth-century capitalist development in Britain, is that technology determines the structure of social power, imparting a certain inevitability and determinism to economic and social development. An alternative view, which I find much more appropriate, is that evolving relations of production have an important influence on the development and diffusion of the forces of production, and that the process of economic development can therefore be better understood as the result of social conflict and compromise rather than as the outcome of the imperatives of technology.

To test the historical validity of Marx's theory of capitalist development, I decided that a thorough case study of the interaction of the forces and relations of production was in order. The result was a detailed historical analysis of the evolution, interaction, and impacts of capital-labor relations and technology in British cotton textiles—the industry that was at the core of the world's first industrial revolution (Lazonick 1979, 1981b, 1986a; Lazonick and Mass 1984).

The first round of case-study research raised questions concerning the impact of industrial organization—the relations among capitalist firms—on capital-labor relations. In the attempt to incorporate more phenomena into the analysis, I carried the study of the cotton industry well into the twentieth century (Lazonick 1983b), confronting along the way a mainstream literature on British economic performance and explanations of Britain's long-term economic decline (see McCloskey 1971; McCloskey and Sandberg 1971; Sandberg 1974; Lazonick 1981a and 1984a; Lazonick and Mass 1984). As the scope of the research broadened and as the nature of the debates changed, my arguments began to be less explicitly focused on how to make use of Marx, and more on what a theory of capitalist development should and can be, quite apart from how Marx and Marxists have approached the subject (Lazonick 1983b, 1984b; Elbaum and Lazonick 1986).

Nevertheless, my efforts to mine the intellectual insights and uncover the analytical weaknesses of Marx have left an indelible—and in my view invaluable—imprint on how I approach economic history, economic theory, and the relation between the two. If my work be called "Marxist," it is not because I adhere to a "Marxist" theory of capitalist development. Rather it is because a critical examination of the Marxian framework has helped me to pose the right questions, search out the right empirical data, and analyze in a coherent fashion complex historical material—often to the point of showing where and why Marx himself went wrong. My purpose here is to sketch the outlines of the Marxian influence in order to demonstrate how, by making use of Marx, historical analysis can yield new theoretical insights, and theory in turn can serve as a guide to empirical research.

This essay focuses upon Marx's analysis of the evolution of capital-labor relations in the rise and consolidation of British industrial capitalism through the 1860s, when Marx published Volume I of *Capital* and Britain became known as the "workshop of the world." The essay begins by addressing a long-standing debate concerning the emergence of a wage-labor force in the British industrial revolution. Mainstream economic historians have tended to argue that British workers were pulled into the factories of the Industrial Revolution by the promise of higher standards of living rather than pushed into them by the erosion of their prior rights to the use of property. Marx clearly puts the push before the pull, arguing that, by the mid-eighteenth century, enclosures of agricultural land in Britain had resulted in a large class of landless workers—that is, a proletariat—who were compelled to turn to wage-labor to gain their sustenance.

Some economic historians have attributed to Marx the notion that, in one fell swoop, enclosures drove the peasants off the land and into the factories. Marx does not put forth such a simplistic view, although one might easily be misled by his overemphasis on the dramatic displacement of peasants as a result of enclosures in the early sixteenth and early nineteenth centuries as well as his inadequate analysis of how a factory labor force was in fact created. Marx's argument is that the transformation of social relations of production and the emergence of a wage-labor force in the *agricultural* sector was the critical *precondition* for the Industrial Revolution characterized by the rise of the factory system. Indeed, as we shall see, Marx seems to be quite comfortable with the view that the pull of higher wages influenced the transfer of labor resources from the agricultural to the industrial sector once the capitalist mode of production was in place.

The social transformation that separated the mass of producers from the means of production is critical for Marx's theory of capitalist development. The basic hypothesis is that producers will only give up control of their laboring capacity to others if they no longer have access to a mode of production in which they can combine their labor-power with their own means of production. The critical implication for the exercise of social power by the capitalist over the worker is that compulsion—the urgent need to make a living—underlies the wage-labor contract—a contract that by all outward appearances is a manifestation that the worker is free to choose.

Marx's analytical framework contains several concepts that illuminate the relation between the development of an industrial labor force and Britain's successful industrialization. On the one hand, the Marxian focus on the importance of proletarianization and relative surplus population directs our attention toward social conflicts over alternative modes of acquiring a subsistence, such as resettlement of land, poor relief, crime, emigration, and domestic industry. On the other hand, Marx's emphasis on the duration of work, the intensity of labor, and mechanization as determinants of productivity directs our attention to the behavioral transformation that was required to get the proletariat to accept the work discipline that, along with automation, became a defining characteristic of the factory form of work organization.

Yet, as I argue in section III, in analyzing the evolution of the factory system in Britain's industrial revolution, Marx is overly impressed by the role of technology in shaping the structure of social power. Since Marx wrote, historians have added considerably to our knowledge of the emergence and development of a factory labor force in Britain.[1] Empirically speaking, we are now in a much better position to assess the weaknesses of the Marxian analysis of the interaction of the forces and relations of production in the rise of industrial capitalism, and modify it accordingly.

Marx emphasizes, and decries, the adverse social impact of industrial capitalism on the worker. But what distinguishes Marx from the well-informed muckraker or the compassionate social historian is his construction of the theory of surplus-value to analyze the economic causes and consequences of (as he calls it) the "subsumption of labor to capital." Section IV outlines and assesses Marx's theory of surplus-value as a microeconomic theory of productivity growth and income distribution under capitalism. In particular, I argue that, despite Marx's own misuses of the theory, its focus on the relation between work effort and pay is essential for analyzing the impacts of the social organization of the capitalist enterprise on the growth of productivity and the distribution of income.

The last section of the essay raises the major implications of my review of Marx's empirical work for analyzing the development of capitalism since his time. Marx predicted the rise of highly concentrated industrial structures, but for the wrong reasons. As with capital-labor relations, he overemphasized the independent impact of technology on industrial organization. As a result, Marx not only attributed to British capitalists social power that they never had, but also ended up believing quite incorrectly that future capitalist development in places such as Germany would in all essentials conform to the nineteenth-century British experience.

Nevertheless, with its focus on the relation between the control of work and the distribution of income, Marx's theory of surplus-value provides an essential starting point for analyzing the role of production relations in creating the modern industrial enterprise. I make use of Marx by integrating his theory of the development of the labor process with the Chandlerian perspective on the strategy and structure of corporate enterprise.

Throughout, I stress the importance of an analysis of social power for understanding the operation and performance of the capitalist economy. Marx's most fundamental conceptual contribution was to distinguish the apparent lack of social power inherent in arm's-length exchange relations from the very real social power inherent in personalized production relations. From this distinction between social relations of exchange and social relations of production, Marx went on to fashion a theory of the interaction of social relations and technology within the production process itself. Based upon my reassessment of Marx in the light of a portion of the available historical material on capitalist development, my intent here is to clarify how we should and should not make use of Marx.

At issue is not just the usefulness of Marx. No other economic theorist has made such a concerted attempt to integrate history and theory or delved so far into the nature of the mechanized production process. Modern economics is greatly—indeed sadly—in need of debate over methodological issues concerning the relations between production and exchange, social power and technology, and history and theory. A critical assessment of Marx's work not only enhances our understanding of British capitalist development, it also enables us to explore how historical research and theoretical reasoning might be united to ensure the relevance of our fundamental assumptions and the rigor of our empirical work.

II. Property Relations

Volume I of Marx's *Capital* is an examination of how capital accumulation occurs in a market environment. Marx begins by assuming a world characterized by commodity exchange in which equality among buyers and sellers prevails and in which the exercise of social-class power appears to have no place (Marx 1977, chs. 1–6).[2] Marx, however, is merely setting up the free market notions of (as he puts it) "Freedom, Equality, Property and Bentham" (p. 280) for a dialectical fall, for he goes on to ask how accumulation of wealth by capitalists such as had taken place in the British industrial revolution could possibly be reconciled with a theory of equal exchange. He answers by constructing a theory in which labor-power, like all commodities, exchanges at its value, but faces social inequality when it passes from the sphere of commodity exchange to the sphere of capitalist production.

In the production process, according to Marx, capitalists exercise considerable social power over the utilization of the labor inputs that they have purchased on the market, extracting more value added from the workers than the level of wages determined by the laws of commodity exchange. What is the source of the power of capitalists over workers? Social power is rooted in social dependence. Marx argues that capitalist control of the means of production makes the propertyless worker much more dependent on securing employment as a wage-laborer than the capitalist is on retaining the services of that particular worker.

Marx was not the first economist to argue that capitalists held the balance of power in their relations with wage-laborers. Adam Smith wrote in 1776:

> What are the common wages of labour depends everywhere upon the contract usually made between those two parties, whose interests are by no means the same. The workmen desire to get as much, the masters to give as little as possible. The former are disposed to combine in order to raise, the latter in order to lower the wages of labor. It is not, however, difficult to foresee which of the two parties must, upon all ordinary occasions, have the advantage in the dispute, and force the other into a compliance with their terms. The masters, being fewer in number, can combine much more easily; and the law, besides, authorises, or at least does not prohibit their combinations, while it prohibits those of the workmen. We have no acts of parliament against combining to lower the price of work; but many against combining to raise it. In all such disputes the masters can hold out much longer. A landlord, a farmer, a master manufacturer, or merchant, though they did not employ a single workman, could generally live a year or two upon the stocks which they have already acquired. Many workmen could not subsist a week, few could subsist a month, and scarce any a year without employment. In the long-run the workman may be as necessary to his master as his master is to him, but the necessity is not so immediate. (Smith 1937, p. 66)

But how did the division of society into capitalist employers and hired workers occur in the first place, and what are the implications of this class division for the development of capitalism? To these questions, Smith provides no answers. Writing on the eve of Britain's industrial revolution, Smith was certainly aware that an historical transformation had taken place, for he contrasts the capitalist economy of his time with "that rude state of society in which there is no division of labor, in which exchanges are seldom made, and in which every man provides everything for himself.... (Smith 1937, p. 259)

In "that rude state of society," Smith goes on to say, "it is not necessary that any stock should be accumulated or stored up beforehand, in order to carry on the business of society." But for the emergence of a modern industrial economy with its characteristic division of labor, previous accumulation is a basic precondition.

The "previous accumulation" explanation does not satisfy Marx because it fails to address the role of social power in creating the preconditions for industrial capitalism. The late fifteenth century is known as the golden age of the peasantry because the vast majority of British workers had escaped the servile status and obligations of the feudal era, but were not yet compelled to seek their subsistence by selling their labor-power to others. In contrast to the feudal mode of production before and the capitalist mode of production after, Marx characterizes the era stretching from the fifteenth century to the early eighteenth century as the petty proprietor mode of production. How, why and when did the petty proprietor mode of production give way to the capitalist mode of production? For Marx, "[s]o-called primitive accumulation...is nothing else than the historical process of divorcing the producer from the means of production" (pp. 874–875).

Marx's argument is that, whatever the stock of capital accumulated prior to the advent of industrial capitalism, this previous (or primitive or original) accumulation in and of itself would not have resulted in the emergence of a wage-labor force, the sine qua non of *capitalist* production and accumulation. Previous accumulation may be a necessary precondition for the emergence of industrial capitalism but is not sufficient to create its characteristic social relation.

An analysis of the origins of the relation between capitalists and wage-laborers is critical for understanding the conditions under which workers sought out their sustenance through wage-labor. It is only when these conditions are specified that we can assess the nature and extent of the social power that capitalist employers exercised over wage-laborers in the production processes of the industrial revolution. Marx's historical analysis of "so-called primitive accumulation" puts considerable weight on the role of agricultural enclosures in creating a landless labor force in Britain. On the basis of relatively little empirical data, Marx was able to discern the main elements of the social transformation that gave rise to a critical precondition for Britain's industrial revolution—the existence of a large, landless population that could potentially be hired as wage-laborers.

My reading of the secondary sources confirms the broad outlines of Marx's arguments (see Lazonick 1974). Enclosures in their various forms represented successful attempts by some landlords and farmers to take advantage of new market opportunities. Taking place by means of individual acts of appropriation in the early sixteenth century, by the early nineteenth century, enclosures occurred through national acts of expropriation. If not in the short run than over the long run, the massive reallocations of access to land that enclosures entailed resulted in the separation of the mass of agricultural producers from the means of production.

Beginning with a well-known article by J.D. Chambers (1953), a number of economic historians have sought to refute the Marxian thesis that the organizational transformation of British agriculture in the sixteenth to eighteenth centuries was responsible for the emergence of a wage-labor force (Ashton 1961, pp. 39, 47; Mingay 1963, pp. 98–99; Harris 1963, p. 24; Chaloner 1964, p. vii; Chambers and Mingay 1966, pp. 90, 98; Landes 1969, pp. 114–115; Deane 1973, pp. 191–192; Turner 1984, pp. 67–80). The critics, it turns out, do not differ substantially with Marx on the facts of agricultural transformation. But by ignoring the historical and theoretical significance of the resultant changes in the social relations of *agricultural* production, virtually all the critiques have missed Marx's main point.

For example, David Landes (1969, p. 115) takes issue with the view propounded by Marx and others that

> explains the accomplishment of so enormous a social change—the creation of an industrial proletariat in the face of tenacious resistance—by postulating an act of forcible expropriation: *the enclosures uprooted the cottager and small peasant and drove them into the mills*. (emphasis added)

Citing Chambers on enclosure and labor supply, Landes goes on to argue:

> Recent empirical evidence has invalidated this hypothesis; the data indicate that the agricultural revolution associated with enclosures *increased the demand for farm labour*, that indeed those rural areas that saw the most enclosures saw the largest increase in resident population. From 1750 to 1830, Britain's agricultural counties doubled their inhabitants. (emphasis added)

Marx does not argue that enclosures uprooted the cottager and small peasant and drove them into the mills. Moreover, the argument that dispossessed landholders remained in agricultural employment after enclosures misses Marx's point. The critical transformation that Marx identifies in his analysis of "the so-called primitive accumulation" is not the *level of employment* before and after enclosure, but rather the changes in *employment relations* caused by the reorganization of landholdings and reallocation of access to land. If one accepts the Marxian premise that the employment of wage-labor is the fundamental and distinguishing social characteristic of capitalism, then it is only of secondary importance to the analysis of the social transformation in production relations whether workers *initially* sold their labor-power in the agricultural or manufacturing sector. If one wants to take on Marx's historical analysis, the issue is the relevance of his emphasis on the separation of the mass of producers from the land as a necessary precondition for the emergence of industrial capitalism.

No one, including Chambers, disputes the fact that those who had the least secure ties to the land prior to enclosure were left landless. But insofar as these newly created proletarians were reemployed as wage-laborers, the social relations of production into which they entered had dramatically changed. As wage-laborers, these workers were now much more responsive to social and economic forces that might push or pull them from one sector to another. Marx (pp. 795–796) argues:

> As soon as capitalist production takes possession of agriculture...[p]art of the agricultural population is...constantly on the point of passing over into an urban or manufacturing proletariat and on the look-out for opportunities to complete this transformation.

As the *first step* in the emergence of a wage-labor force, the significance of enclosures was that these workers had become part of a landless proletariat, their sustenance dependent on securing wage employment in whatever sector of the economy it might be available.

Another popular anti-Marxian argument that misses the importance of the transformation of property relations as a precondition for industrial capitalism is that there is little evidence that *legal* rights to land were not protected during enclosures (Chambers 1953, p. 327; Ashton 1961, p. 39; Mingay 1963, p. 195; Chambers and Mingay 1966, p. 90). Yet Chambers (1953, p. 327n) himself recognizes that "of the poor without legal rights it remains true that [in Arthur Young's words] 'by nineteen enclosure bills out of twenty they are injured, in some grossly injured.'" As E.P. Thompson (1963, p. 218) puts it, "[e]nclosure (when all the sophistications are allowed for) was a plain enough case of class robbery, played according to fair rules of property and law laid down by a Parliament of property-owners and lawyers."

Even if we accept that (by the standards of the times) just treatment was accorded to peasant proprietors who could show legal title to the use of land, nothing is said about the majority of the agricultural population in the eighteenth century—the masses of cottagers, squatters, and agricultural laborers—who had only customary rights. To argue that these people were not treated unfairly because they did not possess legally enforceable property rights is irrelevant to the fact that they were dispossessed by enclosures. Again, Marx's critics have failed to address the issue of the transformation of access to the means of production as a precondition for the Industrial Revolution.

Yet another argument is directed against Marx's (p. 883) statement that the yeomanry had disappeared by 1750. Chambers assumes that Marx means that the yeomanry had descended to the ranks of the proletariat, and seeks to refute Marx by showing that, after enclosures of the late eighteenth and early nineteenth centuries, the number of small farm owners increased, or at least did not greatly decline (Chambers 1953, pp. 325–332).

Chambers, however, fails to comprehend Marx's analysis of the transformation of the social-class structure of British agriculture that preceded the Industrial Revolution. Nowhere does Marx argue that the yeomanry disappeared because they were proletarianized. Rather, when Marx speaks of the disappearance of the yeomanry, he is referring to the demise of a social class of independent peasant proprietors who had secured decent livehoods from their traditional landholdings and who epitomized the petty proprietor mode of production. Taking advantage of the growing commercialization of British agriculture from the fifteenth century on, some were able to climb the social ladder to become landlords or capitalist farmers, while others looked to improve their lot by emigrating. In each case, the British yeoman ceased to be a British yeoman.

It is true that after 1750 some petty proprietors still continued to occupy and work their own land. But in a world of capitalist agriculture, the yeomanry no longer played an important role in determining the course of capitalist development. As a social class in the evolution of British economy and society, the yeomanry had disappeared.

Even if some yeomen did become proletarians, they need not have constituted the primary source of a landless laboring class. Using Gregory King's statistics, we can estimate that cottagers, paupers, and agricultural laborers along with their families made up 55–65 percent of the agricultural population and 40–45 percent of the total population of England

and Wales in 1688 (see Lazonick 1974, p. 22). At this date, there was already a sizeable urban and migrant proletariat. There is also general agreement that smaller tenant-farmers found life difficult both before and after enclosures. Even if we assume that no yeoman lost his land during the first half of the eighteenth century, we still have an abundance of potential proletarians just prior to the industrial revolution (see Saville 1969, pp. 261–262).

Finally, Marx's critics argue that it was population growth, not enclosures that provided the Industrial Revolution with a wage-labor supply (Chambers 1953, p. 338; Chambers and Mingay 1966, pp. 92–93). The argument, however, ignores the dynamic between the forces and relations of production that is the essence of Marx's approach. Population growth is one form of the development of the forces of production. The general Marxian approach to history leads one to ask whether the changes in the social relations of production had an impact on the observed trends toward earlier marriage and larger families after 1750. There is reason to believe that they did. As hired farm laborers ceased to be live-in servants who were treated as part of the family and became wage-laborers subject to much more short-term, impersonal contracts, social constraints on choice of spouse and early marriage may have broken down. At the same time, the growth of domestic industry, probably even more than the use of child labor in the factories, created economic incentives for workers with and without land to have more children (Clarkson 1985; Levine 1985).

Insofar as the rapid rate of growth of Britain's population after the mid-eighteenth century was independent of the changing social relations of production, the fact remains that increasingly the offspring of landless workers were themselves born into a landless condition. In other words, history matters, and unless the critics can show that the major source of the wage-labor force in the British industrial revolution was people who *decided* to forego the subsistence that could be had on viable family farms to earn a living working for others, then Marx's thesis of forcible separation of the producers from the land has not been addressed.

Why have Marx's critics had such difficulty in coming to grips with his arguments concerning the causes and effects of proletarianization? In part, the problem may be that Marx has remarkably little to say about how the first generation of factory workers was in fact recruited, leading his critics as well as many of his followers to conflate the issues of the dissolution of the petty proprietor mode of production and the emergence of a disciplined factory labor force. In part, the problem is Marx's provocative style of discourse, which was undoubtedly intended to make his critics (quite literally) see red. Provoked, the nonsocialist camp has in turn overreacted

—for example, the attribution to Marx of the stance that enclosures uprooted the peasants and drove them into the mills.

The ideological gulf is real. Over one hundred years after Marx sought to dispel the notion that the capitalist economy is simply a world of free and equal exchange relations, economists have instead elaborated even more systematically the individualistic, free-market vision while ignoring the Marxian focus on social power in the production process. The neoclassical theory of the "capitalist" economy makes no qualitative distinction between the corporate enterprise that employs tens of thousands of people and the small family undertaking that does not employ any wage-labor at all. As far as theory is concerned, it is technology and market forces, not structures of social power, that govern the activities of corporate capitalists and petty proprietors alike. Given the dominance of a theoretical vision that treats the inner workings of the production process as a black box, it is not perhaps surprising that economic historians who imbibe the ideology that economic activity under capitalism can be construed as a series—even a general equilibrium—of market exchanges find the Marxian focus on the evolution of relations of production difficult to comprehend.

For Marx, the analysis of the transformation of production relations in the rise of industrial capitalism provides essential historical support for the centrality or social relations of production in the development of capitalism. Moreover, far from ignoring exchange relations, the power of Marx's approach is to show how, as far as labor is concerned, the transformation of production relations based upon new property relations *generated* exchange relations. That exchange relations were thrust upon workers who could no longer get their sustenance through their direct access to land in turn provides the basis for Marx's argument that in capitalist production it is employers rather than employees who hold the balance of power.

III. Work Organization

Marx, therefore, posits a dramatic change in social relations of production as a precondition for the advent of industrial capitalism. He argues, moreover, that the forces underlying this transformation were historically and logically distinct from the rise of the factory system that was to become the characteristic form of the capitalist production process. Without direct access to the means of production, the *proletarianized* worker could no longer be independently employed. But neither was he or she yet an industrial worker, subject to the work discipline of regular work hours and direct supervision that we have come to regard as normal in the capitalist workplace. As Marx emphasizes, the success of industrial capitalism depended upon the extent to which capitalists could exercise control over the working time of their employees. To what extent, at what points in time, and in what ways was capitalist control imposed on the British proletariat?

To analyze these issues, Marx (chs. 14–15) divides the history of industrial capitalism into two phases: manufacturing and large-scale industry. In manufacturing, the forces of production are simply the artisanal skills and tools of the preceding handicraft era. But when these forces of production are brought under the control of the capitalist, productivity growth results from two changes in work organization: cooperation and division of labor. Cooperation and division of labor in turn provide the organizational bases for the further, and most dramatic, development of the forces of production through the introduction of automated machinery, ushering in the era of large-scale industry.

In Marx's view, machinery revolutionizes the mode of production by overcoming the strength and skill constraints that human beings impose on productivity. By transforming the worker from an active force of production to an easily replaceable appendage of an automated system, machinery provides the capitalist with the ultimate weapon for imposing work discipline on workers (ch. 15).

In historical perspective, there are a number of serious problems with Marx's analysis, not the least of which is his notion of "manufacture" as an historical stage preceding the advent of large-scale industry. Marx (p. 455) asserts that "the manufacturing period . . . extends, roughly speaking, from the middle of the sixteenth century to the last third of the eighteenth century." Manufacture arises either from "the assembling together in *one workshop*, under the control of a single capitalist, of workers belonging to various independent handicrafts, through whose hands a given article must pass on its way to completion" or when "[o]ne capitalist simultaneously employs in *one workshop* a number of craftsmen who all do the same work, or the same kind of work, such as making paper, type or needles" (emphasis added) (pp. 455, 456). In other words, Marx defines manufacture as either the vertical or horizontal integration of crafts into one site under the direct coordination and oversight of the capitalist and his managerial agents.

Marx raises the "manufacturing period" to the status of an historical stage in the development of industrial capitalism, but provides no documentation that manufacture, as he defines it, actually existed—let alone dominated the industrial sector—in Britain from the mid-sixteenth century to the late eighteenth century. In the last decades of the eighteenth-century and throughout the nineteenth century, nonmechanized capitalist workshops existed alongside, and at times in competition with, the mechanized factory (Samuel 1977; Hobsbawm 1984). But historical research does not support Marx's claim that "manufacture"—the gathering together of large numbers of workers in one location—constituted a significant form of work organization *prior* to the rise of the factory system in the last decades of the eighteenth century.

What preceded the factory system was not the manufacturing workshop but rather domestic industry based upon the putting-out system (see Pollard 1968, ch. 2; Rule 1981; Berg, Hudson, and Sonenscher 1983; Ramsay 1984, ch. 3; Berg 1985; Clarkson 1985; Landes 1986). In domestic industry (or outwork, as it came to be called once the factory system had made its impression), a small group of workers (typically a family) labored independently in their own workplace (typically a portion of the family home) under the direction of a supervising worker (typically the husband and father).

If, as was usual in the woollen industry of West Yorkshire in the mid-eighteenth-century, the work group supplied all its own tools, workplace, and materials and had direct access to the product market without the intervention of an outside capitalist, then domestic industry was part of the petty proprietor mode of production. When operated under the putting-out system, however, the capitalist who supplied the domestic workers with materials to be transformed had a direct interest in the quality and quantity of work performed in the labor process. The more social power the putting-out capitalist had to further this interest, the more could domestic industry be viewed as belonging to the capitalist mode of production. If, as was increasingly the case during the nineteenth-century, the putting-out capitalist had access to an abundant supply of outworkers as well as a legal system that would help enforce the rapid and complete return of worked-up materials under putting-out contracts, then the control that domestic workers exercised over the actual labor process could be considerably reduced (Thompson 1963, ch. 9; Bythell 1978; Schmiechen 1984).

The putting-out system existed on a large scale in the textile industries that were to lead the rise of the factory system and form the basis of the Industrial Revolution. But outwork was also widespread in diverse manufactures such as nailmaking, watchmaking, and straw-plaiting. As direct access to the land was eroded, domestic industry enabled producers to remain in the rural setting, as capital flowed to the worker rather than vice versa. Whether pursued as a by-employment to supplement income derived from agriculture or as the sole source of family earnings, domestic industry permitted the continuity of the traditional rural lifestyle, including the integration of work-time and family-time. In the workplace, the adult-male domestic worker could continue to be his own boss and direct the work of his wife and children.

Research has shown that the "free-born Englishman" of the eighteenth-century—even those who, by force of circumstances, had to submit to agricultural wage-labor—tenaciously resisted entry into the capitalist workshop (Pollard 1968, ch. 5; Thompson 1967; Rule 1981). In his discussion of primitive accumulation, Marx (p. 927) correctly emphasizes that

> [t]he private property of the worker in his means of production is the foundation of small-scale industry, and small-scale industry is a necessary condition for the development of social production and of the free individuality of the worker himself.

The historical background to the reluctance of eighteenth-century and nineteenth-century workers to enter the capitalist workplace was the independence and individualism of the "free-born Englishman" that developed during the era of widespread distribution of property under the petty proprietor mode of production from the fifteenth-century through the seventeenth-century (MacPherson 1962; Hill 1967).

Reinforcing the tradition of independence was the common eighteenth-century equation of the *workshop* operated for profit with the *workhouse* operated for paupers. Throughout the eighteenth-century, Acts of Parliament promoted the setting up of workhouses in order to make poor relief more punitive; to make the poor pay their own way by forced labor; and, perhaps, to train paupers to be industrious. As Marx (p. 808n) notes, Smith, writing in 1776, used the terms "manufactory" and "workhouse" interchangeably. And as Pollard (1968, pp. 190–193) argues, the popular identification of the capitalist workplace with the public workhouse could only have been strengthened by the heavy reliance of the pioneering factories of the early Industrial Revolution on unfree persons—so-called parish apprentices who had been transformed from wards of local poor law authorities to wards of factory owners.

As in the workshop or factory setting, so too under the putting-out system the interests of domestic workers were to maximize earnings for a minimum of effort, whereas the interests of the putting-out capitalists ran in the opposite directions. At any point in time, the social power that the capitalist and the worker could exercise over the relation between work effort and the distribution of income might be very different depending upon which party controlled the physical production site. In the workshop or factory, the capitalist could set the hours of work and directly monitor the pace of work. If workers were in short supply, they might ignore the factory capitalist's rules and orders. We would therefore expect that the factory would be more successful when the supply of workers was more abundant. But whatever the conditions of labor supply, a great advantage of the workshop or factory for the capitalist was that it put him formally in the position of making compliance with *his* rules and orders a condition of employment in *his* place of work.

Not so in the privacy of the domestic worker's own home, where the direct producer could exercise considerably more control over the organization, duration, and pace of work. For capitalists, domestic industry offered the advantages of relatively low investment in fixed capital and managerial structure, but at the cost of leaving control of the labor process in the hands of the workers. In the eighteenth century, domestic workers could not be counted upon to work hard and steadily when left to their own devices. In contrast to the time-orientation that came to characterize work behavior in the factory setting, work behavior in domestic industry tended to be task oriented, a legacy of peasant agriculture out of which domestic industry grew (Thompson 1967). In effect, task-oriented work behavior meant that during a given period of time workers would produce just enough to maintain their standards of living. As a result, domestic workers were regularly accused of working irregularly and holding onto the capitalists' materials for inordinate periods of time. In addition, aided by the privacy of their own homes, they were also known to supplement their earnings by appropriating a portion of the material put out to them, typically by adulterating or stretching the product to bring it up to the expected weight or size (Marglin 1974, p. 51; Rule 1981; Berg 1985, pp. 221–222, 308–310; Landes 1986).

The social relations of the domestic putting-out system, therefore, were qualitatively different from those of the capitalist workshop or factory. In terms of the management of the labor process, the domestic workers are much better depicted as subcontractors than as wage-laborers. They supplied not only their labor-power but also their place of work, assistants, tools and even in some cases machines. Compared to the wage-laborer who contracted to work for a specific length of time within the capitalist's workplace, the key to the independent status of the domestic worker was his or her control over the day-to-day operation of the labor process.

A flood of labor into domestic employments in the first decades of the nineteenth century, however, eroded the standards of living of the out-workers, while, by the same token, maintaining the commercial viability of the putting-out system as against the alternatives of workshop or factory production (Thompson 1963, ch. 9; Bythell 1969). Despite the use of powerlooms in textile factories from 1798, the growth of the factory system in spinning in the first four decades of the nineteenth century was accompanied by the expansion of handloom weaving carried out under the putting-out system. As late as 1830, the number of handlooms in use may have been as much as four times the number of powerlooms, and the wages of handloom weavers, which had been relatively attractive at the turn of the century, had fallen to poverty levels. The 1830s and 1840s saw the large-scale introduction of powerlooms into factories and a concomitant precipitous drop in the number of handloom weavers.

It was domestic industry rather than the manufacturing workshop, therefore, that preceded the factory and that continued as its prime alternative even as the factory system became firmly implanted during the Industrial Revolution. If, as Marx posits, the factory system had in fact been preceded by some two centuries of manufacture as the dominant mode of work organization, then we might expect that, on the eve of the industrial revolution, British workers would have long since grown accustomed to wage-labor *within* the capitalist workplace.

Yet it was during Marx's period of "manufacture," when, by assumption, men were already entering the capitalist workplace, that the British proletarians were attempting to retain critical dimensions of their free-born status—the right to work under their own direction and to determine their own hours and pace of work—by turning to production within their own homes. With domestic industry rather than the manufacturing workshop as the historical alternative, the problem of attracting workers into a centralized workplace was to have far-reaching implications for the development of British capitalism.

Marx provides little explicit historical analysis of the conditions under which British workers came to be regularly employed in the capitalist workplace. Read out of context, one well-known passage in Marx's analysis of historical changes in the length of working day might be interpreted as referring to the resistence of the "free-born Englishman" to supervised and regulated work. Marx (p. 382) argues:

> Centuries are required before the 'free' worker, owing to the greater development of the capitalist mode of production, makes a voluntary agreement, i.e., is compelled by social conditions to sell the whole of his active life, his very capacity for labour, in return for the price of his customary means of subsistence, to sell his birthright for a mess of pottage.

Read in the context of Marx's analysis of struggles over the length of the working day, however, it is clear that he views the "birthright" that the free worker sells, not in terms of his loss of control over the labor process by entering the capitalist workplace, but rather in terms of the *amount* of his "active life" spent under the direct sway of the capitalist. If, by conflating proletarianization and the creation of a factory labor force, Marx's critics miss the point of his analysis of the transformation of production relations in the rise of capitalism, they would nevertheless be justified in arguing that Marx fails to show how a factory labor force was in fact created.

Quoting his favorite procapitalist ideologue, Andrew Ure, Marx (p. 549) certainly recognizes the problem:

> "The main difficulty" (in the automatic factory) "lay above all in training human beings to renounce their desultory habits of work, and to identify themselves with the unvarying regularity of the complex automation. To devise and administer a successful code of factory discipline, suited to the necessities of factory diligence, was the Herculean enterprise, the noble achievement of Arkwright! Even at the present day, when the system is perfectly organized and its labor lightened to the utmost, it is found nearly impossible to convert persons past the age of puberty into useful factory hands." (Ure 1835, p. 15)

But if, as Marx argues, the period of manufacture, stretching from the sixteenth century to the Industrial Revolution, had preceded the coming of the factory, why had the British industrial labor force not long since renounced "their desultory habits" and become inured to capitalist work-discipline?

Marx's (p. 489) answer is that, under "manufacture," craft unions made up of skilled adult males were able to restrict the extension of division of labor and the employment of unskilled workers, at times retaining "a long period of apprenticeship. . .even where it would be superfluous." "The struggle between the capitalist and wage-labourer," Marx (p. 553) contends, "rages throughout the period of manufacture."

> Since handicraft skill is the foundation of manufacture, and since the mechanism of manufacture as a whole possesses no objective framework which would be independent of the workers themselves, capital is constantly compelled to wrestle with the insubordination of the workers. "By the infirmity of human nature," says our friend Ure, "it happens that the more skillful the workman, the more self-willed and intractable he is apt to become, and of course the less fit a component of a mechanical system in which he may do great damage to the whole." Hence the complaint that the workers lack discipline runs through the whole period of manufacture. (p. 490)

In Marx's view, machinery solves the problem of the insubordination of the workers; hence his emphasis on the transition from manufacture based upon handicraft production to large-scale industry based upon machine production rather than on the transition from worker control of the place of work in domestic industry to capitalist control of the place of work in *either* manufacture or large-scale industry.

According to Marx (pp. 458, 489), machinery does away with both the skilled workers of manufacture and their unions, including restrictive rules and customs concerning the organization of work. Machinery supersedes the need for human strength and skill on the shop floor, substituting the labor of docile women and children for that of the truculent craftsmen. The reserve army of labor is augmented by the greater ability of capitalists to make use of segments of the labor force that are physically weaker and less skilled as well as by technical change that makes less direct labor input necessary per unit of output. The growth of the reserve army of labor in turn forces those who remain employed "to submit to over-work and subjects them to the dictates of capital" (p. 789). Machinery, that is, enables the capitalist to impose discipline on the workers.

Marx's analysis of the *technical* relation between machine technology and the laboring capacities of human beings is extremely insightful. But, when applied to the nineteenth-century British factory, his analysis of the *social* impact of technology on the relative power of capitalists and workers to control the labor process is too extreme. Marx fails to see that the introduction of machinery into a labor process that has relied upon skilled workers is only a necessary, not a sufficient, condition for the elimination of worker control. As I have shown, Marx's source for his classic example of how capitalists in large-scale industry used machinery to dominate workers is the procapitalist ideology of Andrew Ure, not the historical experience of the British cotton industry (Lazonick 1979).

During the conflict-ridden decade of the 1830s, Ure (1835, pp. 23, 368) argued that the effect of the introduction of a new, more highly mechanized technology—the self-acting spinning mule—into the cotton industry was "to discharge the greater part of men spinners, and to retain adolescents and children." He suggested that the self-acting mule would, among other things, "put an end...to the folly of trades' unions," and went on to proclaim: "this invention confirms the great doctrine...that when capital enlists science into her service, the refractory hand of labor will be taught docility."

Ure's message to British workers—the futility of collective action and resistence to factory discipline in the face of inexorable technical change —is certainly contrary to the spirit of Marx's faith in the power of working-class organization. But fixed in the notion that, in the era of large-scale industry, technology had become the driving force in capitalist development, Marx absorbed the Urian ideology some three decades after it was written while ignoring the on-going reality of the factory system. Far from being "taught docility," the mule spinners—now called minders—emerged from the long Victorian boom of the third quarter of the nineteenth century as the best-organized and best-financed union in all of Britain, a position based upon very substantial control over the organization of work (Lazonick 1979, 1981b).

Why were mule-spinning operatives able to retain control over the labor process despite substantial mechanization, and, why was Marx misled about the impact of the new technology on these workers? The answer requires an understanding of how the mule spinners—almost all of whom were adult males—were recruited into cotton-spinning factories in the first place. The mule-spinning machine was invented in 1779, and in the 1780s was used as a hand-powered machine in domestic industry. In the late 1780s, mule workshops arose, and in the 1790s factory production predominated as the mule was attached to waterpower and steampower. In the mule-spinning factory, the mule spinner worked on an internal subcontract system. Transferring into the factory the essentials of the actual organization of work in domestic industry, the mule spinner was paid by the piece, and out of his earnings paid time wages to assistants whom he himself recruited and supervised.

The subcontract system shifted the burden of recruitment and supervision onto the operative spinner, an advantageous arrangement for the capitalist in the early decades of the factory system, when workers other than the most destitute were reluctant to enter the mills and when those who did were as yet undisciplined to factory routine (Pollard 1968, pp. 51–66; Lazonick 1979). The subcontract system permitted the mule spinner, who viewed himself as the practitioner of a craft, to maintain a considerable degree of control over the hierarchical and technical division of mule-spinning labor within the factory. In addition, but for the fact that he could hire and supervise his own children and, in some cases, his wife, the mule spinner might not have permitted them to enter the early factories.

Indeed, the mule spinners themselves—who represented the first important group of adult-male operatives to participate in the factory system—would probably not have been lured into the mills had it not been for the degree of independence that they could retain within its walls. In effect, the early mule spinners were craft workers who, even within the factory environment, were able to establish many of the conditions of independence that characterized domestic industry.

As long as mule spinners were in short supply, they might resist the time-orientation that came to characterize factory life. But the very success of the workers in retaining a measure of independence within the cotton mills served to increase their numbers and reduce resistence to hard and steady work. The demonstrated ability of factory spinners to maintain substantial control over the conditions of work and pay helped to overcome the long-standing aversion of a portion of the "free-born Englishmen" to the factory setting, particularly as the flood of workers into domestic industry after the Napoleonic Wars made that alternative less and less attractive.

In combination with the negative incentive posed by a growing reserve army of labor, positive incentives also served to habituate mule spinners to factory discipline. In answer to Ure's question of "how with. . .surplus hands the wages of fine spinners can be maintained at their present high pitch," a capitalist of the 1830s replied that by maintaining wages above the going market rate, "[a] spinner reckons the charge of a pair of mules in our factory a fortune for life, [and] he will therefore do his utmost to retain his situation, and to uphold the high character of our yarn" (Ure 1835, p. 336; cited in Marglin 1985, pp. 106–107, to explain wage-stickiness). By offering them relatively high wages and secure employment (as well as possible promotion to muleroom overlooker), mule spinners could be enticed to keep regular hours and work at a hard and steady pace.

If mule spinners had only employed their own children as assistants, and had as a result been able to retain the imputed wages of these helpers as family earnings, they might have worked in the irregular manner and with the limited earnings objectives characteristic of domestic industry. But a portion of the mule spinners' gross piece-rate earnings went as time-wages to nonfamily members who typically had to be hired in addition to family members in order to constitute a complete mule-spinning team (Anderson 1976). Just as capitalists had an interest in getting as much work as possible out of their workers for a given wage, so too did the mule spinners—but with the difference that, as the *key operatives* in the spinning team, the mule spinners themselves had to labor long and hard in order to exploit as fully as possible the labor power of their assistants. The social relations of the internal subcontract system, therefore, helped to enforce factory discipline on subcontractor and assistants alike.

The most diligent of the young assistants could aspire to become mule spinners one day. By virtue of their early introduction to factory discipline, therefore, successive generations of mule spinners as well as many other former assistants who remained at lower-paid jobs, acquired the temperament and outlook that came to characterize life-long factory hands.

Hobsbawm (1968, p. 350) argues that "somewhere around the middle of the century we see a conscious adjustment of skilled workers to the 'rules of the game.'" It is critical to note, however, that mule spinners, as well as many other groups of workers who secured considerable job control within the factory setting and became part of the British "labor aristocracy," did not merely adjust to the "rules of the game." Through their collective organizations, they had a preponderant role in *making* the rules. By the 1830s, when a commercially viable self-acting mule finally was available, the internal subcontract system in mule spinning had evolved into a very effective mode of labor management. The adult-male mule-spinning operatives who managed production on the shop floor had themselves become highly productive workers who were willing and able to work regular hours at a steady pace. At the same time, however, as skilled workers entrusted with considerable shop-floor autonomy and what, in retrospect at least, would be seen as managerial responsibility, the mule spinners were able to develop effective collective organizations that could seek to enforce wage agreements and lead the fight for a shorter workday.

It was this collective power rather than any lack of work discipline on the part of mule spinners that the introduction of the self-acting mule was supposed to undermine. In the 1830s and 1840s, the mule-spinning unions were momentarily weakened, and the wages of mule spinners considerably reduced—by the depressions of the 1830s and 1840s as well as by labor-saving technological changes. Nevertheless, going into the long boom of the third quarter of the nineteenth century, the collective organizations of both mule spinners and self-acting minders remained intact. For the minders, whose social power, according to both Ure and Marx, was supposed to have been automated out of existence, what was critical for maintaining control over the conditions of work and pay was the retention of the internal subcontract system that had been the legacy of domestic industry implanted in the factory (Lazonick 1979).

In their virtually universal adoption of the internal subcontract system, the cotton-spinning factory capitalists of the Industrial Revolution left considerable control of the labor process in the hands of their adult-male operatives. With the coming of the self-acting mule, the factory capitalists had little incentive to take away control of the labor process from key shop-floor workers who had in fact themselves become well-disciplined and who were in turn disciplining the younger generation of workers. The strong inclination to continue with the tried and true methods of labor management even on the more automated machinery was further reinforced by the highly competitive conditions of the British cotton industry, which made it very risky for an individual firm to experiment with new modes of work organization. When, in the long boom that followed the hard times of the 1830s and 1840s, prosperity enhanced the power of workers in general to control the conditions of work and pay, self-acting minders were able to use their control over the labor process as well as the competitive fragmentation of their capitalist employers to build their collective organizations and consolidate their internal control (Lazonick 1979, pp. 246–251).

Misunderstanding the conditions under which workers such as the mule spinners entered the factories of the industrial revolution, Marx vastly overrates the social power that British factory capitalists exercised in the labor process and on the labor market (Brown 1977; Samuel 1977; Elbaum and Wilkinson 1979; More 1980; Gray 1981; Wood 1982; Hobsbawm 1984, chs. 11–14; Harrison and Zeitlin 1985). Mistaken in the notion that the "freeborn Englishman" had labored in the capitalist workplace for some two centuries before the Industrial Revolution, and convinced that the development of the forces of production in the form of automated machinery would eliminate any remaining shop-floor resistence, Marx fails to analyze the evolution of the social relations of production under industrial capitalism.

For Marx, the introduction of machinery into the factory not only resulted in the complete subjugation of labor to capital, but also put to an end alternative forms of work organization—in particular, domestic industry. Although Marx does not view domestic industry as an important eighteenth-century precursor of the factory, he recognizes that it *coexisted* with the factory system in the third quarter of the nineteenth century. He views the appearance of domestic industry as a passing phenomenon that cannot withstand the centralizing impact of machinery. His primary empirical examples to illustrate the onward march of machinery and the factory system are the introduction of the sewing machine into the clothing industry and the use of steampower in ribbon weaving. As in the case of the self-acting mule, however, Marx misinterprets the evdience because of his assumption that it is technology rather than the social relations of production that determines the mode of work organization under capitalism.

Like nineteenth-century manufacture, domestic industry is, according to Marx (p. 599), characterized by, on the one hand, the absence of labor-saving machinery, and, on the other hand, "the cheapening of labour-power, by sheer abuse of the labour of women and children, by sheer robbery of every normal condition needed for working and living, and by the sheer brutality of overwork and night-work." But such exploitation of human laboring capacities "finally comes up against certain insuperable obstacles."

> When this point at last has been reached—and this takes many years—the hour has struck for the introduction of machinery, and for a thenceforth rapid transformation of the scattered domestic industries, as well as the manufactures, into factory industries.

Marx's (pp. 599–600) prime example of the transition from domestic industry and manufacture to the factory is the introduction of the sewing machine into the apparel industries. Unlike the self-acting mule, which had been in widespread use for three decades when Marx published *Capital* in 1867, the sewing machine had barely even been introduced in Britain when Marx speculated on its impact on work organization. By the end of the 1860s, there may have been as few as 500 machines in use in all of England, some in small workshops, others in workers' homes, and still others in an army clothing factory (Schmiechen 1984, p. 25).

Marx (p. 601) argues correctly that, through the 1850s, domestic industry was the main form of work organization in apparel production. On the basis of an abundant labor supply set free by large-scale industry and agriculture, surplus-value was produced by a combination of "the minimum wages [sufficient] for a miserable, vegetable existence, and... the extension of the hours of labor to the maximum endurable by the human organism."

But domestic industry as well as small workshops were just "a variegated medley of transitional forms" (p. 602) in the evolution of the apparel factory. "At last," Marx (p. 601) argues, "a critical point was reached."

> The basis of the old method, sheer brutality in the exploitation of the workers, accompanied by a more or less systematic division of labour, no longer sufficed for the extending of markets and for the still more rapidly extending competition of the capitalists. The hour of the machine had struck. The decisively revolutionary machine, the machine which attacks in an equal degree all the innumerable branches of [the wearing apparel] sphere of production, such as dressmaking, tailoring, shoemaking, sewing, hat-making and so on, is the sewing machine.

Marx (p. 603) describes "the system actually prevalent in England in 1867:

> [T]he capitalist concentrates a large number of machines on his premises, and then distributes the product of those machines amongst the domestic workers to work it up [on sewing machines] into its finished form. The variety of these transitional forms does not, however, conceal the tendency operating to transform them into the factory proper. This tendency is nurtured *by the very nature of the sewing-machine*, the manifold uses of which tend to compel the concentration, under one roof and one management, of previously separated branches of a trade. (emphasis added)

In addition to the "very nature of the sewing machine," other forces working toward the concentration of production "under one roof and one management" are, according to Marx (pp. 603–605), the advantages of having vertically related production processes performed in one place, the extension of the Factory Acts even to domestic production if women and children are employed, the overproduction of machine-made goods which forces impoverished domestic workers to sell their own machines, and the overproduction of sewing machines which "causes their producers, who need to sell at all costs, to let them out for so much a week, thus crushing the small sewing-machine owners by their deadly competition."

Marx (p. 603) goes on:

> Constant changes in the construction of the machines, and their ever-increasing cheapness, cause the older makes to depreciate daily and compel their sale in great numbers, at absurd prices, to large capitalists, who are now the only people who can employ them at a profit. Finally, the substitution of the steam-engine for man strikes the final blow in this, as in all similar processes of transformation.

Marx is wrong to assume that the inevitable outcome of the diffusion of the machine was the factory. The author of a history of the London clothing trades argues that "[t]he most important consequence of the invention of the sewing machine was the speedup in work and production, which, in effect, caused a proliferation of the sweating system" (Schmiechen 1984, p. 24). Some large-scale factories were established in Leeds, but the future of the industry was a proliferation of subcontracting and subdivision of labor on the basis of immigrants employed in their homes and small workshops (Thomas 1955; Bythell 1978; Schmiechen 1984). Referring to the same 1864 report of the Children's Employment Commission from which Marx culls his evidence of the rise of the apparel factory, Schmiechen (1984, p. 26) says:

> Early predictions that the sewing machine would encourage the centralization of production in the factory were unfounded. . . . As late as 1915 there was probably no industry as untouched by factory production or in which the methods of production had been standardized so little as the manufacture of clothing.

In the case of the sewing machine, Marx falls victim to his preconception that the forces of production determine the evolution of work organization under capitalism. Far from encouraging the concentration of production under one roof, as Marx argues, "the very nature of the sewing machine"—its flexibility in making many products—made it ideal for outworkers who stood ready to pick up any type of work that was available to them. The extension of the Factory Acts to workshops employing less than fifty people was ineffective because of inadequate inspection and enforcement, and, contrary to Marx, did not favor centralized work organization (Schmiechen 1984, ch. 6).

Marx's argument that price-cutting by sewing-machine makers created "deadly competition" for outworkers simply assumes the superiority of the concentrated workshop or factory. In fact, the practice of letting the sewing machines out "for so much a week" was a calculated marketing effort, first pursued by the Singer Manufacturing Co., to make sewing machines available and affordable to women working in their homes (Davies 1976; Hounshell 1984, ch.2). It is not at all clear why overproduction of machine-made goods would, as Marx argues, compel outworkers to sell their machines (or to whom they would have sold them if they did). Rather than divest themselves of their sources of livelihood during slumps, one would have thought that domestic workers would have become even more dependent on their possession of the sewing machine as a means of production. The "final blow" rendered by the attachment of the steam engine to the sewing machine in fact never took place on a large scale. When and where they appeared, apparel factories based upon the sewing machine tended to use, not the steam engine, but rather electric power, a motor force that could just as well have favored decentralized production.

Even when the steam engine was used as the prime mover in manufacturing it did not necessitate the factory system. In a section of his chapter on machinery and large-scale industry entitled "The Revolutionary Impact of Large-Scale Industry on Manufacture, Handicrafts and Domestic Industry," Marx (p. 589) allows that a machine 'may itself serve as a basis of an industry of a handicraft character." He goes on to argue, however, that

> this reproduction of the handicraft system on the basis of machinery only forms a transition to the factory system which, as a rule, makes its appearance as soon as human muscles are replaced, for the purpose of driving the machines, by a mechanical motive power such as steam or water. Here and there, but in any case only for a time, an industry may be carried on, on a small scale, by means of mechanical power.... In the Coventry ribbon industry the experiment of "cottage factories" was a quite natural and spontaneous development. In the centre of a square surrounded by rows of cottages, an engine-house was built and the engine connected by shafts with the looms in the cottages. In all cases, the power was hired out at so much per loom. The rent was payable weekly whether the looms were working or not. Each cottage held from two to six looms; some belonged to the weaver, some were bought on credit, some were hired. The struggle between the cottage factories and the factory proper lasted over twelve years. It ended with the complete ruin of the 300 cottage factories.

As far as it goes, Marx's account of the coexistence of factories and cottage factories in the Coventry ribbon industry is accurate. But he does not go far enough in his analysis of the reasons for the "complete ruin" of the cottage factories, leaving the impression that, because steam-powered machines were involved, the ultimate triumph of the factory was inevitable.

From the 1840s, when the first steam-powered factories and cottage factories were built, until 1860 when the British ribbon industry was exposed to free trade under the Cobden-Chevalier Treaty, the two modes of work organization did compete with one another. The cottage factories more than held their own: between 1857 and 1860, industry expansion in Coventry took place exclusively in cottage factories, bringing the number to 383 on the eve of free trade (Prest 1960, pp. 95–99).

What determined the failure or success of the two alternative modes of production? The machine technology used in both was identical. The two systems grew up side by side, so there was not much difference in the average vintage of plant and equipment. Total fixed costs of plant and equipment were probably about the same. It is not apparent that the weavers who entered the factories were any more or less skilled than those who worked in their homes.

What distinguished the two systems was not technology but rather the impacts of the different relations of production on the levels of work effort and the distribution of income. To entice workers into the factories as well as to avoid being governed by the piece-rate lists of the outworkers' union, factory capitalists paid predetermined weekly wages instead of piece-rates (Prest 1960, pp. 79, 113–118). The earnings of factory workers, therefore, were not directly dependent upon the amount of work effort that they expended. Moreover, with labor markets tight and workers' organizations strong during the prosperity of the late 1840s and 1850s, wages not only rose but factory owners also had little power to use the threat of dismissal to get more work effort out of their workers.

In the cottage factories, however, not only were workers paid by the piece, giving them a direct monetary incentive to work harder if they chose to do so, but they also had to bear a fixed weekly charge for the rental of the workshop portion of the cottages as well as steam power, whatever the level of output that they produced. In other words, because of the very different distributions of the costs and benefits of production in the two modes of work organization, the outworkers had direct incentives to work hard, whereas the factory workers did not. We can therefore infer that, using the same technology, physical productivity was higher and unit costs lower under the cottage-factory system than under the factory system, explaining the apparent competitive advantage of the cottage factories prior to 1860.

The structures of social power and work incentives changed, however, when free trade enabled French ribbons to flood the British market. In the long run, the whole of the Coventry ribbon trade, not just the cottage factories, was to meet its demise (Prest 1960, p. 119ff). In the short run of the early 1860s, a partial adjustment to the new competition was made by a successful attack on the piece-rates paid to outworkers and the wages paid to factory workers. In the absence of a steady flow of ribbon orders, outworkers had no interest in continuing to pay steam-power charges. The owners of the steam engines made some concessions to try to keep the cottage factories going, but others either closed or reverted to handloom weaving. More important, with the workers' power of collective action and individual exit broken, the factory owners were now able to reap the main benefit that the factory setting could potentially offer: the intensification of work effort by direct supervision within the factory walls. As a result the factories weathered the storm of free trade better than the cottage factories.

Indeed, to create a social setting in which it would be easier to impose work discipline, some of the cottage-factory owners made the transition from domestic industry to the factory with the same workers within the same facilities. As Prest (1960, p. 132) describes the transformation that had occurred by 1861 at a firm that had built its cottage factories in 1857:

> [A] way [was] knocked through the partition walls from one shop to another, and...the top story of each [cottage factory block] was now run as a factory. The weavers might still be working above their own houses but they were no longer working at home. They still made their way up to their factory through their own trap doors, but soon these were to be closed, and the weavers would have to proceed to the factory by leaving their own houses, and walking through the yard to the external staircase in the corner between the two blocks.

In contrast to the case of the London garment trade, therefore, Marx is, strictly speaking, correct to herald the ultimate success of the factory in the case of Coventry ribbon weaving. But he might have added that the factory "triumphed" only when and because the industry entered into permanent decline, wiping out both the viability of the subcontracting system that permitted workers to work in the privacy of their own homes and the social power of factory workers to resist unremunerated intensification of labor. The example of post-1860 Coventry ribbon weaving supports Marglin's (1974) argument that the success of the factory system depended not on technology, but rather on the creation of a social environment conducive to the imposition of work discipline. The economic effectiveness of the factory as a mode of work organization did not occur within a social vacuum, but rather depended on the historical evolution of conditions that determined the relative power of capitalists and workers to structure the relation between work effort and pay.

IV. Surplus-value

In the light of the history of the nineteenth-century British economy, it is fair to conclude that Marx overemphasizes the independent influence of technology as opposed to relations of production in the determination of work organization. Because machinery does change the strength and skill content of work, it can potentially serve as an instrument of social power. How and to what extent it does so, however, depends not only on the nature of the technology but also on the nature of the social environment into which it is introduced.

If Marx does not provide all the correct answers to these questions, he does at least make the exercise of social power in the labor process central to his analysis of the capitalist economy. The main focus of his theoretical work is how capitalists use wage-labor to generate and appropriate surplus-value. Marx's great insight is to recognize that the capitalist production process is a social process in which there is basic coflict of interests between capitalists and workers over the relation between work effort and pay. His error is his failure to analyze closely enough the evolving sources of social power of the two sides in determining the effort-pay relation in the presence of technological change.

Despite Marx's errors of empirical application and theoretical elaboration, his theory of surplus-value remains highly relevant for empirical work because of its focus on key variables that determine the effort-pay relation: the subsistence wage, the duration of work, the intensity of work, and the skill content of work. Given technology, the higher the level of work effort the capitalist can elicit from the worker and the lower the wages he has to pay to get it, the higher the level of surplus-value he can appropriate to himself. Unless the worker gets intrinsic satisfaction from working harder or longer for a given wage, his or her loss is the capitalist's gain. Given the inherent conflict, what has to be understood and analyzed are the sources of social power that the two sides can bring to bear in determining the relation between work effort and pay.

In Marx's general theory of the capitalist economy, the theory of surplus-value must be distinguished from the labor theory of value. The theory of surplus-value, presented in parts Three through Six of volume I of *Capital*, is a microeconomic theory of the sources of productivity growth and the distribution of income within the capitalist production process.

The labor theory of value, which is set forth in parts One and Two of Volume I of *Capital*, is a theory of price determination in the process of market exchange.

Unlike the labor theory of value, which takes technology, skills, and work effort as given, the theory of surplus-value analyzes how productivity changes in a capitalist economy. If inputs are to be transformed into outputs, raw materials, tools, and machines require the active participation of human beings in the production process. Active participation can involve inventing a new process, designing a new product, coordinating the transformation of inputs into outputs, handling a tool, or simply tending a machine. For Marx, the critical transformation of the production process in the development of industrial capitalism is from tool handling to machine tending. The vast majority of workers become mere appendages to the machine. Work loses any intrinsic value, so that the only reward the worker gets is the pay he or she receives. The alienating nature of work brings to the fore the conflict over the relation between effort and earnings.

As a microeconomic theory of a capitalist enterprise operating in a competitive environment, the theory assumes that the only way in which the individual capitalist can raise his profits is to increase the amount of work effort that is elicited from his workers. As a general rule, all market prices, including wages, are given to the individual capitalist. Moreover, in a competitive world a particular capitalist cannot retain privileged access to process or product innovations for any appreciable period of time. But the capitalist does have privileged access to, and control over, the workers he employs. Precisely because the worker is not perfectly mobile but rather dependent upon the capitalist to gain a living, the capitalist is not subject to the dictates of market forces in dealing with the worker in the production process. The more dependent the worker is upon a particular employer, the more power the capitalist has to demand longer and harder work in return for a day's pay. The resultant unremunerated increase in the productivity of the worker per unit of time is the source of surplus-value.

The measure of surplus-value is the difference between the value-added by and the value paid to the worker. As owner of the means of production, the industrial capitalist has a legal right to keep the surplus-value for himself. If the industrial capitalist has borrowed capital or rented productive resources, then he passes along some of the surplus-value to financiers or resource owners, typically on the basis of predetermined rates.

The means of production must be transformed into saleable products at a cost that will yield a gross profit. Given the prices of inputs other than labor power as well as the prices of outputs, surplus-value will depend on the levels of effort and pay for a given quality of labor. According to the labor theory of value, labor-power exchanges for a wage that is determined by the labor-time socially necessary to reproduce the capacity to work. "In contrast...with the case of other commodities," Marx (p. 275) argues, "the determination of the value of labor-power contains a historical and moral element." He then asserts that "[n]evertheless, in a given country at a given period, the average amount of means of subsistence necessary for the worker is a known *datum*."

By taking the value of labor-power as given, Marx is able to focus his attention on the extraction of surplus-value once the worker has entered the capitalist production process. Unfortunately, within Marx's general framework, what should be merely a simplifying assumption becomes a means of portraying the capitalist workplace as a social system unto itself. By assuming that the value of labor-power is given, Marx avoids the analysis of such items as the structure and size of the family and the resultant norms for family and supplementary wages; the role of the state in the provision of social services that may partially substitute for the market wage; the collective power of workers to obtain a permanently higher subsistence wage or to prevent the establishment of a permanently lower one, including the power of workers from one "historical and moral" background to protect their wages from erosion by the influx of workers from another "historical and moral" background; and the nature of skills, training, and education required by the historical evolution of work organization itself.

In short, the investigation of the determinants of the value of labor-power is critical for understanding the evolving relation between economy and society. Marx's failure to analyze the wider social processes that determine the value of labor-power leads him to underestimate the impact of institutions such as the family, school, and unions on the structure of social power within the capitalist enterprise (Lazonick 1978).

Reading Volume I of *Capital*, one gets the impression (by no means dispelled by Marx's other writings) of a working class rendered increasingly defenseless by nineteenth-century capitalist development. Even the adult-male worker has no time for cultural and political activities, as capitalist domination transforms "his lifetime into working-time." The working-class family is torn apart as capitalist exploitation drags "his wife and child beneath the wheels of the juggernaut of capital" (p. 799). Competing with the cheap labor of women and children, men can no longer earn the family wage that forms the material foundation of the working-class family. Schooling for working-class children bears no relation to the needs of production, but only exists to comply with stipulations of the Factory Acts. After the achievement of the "normal" ten-hour working day through state legislation in the 1840s, trade unions no longer have an important institutional role to play in determining the generation and appropriation of surplus-value.

Such conclusions are unwarranted. The working-class family was far from destroyed by capitalist development. To be sure, as Marx stresses, capitalists were able to use the structure of the patriarchal family to pay women and children wages far below those of adult males. But adult males were also able to use the same structure to support their claims to earnings to support a family. Labor movements in defense of the standard of living of the working-class family, as well as state legislation such as the Factory Acts, were based upon patriarchal relations and attitudes—namely, that women and children were unfree persons, that a woman's place was in the home, and that a man had the right to and need for a wage that would permit him to support a family. Insofar as these movements were successful, they served to consolidate the role of the family as the basic unit for the material and cultural reproduction of the labor force.

Unions, moreover, did not merely fight defensive battles against a dominant capitalist class, as Marx argues in *Value, Price, and Profit* (1935, p. 61). Gaining power in the long boom of the third quarter of the nineteenth-century, unions were able to win electoral reform that, in 1867 (the same year that *Capital* was first published), extended the vote to a large proportion of the adult-male workers. With this political power, the working class was able to secure legislation that protected the position of the labor movement in industry and extended the rights of workers as citizens to a decent standard of living, influencing both the share of the working class in the social product and the extent to which that share was dependent on the wages that were wrested from capitalist firms.

Taking the value of labor power as given, however, Marx goes on to analyze the determinants of labor productivity within the capitalist enterprise. Employing labor at an externally determined wage, the capitalist faces the problem of getting work effort out of the workers he has hired. At stake are not only unit labor costs but, insofar as the utilization of physical capital depends upon work effort, unit capital costs as well.

Marx analyzes two dimensions of work effort: duration and intensity. Given the daily wage and the amount of labor performed per working hour, the capitalist can increase surplus-value by extending the length of the working day. Or, holding the wage and the working day constant, surplus-value can be augmented by increasing the intensity of work.

For Marx, duration and intensity are two very different ways of increasing surplus-value. Like the subsistence wage, the normal length of the working day is determined by forces beyond the bounds of the enterprise, whereas the intensity of labor is determined by the exercise of social power within the capitalist enterprise itself.

As Marx (p. 344) argues, "in the history of capitalist production, the establishment of a norm for the working day presents itself as a struggle over the limits of that day, a struggle between collective capital, i.e., the class of capitalists, and collective labor, i.e., the working class." In chapter 10 of *Capital*, Marx gives a lucid account of the struggle over the length of the working day in the rise of capitalism and its culmination in the Factory Acts of the 1830s and 1840s.

As we have seen, Marx ignores the role of domestic industry as a means by which workers maintained significant control over the length of the working day in the eighteenth and early nineteenth centuries. As a result, he in effect *underrates* the importance of the factories of the early Industrial Revolution as a means of extending the hours of labor.

But his account of the configuration of social forces surrounding the passage of the various Factory Acts in the first half of the nineteenth-century is historically accurate. Marx describes the lengthening of the hours of work in the early stages of the Industrial Revolution; the ineffectiveness of the pre-1833 factory legislation because of lack of enforcement mechanisms; the growing movement of the operatives for a shorter working day; the progression from legislation covering children to legislation covering women, and how, as a result, the working day of men became de facto fixed at ten hours; attempts by capitalists to prolong the working day for adults under the Factory Acts by using children in shifts; the interest of the state in ensuring the long-run reproduction of a healthy labor force; and the increasing tendency for those factory owners who could more easily adjust to a shorter working day to support the movement for effective legislation as a means of putting pressure on competitors who were less capable of maintaining profits with the hours of labor restricted.

The result of the Factory Acts was the creation of a normal working day that, in Marx's view, could, like the subsistence wage, henceforth be taken as given in the analysis of the determinants of surplus-value. The formal elements of the wage contract—the wage and the hours of work—were now set, but the problem of getting work effort out of the workers had just begun. The remainder of Marx's analysis of capitalist production concerns the ways in which capitalists can gain control over workers and extract surplus-value in the labor process with the wage and working day fixed.

The methods of capitalist work organization that permit the extraction of surplus-value are cooperation, division of labor, and machinery. By introducing these methods, according to Marxian theory, the owner of the means of production turns himself into an industrial capitalist. How do cooperation, division of labor, and machinery increase the physical productivity of labor and, hence, the production of surplus-value? Specifically, in the light of the discussion in Section III of the historical development of capitalist work organization in Britain, what is Marx assuming about the structure of social power and its impact on the relation between work effort and pay when he argues that cooperation, division of labor, and machinery augment the surplus-value extracted from each worker?

According to Marx (pp. 439, 453), cooperation occurs whenever the capitalist gathers a large number of workers together under his direction. As a source of productivity growth under manufacture, cooperation takes the preexisting handicraft methods of production and division of labor as given (p. 454). As Marx (p. 439) says:

> [M]anufacture can hardly be distinguished, in its earliest stages, from the handicraft trades of the guilds, except by the greater number of workers employed by the individual capitalist. It is merely an enlargement of the workshop of the master craftsman of the guilds.

Marx (p. 447) argues that "[w]hen the worker cooperates in a planned way with others he strips off the fetters of his individuality, and develops the capabilities of his species," thus unleashing the "productive power of social labor." Marx gives four distinct reasons why cooperation unleashes this productive power. First, economies of scale in the use of fixed capital are realized (pp. 442–443; also 446). Second, relatively large numbers of laborers working in concert can now perform tasks that could not be done within the strict confines of handicraft (or peasant) production because of "the physical constitution of the object of labor" relative to the laboring capacities of the individual worker (pp. 443; 445–446). Third, man is "a social animal" and "mere social contact begets in most industries a rivalry and a stimulation of the "animal spirits," which heightens the efficiency of each individual worker" (pp. 443–444). Fourth, time and motion can be saved when certain tasks are done cooperatively (p. 444).

As a source of productivity growth, the last reason—the saving of time and motion—really belongs under the heading of division of labor, and shall be discussed in that context below. As for the other three reasons, let us examine each of them in turn to see what assumptions are being made about the nature of the underlying relations of production and the determination of the intensity of work.

To illustrate how cooperation yields economies of scale, Marx (p. 442) argues:

> A room where twenty weavers work at twenty looms must be larger than the room of a single weaver with two assistants. But it costs less labour to build one workshop for twenty persons than to build ten to accommodate two

weavers each; thus the value of the means of production concentrated for use in common on a large scale does not increase in direct proportion to their extent and useful effect.

If one asssumes that work intensity and wages are the same in both the concentrated and decentralized work settings, then the cooperative mode will yield lower unit costs. But our discussion of the coexistence of outwork and factory work in British textiles revealed that the assumption of equal work effort does not necessarily hold. Rather, to say anything about relative work intensities, one has to make further assumptions about the structures of social power that prevail in each of the two work settings.

The second reason—that the capitalist can extract surplus-value from new tasks that can be performed cooperatively, but not individually—simply says that the capitalist can appropriate the surplus-value from cooperative labor because he owns the means of production. It does not tell us why cooperative labor generates surplus-value. Only the third reason—that man is "a social animal"—speaks to the impact of cooperation on work effort within the capitalist mode of production. Marx assumes that when capitalists, as the owners of the means of production, bring together large numbers of proletarianized workers under their control, they are able to appropriate the "socially productive power of labor as a free gift" (p. 451).

But Marx is assuming what has to be proved. When proletarianized workers have entered the capitalist workplace, why should they direct their "animal spirits" to working more "efficiently" for the capitalist, with whom they supposedly have antagonistic relations? Why not direct their "animal spirits" (derived from "mere social contact") to struggle against the capitalist whose only interest is the exploitation of their labor? Why not use their collective power to restrict output and preserve their own capacities to work (and live) rather than present capital with a "free gift" of the social power of their labor?

Marx's answer appears to go beyond "mere social contact" among workers to direct supervision. The capitalist must not only own the cooperative production process, but must also organize the appropriation of surplus-value from it. Hence capitalist production must be, as Marx (p. 451) puts it, despotic. Supervision "is made necessary by the capitalist, and therefore antagonistic, character of [the cooperative labor] process." As the enterprise expands its scale, the capitalist "hands over the work of direct and constant supervision of the individual workers and groups of workers to a special kind of wage-laborer," namely managers, foremen, and overseers "who command during the labor process in the name of capital."

But why, against the worker's resistence to exploitation of their labor-power, does direct supervision succeed in intensifying labor to the point where it more than compensates for the costs of managers, foremen, and overlookers? Ironically, Marx (p. 451) posits a solution to the problem of work effort that rests not on the social nature of production, but rather on the social nature of exchange! The capitalist makes individual contracts with, say, 100 workers:

> Being independent of each other, the workers are isolated. They enter into relations with the capitalist, not with each other. Their cooperation only begins in the labour process, *but by then they have ceased to belong to themselves*. On entering the labour process they are incorporated into capital. As co-operaters, as members of a working organism, *they merely form a particular mode of existence of capital*. Hence the productive power developed by the worker socially is the productive power of capital. The socially productive power of labour develops as a free gift to capital whenever the workers are placed under certain conditions, and it is capital which places them under these conditions. (emphasis added)

With cooperation as its basis, division of labor become, in Marx's view, the means of raising surplus-value during the period of "manufacture." Here the intensity of labor would surely seem to be important, because Marx (pp.457–458) states that "[w]hether complex or simple, each operation has to be done by hand, retains the character of a handicraft, and is therefore dependent on the strength, skill, *quickness and sureness* with which the individual manipulates his tools" (my emphasis).

Marx draws upon the famous analysis of Adam Smith to explain how a greater fragmentation of tasks leads to higher labor productivity. In *The Wealth of Nations*, Smith (1937, bk. 1, ch. 1) argues that, by means of the division of labor, the worker (i) becomes more adept at doing one simple task; (ii) saves time moving from task to task; and (iii) becomes more inventive. Smith views the sources of productivity growth that flow from increased division of labor as purely technical in nature. He pays no attention to the impact of the social relations of the workplace on the generation or appropriation of productivity gains (see Marglin 1974).

Marx, unfortunately, follows Smith all too closely in explaining the impact of division of labor on the extraction of surplus-value. Marx argued that "a worker who performs the same simple operation for the whole of his life converts his body into the automatic, one-sided implement of that operation," and that as a result "in comparison with the independent handicraft, more is produced in less time" by the worker in capitalist production. Marx (p. 458) goes on to say:

> The worker's continued repetition of the same narrowly defined act and the concentration of his attention on it teach him by experience how to attain *the desired effect with the minimum of exertion*. But since there are always several generations of workers living at one time, the technical skill, the tricks of the trade thus acquired, become established, and are accumulated and handed down. [emphasis added)

In essence, Marx is making a learning-by-doing argument: productivity advances result from the increasing ability of experienced workers to produce more per unit of time *with the same expenditure of work effort* (see Helper and Lazonick 1984; Lazonick and Brush 1985).

But the fact that workers become more adept at performing a particular task does not tell us anything about "the quickness and sureness" with which they actually apply their "strength and skill" within the capitalist labor process (see Lazonick 1983a, 1984b). Is it not likely that even when their labor has been divided, wage-laborers will use the development of their particular laboring capacities and their intimate understanding of a particular part of the production process—the "tricks of the trade" that they pass down from generation to generation—to control the pace of work and thereby reap for themselves productivity gains in the form of on-the-job leisure? Alternatively, is it not likely that wage-laborers will form craft unions, the express purpose of which is to control not only the level of effort, but also the relation between effort and pay? We need only look to the history of nineteenth-century British capitalist production, summarized in section III, to answer these questions. In industry after industry, key groups of British workers did come to exercise substantial control over the relation between work effort and pay within the capitalist enterprise.

Like Smith, however, Marx gives the impression that the technical division of labor of a cooperative labor process in and of itself—that is quite apart from the particular social relations of production—solves the problem of getting work effort out of the worker. As Marx (p. 469) argues:

> The habit of doing only one thing converts [the specialized individual worker] into an organ which operates with the certainty of a force of nature, while his connection with the whole mechanism compels him to work with the regularity of a machine.

The forces of production, including the worker's mindless expenditure of his or her labor-power, ensure that high levels of work effort are forthcoming.

If the exercise of social power enters into Marx's analysis of the relation between division of labor and effort, it is because capitalists use division of labor to reallocate unskilled work away from men, who had made these tasks integral to their craft, to women and children. Given the patriarchal relations of the family, women and children can be employed for lower wages than men and have less social power to resist attempts to intensify their labor. Surplus-value is thereby enhanced.

It can also be argued that the real advantage of the technical division of labor that Smith and (following him once again) Marx (p. 460) attribute to time saved in moving from task to task is the greater ease with which supervisors can oversee workers who have no business but to stay put at a particular post throughout the working day, producing a particular component of a larger product. Conversely a worker who is permitted, say, to fetch supplies to be used in his or her primary task may use the opportunity of moving from place to place to control the pace of work (see Lazonick 1983a).

Marx (p. 483), quoting Smith, stresses the detrimental effects that the extreme division of labor in the workplace can have on the intellectual development of workers. We must assume that Marx is thinking of unskilled workers, for he recognizes that however far the division of labor goes under manufacture, there always remain certain skills that cannot be simply divided away. Hence Marx (p. 460) emphasizes the distinction between skilled workers (mainly men) and unskilled workers (mainly women and children) under manufacture, arguing—and this relates to Smith's controversial third reason (see Rosenberg 1965; Marglin 1974)—that the technical division of labor clarifies possible improvements and adaptations of particular tools, enabling "the specialized workers... themselves [to take] an active part" in the development of technology.

As we have seen, Marx (p. 490) stresses the constraints that the social power of skilled workers place upon the extraction of surplus-value, arguing that "the complaint that the workers lack discipline runs through the whole period of manufacture." In large-scale industry, however, the introduction of machinery is supposed to resolve the problem of discipline by making the skilled workers superfluous.

Marx (pp. 535–536) portrays the determination of work effort in large-scale industry as simply derivative of changes in the length of the working day and mechanization, rather than as a direct outcome of capital-labor conflict. He argues that "the efficiency of labor-power is in inverse ratio to the duration of expenditure." He introduces factual evidence that, when the working day is shortened from 12 to 11 hours, output per working day actually increases "entirely as a result of steadier application to the work and a more economical use of time on the part of the worker." But he does not explore changes in capital-labor relations that may have influenced this result. At best, he adopts a "human-relations" perspective on how the "animal spirits" of the workers are raised, arguing that

> [t]he moral element played an important part in the. . .experiments. The workers told the factory inspector: "We work with more spirit, we have the reward ever before us of getting away sooner at night, and one active and cheerful spirit pervades the whole mill, from the youngest piecer to the oldest hand, and we greatly help each other." (p. 536n)

Machinery, however, is a more potent means of permitting the intensification of labor because the production process is no longer reliant upon the physical strength and craft skills of workers. Machinery increases surplus-value by reducing the amount of work effort required per unit of output, while at the same time making the workers needed to tend these machines easily replaceable, and hence subject to speed-up and stretch-out. Quite apart from the cutting of the wage bill that results from the use of cheaper segments of the labor force, Marx (pp. 536–538) assumes that capitalists are able to increase surplus-value by running machines so fast that complementary labor-power is compelled to work with the maximum effort that is humanly possible. As a result, unit labor costs are lowered and fixed-capital costs are spread over more output per unit of time.

Marx makes no mention of worker resistence to unremunerated intensification of labor. As we have seen in the case of the self-acting mule, Marx fails to see that the introduction of machinery into the capitalist labor process is only a necessary, not a sufficient, condition for the displacement of worker control over the relation between work effort and pay.

Marx's assumption that mechanization enables the capitalist to intensify work effort to its physical maximum has led most Marxists to ignore the relation between mechanization and the intensity of labor. Like most economists, they rarely ask why machinery results in increases in labor productivity, even though one of Marx's most important contributions to our understanding of production is to reveal the answer (pp. 492–508). Simply put, mechanization overcomes the constraints on productivity inherent in human labor by embodying the strength and skill requirements of work in much more durable and precise machines. After mechanization, the same task can be performed as well as it could be before *with less expenditure of work effort* on the part of the operative. Such technological change should properly be called *effort-saving* (Lazonick 1984b).

The introduction of effort-saving machinery does not *ensure* either increased physical labor productivity or surplus-value. The sufficient condition for increased labor productivity is that remaining workers be unable to reap (or eliminate, depending on one's perspective) all of the productivity gains by a combination of more leisurely work and higher pay. If surplus-value is to increase subsequent to the introduction of an effort-saving technology, high levels of work effort will have to be restored without the inordinate use of income incentives. Furthermore, because capital costs are incurred in the process of technological change, the ability of capitalists to restore (or, in the presence of very high capital costs, augment) the level of work effort received for a given level of earnings is a precondition for the introduction of the technology in the first place (Lazonick 1984b). Struggles over the intensity of labor and its relation to pay are, therefore, integral to the on-going process of capitalist accumulation.

Marx avoids an analysis of how the evolving structure of capital-labor relations affects the determination of the relation between effort and pay. He views the intensification of labor subsequent to the introduction of machinery as nonproblematic because of two built-in mechanisms—one external to the labor process and one internal—that push the intensity of work to its maximum.

The external mechanism has already been mentioned: the introduction of machinery is assumed to create an industrial reserve army that stands ready to take the jobs of those still fortunate enough to have them, forcing the employed to submit to the demands of supervisors for more intense labor. Even assuming the existence of an industrial reserve army, the argument is problematic for both technical and social reasons. The technical reason is that the firm has to concern itself with the costs of high levels of turnover. There are transactions costs of hiring and training new workers (which can result not only in short-run productivity declines but also in the wastage of raw materials and damage to equipment). Such costs can be considerable, and even then the firm has no assurance that, over the long run, it will end up with more productive workers. The social reason is that, even with the introduction of "deskilling" technology, workers, as "social animals," *cooperate* with each other, formally in unions or informally on the shop floor, to control the relation between effort and pay, their purpose being to protect themselves from unrenumerated overwork.

Marx's internal mechanism is payment by the piece—a form of wage payment that, unlike time wages, supposedly overcomes restriction of output by workers. It is his view that, by mid-nineteenth-century, piece-rates had become "the general rule" in British "large-scale industry," in part because in "workshops which are subject to the Factory Acts,... capital can increase the yield of the working day only by intensifying labor" (p. 699). Taking as given the technical productivity of workers and the piece-rate, Marx (p. 695) argues that "it is naturally in the personal interest of the worker that he should strain his labor-power as intensely as possible" and that "this in turn enables the capitalist to raise the normal degree of intensity of labor more easily." As he goes on to argue, "the wider scope that piece-wages give to individuality tends to develop both that individuality, and with it the worker's sense of liberty, independence, and self-control, and also the competition of workers with one another" (p. 697).

This competition (now both internal to the labor process as well as external in the form of a reserve army of unemployed) in turn provides capitalists with the opportunity to lower piece-rates. Should workers in a particular craft be capable of protecting "a particular rate of piece-wage [that] has for a long time been fixed by tradition"—an "exceptional" circumstance according to Marx (p. 697)—capitalists may have "recourse to the forcible transformation of piece-wages into time-wages."

Marx, therefore, recognizes that the relation between effort and pay for a given technology is a source of capital-labor conflict. But he assumes either that workers compete with one another in blind pursuit of individual gain, resulting in unremunerated intensification of labor (and hence an increase in surplus-value), or that, in "exceptional cases," capitalists are forced to scrap the piece-rate system. Contrary to Marx, in virtually all cases of "large-scale industry" in nineteenth-century Britain, key groups of workers were better able to divide and conquer their capitalist employers than vice versa. Far from blindly competing with one another, as Marx assumes, these workers—the so-called "aristocracy of labor" and even some other groups of workers who were not so highly paid—were in general far better organized than their capitalist counterparts. Through the power of their unions, they maintained considerable job control in the labor process and enforced piece-rate lists; as a result they played an active and critical role in the determination of the relation between effort and earnings.

Ignoring the evolution of job control in nineteenth-century British capitalism, the bottom line of the Marxian analysis is that all-powerful capitalists are able to intensify labor to the limit for a given wage. Marx (pp. 697–698) concludes that "the piece-wage is the form of wage most appropriate to the capitalist mode of production." Although he recognizes that capitalists will have an interest in *unremunerated* intensification of labor (and indeed might be forced into it by competition from other capitalists, particularly from more technologically progressive ones), he sees the individualistic actions of workers as self-defeating. He offers no reason to believe that collective action will enable workers to control the relation between effort and earnings over the long run.

Marx also considers the more dynamic case of the use of payment systems in the presence of technological change. When the productivity of labor rises because of the introduction of a new technology, the piece-rate is cut proportionally, leaving the worker's earnings unchanged. The result of the change in the piece-rate is, in Marx's words, "purely nominal." The implication is that the level of work effort is also left unchanged—which will only be the case if output per worker rises just enough to offset the effort-saving impact of the technological change.

There is no reason to expect such a result. One cannot even assume that managers (or industrial engineers) know a priori the extent of the effort-saving effect of any particular technological change (Lazonick 1984b). Workers in a particular workplace will have a collective interest to conceal from management the true impact of a change in technology on the level of work effort required to produce a given amount of output, for by so doing they lessen the extent of the piece-wage cut that management *thinks* is "purely nominal"—the cut that will leave the relation between effort and earnings unchanged. Because it is workers, not managers, who are actually doing the work, access to information on the effort-saving potential of a machine will be asymmetric, giving workers a distinct advantage in determining the pace of work. In addition, workers through their unions will attempt to exert industry-wide control over the relation between effort and pay on a newly diffused technology. The resultant relation between effort and earnings will depend upon the exercise of social power, not upon abstract "laws" of proportional change.

Marx (p. 700) recognizes that "purely nominal" rate-cutting subsequent to technological change "leads to constant battles between the capitalist and the worker," as capitalists, in fact, try to use the opportunity to appropriate unremunerated effort, or as workers press for a share of real productivity gains. From Marx's analytical perspective, however, these battles are of little consequence to the long-run development of capitalist production for two reasons. First, deskilling and labor-displacing technology in combination with the individualism of workers is continually pushing intensification of labor to the maximum consistent with laboring capacity. Second, although conflict *within* the labor process persists, it is, like all collective actions on the part of workers, purely defensive. It does not permit particular collectivities of workers to protect themselves from the forces of the labor market or technology, nor does it permit workers in general to raise the "historical and moral" value of labor-power. The capitalists of Marxian theory, therefore, have not only an incentive to continually "revolutionize" the labor process by means of technological change, but also the unfettered ability to do so.

V. Relations and Forces of Production

One of the most intelligent critics of Marxist economics has said:

> The difference between a scientist and a prophet does not lie in what some great man says but in how it is received. The duty of the pupils of a scientist is to test his hypotheses by looking for evidence to refute them, while the duty of the disciples of a prophet is to go on repeating his very words. (Robinson, 1980, p. 202)

The purpose here has been to treat Marx as a scientist rather than a prophet. Because Marx was a "great man," the value of his work does not vanish with criticism; it can potentially be strengthened by it.

"Great men"—those who, in Kuhnian fashion (Kuhn, 1970), put forth seminal and coherent worldviews within which the importance of previously ignored phenomena can be demonstrated—are few and far between in the social sciences. We can follow Joseph Schumpeter (1949) —another "great man," who was a critical admirer of Marx—in distinguishing between a "prescientific" vision of how the world works and theoretical analysis that seeks to impart scientific rigor to the broader perspective. A great social scientist cannot do one or the other; he or she must do both.

The greatness of Marx is his vision of economic development as the outcome of the interaction of social structure and technology. Impressed by the unprecedented industrial development of the first half of the nineteenth-century, the vision led Marx to focus on the interaction of the relations and forces of production in contrast to a growing tendency of social analysts to view the new industrial world as one in which impersonal market forces predominated.

Marx's focus on production in turn led him to study the works of the classical economists, whom he criticized for the sake of developing more sophisticated and relevant theory—in much the same manner that I have attempted to make use of Marx. Marx's major advance over classical economists such as Adam Smith and David Ricardo was his emphasis on the role of social power in the operation of the capitalist production process. In particular, Marx's basic criticism of Ricardian theory was its failure to distinguish between the capacity to work (labor-power) and work actually performed (labor-embodied), and hence its inability to develop a theory of surplus-value that was logically consistent with a theory of equal exchange.

The distinction between labor-power and labor-embodied brings the problem of work effort and the exercise of social power to the center of the Marxian theory of production, and differentiates it from both classical and neoclassical economic theory in which the relations between labor inputs and final outputs are technically determined. For Marx, the distinction between labor-power and labor-embodied lays the basis for the theory of surplus-value, which sets out a fundamental theoretical framework for analyzing the relations among work effort, skill, technology, wages, and profits. The greatness of Marx is not only that he constructs such a theory but also that, in keeping with his materialist conception of history, he makes an attempt to generate and validate his theoretical ideas on the basis of the historical experience of the foremost capitalist nation of the time.

The strengths of Marx's work, therefore, are his overarching vision of economic development and social change, his general theoretical framework for analyzing capitalist production, and his methodological approach. The weaknesses arise when he lets his theory take on a life of its own, so that theory tends to determine "history" rather than vice versa.

Marx's basic problem was that he was overinfluenced by the intense class-conflict of the first half of the nineteenth-century, during which rapid industrial change and frequent periods of boom and bust played havoc with the economic security and well-being of the British working class. Marx's view of the world was particularly influenced by Engels' (1969) first-hand account of the condition of the British working class in the early 1840s—a time when British industrial workers were suffering from one of the worst cyclical downturns of the first half of the nineteenth-century. In a largely accurate portrayal of the plight of various strata of the British working class in the "hungry forties," Engels stressed the role of labor-displacing machinery as the source of the workers' misery (see Sherwood 1985). When combined with the testimony contained in government enquiries into work conditions—many of them undertaken before mid-century and many of the later ones dealing with occupations that were outside the factory system—Engels' depiction convinced Marx that British capitalists were exploiting British workers to the point where they had "nothing to lose but their chains." These accounts in turn undoubtedly led Marx to accept as fact the ideological pronouncements of Andrew Ure.

In the conflict-ridden 1830s, Ure's utterances reflected the world that many British capitalists hoped would come to pass rather than the world in process of evolution (Lazonick 1979). Overly influenced by the intense class conflict of the first half of the century as well as by procapitalist ideology that proclaimed the unmitigated triumph of capital, Marx predicted increasing misery for the mass of British workers: their lifetimes would be transformed into working time and they would become appendages to the machine. But, when he was working out the theories that appear in *Capital*, Marx misunderstood the evolution of both the collective power of British workers and the competitive fragmentation of British capitalists during the industrial revolution and into the 1850s and early 1860s.

Throughout the first half of the nineteenth-century, as we have seen, adult-male operatives played key roles in the coordination and control of the labor process, even as they were buffeted about by periodic industrial downturns. In the long boom of the third quarter of the nineteenth-century, however, these workers were to build their collective organizations on the foundations of shop-floor control of work organization. As they sought to regulate the relation between effort and earnings, they confronted capitalists who, more divided by market competition than united by class interest, opted for collective accommodation with well-organized groups of workers, such as the mule spinners, rather than jeopardize current profits during prosperity by engaging in industrial conflict.

During a period in which British industry dominated the world economy, most British capitalists came to support the *industry-wide* enforcement of collective bargaining agreements because it assured them that all their competitors would be governed by the same basic labor-cost conditions. The Liberal-Labour alliance that brought together industrial capitalists and the "New Model" unions in the political arena enabled the labor movement to make legislative gains that greatly enhanced the ability of workers to organize unions; build up strike funds; and, when necessary, stage prolonged strikes (Lazonick 1979; Elbaum and Lazonick 1986).

The result was the emergence of a so-called "labor aristocracy" in the middle decades of the nineteenth-century. These workers, whom Hobsbawm (1968, p. 290) has estimated made up 10 to 20 percent of the British labor force in the late nineteenth-century, labored long and hard. In return for their high levels of work effort, the "labor aristocrats" were, by the standards of the time, decently paid. Within the workplace, where they combined knowledge of production with control over work organization, the labor aristocrats cannot accurately be described as mere appendages to the machine. Outside the workplace, moreover, industrial workers had opportunities for cultural and political development even under the ten hour day. Contrary to Marx, their lifetimes were not reduced to working time.

Gross exploitation of workers abounded in late nineteenth-century Britain, but it was in domestic industry and small "sweatshops," not in large-scale factories. Where the factory system was most developed, the introduction of effort-saving machinery into the workplace meant that the conflict over the relation between effort and pay was not necessarily a zero-sum game. Industrial-relations structures that would ensure both capitalists and workers acceptable shares of potential productivity gains through the introduction of new methods of production could promote the diffusion of those methods and actual realization of the productivity gains which could then be shared out. Cooperative relations of production, that is, could create a basis for the development of the forces of production.

Opting for cooperative production relations with powerful groups of organized workers, British industrialists came to accept significant worker control over the management of their labor processes. From the fourth quarter of the nineteenth-century, when intermittant but at times prolonged recessions occurred and British industry began to feel the threat of foreign competition, many British capitalists tried to challenge the power of unions (see Brown 1977). But they were unable to replace job control by top-down managerial control as was being done by competitors in, among other places, the United States, Germany, and Japan. Despite the continued introduction of many deskilling technologies, the power of union organization developed earlier had become too great. When Parliament and the judiciary sought to undermine the union movement—most notably by means of the Taff Vale decision that signaled financial ruin for any union engaged in a prolonged strike—workers turned en masse to build a political party that would represent their interests.

The persistence of structures of social power inherited from the nineteenth-century made it exceedingly difficult for twentieth-century British industry to meet the powerful international challenges from industries with more coordinated managerial control over the introduction of mass production technologies (Elbaum and Lazonick 1986; Lazonick 1986b). The capacity for British production relations characterized by job control to promote the development of the forces of production reached its limits. Given the productivity standards set by international competition, old procedures of distributing the costs and benefits of productivity growth between workers and capitalists were not necessarily sufficient to give capitalists the incentive to invest in the new technologies. Vested interests —in particular the stake that British workers had in job control and the historic underdevelopment of British management—stood in the way of transforming relations of production in ways that would promote the diffusion of advanced production methods. Instead, British managers and workers sought to adapt to international competition on the basis of the existing structures of social power, and this resulted in further entrenchment rather than transformation of the traditional relations of production.

Fixed in his views that the forces of production were securing the domination of capitalists over workers and that, as a result, the production process was evolving into a social system unto itself, Marx fails to analyze the ways in which relations of production were actually evolving in his own time (Lazonick 1979; MacKenzie 1984; Sherwood 1985). Instead he stresses the role of a rising organic composition of capital—the ratio of nonhuman to human inputs per unit of output—in reproducing capitalist domination over workers, in creating accumulation crises, and in fostering the concentration and centralization of capital. That is, the rising organic composition of capital permits Marx to make technology rather than production relations the main link between his theory of surplus-value and his theory of capital accumulation.

The argument that the rising organic composition of capital accounts for the inherent tendency for competitive capitalism to evolve into "monopoly" capitalism is of particular importance in the history of Marxist theory because Marx can be credited with using his theory of capital accumulation to predict the rise of big business before its actual appearance.

According to Marx (pp. 778–779), "the two most powerful levers of centralization [are] competition and credit."

> The battle of competition is fought by the cheapening of commodities. The cheapness of commodities depends, all other circumstances remaining the same, on the productivity of labor, and this depends in turn on *the scale of production.* Therefore *the larger capitals beat the smaller.* (p. 777) [my emphasis]

In the Marxian analysis, credit enables *some* capitalists to update their plant and equipment as well as to acquire cheaply the plant and equipment of weaker firms that can no longer meet the competition (pp. 777–780).

In historical perspective, however, the Marxian argument cannot account for the tenacity of competitive forms of industrial organization in Britain. In staple industries as diverse as steel and textiles, British capitalists found themselves trapped in "competitive equilibrium," in large part because the imposition of job control across firms in an industry made it very difficult for any one firm to achieve a distinct competitive advantage through the lowering of unit costs (Elbaum and Lazonick 1986). Thus, well into the twentieth-century, the structure of these industries was characterized not by monopoly capitalism, but by competition, to the point where constituent firms were discouraged from engaging in modernization.

It is true that in the United States oligopolistic structures did emerge out of competitive conditions. The imperative of a rising organic composition of capital provides an insufficient explanation for this transition, however, because it totally ignores the organizational transformation, and the structure of social power inherent in it, that characterized the rise of big business.

It is generally the case that the adoption of more advanced technology increases the firm's capital-labor ratio and requires a greater precommitment of resources. But a firm that invests in capital-intensive technology will not automatically secure lower unit costs and competitive advantage. If the investing firm does not have the *organizational* capacities to utilize the fixed capital at its disposal—that is, if it cannot generate and appropriate surplus-value by coordinating and controlling the efforts of its employees—then it might well find itself at a competitive *disadvantage* compared to a labor-intensive operation that is less burdened by fixed costs. To understand how large-scale precommitments of capital to advanced methods of production can be transformed from a potential competitive burden into an actual competitive advantage requires an analysis of the types of relations of production that permit the effective *utilization* of technology.

A relevant theory of the rise of corporate capitalism (a much better description of the nature of the new production relations than "monopoly capitalism") must begin with an intimate knowledge of the history of the place and period in question. With this knowledge, generalizations that have empirical foundations and testable content can then be made. In the *Visible Hand*, Chandler (1977) provides an historical analysis of the emergence of corporate enterprise and oligopolistic industrial structures in the United States between 1880 and 1920. He argues that the firms that came out on top were those that were able to cut costs dramatically by a strategy of vertical integration, redesign of plant layout, standardization of inputs, and mechanization of heavy and skilled work. As a result, these firms (as epitomized by Carnegie Steel) were able to reap enormous internal economies that were decisive in the competitive struggle.

Like most other economists, Marxists tend to view the internal economies that permit some firms to gain a distinct competitive advantage over others as scale economies that derive from the imperatives of technology, without any analysis of the structures of social power that permit the effective utilization of "scale." Chandler's historical analysis confronts this perspective by demonstrating the importance of a distinct class of internal economies—*economies of throughput*.

To use the terminology from Chandler's earlier work, *Strategy and Structure* (1962), an enterprise may embark on an investment strategy but the more ambitious this strategy in terms of process, product, and geography, the more critical will be the development of a managerial structure that can coordinate the flows of inputs—including the work effort of employees—and the distribution of outputs in order to justify the large-scale commitment of capital. Indeed, the very investment in a bureaucracy to achieve high levels of throughput will in itself only serve to increase the precommitment of capital, making the achievement of high levels of throughput all the more critical to enterprise success. The firm, as distinct from its employees, moreover, needs to accomplish high *levels* of throughput while retaining some of the resultant productivity gains for itself, if it is to reap *economies* of throughput. To inject the Marxian insight into the Chandlerian framework, economies of throughput assume not only high levels of work effort on the part of employees but also high levels of *unremunerated* effort—that is, surplus-value.

To say that the profits of the firm, or its ability to undercut the prices of its rivals, depends upon unremunerated work effort is to say that the relation between effort and earnings is not determined solely by market forces. In capitalist enterprises, employees contribute their work effort not only in return for a wage or salary but also because of loyalty to the firm or (what may amount to the same thing) because of the promise of job security and career advancement that the particular firm can offer. Once an employee has committed himself or herself to an organization that can offer more than this week's or this year's earnings for this week's or this year's effort, the employee becomes dependent upon the enterprise, and hence prone to be "exploited" by it because of a diminution of his or her ability to use the market to extract full remuneration for the value added by his or her work effort. In Western capitalist economies, it is only the exceptional employee who can *successfully* use the threat of exit from the firm in order to extract "full," that is, market-determined, remuneration for his or her services, in part because of the cost of using the market but also in part because that employee's productivity is not independent of the specific organization within which his or her capabilities have been developed and utilized. (For an elaboration on this theme, see Lazonick 1986c) In modern-day Japanese industry, which has certainly been successful in mobilizing the efforts of its workers to gain international competitive advantage, for any "permanent employee" even to threaten to use the market to enhance his or her rewards from the firm would immediately spell the end of that employee's association with the organization.

In basing his theory of capitalist development on the experiences of the world's first industrial nation, Marx could not garner the insights that come from cross-national historical comparisons of the rise of capitalist economies from the late nineteenth-century on. Even with access to the same forces of production, relations of production will differ markedly from one political and cultural context to the next. In terms of the Marxian notion of surplus-value, the success or failure of capitalist enterprise will therefore differ across regions and nations because different cultural and political contexts will yield different structures of social power, which will in turn yield different relations between effort and monetary rewards.

Once we recognize that the capitalist enterprise functions differently because of variations in social context, it becomes evident that we require a theory of capitalist development that explores the nature and impact of these social differences rather than a theory that serves as an intellectual excuse for pretending these differences do not exist. If a theory is to be, and remain, relevant, it must stay in touch with the reality it is supposed to be analyzing. Theory must not be allowed to take on a life of its own.

Even though Marx generated his theory of capitalist development by studying the history of the rise of capitalism, he ultimately came to regard his theory as a set of laws from which determinate solutions could be derived rather than as a framework for exploring further the complexities of social reality. With technology as the driving force of economic development and class conflict and social relations of production pushed into the background, Marx came to view his theory as a determinate model of capitalist development that could be applied to all times and all places where private property and wage-labor could be found.

Marx generated his theory of capitalist development by studying the British experience. But when his work was done—specifically when he wrote the Preface to the First Edition of *Capital*, published in German—Marx sought to justify his focus on the British experience by arguing that it was merely illustrative of the course of development awaiting Germany. "Until now," Marx (p. 90) argued,

> [the] *locus classicus* [of the capitalist mode of production] has been England. This is the reason why England is used as the main illustration of the theoretical developments I make. If, however, the German reader pharisaically shrugs his shoulders at the condition of the English industrial and agricultural workers, or optimistically comforts himself with the thought that in Germany things are not nearly so bad, I must plainly tell him: *De te fabula narratur*.

Theory has detached itself from reality and taken on a life of its own. Marx (pp. 90–91) continues:

> Intrinsically, it is not a question of the higher or lower degree of development of the social antagonisms that spring from the natural laws of capitalist production. It is a question of these laws themselves, of these tendencies winning their way and working themselves out with *iron necessity*. The country that is more developed industrially only shows, to the less developed, the image of its future.

There are many things to be learned about the relation between theory and history from the serious study of Marx. But the notion of "natural laws of capitalist production. . .winning their way and working themselves out with iron necessity" is not one of them. Marx supplied valuable insights into the nature of the conflict between capitalists and workers in the labor process as well as the nature of technology. In the British case that stands at the center of his analysis, however, he failed to discern the considerable power that British workers exercised over the division and coordination of labor and the utilization of technology in the nineteenth-century. The serious weaknesses of Marx's analysis of the evolution of nineteenth-century industrial capitalism should make one rather wary of using his theoretical distillation of the British experience as the appropriate model for analyzing later-developing capitalist economies.

The British experience demonstrates that structures of social power shape the development, diffusion, and utilization of technology. Successful capitalist development in the economies of Germany, the United States, and Japan has been based upon structures of social power that, in historical and comparative perspective, reveal a serious underdevelopment of British managerial coordination and control persisting well into the twentieth-century (Chandler 1980; Elbaum and Lazonick 1986; Lazonick 1986b). The nature of successful development in the twentieth-century cannot merely be extrapolated from the history of the world's first industrial revolution—even when we get the story right. Only by comparing and contrasting the dramatic social and technological changes in the development of capitalism in various national economies over the past hundred years can we begin to put forth, and test the empirical limits of, theoretical generalizations. If a relevant theory of economic development is what is wanted, the future of economic history is to explore and compare the dynamic interaction of the forces and relations of production in widely varying cultural and political contexts. The Marxian theory of surplus-value points us in the right direction. But only the rigorous study of comparative historical experiences can ensure that we stay on the relevant theoretical path.

Notes

1. The volume of historical research on the topics covered in this essay is substantial, and no attempt is made to cite all the relevant literature. I refer to recent surveys (e.g., Rule 1981; Berg 1985) and analytical works (e.g., Marglin 1974; Landes 1986) in which more complete references to the historical material can be found.

2. Unless indicated otherwise, all references to Marx are to the 1977 Vintage Books edition of the Fowkes translation of *Capital* Volume I. I should also make clear at the outset that I am not here engaged in an exercise in Marxology. My concern is rather the relation between history and theory in *Capital*, Marx's most systematic, central, and mature work. For the issues of the nature of capitalist production that concern me, moreover, virtually all the relevant material is in Volume I, the only one of the three volumes of *Capital* that Marx published during this lifetime.

References

Anderson, Michael. 1976. Sociological history: The Industrial Revolution and the working-class family. *Social History* 3:317–334.
Ashton, T.S. 1961. *An Economic History of England: The 18th Century*. London: Methuen.
Berg, Maxine. 1985. *The Age of Manufactures, 1700–1820*. London: Fontana.
Berg, Maxine, Pat Hudson, and Michael Sonenscher, eds. 1983. *Manufacture in Town and Country before the Factory*. Cambridge: Cambridge University Press.
Braverman, Harry. 1974. *Labor and Monopoly Capital*. New York: Monthly Review Press.
Brown, Geoff. 1977. *Sabotage*. Bristol: Spokesman Books.
Bythell, Duncan. 1969. *The Handloom Weavers*. Cambridge: Cambridge University Press.
Bythell, Duncan. 1978. *The Sweated Trades*. New York: St. Martin's Press.
Chaloner, W.H. 1964. Preface to the second edition, of A. Redford, *Labor Migration in England, 1800–1850*. Manchester: Manchester University Press.
Chambers, J.D. 1953. Enclosure and labor supply in the Industrial Revolution. *Economic History Review* 2nd ser. 5:319–343.
Chambers, J.D., and G.E. Mingay. 1966, *The Agricultural Revolution, 1750–1880*. London: Batsford.
Chandler, Jr., Alfred D. 1962. *Strategy and Structure*. Cambridge: M.I.T. Press.
Chandler, Jr., Alfred D. 1977. *The Visible Hand*. Cambridge: Harvard University Press.
Chandler, Jr., Alfred D. 1980, The growth of the transnational industrial firm in the United States and the United Kingdom: A comparative analysis. *Economic History Review* 2nd ser. 33:396–410.
Clarkson L.A. 1985. *Proto-industrialization: The first phase of industrialization?* London: Macmillan.
Davies, Robert B. 1976. *Peacefully Working to Conquer the World*. New York: Arno Press.
Deane, Phyllis. 1973. Great Britain. In C. Cipolla (ed.), *The Fontana Economic History of Europe*, Vol. 4, Part One. London: Collins.
Engels, Frederick. 1969. *The Condition of the Working Class in England*. London: Panther.
Elbaum, Bernard, and William Lazonick. 1986. An institutional perspective on British decline. In Elbaum and Lazonick (eds.), *The Decline of the British Economy*. Oxford: Oxford University Press.
Elbaum, Bernard, and Frank Wilkinson. 1979. Industrial relations and uneven development: A comparative study of the American and British steel industries. *Cambridge Journal of Economics* 3:275–303.
Gray, Robert. 1981. *The Aristocracy of Labour, c. 1850–1914*. London: Macmillan.
Harris, R. 1963. *A Short History of 18th Century England*. New York: Mentor.
Harrison, Royden, and Jonathan Zeitlin, eds. 1985. *Divisions of Labour: Skilled Workers and Technological Change in Nineteenth-Century Britain*. Brighton:

Harvester.

Helper, Susan, and William Lazonick. 1984. Learning curves and productivity growth in institutional context. Harvard Institute of Economic Research Discussion Paper No. 1066 (June).

Hill, Christopher. 1967. Pottage for freeborn Englishmen: Attitudes to wage labor in the sixteenth and seventeenth centuries. In C.H. Feinstein (ed.), *Socialism, Capitalism, and Economic Growth*. Cambridge: Cambridge University Press.

Hobsbawm, E.J. 1968. *Labouring Men*. London: Weidenfeld & Nicolson.

Hobsbawm, E.J. 1984. *Workers: Worlds of Labor*. New York: Pantheon.

Hounshell, David. 1984. *From the American System to Mass Production, 1800–1932*. Baltimore: Johns Hopkins University Press.

Kuhn, Thomas. 1970. *The Structure of Scientific Revolutions*, 2nd ed. Chicago: University of Chicago Press.

Landes, David. 1969. *The Unbound Prometheus*. Cambridge: Cambridge University Press.

Landes, David. 1986. What do bosses really do? *Journal of Economic History* 46:585–593.

Lazonick, William. 1974. Karl Marx and enclosures in England. *Review of Radical Political Economics* 6:1–32.

Lazonick, William. 1975. Marxian theory and the development of the labor force in England. Ph.D. thesis, Harvard University.

Lazonick, William. 1978. The subjection of labor to capital: The rise of the capitalist system. *Review of Radical Political Economics* 8:1–31.

Lazonick, William. 1979. Industrial relations and technical change: The case of the self-acting mule. *Cambridge Journal of Economics* 3:231–262.

Lazonick, William. 1981a. Factor costs and the diffusion of ring spinning in Britain prior to World War I, *Quarterly Journal of Economics* 96:89–109.

Lazonick, William. 1981b. Production relations, labor productivity, and choice of technique: British and U.S. cotton spinning. *Journal of Economic History* 41:491–516.

Lazonick, William. 1983a Technological change and the control of work: The development of capital-labor relations in U.S. mass production industries. In Howard Gospel and Craig Littler (eds.), *Managerial Strategies and Industrial Relations*. London: Heinemann.

Lazonick, William. 1983b. Industrial organization and technological change: The decline of the British cotton industry. *Business History Review* 57:195–236.

Lazonick, William. 1984a. Rings and mules in Britain: Comment. *Quarterly Journal of Economics* 99:393–398.

Lazonick, William. 1984b. Work effort, pay, and productivity: Theoretical implications of some historical research. Photocopy, Harvard University (April).

Lazonick, William. 1986a. The cotton industry. In Bernard Elbaum and William Lazonick (eds.), *The Decline of the British Economy*. Oxford: Oxford University Press.

Lazonick, William. 1986b. Strategy, structure and management development in the

United States and Britain. In Kesaji Kobayashi (ed.), *The Development of Managerial Enterprises*. Tokyo: University of Tokyo Press.
Lazonick, William. 1986c. A conception of the capitalist economy. Photocopy, Harvard University (February).
Lazonick, William, and Thomas Brush. 1985. The "Horndal Effect" in early U.S. manufacturing. *Explorations in Economic History* 22:53–96.
Lazonick, William, and William Mass. 1984. The performance of the British cotton industry, 1870–1913. *Research in Economic History* 9:1–44.
Levine, David. 1985. Industrialization and the proletarian family in England. *Past and Present* 107:168–203.
MacKenzie, Donald. 1984. Marx and the machine. *Technology and Culture* 25:473–502.
MacPherson, C.B. 1962. *The Political Theory of Possessive Individualism: Hobbes to Locke*. Oxford: Clarendon Press.
Mandel, Ernest. 1968. *Marxist Economic Theory*. New York: Monthly Review Press.
Marglin, Stephen. 1974. What do bosses do? The origins and functions of hierarchy in capitalist production. *Review of Radical Political Economics* 6:33–60.
Marglin, Stephen. 1985. *Growth, Distribution, and Prices*. Cambridge: Harvard University Press.
Marx, Karl. 1935. *Value, Price, and Profit*. New York: International Press.
Marx, Karl. 1977. *Capital* Vol. I. New York: Vintage.
McCloskey, Donald, ed. 1971. *Essays on a Mature Economy: Britain after 1840*. London: Methuen.
McCloskey, Donald, and Lars Sandberg. 1971. From damnation to redemption: Judgments on the late Victorian entrepreneur. *Explorations in Economic History* 9:89–108.
Mingay, G.E. 1963. *English Landed Society in the Eighteenth-Century*. London: Routledge & Kegan Paul.
More, Charles. 1980. *Skill and the English Working Class, 1870–1914*. London: Croom Helm.
Pollard, Sidney. 1968. *The Genesis of Modern Management*. Harmondsworth: Penguin.
Prest, John. 1960. *The Industrial Revolution in Coventry*. London: Oxford University Press.
Ramsay, G.D. 1984. *The English Woolen Industry, 1500–1750*. London: Macmillan.
Robinson, Joan. 1980. *Further Contributions to Modern Economics*. Oxford: Basil Blackwell.
Rosenberg, Nathan. 1965. Adam Smith on the division of labour: Two views or one? *Economica* n.s. 32:127–139.
Rule, J.G. 1981. *The Experience of Labour in Eighteenth-Century English Industry*. New York: St. Martin's.

Samuel, Raphael. 1977. Workshop of the world: Steam power and hand technology in mid-Victorian Britain. *History Workshop Journal* 3:6–72.

Samuelson, Paul. 1962. Economists and the history of ideas. *American Economic Review* 52:1–18.

Sandberg, Lars. 1974. *Lancashire in Decline*. Columbus: Ohio University Press.

Saville, John. 1969. Primitive accumulation and early industrialisation in Britain. In Ralph Miliband and John Saville (eds.), *Socialist Register 1969*. London: Merlin.

Schmiechen, James A. 1984. *Sweated Industries and Sweated Labor*. Urbana: University of Illinois Press.

Schumpeter, Joseph. 1949. Science and ideology. *American Economic Review* 39:345–359.

Sherwood, John. 1985. Engels, Marx, Malthus, and the Machine. *American Historical Review* 90:837–865.

Smith, Adam. 1937. *An Inquiry into the Nature and Causes of the Wealth of Nations*. New York: Modern Library.

Sweezy, Paul. 1968. *The Theory of Capialist Development*. New York: Monthly Review Press.

Thomas, Joan. 1955. A history of the Leeds clothing industry. *Yorkshire Bulletin of Economic and Social Research*. Occasional Paper No. 1 (January).

Thompson, E.P. 1963. *The Making of the English Working Class*. New York: Vintage.

Thompson, E.P. 1967. Time, work-discipline, and industrial capitalism. *Past and Present* 28:56–97.

Turner, Michael. 1984. *Enclosures in Britain, 1750–1830*. London: Macmillan.

Ure, Andrew. 1935. *The Philosophy of Manufactures*. London: Knight.

Wood, Stephen, ed. 1982. *The Degradation of Work?: Skill, Deskilling and the Labour Process*. London: Hutchinson.

7 LABOR HISTORY AND LABOR ECONOMICS

Gavin Wright

What would a modern economist want to learn from American labor history? Economists interested in long-term growth and development might want to begin with the material conditions of the laboring classes, the growth of worker real incomes and living standards in relation to general economic progress. This sort of interest would not stop at the consumption of goods as conventionally defined, but would include other components of economic welfare, such as long-term trends in conditions of work: hours, safety, job security, workpace, and perhaps more elusive aspects of "job quality." For the analytically minded economist of today, however, learning these bare facts would only be the beginning. The modern economist would then want to know something about what kind of market or nonmarket mechanisms generated these results. Have worker preferences changed, for example, regarding the trade-offs among money income, job security, shorter hours, and better working conditions? How has the labor market priced these job attributes at different historical periods? If some improvements in the conditions of workingmen's lives have been purchased only at an economic cost, what was this cost, and what were the implications for national economic progress?

Today's macroeconomist, concerned about wage stickiness and the persistence of unemployment, might have a different set of questions. He or she might want to learn about the development of the labor market itself: How have employers and workers made contact with each other? What forms of labor contracts prevailed at different times? Were workers paid by time, by piece, or in some other way? Did the typical worker have one employer for a lifetime, or many? Such an economist would be especially interested in the effects of labor unions on all of these dimensions, on wages, on the mix between wage and nonwage goals, on turnover and wage structure, as well as on productivity and the choice of technique in production. Labor economists concerned about the economic welfare of women and members of minority groups would also want to know how the labor market has processed the productive potential of women and minority workers at different phases of history, and how the market's performance has been affected by unions and other forms of collective choice. To be sure, not every modern economist has the awareness to know that he or she ought to be well-informed about these historical aspects of labor economics. But if the world were as it should be, the disciplines of economic history and labor history would at least serve as inveterate reminders of the importance of history for contemporary labor issues.

Alas, an eager and historically curious modern economist might read many pages of labor history and labor economics, and find few if any of these questions answered. The sad state of affairs that has prevailed for the past quarter-century is that labor history and labor economics have almost nothing to do with each other. *Labor Economics* has become a thoroughly unhistorical branch of applied microeconomics; recent textbooks and journals cover virtually no historical topics, not even the traditional histories of labor union development.[1] Over roughly the same period, *Labor History* has enjoyed a great revival and growth as a field of study, but with overwhelming concentration on social and political themes. A recent survey notes that "there is a paucity of economic analysis in recent writings on labor history" (Montgomery 1980, p. 493), and in many cases "active hostility to" might be substituted for the word "paucity." Not only do labor historians and labor economists take almost no notice of each other's work, but even the more specialized subfield of *Industrial Relations* (descended from the older historical/institutional school of labor economics) today has little connection to labor history. Two recent books summarizing recent research on "labor in the twentieth-century" in the two disciplines—historian James R. Green's *The World of the Worker* (1980) and John Dunlop and Walter Galenson's *Labor in the Twentieth-Century* (1978)—have been aptly called the "scholarly equivalent of ships passing in the night" (Zieger 1983, p. 59).

The field of *Economic History*, which might have been expected to serve as the liaison between these schools, has until recently paid little attention to labor history. The "new economic history" has fixed its attention on economic growth. technology, railroads, banking, business cycles, slavery, agriculture, and demography; but it has largely neglected labor history. All of these subjects do, of course, relate to labor in one way or another, but because labor history has not been the central focus, historical economists have tended to treat labor and labor markets in highly abstract and simplified ways. An example would be the analysis of "labor scarcity" in the literature concerned with American technological development. And, of the small amount of new economic history that does take up labor topics, much or perhaps most has followed the "applied micro" tack of contemporary economics quite closely, and hence has not helped bridge the gap between schools.

This essay begins by considering the reasons for this sad condition, but it does not dwell on the negative. The segregation of approaches to labor issues is itself historical in its origins, but most of the original reasons for incompatability are no longer of great relevance. Later sections go on to argue that labor history would benefit from an infusion of economics; but equally, history is essential to a satisfactory understanding of many phenomena in contemporary labor economics. Indeed, the payoffs to cross-fertilization at the margin are sufficiently high that things are beginning to change. The case for a new hybrid is best argued by illustration,a task pursued here by pointing to the early results of recent studies of labor topics by economic historians.

Approaches to Labor

At one time labor history and labor economics were not separate but unified, in the "institutional" or Wisconsin school associated with the name of John R. Commons. Indeed, what current labor history and labor economics have in common is that they both developed in reaction to the dominance of these institutionalists. Labor history reacted against the conservative political stance of the Wisconsin school and the labor organizatons for which labor economists seemed to be the academic spokesmen: that is, against the comfortable assertion that American workers have always shared middle-class material goals, the emphasis on union history and labor leaders rather than ordinary workers, the neglect of women and minorities. Restoring these imbalances has been the central focus of the "new labor history," led by such figures as David Brody, David Montgomery, and the late Herbert Gutman.[2] Modern labor economics, by contrast, emerged as a reaction to the isolation of the labor field from mainstream trends in economics generally. A transitional generation in the 1940s and 1950s adopted an eclectic synthesis of institutionalism and economic analysis, the best-known names being Clark Kerr, John Dunlop, Melvin Reder, Albert Rees, Lloyd Ulman, and Lloyd Reynolds. But with the publication of H. Gregg Lewis's *Unionism and Relative Wages* in 1963 and the rise of the theory of human capital at the University of Chicago (developed by Theodore Schultz and Gary Becker, and operationalized by Jacob Mincer), an exclusively market-based neoclassical approach came to dominate the field in the 1960s and 1970s. In this work, institutions are treated implicitly, or regarded as mere endogenous vehicles for the operation of market forces. Robert Hall has written that "the central argument of good economics in general and the theory of human capital in particular [is] that economic forces determine institutions and not the other way around" (quoted in Osterman 1984, p. 5), which is a succinct statement of the currently prevailing view. To some extent therefore the ascendance of neoclassical labor economics was part of a broader development, the absorption of applied fields like labor and industrial organization (and economic history, for that matter) into a unified methodological approach.

Much of the separateness of labor history and labor economics may be simply explained by the fact that the two groups are interested in different things. Whereas the early historical labor economists were intensely interested in economic justice, today's labor historians are not mainly concerned with material standards or economic performance. Labor historians are interested in "social relations," in consciousness, in cultural values, and political organization. They want to know why there is "no socialism in America." Why were American construction workers bashing the heads of war protesters in 1970, while European workers were on the streets in protest?[3] For all its imperialistic tendencies, economics does not really have much that is distinctive or compelling to say about subjects like this. Labor economists, on the other hand, are interested in the effects of policies and behavior on *economic* performance: wages, unemployment, productivity, etc. They are specialists. Many labor economists are careful to differentiate their field from industrial relations in terms of interests and subject matter rather than doctrine: broad issues of labor markets and resource allocation versus a narrower speciality in collective bargaining. Certainly the differences in underlying interests are real and substantial, and it would be folly to propose that these disciplines should be amalgamated into "one big union."

But everyone involved knows that this resolution is not the whole story. People choose subjects to study because they think those subjects are important. Labor historians would surely not devote such close attention to "workers' revolts" and the "struggle for control of the workplace," if they thought these movements had no potential effect on wages and working conditions. Indeed, a continuing theme in the very working-class cultures so cherished by labor historians is the *rejection* of marketplace values and principles, the "unregulated, unlimited operation of the vaunted 'law of supply and demand'" (quoted in Jackson 1984, p. 114). The sentiments were well expressed in the foreword to a 1893 book entitled *The Economy of High Wages:*[4]

> No sophistry is more demonstrable than that contained in the phrase "the labor market," a phrase which grates upon the ear and offends the moral sense—for it seems to classify men with machinery, and fails to take into account human impulses and feeling, the heart and brain in their effect upon the energy and excellence of human industry.

We can see in statements like this a conceptual blur which is often found in labor history, an imprecise distinction between normative and positive statements. Does this writer mean to say merely that the wages of labor *ought* not to be determined in a labor market, or does he also mean to say that in fact they *are* not so determined? Often the latter is implied as well as the former. Or, the implied position may be that wages are in fact market-determined but need not be. In this case, the writer gives a clue by stressing that "low wages do not mean cheap production." If so, the economist wants to know, then why do employers pay low wages (as workers and much of labor history implies they did)? Can wages be raised without limit? Or if there is a limit, how do we know historically when we have reached it? Thus, with only a little probing, we find that there really are underlying differences of opinion about the nature of historical reality. There is plenty of room for debate. The trouble is, the debate never happens, because historians do not often confront the economic issues directly, and economists do not pay much attention to labor history.

The above comments are not meant to imply that there is no dissent within these fields. On the economic side, in addition to the division between labor economics and industrial relations, an active minority has pursued in recent years a blend of institutionalism and radicalism centered on the concept of "segmented labor markets" (Doeringer and Piore 1971; Rumberger and Carnoy 1980; Reich 1984). There have been some notable historical studies based on this perspective, whose central theme (drastically simplified) has been that work assignments, job structures, and even technologies have evolved as ever-more-sophisticated managerial devices for the purpose of securing individually compliant and collectively ineffective workers (Stone 1974; Marglin 1974; Edwards 1979; Gordon,

Edwards, Reich 1982). Though these are important books that should be taken seriously, they unfortunately do not bridge the disciplinary gap now under discussion. They don't try to. The authors are so estranged from the neoclassical mainstream that they (like the historians) tend to reject labor-market analysis out of hand, emphasizing only one direction of causation, from managerial strategy to worker control. At the same time, their work is sufficiently sweeping and abstract that professional historians often do not find it impressive (Schatz 1984). Part of the problem, though, is that there is not a large body of relevant historical research for them to draw upon. Most of the rest of the dissenting literature in labor economics has little historical content. A recent collection of "Modern Views" of the field (most of them critical) contains not a single historical study (Darity 1984).

But the problem is deeper than the simple fact that neither mainstream economists nor their critics devote much serious study to the historical past. The adversarial relationships among these schools diminish the entire quality of debate, inducing both camps to concentrate on defending the ability of their "paradigm" to "account for" various phenomena and bodies of evidence. Even radicals and institutionalists seem willing to don pseudo-scientific hats and perform "empirical tests of the segmented labor market hypothesis," while neoclassical/human capital theorists respond that these "challenges to orthodoxy" have yet to generate unambiguous "refutable hypotheses" (Cain 1976; Reich 1984; Hoffman 1984). In introducing his recent collection, William Darity notes that "institutions" have now become "only a temporary puzzle" to neoclassical theorists, citing Walter Oi's well-known article on "Labor as a Quasi-Fixed Factor" (Oi 1962). Oi was able to rationalize many labor policies that appear to be institutional (occupational differences in employment stability, discriminatory hiring and firing) on the grounds that each firm's labor force is relatively fixed in the short run. Darity comments that institutionalists will always be "confronted with this vulnerability" (p. 6). But why should this be considered a "vulnerability" rather than a helpful insight into the reasons behind certain institutionalized practices? Often the contending schools are merely offering alternative vocabularies to describe essentially the same behavior. But treating the subject as a contest of "paradigms" tends to submerge the real issues, which are how and why the labor force became "quasi-fixed," and what it would take to change these "institutionalized" practices once they are in place. These questions are intrinsically historical.

Where in this spectrum of contending schools is there room for the common-sense view that economic institutions arise in response to the pressures and conditions of a particular era, some of which may be eternal but many of which are fleeting? Once in place, institutions change relatively slowly and incrementally as new pressures develop. An institution which evolves from decades of incremental change may be far from ideal. But in the meantime many kinds of behavior, by employers and workers, will have adapted to the institution rather than vice versa: workers adapt their skills, their effort level, their leisure-time activities to the job definitions and promotion system; employers adapt hiring standards, supervision, and technological strategies to the same systems. The adaptations may approximate a kind of equilibrium which, at any point in time, may be rationalized any way you want. But at that point in time, no "empirical test" of the "institutional hypothesis" will tell us anything useful. Unless you know the beginnings of the institution and have traced through adaptations on both sides, you will not understand the equilibrium you have observed. Thus, the proper alternative to neoclassical labor orthodoxy is not "institutional economics" but economic history.

In my view this perspective is more reasonable on its face than any of the other contending positions. But issues like this may be debated in the abstract indefinitely, without noticeable effect. Rather than continue an abstract or theoretical argument, the rest of the essay proceeds by taking up concrete cases, advancing two propositions: labor economics needs labor history, and labor history would benefit from more economics. Reflecting limits of space, time, and author's knowledge, the examples are taken exclusively from American history, but the underlying methodological argument is intended to be more or less general.

Labor Economics Needs Labor (Economic) History

The assertion that economic history has neglected labor is only true for industrial wage earners, the group that has traditionally been at the center of attention for labor historians. Slavery is of course a form of labor organization that has by no means been neglected by economic history; and, going back still further, indentured servitude is a labor contract form that has been extensively analyzed by David Galenson (1981, 1984) and other historical economists. Postslavery labor systems in the South, especially sharecropping and other varieties of tenancy, have also been closely studied (Alston and Higgs 1982; Ransom and Sutch 1977; Shlomowitz 1979, 1984), and in some ways this agricultural example offers a better historical laboratory for labor-market study than do the industrial cases. The aftermath of the violent abolition of slavery gives us a dramatic picture of a world with no established labor markets or labor institutions:

no guideposts, no understandings, no recognized terms or categories, no standard contract forms, no clear enforcement machinery. As one might expect, the situation was chaotic. All parties were free to subscribe to any mutually agreeable arrangements they may have wanted (and a host of experimental forms appeared), labor was mobile, and employers were numerous enough to approximate competitive demand conditions. Yet there were violent disputes, innumerable claims of cheating and bad faith on both sides, and production was negligible. Harold Woodman quotes a partial list of disputed issues compiled in 1866 by an official of the Freedmen's Bureau, which is worth reproducing:

> are the freedpeople to work Saturdays or not,—the *date* of the termination of the contract,—whether at a specified time, or when the crops are gathered;—whether those under contract for a portion of the crop shall be required to do other work on the plantation;—and when part of the crop is the consideration, whether or not it is to be *fed* out of prior to gathering and dividing the same, if so some provision to be made for the settlement of the same at the division;—whether the fences are to be kept in repair or not, and if so, *what* fences and the probable number of new rails required;—whether medical attendence [sic] is to be furnished or not, and if so *what* kind;—is a physician to be employed, or only such attendence [sic] and medicines as were commonly kept and given by the planter upon his premises previous to emancipation;—whether an overseer is to be employed, and by whom he is selected;—when the freedpeople are working for a portion of the crop, or rent land, and the owner of the land furnishes all stock and tools, if animals die or tools are broken, who bears the loss;—the kind and quantity of rations, quarters, or clothing when furnished;—the number of hours that constitute a days [sic] labor, in Summer and in Winter;—whether the women and children are to work or not, if not, at whose expense they are to be fed and clothed; how wages are to be paid, monthly or otherwise, and the amount retained, if any, and *when* the retained wages are to be paid; when working for a portion of the crops, what such portion is, whether the crop in kind or proceeds, by whom to be divided, when and how;—who is to furnish rope and bagging; who is to do the ginning, and when time is lost through sickness or by other causes, avoidable or unavoidable, who is to bear the loss, the planter or the freedpeople. (quoted in Woodman 1984, p. 535)

The list serves as a reminder of how much we tend to take for granted in labor markets, how much is determined not directly by bargain but by precedent and rule-of-thumb. Labor economists will immediately point out that most of these items are arbitrary, they could go one way or the other and net wages can adjust accordingly. But the postslavery chaos reminds us how enormously costly and inefficient it would be if employers and workers actually had to negotiate every detail of every work situation every time. A well-developed labor market is itself an institution, which emerges over the course of time and helps to regularize communications and contracts between parties. By their very nature, labor markets are subject to "increasing returns," which is to say that they function more efficiently when terms and categories are standardized into a few recognizable packages. There is no one "labor-market system"; labor markets can evolve in many different directions, but not in all directions at once.

Economist Thomas Sowell attributes much of the slow economic progress of American blacks after emancipation to the weakness of black cultural heritage. As he puts it, blacks in both Brazil and the United States "showed remarkably similar historical patterns of resistance to the *inherent requirements and constraints of labor markets*. . . including a reluctance to accept responsibility and self-discipline, and preoccupation with status aspects of work" (Sowell 1983, p. 141, emphasis added). But what *is* a labor market, and what are its "inherent requirements and constraints"? Sowell uses expressions like "the power of the market" and the "systemic logic of the market" quite freely, but when we search his pages to find out what this powerful entity might actually be, we find the following:

> A market is not a specific set of institutions but simply the freedom to choose among existing institutions, or to create new institutions, contracts, or relationships to meet one's economic purposes. (Sowell 1983, p. 165)

This is a clear statement of a viewpoint held implicitly by most modern labor economists: the "labor market" does not mean any particular thing, it is just a catch-all term for any and all transactions between employers and workers. In that case, however, how can we speak with any authority about "inherent requirements and constraints"? An alternative view is that real-world labor markets are mechanisms for processing large quantities of information about people and jobs; well-functioning markets tend over time to select a small number of standard contract forms from an infinite array of possibilities. The contract forms may certainly change, and if they are grossly out of line with the desires of employers or workers, *something* will change. But it is just as plausible that both parties will find it easier to adapt their behavior to the prevailing market structures than the other way around. This logic is well illustrated by the postbellum Southern case.

In fact, historical research on Southern labor markets suggests that Sowell's diagnosis is quite wrong. Despite a long historical tradition denying the existence of labor markets in the postbellum South, the evidence from firm and plantation records and the federal census indicates that black labor was highly mobile, and wage surveys show that the market for unskilled labor (which was closely linked to local markets for sharecroppers) functioned effectively to equalize black and white wages (Higgs 1977, 1978a; Wright 1985). Indeed, in that market blacks were often favored by employers, who complained that *white* laborers were "preoccupied with status aspects of work." The problem for blacks was not maneuvering *within* the labor market, it was overcoming the barriers to getting *out* of the labor market, such as the capital requirements for moving up the farm ladder, or the racial restrictions on skilled or supervisory jobs in industry. There was a labor market, but the way in which it evolved was not necessarily neutral. Sharecropping clearly emerged in the postwar years from a process of labor market competition among alternative arrangements. But once this particular form had crystallized as the standard (for married men without capital), variations in supply and demand were typically accommodated by (for example) adjusting the size of the plots rather than changing the share or the contract form itself. The institution of plantation sharecropping subsequently influenced the technological evolution of Southern agriculture over three-quarters of a century (Whatley 1985).

One of the formulations often used by economists to deny the lasting influence of history is to argue that times of dispute and institutional flux are merely periods of disequilibrium. Robert Higgs analyzes a later phase of Southern economic history in precisely this fashion (Higgs 1978b, pp. 111–116). Suppose we start in a state of equilibrium, he argues, in which the going wage rate "clears the market." Then, "suppose that something alters the situation, for example, that many workers migrate away from the area.... The outcome of [the] adjustment process is that *eventually* a new equilibrium will be established: fewer workers will be employed than before, and the new prevailing wage rate will be higher than before. The labor market will accommodate itself, so to speak, to the new reality of a smaller labor force." In a statement that is not necessarily representative but does express views economists usually hold implicitly, Higgs goes on to say:

> The adjustment to disequilibrium...comprises much of the behavior of prime concern to historians, sociologists, politicians, and ordinary people. The adjustment may include social protests, political struggles, personal and group conflicts, violence, suffering, heroism, cruelty, and all sorts of human difficulties, triumphs, and tragedies. The economist contents himself in the knowledge that the outcome of all this kicking and squealing is foreordained. But the actors in the human drama often learn slowly and struggle vigorously against the inevitable. (Higgs 1978b, p. 112)

Several things about this quotation are interesting. The first is that Higgs assumes implicitly that a labor market is a "local" market; this is a common usage often found in labor economics texts, which refer to migration as "moving from one labor market to another" (Fleisher and Knieser 1984,

p. 350). But many labor markets are not local at all. Today's markets for skilled professionals are national or even global. In the nineteenth-century, markets for *unskilled* workers functioned over long distances as well, which is to say that job information was conveyed through formal and informal channels, and streams of workers moved back and forth along regular paths, in response to changes in demand. Far from being compelled to pay a higher wage by "the reality of a smaller labor force," employers had the alternative of broadening the geographic scope of their labor market by expanding recruitment efforts (at a cost, to be sure). Change in the scope of labor markets has been a central phenomenon in American history, but it is not one to which labor economics has given explicit attention. Perhaps the reason is that the topic is fundamentally historical. A clear example is the continuing separateness of northern and southern unskilled labor markets well into the twentieth-century, despite high rates of labor mobility in response to market incentives within each region (Wright 1986).

A second assumption in the quotation is that only a change in the wage rate can restore equilibrium; all other changes are ephemeral. But this assumption has no theoretical or empirical foundation. Employers often find nonwage adjustments to be easier and more effective, and the possibilities are endless: they may change the workload, as the Waltham mills did after the coming of the Irish (Lazonick and Brush 1985); they may change the length of the standard workday, as employers did during World War I; they may change their hiring standards, or the criteria by which workers are promoted to more advanced jobs, as the Ford Motor Company did at the time of the Five Dollar Day (Meyer 1981); they may institute night shifts (Shiells and Wright 1983); they may offer binding promises of job security, such as seniority systems, as numerous employers did well before unionization (Slichter 1929, Schatz 1983); and so on. For some purposes it may be harmless to compress all these adjustments into a "wage-change-equivalent," but in general such a procedure is not legitimate—different packages will attract different workers, and will have different implications for costs and productivity. In the present context, the important point is that different packages will have different degrees of reversibility; hence the choice made at one point in time will continue to affect the choices made in the future. It follows that to really understand the labor arrangements of today, you have to know their history.

Capital, Skill, Technology, and Jobs

Which kinds of labor-market adjustments are easiest, and which are reversible, will depend on particular historical circumstances. But it is important to be precise about whose perspective and time horizon are under examination, distinctions emphasized in most economic analysis: an individual firm may be able to adjust work loads and hiring standards readily, but it is not likely to be in a position single-handedly to invent a whole new technology in response to labor-market pressures, and even the implementation of previously existing technologies may be difficult and time consuming, especially if major capital investments are involved. Just the same, at a higher level of aggregation and over a longer time period, technological change has to be counted as a form of labor-market adjustment. Technological *search* is an economic activity, in that it absorbs resources and requires choice. If enough firms are pursuing similar search strategies with a similar labor-market character, the aggregate effect over time may constitute a collective labor-market adjustment. If there is a specialized "technology industry," like the machine-tools industry which developed early in the course of American industrialization, its research strategies will be influenced by the labor-market positions of its prospective customers, which is to say the "typical" firms in the economy as a whole. Induced-technological changes like this are intrinsically historical: they are cumulative, within limits they are self-reinforcing because of increasing-returns effects, and they are largely irreversible because that is the nature of "learning."[5]

Modern labor economists do not approach the subject in this spirit at all, but abide by the age-old assumption that technology and its factor demands are exogenous to the economy. The modern approach is much more sophisticated than the old concept of "skill requirements"; but the deeper underlying notion that relative demands for something called "skill" or "human capital" are *technologically determined* is more firmly entrenched than ever. An example is the hypothesis of Capital-Skill-Complementarity, which dates from a seminal article of that title by Griliches (1969). Since that time, literally dozens of econometric studies have confirmed the finding that capital and skilled labor are complements in production, whereas capital and unskilled labor are substitutes; a rare case of consensus in applied econometrics (Hamermesh and Grant 1979). To a modern economist, as perhaps to most modern people, it seems inherently plausible that more physical capital embodying more advanced technologies should require more technicians, machinists, engineers, and scientists, and little or no raw labor. And even some historical economists, notably Jeffrey Williamson and Peter Lindert (1980), have applied assumptions of this nature to interpretations of long-term trends in the premium for skill in the labor market.

The prevailing views among labor historians could not be more different. A favorite buzzword in that camp is "deskilling," the term coined by Harry Braverman (1974) to describe a deep underlying capitalist tendency to *reduce* skill requirements in production, as a way of lowering costs and increasing management control. If there were any correlation between capital and skill in the nineteenth-century, according to these historicans, it would be inverse: the use of capital in conjunction with *unskilled* labor to replace skilled artisans and craftsmen. Is this an example of conspiratorial mythology, which objective statistical evidence has now refuted? True, much of the historical literature does not have the econometric rigor of contemporary labor economics, but many kinds of stuides indicate that the nineteenth-century pattern was indeed different. A detailed review of the early industrial history of Massachusetts finds no positive association between industrialization and skill intensity (Field 1980). Skill-saving was one of the hallmarks of the "American system" of technology analyzed by Nathan Rosenberg (1969, 1976), and the most recent econometric study of these sectors tentatively concludes: "Skilled labor appears to have been a better substitute for capital than unskilled labor was" (James and Skinner 1985, pp. 523–524). Numerous case studies of technological change describe efforts to develop "user friendly" machinery which could be operated by inexperienced, untrained workers (Erickson 1957). Ring spinning technology, an American innovation, had precisely this property as contrasted with mule spinning, the English technique (Saxonhouse and Wright 1984). To be sure, "technological progress" is by no means equivalent to "capital accumulation." But many observers in the nineteenth-century perceived a self-evident complementarity between capital and *unskilled* labor, which the American example vividly illustrated (Harley 1974). Certainly the two capital-intensive industries at the core of American industrial development, railroads and steel, were voracious demanders of unskilled labor. A study of American manufacturing exports before 1914 finds that they did tend to be capital intensive, but not skill intensive (Eysenbach 1970).

My object here is surely not to argue that the modern econometric studies are simply mistaken, still less to advance a new overarching interpretation of the historical connections among capital, technology, and skill, but to point out some lessons for the study of economics and history. The first lesson is the need for historical perspective on structural or technological relationships in the economy "Capital-skill-complementarity" is not a universal technologically detemined "fact." The recent findings reflect the American labor-market context of the last half-century or so, during which there has been continuing upward pressure on unskilled wages (from both market and nonmarket sources) and on the wages of production workers relative to nonproduction workers, while the educational levels of the labor force generally have been rising. Before 1914, however, the additions to the industrial labor force were overwhelmingly young unskilled immigrants with little education; and the jobs thrown up by the industrial system were adapted to this fact. As one labor historian describes the trends at the leading automobile manufacturer: "Ford engineers and toolmakers attempted to select, design and construct machine tools and attachments to *match the skill level of the labor force*"(Meyer 1981, p. 26, emphasis added).

In my view it is basically mistaken to think that "skill requirements" or "skill premia" are technologically determined: job attributes are among the more malleable components of an economic structure, at least on technological grounds. There is no reason why advanced technologies cannot be designed to utilize inexperienced, unskilled workers—systems (as has been said of McDonald's) "designed by geniuses to be run by idiots." Even within a common basic technology, like textiles in the nineteenth-century, comparative studies show great variation in the structure of job assignments and wages (Saxonhouse and Wright 1984).[6] One often hears that child labor disappeared for economic reasons, that the jobs were really destroyed by technology rather than legislation. Such a claim is an absurdity: modern technologies could make far better use of child workers today than any techniques available to nineteenth-century employers. In Southern textiles, the job of "doffer" (replacing spindles) was performed by adolescent boys in the 1890s, but by adult men in the 1930s; not because the "skill requirements" had increased, but because the labor force had "grown up," and job assignments had adjusted accordingly. Thus, the practice followed by Williamson and Lindert of measuring the "skill premium" over long periods of time by dividing the wage rate for a so-called "skilled" job by a laborer's wage, with no reference to who held these jobs or how the job content had changed, is dubious.

The deeper lesson is that the concept of "skill" is slippery and ambiguous, and really should be defined in historical context. There are skills and skills. They may be narrowly specific to a particular process, like puddling and capping and mule spinning, and hence vulnerable to obsolescence; or they may be general and flexible, what Theodore Schultz calls "learning how to learn." Skill levels may be institutionalized in particular job designations, or tests of competence, or markets; or they may be implicit, subjective, revealed only with uncertainty over an extended period. The theory of human capital is very flexible, and offers great insights into labor market phenomena, but the attempt to compress all of these dimensions into one metric obscures much of the interesting history of labor-market development in relationship to skills of various kinds. Very often some skill differentials are going up at the same time that others are going down (Shergold 1977; Elbaum 1984; Grosse 1982).

It is even more dangerous to use terms like "skill" and "human capital" as catch-all expressions for all aspects of labor quality. Studies of early industrialization persistently show that increased factory experience on the part of so-called "unskilled" workers is a significant component of historical productivity growth (Saxonhouse 1977; Wright 1981; Lazonick and Brush 1985); yet this may be a matter of psychological adaptation or socialization, a process that by its very nature cannot readily be anticipated or priced in the labor market. The very categories used to designate levels of skill may change belatedly, in recognition that the rank of certain attributes has risen while others have declined. For example, the category of "semiskilled worker" emerged in the twentieth-century as a way of distinguishing machine-tending jobs (which may require patience, alertness, dexterity) from traditional labor (which was more likely to require physical strength and endurance).

Some economists may say that problems like these are merely index-number problems, no different in principle from similar difficulties that plague long-term measures of the capital stock or economic growth. For many purposes one might want to gloss over all of these issues in the way that growth accountants generally do, if the purpose is to contrive an overall index of skill or human capital through history. But labor markets too are measuring rods for skills, and real-world labor markets are selective in their rewards to different dimensions of skill (or other human attributes). It follows that a country concerned about its educational system and the productivity of its citizens is a country that should know more about the history of its labor markets.

The contradiction in the position of modern labor economists is fundamental: they do not study labor history because they feel that the institutions and behavior of former times are so different and so remote from modern experience that they have no relevance for today's issues. Yet they try to make their models as institution-free as possible, so that they have no idea exactly what it is about their analysis that is, in fact, historically specific. Textbooks may acknowledge that their analysis applies only to "modern" labor markets (Hamermesh and Rees 1984, p. xii), but they do not say what it is that makes them "modern". If it is indeed true that labor markets in the past were so very different from those of today, what is to say that equally momentous structural changes will not occur in the future?[7] History has no magic crystal ball by which to forecast the future, but an economics without history amounts to a denial that our generation is also living in historical time, a reality which to future generations will seem obvious.

But Labor History Would Benefit from More Economics

Despite emphasis in the preceding pages on institutional aspects of labor markets and on the enduring influence of history, this section argues for an infusion of economic analysis into labor history. The analysis should be historically specific, which means the analyst needs a sense of historical context. But it is economic analysis just the same. My central proposition is this: much of the struggle and conflict in American labor history has not been a direct tug-of-war between capital and labor over division of the surplus; the conflict has instead been over the scope and operation of labor markets. To understand the issues and their effects, therefore, we have to analyze the markets as markets.

We might begin with the elemental matter of wages, a subject given remarkably little attention by the new labor history. Sympathetic as most of them are to the struggles of labor, labor historians tend to give brief and grudging acknowledgement at best to the fact that for the most part American workers have been well paid, and real wages have indisputably risen over the long haul. The basic real-wage estimates constructed by Long (1960) and Rees (1961) show only brief periods of decline for manufacturing workers since 1865, and a secular increase in excess of 1 percent per year. Before 1860 the trends are less clear, but here too the longer series show an increase in real wages over the first half of the century as well (Adams 1982; David and Solar 1977). For a country with such an optimistic labor history, one might suppose that the relative absence of militant labor organization hardly needs explanation.

A closer look at the evidence, however, suggests some of the reasons why American workers and their historians have taken such a dim view of the labor market as a form of social organization. The first interesting feature of the trend is that prior to World War I, very little of the increase came through a rise in nominal wages. In the nineteenth-century, the only periods of marked increase in nominal wages were periods of general inflation (1812–1815, 1830–1837, 1860–1865), all of which were periods of stability or decline in real wages. The bulk of the increase came from the denominator, the cost of living. It would be a mistake to jump to the conclusion that the entire increase is institutional in character, the artifact of sticky wages and declining costs of living—"money illusion" over a century is not very plausible. But it is still noteworthy that nineteenth-century labor markets basically were not called upon to perform the function of passing the fruits of progress on to workers as a group. Much of the increase in real wages derives from declines in transportation and distribution costs, which allowed the terms of trade for all sectors to improve simultaneously. When the background price-level conditions changed after 1900, the labor market did not move smoothly into a pattern of regular wage increases, but went through turbulence, conflict, and bouts of high turnover as the vehicle for extracting wage increases.

A second observation about the real-wage trends is that these are *average* wages for the *average* worker for the entire country; they don't correspond to any particular group or cohort of workers, they are not standardized for changes in worker attributes (age, sex, experience, education), and they are not keyed to terms of actual transactions. Hence these series lack clear analytical interpretation; they are not exactly measures of economic welfare, but they are not indicators of the "price of labor" either. It would indeed be difficult to develop a long-term aggregate wage index that did correspond to the terms of the labor market, because these terms did not stay fixed. The "hourly wage," for example, is a modern concept; the large cotton mills of Massachusetts only began to quote and compute wages by the hour in the 1870s,in direct response to legislation limiting the length of the work day (Shiells 1985). Most nineteenth-century wages were daily wage rates, despite the fact that the length of the work day varied seasonally. Indeed, given the widely shared view that America was the land of high wages and labor scarcity, it is striking that the standard length of the American work day was longer than in the dark, satanic mills of England. Some labor economists have begun to construct elaborate "hedonic real-wage" indexes which give utility weights to various components of labor's welfare (Pencavel 1979), and these could in principle be applied historically (cf. David and Solar 1977). But the potential contributions of economics to labor history probably do not lie in refinements of the concepts and measurement of human welfare so much as in analysis of the labor market as a market.

What we do know is that the labor markets for early industrialization were regional or local, and that New England was the low-wage region of the country. In contrast to the usual pattern in modern times, where migration pours into an industrializing area, American industry first flourished in a region characterized by outmigration for decades. The technologically advanced Lowell-Waltham mills recruited young girls from the declining farms of northern New England; at the same time, unmechanized labor-intensive industries like boots and shoes and palm-leaf-hats also grew up, using putting-out systems and characterized by wide variance in labor earnings from one community to another (Lebergott 1964, p. 132; Field 1978). Even before the coming of the Irish in the late 1840s and 1850s, these localized labor transactions were marked by disputes over the practice of employing outworkers in the countryside as a way of restraining wages in the towns (Faler 1981, pp. 174–176). This was one of the key issues in the great Lynn strike of 1860. Here we have an early example of a struggle over the geographic scope of labor market, where workers thought there was an implicit understanding that theirs was a bargain between local employers and local employees, but over time the pool of competing workers was broadened. At every point in time they may have received the "going wage" in a "competitive labor market," but the boundaries of that market kept changing.

Though real wages in the region probably did rise across the first half of the century, from the mid- 1840s onward there is abundant evidence that conditions of labor in New England (in contrast to the rest of the country) deteriorated. The visible decline in average real wages understates the matter: work loads increased, hours were lengthened, the experience-earnings profile flattened, and most of the highly touted trappings of Waltham paternalism were scrapped (Dublin 1979; Lazonick and Brush 1985; Faler 1981, pp. 77, 99). It seems far more plausible to consider this trend as a labor-market phenomenon, the effects of a massive inflow of cheap Irish labor, than to invoke such demons as "intensified competition," "moral decline," or a compulsive urge to "degrade the worker" on the part of millowners. In many seaboard cities, immigrants virtually *became* the working class. But what historians do not always appreciate is that even where immigrant workers were not directly employed (as at Lynn), labor-market links served to establish the "immigrant wage" as the going wage for unskilled labor. It is not surprising that where native-born workers toiled in these markets, they were seen to be degraded and poorly paid. Unless, that is, they were able to claim a recognized skill and compete in a narrower market which recognized and rewarded that skill.

Now to say that these developments were labor-market phenomena is not to say that they were natural, inevitable, or beyond debate and evaluation. The scope and terms of labor markets are influenced by a host of public policies, from national immigration and transportation systems to local public schools and social services to state laws governing labor contracts. If citizenship means anything at all, the terms by which new persons are admitted into a jurisdiction must be governed by some kind of public policy. This is not merely hypothetical: the antebellum South remained largely untouched by foreign workers, even during periods of strong demand and rising labor costs, because the dominant political interests were hostile to immigration (Wright 1979, pp. 676–679). The point is, however, that once effective labor-market channels are established in an area, it is likely to be extremely difficult for one employer to deviate from the market, just as it is difficult for groups of workers to withstand the market's pressures. Though the story may still be told as a series of local struggles, the determinants of the outcomes should be analyzed at a level of aggregation commensurate with the scope of the relevant labor market. Labor historians do not always seem to realize this.

From 1865 onward it is clear that the real wages of unskilled as well as skilled labor were steadily rising, in all parts of the country outside of the South. Yet the issues laid out in the earlier New England history continued to be the essence of the labor struggle for the country—defining the proper geographic scope of a labor market, recognizing and rewarding particular skills. Increasingly the Amercian manufacturing labor force came to be dominated by immigrants. Chicago, for example, had a unique pattern of industrialization in the midst of relative scarcity of unskilled labor down to the 1870s; after that time, regular flows of immigrant labor began to reach the city, and their wage came to define the base wage for unskilled workers (David 1986). The methodological criticism expressed in the previous section should not be taken as a dissent against Williamson and Lindert's general characterization of the late nineteenth-century as an era of relatively cheap unskilled labor and high skill premia (Williamson and Lindert 1980; Shergold 1982). This pattern is interpreted here as an indication that the market for unskilled labor was not an American market at all, but an Atlantic market. Comparisons of absolute wage levels between countries are difficult or impossible, but the evidence is that unskilled labor markets were linked across the ocean, among the industrializing countries of the world. Americans do not sufficiently appreciate that the growth of real wages in this country over the period 1870–1913 was not significantly greater than that in such countries as Germany, Sweden, England, and France (Brown and Browne 1968), and this tendency to equivalence might be even clearer if the real wage indexes were designed to isolate unskilled labor. Immigrants taking industrial jobs were mobile, hard-working, interested in pecuniary goals, often planning a return to their mother country after accumulating savings (Piore 1979). As flows of information, finance, and people came to move regularly on well-established channels in both directions, it is not overstating the case to say that a trans-Atlantic market in unskilled labor existed and defined the basic American wage.

The markets for skilled labor were quite different. These were more local, but continually threatened by geographic extension on the one hand

and by technological displacement on the other. Given the pervasive dualism in the labor market, it is not surprising that older, skilled workers lived under the threat of deskilling technologies, of finding that the mule-spinning machines had been destroyed over the weekend and replaced by rings (as one oft-repeated anecdote goes), or that a machine-tools producer had invented "Cox's capper," which at one stroke destroyed the value of precious craft secrets and skills (Brown and Philips 1985). But if the proper interpretation of this trend is that it was an effort to "adapt the technology to the available labor force," then we should not expect to find that previously skilled, experienced workers were in fact reduced to destitution, unemployment, or the status of unskilled laborers. If experience and maturity have productive value (as they undoubtedly do), only a perverse labor market would offer no decent employment to such people. Here is a challenge to labor and social historians: how many real live individual cases can you document, of individuals displaced and drastically demoted by new technology? Many authors write as though this were the standard experience, but they rarely produce a concrete case. (An independent arbitrator will have to determine whether "unemployed cigar makers" who become labor leaders may be counted.) Though the number of hardship cases is undoubtedly greater than zero, on the whole it seems more likely, as Andrew Dawson (1979) argues, that skilled native-born workers were able to maintain their labor market niche successfully. A lively debate among economic historians has arrived at the conclusion that pre-World War I labor markets did offer a premium to the native born, even after adjusting for objective criteria such as age, sex, and education (Higgs 1971; Hill 1975; McGouldrick and Tannen 1977; Blau 1980; Hannon 1982a,b).

But *where* could these skilled workers ply their trades, under whose direction, and at what pace? These were the sorts of issues raised by labor organizations during this era. Again the geographical dimension was paramount. In a classic of the old labor history which has been somewhat neglected by the new, Lloyd Ulman showed in *The Rise of the National Trade Union* (1955) that national federations of local craft unions emerged precisely to deal with the problems posed by the "traveling member." On the one hand, management continued to attempt to bring in "outside" people to break strikes or undermine local wages. On the other, a local union could hardly ask a skilled craftsman to respect its jurisdiction, unless he were given some assurance that his skill level (or "priority") would be acknowledged and credited in other cities. Working out an orderly mechanism for intercity movement, equalizing city wage levels (but at union scale), and stabilizing labor relations in particular crafts and communities—these were the central objectives of the skilled-craft unions, often achieved with considerable success. Being locally based as they were, it is not surprising that these unions often had community support during labor disputes, as Gutman and others have emphasized. But in trades like printing and carpentry, most employers came to accept the unions with reasonable tolerance, since they stabilized labor supply and labor standards, and support for complete unionization in a community protected employers against "unfair" local competition (Jackson 1984). It is often said that the American labor force has always been highly mobile, but the evidence from social mobility studies (e.g., Thernstrom 1964, 1973) is that the high rates of *geographic* mobility were found among young, unskilled, propertyless workers, especially immigrants. Obtaining a skill or a home greatly reduced the probability of moving. The concept of "property rights" in a job had real meaning for these workers, and was closely linked to developing a "stake in the community." One can imagine many other institutional arrangements that might have accomplished these objectives, but in fact they were achieved by craft unions if at all.

The dimension of geography in labor markets has been stressed here, in part as a way of pointing out that this issue had a meaning and saliency separable from the ethnic and racial hostility with which it was so often linked. It is chilling to go back to Commons' 1909 article and find him railing against the "competitive menace" of the "Chinaman" and the "foreign immigrant" as stridently as he does against "prison labor, child labor, and long hours of labor" (Commons 1909, pp. 76, 80). Labor historians have found many inspiring examples of interracial cooperation and egalitarianism in pre-World War I American labor history , but the darker chapters of racism, prejudice, and hostilities are part of the story too. Rather than giving exclusive attention to reconstructing the values, attitudes, and political belief systems of the working class, it would be useful to devote more consideration to the economic structures that tended to exacerbate or (alternatively) to ameliorate these animosities.

Internal Labor Markets, Collective Goods, and Industrial Unionism

Historians may think of economists as people who go around quoting the law of supply and demand all the time, but if they would look more closely, they would find proponents of a diverse set of labor-market models which might be helpful in interpreting certain chapters of labor history. One of the most directly relevant of these models is the proposition that a primary function of unions is to negotiate "public" or "collective" goods at the workplace; that is, attributes of work that by their very nature must be experienced jointly, such as the speed of the assembly line, cotton lint in the air, or the risk of catastrophic accidents (Freeman and Medoff 1984; Flanagan 1983; Duncan and Stafford 1980). These choices may of course be determined by the markets, but in that case they will effectively be determined by the preferences of the "marginal worker," the one just on the verge of coming or going. A collective choice mechanism will give more weight to the views of intramarginal workers (perhaps the median or average workers), who are not about to leave but may still have strong views about workplace public goods. The list of collective goods properly includes not just environmental issues but the general set of company labor "policies"—procedures for hiring, firing, and promoting; systems of monitoring and supervision; fringe benefits, etc. This perspective on unions is thus consistent with the labor historians' emphasis on workers' control and work intensity as opposed to wages.

A second new development in labor economics that is relevant for labor history (actually a new formulation of an old body of thought) is the concept of the "efficiency wage": the general proposition is that if productivity depends on the wage paid by the firm, a rational firm will pay a wage above the market rate, even though unemployed workers are available (Yellen 1984; Weiss 1980; Bowles 1985). Why should productivity depend on the wage? Mechanisms may include (a) costly turnover (usually related inversely to the wage); (b) effort (employees may work harder if the cost of losing their job is high); (c) selection (a better quality worker is attracted at a higher wage, and management can impose more demanding standards). In addition to rationalizing some apparent institutional rigidities in the labor market, these models raise the possibility of multiple equilibria: a given firm may find that *either* a low-wage-low-quality-high-turnover package or a high-wage-high-quality-low-turnover combination is internally consistent and at least locally optimal.

Economists have developed models like these in an effort to understand the operation of modern labor markets more realistically, but very little work has considered the origins and development of "efficiency-wage" policies and related structures. A marriage of theory and history would be far more powerful. The crucial period is roughly from 1910 to 1940, when American labor markets underwent marked structural change. An important new book by Sanford Jacoby entitled *Employing Bureaucracy* (1985) traces in detail the rise of centralized personnel departments and formalized labor relations policies in U.S. companies during this time. He also details numerous incentives to reduce turnover and raise productivity, such as the institution of job ladders and internal promotion plans (the so-called "internal labor market").[8] Economists can rationalize such policies in various ways. The obvious question, however, is why employers moved so sharply away from their former polices at this particular historical juncture? Economists are inclined to invoke the labor requirements of modern technology, while employers themselves were inclined to credit their own enlightenment (Gitelman 1984); business historians appeal to the imperatives of large corporate enterprises; and radical economists attribute these policies to antiunion divide-and-conquer strategies by management (Stone 1974; Edwards 1979). Jacoby stresses that the new policies came in two waves, during World War I and after 1933, and argues that they were a response to crisis—specifically, the threat of union recognition. Though this interpretation undoubtedly contains much truth, it can easily be overdone. Jacoby's own figures show that most of the new departments and policies were retained in the 1920s, though the period of crisis was safely past. And even if this fact is itself explained by an incipient though submerged threat of unionism in the 1920s, we still have to ask what it was about the American labor force after 1914 that made it so much more responsive to the appeal of unionism than it had been in earlier times.

A deeper underlying change was in the composition and priorities of the labor force itself. American workers in the 1920s were more mature, more experienced, more American, more educated, more stable geographically, and above all more thoroughly committed to industrial work as a career, than ever before (Jacoby 1983). Perhaps some of these changes were the result of the new labor policies, of course, but more fundamentally they were the result of the long slow accumulation of experience and the emergence of a substantial core of American-born or Americanized industrial workers, the U.S. version of the "making of the working class." By the 1920s and probably earlier, labor markets were no longer well matched to the labor force, neither to the kinds of jobs desired nor to making the best use of its productive potential. Superimposed on these gradual and quasi-demographic processes was the more dramatic experience of World War I, when a sudden cutoff of immigrant labor was followed by nearly seven years of tight labor-market conditions. The drastic overhaul of their labor policies that was forced on firms during these turbulent times pushed many of them from a low-wage equilibrium before into a high-wage equilibrium after; the adaptation was sufficiently complete that most of the changes were not reversed even after the end of the wartime boom in 1920. If this had not been so, it is doubtful that American business would have accepted as passively as it did the legal imposition of immigration restriction in 1920, made permanent in 1924.

The important point is that a corporation's policies for wage structure, job design, promotion, and the like have the character of "public goods": they may accommodate the desires of the majority group among the labor force, but they cannot satisfy everyone. Take the question of work hours. Many labor historians write as though the long struggle for a shorter work week were a simple matter of good versus evil. But most of the time, implicitly or explicitly, there is a trade-off between hours and take-home pay. For immigrant workers, living away from home for the purpose of making money, and planning to return as soon as they have reached their target, long hours may be exactly what they want. Married men with families might even feel the same way, if household needs were barely covered by earnings. For the steel industry, which was notorious for long hours and harsh working conditions, David Brody reports:

> Particularly where wage rates were falling, steelworkers preferred the extra hours. Nothing mattered more than the maintenance of accustomed living standards. On occasion, workers actually requested the return of a longer schedule. (Brody 1960, p. 94)

What we are seeing after 1914, therefore, is a shift in workplace public goods towards the preferences of the stabler, more permanent workers, in response to a change in the center of gravity of worker preferences. From this vantage point, it is correct to associate the changes in policy with the "threat of unionism," because the same traits would incline workers to see the benefits of organization for long-term improvements. As one contemporary observer remarked: "After a lapse of 50 years, the theory of a worker, consistently urged by workers, had been adopted as a practical business method by a few of the leading industrialists of America" (Cahill, 1932, p. 17). But of course the view "consistently urged by workers" was the view of the labor movement, which had always been the spokespiece for the stabler, more permanent, more committed industrial workers.

Labor historians have been extremely reluctant to accept the reality that American workers were well-off during the 1920s. Their reluctance stems from their focus on the success of labor organization, by which criterion the 1920s were indeed "lean years" (Bernstein 1960); the strikes of 1919 were decisively beaten, and union membership dwindled through the decade. But some are inclined to go further, implying that the much-touted "high wage" thinking was little more than a rhetorical fraud. A recent article by Frank Stricker entitled "Affluence for Whom?" (1983) argues that "our picture of the 1920s as a period of prosperity for workers must be radically qualified" (pp. 8–9). In some ways Stricker simply chooses to look at things negatively: he stressed the modest rate of growth in hourly earnings over 1923–1929, glossing over the fact that these were increases built onto what was already an extraordinary wartime peak. He applies what are essentially modern middle-class standards of nutrition and poverty, without regard for the historical subjectivity of these norms. But the real problem is that Stricker's analysis has no conception of the labor market. If large corporate employers are going to pay high wages and offer fringe benefits and retain workers for years (i.e., if they are going to pay an "efficiency wage"), one can expect as a direct consequence that they will be much more careful about expanding employment, that they will look more closely at the people they do hire, and that they will redirect their energies toward technologies and organizational systems that can save labor above all else. This is just what we see in the 1920s: manufacturing output expands by leaps and bounds, but almost all of the growth is in productivity rather than new employment; workers who landed one of these "good jobs" enjoyed unprecedented affluence, but workers who were uneducated, black, or unlucky had real trouble gaining a decent share of this new output. Ultimately therefore Stricker is not wrong but right. The picture from the 1920s is mixed, depending on who you were and where you happened to land a job. Nonetheless the systems of "welfare capitalism" achieved a certain social as well as economic stability. David Brody (1980a, ch.2) has raised the heretical possibility that these company-initiated labor systems might have continued to function and develop successfully, if it had not been for the accident of the Great Depression.

But the Great Depression did happen, and with it came another wholesale reorganization of American labor markets. This time explicit public policy was clearly involved, from the labor provisions of the NIRA (1933–1935) to the Wagner Act (1935) which laid the legal basis for the CIO organizing efforts of the late 1930s, to the Fair Labor Standards Act (1938) which institutionalized the forty-hour week and the federal minimum wage. An apparently anomalous feature of the decade of the 1930s, which has puzzled macroeconomists ever since, is that real hourly wages rose, beginning in 1933 and continuing to the 1940s, though unemployment was at all times massive. Since the wage increases predate unionism, they have received little acknowledgement from labor historians. Economist Michael Weinstein (1980) attributes the 1933–1935 increase to the NIRA (which in effect imposed an across-the-board hourly wage increase while encouraging price increases at the same time), and argues that it set back economic recovery. After the demise of NIRA in 1935, measures were taken to prevent wages from falling or to increase them, such as the work relief programs, the Davis-Bacon Act, FLSA, and of course, the Wagner Act and unionization. Even these explicit policies may be too narrow to capture the full range of political and public-opinion pressures to maintain or increase wages during the 1930s (Bailey 1983).

How can we explain a set of policies that seems from a labor-market perspective to be a perverse response to unemployment? Political rhetoric often asserted that higher wages were needed to augment purchasing power and consumer spending, but these claims cannot be taken at face value. Though a full consideration of the issue would take us too far afield, there is little theory or evidence to support such an effect in general, and certainly not when simultaneous measures are enacted to raise the prices of farm and manufactured goods. Perhaps most supporters had no specific analysis of economy and society in mind, but it seems to me that a consistent conception of the ideal labor market was implicit in all of these measures, and this concept was only coincidentally related to the Depression. Superimposed on the Depression was a longer-term transition, a collective choice by the United States to move to a "high-wage" basis; by which is meant that among the array of possible quantity-quality combinations firms might choose, they were to operate at the high-quality end. This meant upgrading labor standards and redefining jobs to make them appropriate for educated, able-bodied, adult American males; not women, children, or unskilled immigrants. Children belonged in school, women belonged at home, and foreigners belonged in their own countries.

Legions of labor economists have demonstrated that the minimum wage reduces employment opportunities for teenagers, especially for poor, uneducated teenagers, and many have said that the law "hurts the very people it was intended to help." Far from it. One of the clear purposes of the minimum wage was precisely to reduce or eliminate such jobs, to stop employers from "using youth as a bludgeon to defeat those things [for] which the trade union movement has fought for many years" (quoted in Osterman 1980, p. 70). Union leaders understood that detailed job specifications were not dictated by technology, but could be rearranged so that an employer could pay an adult male wage and get his money's worth. Lawrence Kahn (1980) presents the example of the San Francisco longshoremen in the 1930s, where unionization and wage increases were promptly followed by "decasualization," upgrading, an internal labor-market procedure, and associated productivity increases.

But are these labor-market policies really collective goods in any reasonable sense of that term, rather than rationalization for special interests? Large corporate employers could offer "efficiency wages" voluntarily if they chose to, but why should this strategy be imposed on the entire country? Take the example of teenage labor. Child labor reformers had long known that their program was not always popular with child workers and even less so with their parents. To the reformers, this was irrelevant: parents should not be allowed to exploit their children, and it is in the very nature of education that children do not know their own long-run best interests. If educational opportunities are expanded so that young people can raise themselves in time to a "human capital" level that commands the higher wage, is the policy unjustified? The case of women workers is less clear-cut, but the rationale was essentially similar: high wage advocates believed that *if* the wage of the male head of household were raised to a level consistent with a decent middle-class living standard, then husbands would *want* their wives to be home doing housework and giving children a proper upbringing. From a modern feminist perspective, this conception of a "family wage" smacks of male chauvinism, a way of keeping women out of the workforce and reinforcing the subservient status of "sacred motherhood" (Boris 1985; Hartmann 1979; May 1982). This may be so. But high-wage advocates firmly believed that most women would also make the choice to stay at home with the children, if they could afford it. Reformers were supported in this view, not just by the fact that most female political activists and women's organizations shared it, but by the objective facts of household behavior—cross-sectional patterns of women's labor-force participation consistently showed that most married women who were working were from poor families, trying to "make ends meet" because their husbands' earnings were so low (Goldin 1984). If child welfare, education, and the quality of life are legitimately objects of social concern and public policy, then the New Deal labor market was a collective good. If restrictions on the labor force imposed a short-term cost on the economy, this was a price society should be willing to pay for the social benefits. But the costs were not thought to be large, because upgrading jobs can raise productivity, as claimed in the efficiency-wage arguments. And for the longer haul, a better-educated work force can ultimately advance to levels that would otherwise be unreachable.

This broad interpretation is consistent with the evidence that despite the bitter organizing struggles of the late 1930s, there was a substantial overlap between the goals of industrial unions and the types of labor-market and labor-relations policies toward which large employers were moving. Recent studies show that de facto seniority systems are almost as widely used in nonunion settings as in unionized shops, and these seems to have much more the character of making jobs attractive than of merely recording the association between productivity growth and experience (Abraham and Medoff 1984, 1985; Mills 1985). The point would be stronger if it were pointed out that many employers instituted seniority systems well before unionization, to attract and retain workers (e.g.,

Schatz 1983, p. 20).[9] This is not to say that unionization was a trivial matter—an "implicit contract" is one thing while an explicit seniority right, enforceable through a grievance procedure, is another. Similarly, current research shows that labor turnover is lower in unionized than in nonunion firms (Freeman and Medoff 1984). But this correlation has two sources: workers who have a long-term commitment to a plant or community are more likely to unionize; but a union, once established, reshapes the workplace in the interests of the longer-term, intramarginal workers, and thus rewards and reinforces the original inclination to stay put. Thus unions make a difference, but the labor-market structure handed down from the days of the New Deal should not be viewed as the result of an exogenous union 'interference" with market forces. Instead, unionization was itself an endogenous part of a larger transition in American labor markets, rooted in an underlying change in the composition of the labor force but then embodied in a collective choice by the country.

The purpose of these comments is to understand rather than to defend these policies. It is likely that the wage increases of the 1930s did retard recovery. The high-wage economy made it much harder for blacks coming north after 1940 to follow in the upwardly mobile footsteps of the immigrant groups who preceded them. And the conception of "woman's place" was out of date within a generation if not before. Nonetheless this was the labor-market structure that defined American labor markets in the postwar era, and for its day, one can argue that it reflected an accurate reading of majority sentiment. Like many other institutions, it has become out of date with the passage of time. But if one is setting out to reform the labor market, it is best to know that the existing institutions did not stem merely from ignorance and excessive influence by special interest groups.

Conclusion

The interpretations offered here are tentative, inspired by recent research in both labor history and labor economics, but by no means backed by the kind of thorough and rigorous documentation they deserve. They are only a sampling of the many topics in American labor history that would be enhanced by a marriage of theory and history, and which would in turn inform and illuminate current discussions of labor and labor policies. To speak of a marriage of theory and history is not to call for an actual amalgamation of the fields of labor history and labor economics, an unlikely prospect in any case. The parent disciplines of history and economics represent genuinely different intellectual traditions. Economics focuses on dimensions of rationality and efficiency, while history addresses matters of consciousness and human feeling. It is healthy for traditions like these to confront each other continually, and one should not expect or hope for a grand convergence. What is unhealthy is mutual ignorance and hostility, unawareness on both sides of the solid core of understanding within each school.

The real opportunity for growth is within the field of economic history, which alone offers the promise of developing a labor economic history which is both analytical and empirical, to which both labor history and labor economics can turn for enlightenment and provocation. Already many well-trained economists and historians are beginning to fill this intellectual vacuum, including many whose writings have been neglected or barely mentioned here. But it often takes a certain collective consciousness to capture the potential joint benefits of mutually valuable research across disciplinary lines. Encouraging this consciousness has been the modest hope of this essay.

Notes

1. Textbook examples include Hamermesh and Rees (1984), Ehrenberg and Smith (1985), Fleisher and Knieser (1984). The *Journal of Labor Economics*, established in 1983, has yet to publish an article on labor history. [Note: This barrier was overturned, however, with the appearance of an article by Claudice Goldin in the January 1986 issue.] A bibliography in labor economics published in 1978 (Azevedo 1978) contains neither a section nor an index entry on labor or economic history.

2. The most influential works are Brody (1980a), Montgomery (1979), and Gutman (1977), each of which collects articles published over an extended period. Useful surveys of the "new labor history" include Montgomery (1980), Brody (1980b), and Wilentz (1984).

3. This stimulus is noted specifically by Schatz (1983).

4. The excerpt is from the "Introductory Letter" by Hon. T. F. Bayard, Late Secretary of State, USA.

5. The best references on the subject of this paragraph are Rosenberg (1969, 1976), David (1974, 1985), Arthur (1983), Nelson and Winter (1982).

6. A similar analysis, demonstrating the wide scope for "women's place" in inudstrial employment, depending on background conditions in industry history, is presented in Milkman (1983).

7. An example of the potential for enlightenment from even very simple historical comparisons, on the issue of wage flexibility, may be found in Mitchell (1985a,b).

8. Useful earlier studies include Brandes (1976) and Nelson (1975), and the contemporary article by Slichter (1929).

9. It should not be thought that the simple establishment of the seniority principle is the end of the story. The principle is merely the opening of a subsequent set of decisions about the width of "seniority districts," whether seniority applies between plants within a firm, to promotions as well as to layoffs, and so on. As early as 1940, an observer noted that "an infinite variety of combinations fo plant and department seniority [may be] found in the new union agreements (Harbison 1940, p. 857).

References

Abraham, Katharine, and James L. Medoff. 1984. Length of service and layoffs in union and nonunion work groups. *Industrial and Labor Relations Review* 38:87–97.

Abraham, Katharine, and James L. Medoff. 1985. Length of service and promotion in union and nonunion work groups. *Industrial and Labor Relations Review* 38:408–420.

Adams, Jr., Donald R. The standard of living during American industrialization: Evidence from the Brandywine region, 1800–1860. *Journal of Economic History* 42:903–917.

Alston, Lee J., and Robert Higgs. 1982. Contractual mix in Southern agriculture since the Civil War. *Journal of Economic History* 42:327–353.

Arthur, Brian. 1983. On competing technologies and historical small events. Stanford University (November).

Azevedo, Ross. 1978. *Labor Economics: A Guide to Information Sources*. Detroit: Gale Research Company.

Bailey, Martin Neil. 1983. The labor market in the 1930s. In James Tobin (ed.), *Macroeconomics: Prices and Quantities*. Washington: Brookings. Pp. 21–62.

Bernstein, Irving. 1960. *The Lean Years: A History of the American Worker, 1920–1933*. Boston: Houghton-Mifflin.

Blau, Francine. 1980. Immigration and labor earnings in early twentieth-century America. *Research in Population Economics* 2:21–41.

Boris, Eileen. 1985. Regulating industrial homework: The triumph of "Sacred Motherhood." *Journal of American History* 71:745–763.

Bowles, Sam. 1985. The production process in a competitive economy. *American Economic Review* 75:16–36.

Brandes, Stuart D. 1976. *American Welfare Capitalism*. Chicago: University of Chicago Press.

Braverman, Harry. 1974. *Labor and Monopoly Capital*. New York: Monthly Review Press.

Brody, David. 1960. *Steelworkers in America: The Nonunion Era*. Cambridge: Harvard University Press.

Brody, David. 1980a. *Workers in Industrial America: Essays on the Twentieth-Century Struggle*. New York: Oxford University Press.

Brody, David. 1980b. Labor history in the 1970s: Towards a history of the American worker. In Michael Kammen (ed.), *The Past Before Us*. Ithica, NY: Cornell University Press.

Brown, E.H., and Margaret Browne. 1968. *A Century of Pay*. New York: St. Martin's Press.

Brown, Martin, and Peter Philips. 1985. The evolution of labor market structure. *Industrial and Labor Relations Review* 38:392–407.

Cahill, Merion Cotter. 1932. *Shorter Hours: A Study of the Movement since the Civil War*. New York: AMS Press. (Reprint 1971.)

Cain, G.G. 1976. The challenge of segmented labor market theories to orthodox theory. *Journal of Economic Literature* 14:1215–1257.

Clark, Gregory. 1984. Authority and efficiency: The labor market and the managerial revolution of the late nineteenth-century. *Journal of Economic History* 44:1069–1083.

Commons, J.R. 1909. American shoemakers, 1648–1895. A sketch of industrial evolution. *Quarterly Journal of Economics* 24:39–83.

Darity, Jr., ed. William 1984. *Labor Economics: Modern Views*. Boston: Kluwer-Nijhoff.

David, Paul A. 1974. *Technical Choice, Innovation and Economic Growth*. New York: Cambridge University Press.

David, Paul A. 1985, CLIO and the Economics of QWERTY, *American Economic Review* 75, 332–337.

David, Paul A. 1986. Industrial labor market adjustment in a region of recent settlement: Chicago 1848–1868. In Peter Kilby (ed.), *Quantity and Quiddity: Essays in Honor of Stanley Lebergott.* (Forthcoming.)

David, Paul A., and Peter Solar. 1977. A bicentenary contribution to the history of the cost of living in America. *Research in Economic History* 2:1–80.

Dawley, Alan. 1976. *Class and Community: The Industrial Revolution in Lynn*. Cambridge: Harvard University Press.

Dawson, Andrew. 1979. The paradox of dynamic technologic change and the labor aristocracy in the United States, 1880–1914. *Labor History* 20:325–351.

Doeringer, Peter, and Michael Piore. 1971. *Internal Labor Markets and Manpower Analysis*. Lexington, MA: Heath.

Dublin, Peter. 1979. *Women at Work: The Transformation of Work and Community in Lowell, Massachusetts, 1826–1860*. New York: Cambridge University Press.

Duncan, Greg, and Frank Stafford. 1980. Do union members receive compensating wage differentials? *American Economic Review* 70:355–371.

Dunlop, John, and Walter Galenson, (eds.). 1978. *Labor in the Twentieth-Century*. New York: Academic Press.

Earle, Carville, and Ronald Hoffman. 1980. The foundation of the modern economy agriculture and the costs of labor in the United States and England 1800–1860. *American Historical Review* 85:1055–1094.

Edwards, Richard. 1979. *Contested Terrain: The Transformation of the Workplace in the Twentieth-Century*. New York: Basic Books.

Ehrenberg, Ronald G., and Robert S. Smith. 1985. *Modern Labor Economics*. 2nd Glenview, IL: Scott, Foresman.

Elbaum, Bernard. 1984. The making and shaping of job and pay structures in the iron and steel industry. In Paul Osterman (ed.), *Internal Labor Markets*. Cambridge: M.I.T Press. Pp. 71–107.

Erickson, Charlotte. 1957. *American Industry and the European Immigrant, 1860–1855*. Cambridge: Harvard University Press.

Eysenbach, Mary Locke. 1970. *American Manufacturing Exports, 1870–1914*. Ph.d. thesis, Stanford University.

Faler, Paul G. 1981. *Mechanics and Manufacturers in the Early Industrial*

Revolution: Lynn, Massachusetts, 1780–1860. Albany: State University of New York Press.

Fearn, Robert. 1981. *Labor Economics: The Emerging Synthesis*. Cambridge: Winthrop.

Field, Alexander James. 1978. Sectoral shift in antebellum Massachusetts: A reconsideration. *Explorations in Economic History* 15:146–171.

Field, Alexander James. 1980. Industrialization and skill intensity: The case of Massachusetts. *Journal of Human Resources* 15:149–175.

Flanagan, Robert J. 1983. Workplace public goods and union organization. *Industrial Relations* 22:224–237.

Fleisher, Thomas, and Belton Knieser. 1984. *Labor Economics: Theory, Evidence and Policy*. 3rd ed. Englewood Cliffs, NJ: Prentice-Hall.

Freeman, Richard, and James L. Medoff. 1984. *What Do Unions Do*? New York: Basic Books.

Galenson, David. 1981. *White Servitude in Colonial America: An Economic Analysis*. Cambridge: Cambridge University Press.

Galenson, David. 1984. The rise and fall of indentured servitude in the Americas: An economic analysis. *Journal of Economic History* 44:1–26.

Gersuny, Carl, and Gladis Kaufman. 1985. Seniority and the moral economy of U.S. automobile workers, 1934–1946. *Journal of Social History* 18:463–475.

Gitelman, Howard M. 1984. Being of two minds: American employers confront the labor problem, 1915–1919. *Labor History* 25:189–216.

Goldin, Claudia. 1984. The historical evolution of female earnings, functions and occupations. *Explorations in Economic History* 21:11–27.

Goldin, Claudia, and Kenneth Sokoloff. 1982. Women, children and industrialization in the early republic. *Journal of Economic History* 42:741–749.

Goldin, Claudia, and Kenneth Sokoloff. 1984. The relative productivity hypothesis of industrialization: The American case, 1820 to 1850. *Quarterly Journal of Economics* 99:461–487.

Gordon, David M., Richard Edwards, and Michael Reich. 1982. *Segmented Work, Divided Workers: The Historical Transformation of Labor in the United States*. New York: Cambridge University Press.

Green, James, R. 1980. *The World of the Worker: Labor in Twentieth-Century America*. New York: Hill and Wang.

Griliches, Zvi. 1969. Capital-skill complementarity. *Review of Economics and Statistics* 51:465–468.

Grosse, Scott D. 1982. On the alleged antebellum surge in wage differentials: A critique of Williamson and Lindert. *Journal of Economic History* 42:413–426.

Gutman, Herbert G. 1977. *Work, Culture and Society in Industrializing America*. New York: Vintage.

Hamermesh, Daniel, and James Grant. 1979. Econometric studies of labor-labor substitution and their implications for policy. *Journal of Human Resources* 14:518–542.

Hamermesh, Daniel, and Albert Rees. 1984. *The Economics of Work and Pay*. 3rd ed. New York: Harper & Row.

Hannon, Joan Underhill. 1982a. Ethnic discrimination in a nineteenth-century mining district. *Explorations in Economic History* 19:28–50.

Hannon, Joan Underhill. 1982b. City size and ethnic discrimination: Michigan agricultural implements and iron working industries, 1890. *Journal of Economic History* 42:825–845.

Harbison, Frederick H. 1940. Seniority in mass-production industries. *Journal of Political Economy* 48:851–864.

Harley, C.K. 1974. Skilled labor and the choice of technique in Edwardian industry. *Explorations in Economic History* 11:391–414.

Hartmann, Heidi. 1979. The unhappy marriage of Marxism and feminism. *Capital and Class* 8:1–33.

Higgs, Robert. 1971. Race, skill and earnings: American Immigrants in 1909. *Journal of Economic History* 31:420–428.

Higgs, Robert. 1977. Firm-specific evidence on racial wage differentials and workforce segregation. *American Economic Review* 67:236–245.

Higgs, Robert. 1978a. Racial wage differentials in agriculture: Evidence from North Carolina in 1887. *Agricultural History* 52:308–311.

Higgs, Robert. 1978b. Race and economy in the South, 1890–1950. In Robert Haws (ed.), *The Age of Segregation*. Jackson: University Press of Mississippi. Pp. 89–116.

Hill, P.J. 1975. Relative skills and income levels of native and foreign-born workers in the U.S. *Explorations in Economic History* 12:47–60.

Hoffman, Saul, 1984. Comment on chapters by Blau and Datcher. In William Darity, Jr., (ed.), *Labor Economics*. Boston: Kluwer-Nijhoff.

Jackson, Robert Max 1984. *The Formation of Craft Labor Markets*. Orlando, FL: Academic Press.

Jacoby, Sanford. 1983. Industrial labor mobility in historical perspective. *Industrial Relations* 22:261–282.

Jacoby, Sanford. 1984. The development of internal labor markets in American manufacturing firms. In Paul Osterman (ed.), *International Labor Markets*. Cambridge, MA: M.I.T Press. 23–69.

Jacoby, Sanford. 1985. *Employing Bureaucracy*. New York: Columbia University Press.

James, John A., and Jonathan S. Skinner. 1985. The resolution of the labor-scarcity paradox. *Journal of Economic History* 45:513–540.

Kahn, Lawrence. 1980. Union and internal labor markets: The case of the San Francisco longshoremen. *Labor History* 21:369–391.

Kerr, Clark. 1983. The intellectual role of the neorealists in labor economics. *Industrial Relations* 22:298–313.

Lazear, Edward P. 1979. Why is there mandatory retirement? *Journal of Political Economy* 87:1261–1284.

Lazonick, William, and Thomas Brush. 1985. The "Horndahl Effect" in early U.S. manufacturing. *Explorations in Economic History* 22:53–96.

Lebergott, Stanley. 1964. *Manpower in Economic Growth*. New York: McGraw-Hill.

Lewis, H. Gregg. 1963. *Unionism and Relative Wages in the United States*. Chicago: University of Chicago Press.

Long, Clarence. 1960. *Wages and Earnings in the United States, 1860–1890*. Princeton, NJ: NBER.

Marglin, Stephen A. 1974. What do bosses do? The origins and functions of hierarchy in capitalist production. *Review of Radical Political Economic* 6:33–60.

May, Martha. 1982. The historical problem of the family wage: The Ford Motor Company and the five dollar day. *Feminist Studies* 8:399–424.

McGouldrick, Paul, and M.B. Tannen. 1977. Did American manufacturers discriminate against immigrants before 1914? *Journal of Economic History* 37:723–746.

McNulty, Paul J. 1980. *The Origins and Development of Labor Economics*. Cambridge, MA: M.I.T Press.

Meyer, Stephen, III. 1981. *The Five Dollar Day: Labor Management and Social Control in the Ford Motor Company, 1908–1921*. Albany: State University of New York Press.

Milkman, Ruth. 1983. Female factory labor and industrial structure: Control and conflict over "women's place" in auto and electrical manufacturing. *Politics and Society* 12:159–203.

Mills, D. Quinn. 1985. Seniority versus ability in promotion decisions. *Industrial and Labor Relations Review* 38:421–425.

Mitchell, Daniel J.B. 1985a. Wage flexibility in the United States: Lessons from the past. *American Economic Review* 75:36–40.

Mitchell, Daniel J.B. 1985b. Wage flexibility: Then and now. *Industrial Relations* 24:266–279.

Montgomery, David. 1979. *Workers' Control in America*. Cambridge: Cambridge University Press.

Montgomery, David. 1980. To study the people: The American working class. *Labor History* 21:485–512.

Nelson, Daniel. 1975. *Managers and Workers*. Madison: University of Wisconsin Press.

Nelson, Richard R., and Sidney G. Winter. 1982. *An Evolutionary Theory of Economic Change*. Cambridge: Belknap Press.

Oi, Walter. 1962. Labor as a quasi-fixed factor. *Journal of Political Economy* 70:538–555.

Osterman, Paul. 1980. *Getting Started: The Youth Labor Market*. Cambridge, MA: M.I.T Press.

Osterman, Paul, ed. 1984. *Internal Labor Markets*. Cambridge, MA: M.I.T Press.

Ozanne, Robert. 1980. Trends in American labor history. *Labor History* 21:513–521.

Pencavel, John. 1979. Constant-utility index numbers of real wages: Revised estimates. *American Economic Review* 69:240–243.

Piore, Michael. 1968. The impact of the labor market upon the design and selection of productive techniques within the manufacturing plant. *Quarterly Journal of*

Economics 82:602–620.
Piore, Michael. 1979. *Birds of Passage: Migrant Labor and Industrial Societies*. New York: Cambridge University Press.
Price, Richard. 1984. Theories of Labor Process Formation. *Journal of Social History* 18(Fall):91–110.
Ransom, Roger, and Richard Sutch. 1977. *One Kind of Freedom*. New York: Cambridge University Press.
Rees, Albert. 1961. *Real Wages in Manufacturing, 1890–1914*. Princeton, NJ: NBER.
Reich, Michael. 1984. Segmented labor: Time series hypotheses and evidence. *Cambridge Journal of Economics* 4:63–82.
Rosenberg, Nathan. 1976. *Perspectives on Technology*. New York: Cambridge University Press.
Rosenberg, Nathan, ed. 1969. *The American System of Manufactures*. Edinburgh: Edinburgh University Press.
Rumberger, Russell W., and Martin Carnoy. 1980. Segmentation in the U.S. labor market. *Cambridge Journal of Economics* 4:117–132.
Saxonhouse, Gary. 1977. Productivity change and labor absorption in Japanese cotton spinning, 1891–1935. *Quarterly Journal of Economics* 91:195–219.
Saxonhouse, Gary, and Gavin Wright. 1984. Two forms of cheap labor in textile history. In Saxonhouse and Wright (eds.), *Technique, Spirit, and Form in the Making of the Modern Economies: Essays in Honor of William N. Parker*. Greenwich, CT: Jai Press:3–31.
Schatz, Ronald W. 1983. *The Electrical Workers: A History of Labor at GE and Westinghouse 1923–1960*. Urbana: University of Illinois Press.
Schatz, Ronald W. 1984. Labor historians, labor economics and the question of synthesis. *Journal of American History* 71:93–100.
Shapiro, Carl, and Joseph Stiglitz. 1984. Equilibrium unemployment as a worker discipline device. *American Economic Review* 74:433–444.
Schoenhof, Jacob. 1893. *The Economy of High Wages*. New York.G.P. Putnam's Sers (Reprinted 1974, New York: Garland).
Shergold, Peter R. 1977. Wage differentials based on skill in the United States, 1899–1914: A case study. *Labor History* 18:485–508.
Shergold, Peter R. 1982. *Working Class Life: The "American Standard" in Comparative Perspective, 1899–1913*. Pittsburgh: University of Pittsburgh Press.
Shiells, Martha. 1985. *Hours of Work and Shift Work in the Early Industrial Labor Markets of Great Britain, the United States, and Japan*. Ph.D. thesis, University of Michigan.
Shiells, Martha, and Gavin Wright. 1983. Night work as a labor market phenomenon: Southern textiles in the interwar period. *Explorations in Economic History* 20:331–350.
Shlomowitz, Ralph. 1979. The origins of Southern sharecropping. *Agricultural History* 53:557–575.
Shlomowitz, Ralph. 1984. "Bound" or "Free"? Black labor in cotton and sugar

cane farming, 1865–1880. *Journal of Southern History* 50:569–596.

Slichter, Sumner. 1929. The current labor policies of American industries. *Quarterly Journal of Economic* 43:393–435.

Sowell, Thomas. 1983. *The Economics and Politics of Race: An International Perspective*. New York: Morrow.

Stone, Katherine. 1974. The origins of job structures in the steel industry. *Review of Radical Political Economics* 6:61–97.

Stricker, Frank. 1983. Affluence for whom? Another look at prosperity and the working classes in the 1920s. *Labor History* 24:5–33.

Thernstrom, Stephan. 1964. *Poverty and Progress: Social Mobility in a Nineteenth-century City*. Cambridge: Harvard Uinversity Press.

Thernstrom, Stephan. 1973. *The Other Bostonians*. Cambridge: Harvard University Press.

Ulman, Lloyd. 1955. *The Rise of the National Trade Union*. Cambridge: Harvard University Press.

Weinstein, Michael. 1980. *Recovery and Redistribution Under the NIRA*. Amsterdam: North-Holland.

Weiss, Andrew. 1980. Job queues and layoffs in labor markets with flexible wages. *Journal of Political economy* 88:526–538.

Whatley, Warren. 1985. A history of mechanization in the cotton south: The institutional hypothesis, *Quarterly Journals of Economics* 100:1191–1215.

Wilentz, Sean. 1984. Against exceptionalism: Class consciousness and the American labor movement. *International Labor and Working Class History* 26:1–24.

Williamson, Jeffrey, and Peter Lindert. 1980. *American Inequality*. New York: Academic Press.

Woodman, Harold. 1984. How new was the new South? *Agricultural History* 58:529–545.

Wright, Gavin. 1979. Cheap labor and Southern textiles before 1880. *Journal of Economic History* 39:655–680.

Wright, Gavin. 1981. Cheap labor and Southern textiles, 1880–1930. *Quarterly Journal of Economics* 96:605–629.

Wright, Gavin. 1986. Postbellum Southern labor markets. In Peter Kilby (ed.), *Quantity and Quiddity: Essays in Honor of Stanley Lebergott*. Middletown, CT: Wesleyan University Press.

Yellen, Janet. 1984. Efficiency wage models of unemployment. *American Economic Review* 74:200–205.

Zahavi, Gerald. 1983. Negotiated loyalty: Welfare capitalism and the shoeworkers of Endicott Johnson 1920–1940. *Journal of American History* 70:602–620.

Zieger, Robert H. 1983. Industrial relations and labor history in the eighties. *Industrial Relations* 22:58–70.

Index

For Product Safety Concerns and Information please contact our EU
representative GPSR@taylorandfrancis.com
Taylor & Francis Verlag GmbH, Kaufingerstraße 24, 80331 München, Germany

www.ingramcontent.com/pod-product-compliance
Ingram Content Group UK Ltd.
Pitfield, Milton Keynes, MK11 3LW, UK
UKHW022207190926
475702UK00003B/236
9781138535794